EDUCATIONAL POLICY
AND MANAGEMENT

Sex Differentials

EDUCATIONAL PSYCHOLOGY

Allen J. Edwards, Series Editor
Department of Psychology
Southwest Missouri State University
Springfield, Missouri

The list of titles in this series continues on the last page of this volume.

EDUCATIONAL POLICY AND MANAGEMENT
Sex Differentials

Edited by

Patricia A. Schmuck
W. W. Charters, Jr.
Richard O. Carlson

Division of Educational Policy and Management
College of Education
University of Oregon
Eugene, Oregon

ACADEMIC PRESS
A Subsidiary of Harcourt Brace Jovanovich, Publishers
New York   London   Toronto   Sydney   San Francisco   1981

ACADEMIC PRESS, INC.
111 Fifth Avenue, New York, New York 10003

United Kingdom Edition published by
ACADEMIC PRESS, INC. (LONDON) LTD.
24/28 Oval Road, London NW1 7DX

Library of Congress Cataloging in Publication Data
Main entry under title:

Educational policy and management.

   (Educational psychology)
   Includes bibliographies and index.
   1. Women school administrators--United States.
2. Sex discrimination in education--United States.
I. Schmuck, Patricia A. II. Charters, W. W. (Werrett
Wallace), Date. III. Series.
LB2341.E37   371.2'088042   81-10878
ISBN 0-12-627350-2   AACR2

PRINTED IN THE UNITED STATES OF AMERICA

81 82 83 84   9 8 7 6 5 4 3 2 1

CONTENTS

PART III

THE STRUCTURE OF CAREERS IN EDUCATION

Chapter 6

The Sex Dimension of Careers in Educational Management: Overview and Synthesis — 117

Richard O. Carlson and Patricia A. Schmuck

Chapter 7

Jobs and Gender: A History of the Structuring of Educational Employment by Sex — 131

David B. Tyack and Myra H. Strober

Chapter 8

Ambitions and the Opportunity for Professionals in the Elementary School — 153

Thomas D. Jovick

CONTRIBUTORS

Numbers in parentheses indicate the pages on which the authors' contributions begin.

Richard O. Carlson (117), Division of Educational Policy and Management, College of Education, University of Oregon, Eugene, Oregon 97403

W. W. Charters, Jr. (3, 35, 307), Division of Educational Policy and Management, College of Education, University of Oregon, Eugene, Oregon 97403

Sakre K. Edson (169), Division of Educational Policy and Management, College of Education, University of Oregon, Eugene, Oregon 97403

Karen N. Gaertner (199), Department of Organizational Behavior, The Weatherhead School of Management, Case Western Reserve University, Cleveland, Ohio 44106

Marilyn Gilbertson (297), Kingswood, South Australia 5062

Barbara Hutchison (99), Northwest Regional Educational Laboratory, Portland, Oregon 97204

Pamela Jacklin (55), Stoel, Rives, Boley, Fraser, and Wyse, Attorneys at Law, Portland, Oregon 97204

Miriam Johnson (235), Department of Sociology, University of Oregon, Eugene, Oregon 97403

Thomas D. Jovick (153, 307), Department of Human Resources, State of Oregon, Mental Health Division, Salem, Oregon 97310

Susan C. Paddock (187), College of Education, Arizona State University, Tempe, Arizona 85281

Nancy J. Pitner (273), Division of Educational Policy and Management, College of Education, University of Oregon, Eugene, Oregon 97403

Patricia A. Schmuck* (3, 73, 117, 221), Division of Educational Policy and Management, College of Education, University of Oregon, Eugene, Oregon 97403

Charol Shakeshaft (9), Educational Administration, Hofstra University, Hempstead, New York 11550

Jean Stockard (235), Department of Sociology and Division of Educational Policy and Management, University of Oregon, Eugene, Oregon 97403

Myra H. Strober (131), Center for Research on Women, School of Education, Stanford University, Stanford, California 94305

David B. Tyack (131), School of Education, Stanford University, Stanford, California 94305

Margaret Wheatley (255), L'Alberi, Amesbury, Massachusetts 01913

Spencer H. Wyant (73), Consulting Exchange, College of Education, University of Oregon, Eugene, Oregon 97403

*Present address: c/o Roland Vandenberghe, Katholieke Universiteit Leuven, Faculteit der Psychologie en Pedagogische Weternschappen, Vesaliusstraat 2, 3000 Leuven, Belgium.

PREFACE

Despite the popularity of television in its role of dramatizing history, most historical developments of importance do not reach us with such visual impact. We are privileged to be witnesses to a series of social changes that are rapidly leading to a new definition of the meaning of being male and female in our twentieth-century Western world.

This book focuses on this development as it relates to men and women in school administration and is the natural culmination of our interest in sexual roles in schools. W. W. Charters, Jr., first wrote about the topic in 1963 in his chapter "The Social Background of Teaching" in the first *Handbook of Research in Teaching*. In 1974, Patricia A. Schmuck investigated the barriers facing women in school administration in her dissertation *Sex Differentiation in Public School Administration*. This research led to the Sex Equity in Educational Leadership Project, aimed at increasing the number of female administrators in Oregon public schools. In 1979, the National Institute of Education provided us with the opportunity to further our knowledge and to propose new directions for research.

The works of the contributing authors are divided into four parts: Dissertation Research, Policies and Practices, The Structure of Careers in Education, and School Organization. Many differing perspectives and methodologies are represented, and the reader will find both theoretical and data-based studies in the traditions of behavioral science, as well as of the newer feminist approach.

Although the editors have had the major responsibility for the selection and preparation of chapters in this book, we wish to acknowledge the contributions of other colleagues. Jane Arends and Thomas Jovick participated in the early stages of the book's creation. Chris Keyes, Ellen Kehoe, Ken Duckworth, Roger Rada, and Helen Washburn took part in the discussions and provided valuable critiques of various chapters in a student–faculty seminar at the Center for Educational Policy and Management in the spring of 1980. Ellen McCumsy and Connie Hixson assisted in typing and organizing the book. Finally, we thank all the authors whose contributions form the substance of this book. These contributors are clearly prime movers in what we hope will be a changing scenario concerning sexual roles in public schools.

The Center for Educational Policy and Management (CEPM) at the University of Oregon is supported in part by funds from the National Institute of Education (NIE). The Center employs authorities from a variety of professional fields who are encouraged to express freely their views on various subjects. Any opinions expressed in this publication, therefore, do not necessarily reflect those of the Center, nor do they necessarily represent the policies or positions of the National Institute of Education. No official endorsement, therefore, should be inferred from either of these organizations.

PART I

PART I
DISSERTATION RESEARCH

Introduction

THE SEX DIMENSION—AN OVERVIEW

Patricia A. Schmuck and W. W. Charters, Jr.

This book includes criticism and suggestions for corrective action. Our view is that the focus of research in educational leadership has been biased toward the study of male society. Not only have women been ignored as subjects in most such research, but little attention has been paid to the factors that differentiate males' experiences from females' experiences in educational institutions. Our purpose in this book is to rectify the bias of previous research and to demonstrate that empirical knowledge and theory about the sex dimension in educational management and policy making have a greater scope and breadth. One of the struggles, and indeed one of the sources of intellectual excitement, has involved questioning past assumptions and formulating new questions concerning the respective roles of women and men in the educational hierarchy.

It is perplexing to us that the profession traditionally open to women lags behind when it comes to research about the role of women in policy and management. There is already a substantial amount of literature discussing settings other than educational institutions (Kanter, 1977; Hennig & Jardim, 1977; Bartol, 1976). While a few published books focus on the general topic of sex roles in education (Frazier & Sadker, 1973; Harrison, 1973; Pottker & Fishel, 1977; Stockard *et al.*, 1980), fewer have systematically investigated the topic of adult professionals (Gross

3

& Trask, 1976; Bicklin & Brannigan, 1980). Although research has lagged, a substantial effort is being made to correct the imbalance of the sexes in educational management. Active feminists, women and men within the profession, are attempting to create a more equitable system of hiring, and federal and state legislation is attempting to provide equal access in employment. There is, in fact, considerably more information from activists than from the research community. This is due, in part, to grants from the Women's Educational Equity Act (WEEA) of the Office of Education that have been directed toward social action (Adkison, 1979; Schmuck, in press; Stockard, in press; Smith, Kalvelage, & Schmuck, in press).

In April 1979, members of six WEEA projects on educational leadership met at Asilomar, California, to pool their knowledge and resources at a state-of-the-art-conference (WEEA, 1979). Although these individuals were interested in direct social change, their persistent message was the lack of substantive information from which action plans could be developed and implemented. In a monograph recording their shared learnings, they said:

> We have learned a great deal about impacting individuals and systems, and the group hopes that decision makers can capitalize on our considerable knowledge base and build upon it. In addition, we have identified significant knowledge gaps about social processes in educational systems that only basic research can fill. The importance of that basic knowledge for those concerned with developing, validating, demonstrating, and disseminating cannot be ignored [WEEA, 1979, p. 13].

The call by those on the forefront of change for needed research on the sex dimension was clear, and the editors of this book hope to fill some of the acknowledged gaps.

SUBSTANCE OF THE TEXT

Some of the original theory papers and research studies that make up this book were prepared for a seminar series conducted in 1978–1979 at the Center for Educational Policy and Management at the University of Oregon; some are reports of research, and some were originally prepared as dissertations. We hope the material will be of use to educational researchers, to researchers on women's roles, to educational practitioners engaged in implementing policy, to graduate students in search of dissertation topics, and to social activists. The book is divided into four parts that discuss dissertation research, policy and practice, the structure of educational careers, and school organizations. The first chapter in Part I, by Charol Shakeshaft, is an analysis of all the doctoral dissertations from 1973 to 1979 on the subject of women in educational administration. Dissertations have been a primary source of information, and the summaries of what has already been studied and suggestions about unexplored areas should be of assistance to others. Parts II, III, and IV include lead chapters synthesizing relevant research, summarizing the contributions of each reading, and making suggestions for future research.

Part II contains four readings on policy. Pamela Jacklin describes policy at the formal level, providing a history of laws regarding sex discrimination. Barbara Hutchison discusses policy at the informal level, describing a project on the development of nonsexist curriculum materials. Although curricular materials are not included in Title IX regulations, the manufacture of materials is an important issue in policymaking. Patricia Schmuck and Spencer Wyant present information about the informal policies that govern the hiring of school administrators. While there are increasingly stringent requirements about hiring, the fact is that most school districts have a great deal of latitude in their administrative hiring.

Part III, on careers, includes five readings representing different perspectives and methodologies. David Tyack and Myra Strober put the problem into a historical perspective. They show the historical social trends that set the stage for the current unequal male–female representation in the work force of teachers and educational administrators. Thomas Jovick investigates the effects of a school structure on personal ambitions and job opportunities, and Karen Gaertner focuses on the patterns of career mobility of males as compared with those of females in educational administration. Jovick's perimeters are the boundaries of a school building, and Gaertner covers movement by occupational position in an entire state, but both focus on the opportunities available within a system. Sakre Edson and Susan Paddock examine the careers of women in educational administration, Edson focusing on the career plans of female aspirants and Paddock concentrating on the attributes and career paths of women who have already arrived in administrative positions.

Part IV, on school organization, addresses the structural features of schools and how they affect the roles of males as compared with those of females. Jean Stockard and Miriam Johnson, in the lead chapter, present a blend of sociological and psychoanalytic theory. Their work is an example of a new feminist perspective. Margaret Wheatley, a colleague of Rosabeth Moss Kanter, has applied Kanter's perspective to school organizations. Wheatley describes how opportunity and power structures in schools influence the positional status and behavior of males as compared with that of females within an organization. The other chapters are data based. Nancy Pitner compares three female superintendents to three male superintendents. The chapter by Marilyn Gilbertson and the chapter by W. W. Charters, Jr., and Thomas Jovick explore the interactional relationships between male and female elementary school principals and teachers. Gilbertson studied four principals using observational measures, and Charters and Jovick present data from a large sample of schools using varied instruments.

This book offers both theoretical and data-based readings, and it represents both the traditional views of behavioral science and the new feminist approaches. Broad social views as well as more narrow school situations are presented in discussions of the issues. We hope the book serves as an example and an inspiration for the discovery of new directions, in the formulation of new concepts in the production of further research regarding educational policy and management.

REFERENCES

Adkison, J. (1979). *ICES Structure: Linking Organizations for Educational Equity.* The University of Kansas, Lawrence.

Bartol, K. (1976). *Male Versus Female Organizational Leaders: A Review of Comparative Literature.* Faculty Research Working Papers Series, WP-76-24, Syracuse University, Syracuse, N.Y.

Bicklin, S., and Brannigan, M., eds. (1980). *Women and Educational Leadership.* Lexington Books, Lexington, Mass.

Frazier, N., and Sadker, M. (1973). *Sexism in School and Society.* Harper & Row, New York.

Gross, N., and Trask, A. (1976). *The Sex Factor and the Management of Schools.* Wiley, New York.

Guttentag, M., and Bray, H. (1976). *Undoing Sex Stereotypes.* McGraw-Hill, New York.

Harrison, B. (1973). *Unlearning the Lie.* Liveright, New York.

Hennig, M., and Jardim, A. (1977). *The Managerial Woman.* Doubleday (Anchor Books) Garden City, N.Y.

Kanter, R. M. (1977). *Men and Women of the Corporation.* Basic Books, New York.

Pottker, J., and Fishel, A. (1977). *Sex Bias in the Schools.* Fairleigh Dickinson University Press, Cranbury, N.J.

Schmuck, P. A. (in press). *Sex Equity in Educational Leadership: The Oregon Story.* Education Development Center, Newton, Mass.

Smith, M. A., Kalvelage, J., and Schmuck, P. (in press). *Sex Equity in Educational Leadership: Women Getting Together and Getting Ahead.* Education Development Center, Newton, Mass.

Stockard, J. (in press). *Sex Equity in Educational Leadership: An Analysis of a Planned Social Change Project.* Education Development Center, Newton, Mass.

Stockard, J., Schmuck, P., Kempner, K., Williams, P., Edson, S. K., and Smith, M. A. (1980). *Sex Equity in Education.* Academic Press, New York.

WEEA, (1979). *Women's Educational Equity Act: A State of the Art Conference on Women and Educational Leadership.* Unpublished paper, Women's Program Staff, Washington, D.C.[1]

[1]The participants of the conference included Marilyn Farris and Dorothy Sanders, Female Leaders for Administration and Management in Education, Dallas, Texas; Lois Sindelar, Monica Kittock-Sargent, and Marian Lohman, Women in School Administration, Billings, Montana; Judith Adkison and Jerry Bailey, Dawn Eros—a Project of Internship, Certification, Equity-Leadership, and Support, Lawrence, Kansas; Nancy Evers and Nancy Kaminsky, Developing Interpersonal Competencies in Educational Leadership, Cincinnati, Ohio; Sallyann Poinsett, Women in Leadership Learning, Lake Forest, Illinois; and Sakre K. Edson, Rita Pougialis, and Patricia Schmuck, Sex Equity in Educational Leadership, Eugene, Oregon.

Chapter 1

WOMEN IN EDUCATIONAL ADMINISTRATION: A DESCRIPTIVE ANALYSIS OF DISSERTATION RESEARCH AND A PARADIGM FOR FUTURE RESEARCH

Charol Shakeshaft

I cannot stress how important for the future of education . . . and the future of human experience it is for us to take the development and explication of a feminine perspective in educational research seriously and devote all our talents and energies collectively to its accomplishment [Anton, 1979].

By 1980 it became clear that women were being researched. In a number of disciplines, the study of women had been opened for reconsideration and revision, and the result was an outpouring of books and articles based on research on women. Once ignored by the researcher, women had been for several years the subject of numerous research studies, and hence, women's issues became one of the fastest growing areas of research in the social sciences (Daniels, 1975). Such projects would at one time have been considered unscholarly or harmful to the researcher's career, but now women's issues have become respectable. "Far from being a mere 'flash in the scholar's pan,' the quantity and quality indicate that research on women will continue to flourish" (Moore & Wollitzer, 1979, p. 2).

As research on women has intensified, researchers have become increasingly concerned about how appropriate the existing methodologies are for the study of women. In one of the earliest critiques, Carlson (1972) argued that current research paradigms—which she characterized as involving manipulation, quantification, and control—not only impose

9

restraints on the understanding of female psychology, but also lead to a general impoverishment of meaningful statements about human personality. Lloyd (1976) documented the impact of societal norms on the definition of sex differences in psychology, sociology, and anthropology. She emphasized a number of methodological issues: the survival of spurious "facts" through repeated publication, the failure to report sex differences, and the consequences of employing the traditional null-hypothesis strategy. Anton echoed the inappropriateness of the null hypothesis for the study of sex differences.

> In the null hypothesis, we assume things are the same and are surprised if they turn out to be different. In research on sex differences, we should be surprised if they turn out to be the same. We should talk about not one normal distribution, but two; and develop quantitative methods for comparing, contrasting, finding, and proving similarity rather than proving differences [1979].

Within a number of disciplines, researchers are searching for a feminist perspective from which to undertake research on women. This chapter extends the inquiry into the field of educational administration, which has followed the lead of other social science disciplines in generating research on women. The bulk of this research has concentrated on treating women as a separate group—for perhaps the first time. Issues pertaining to underrepresentation in administrative hierarchies, the career paths of female administrators, sex discrimination in educational institutions, and methods for increasing women's participation at the decision-making level have all been treated in a number of studies. Although the woman administrator was one of the most researched topics in the discipline during the 1970s, no definitive work has undertaken to discuss the results of these studies. There are, instead, numerous studies from various disciplines on overlapping or related topics, and the ambitious researcher will find them in various journals, in research reports, and in unpublished dissertations.

Because of the quantity of research already done and the expectation that this is an area of inquiry ripe for further research, it becomes important to synthesize what has been undertaken, not only to know what has been done, but also to see in what direction the research is moving. In their bibliographic review of research on women administrators from 1970 to 1978, Moore and Wollitzer (1979) found fewer than 50 studies in the general literature to review. They did not attempt, however, to study the dissertation research. A search of this literature from 1973 to 1978, turns up close to 120 dissertations on the woman administrator in education. Thus, dissertations appear to be very fertile ground for the study of the administrative behavior of women in education. Dissertation literature is an appropriate genre for the integration of studies for at least two other reasons. Dissertation research, by its very nature, indicates the trends of a discipline. It reflects the newest directions and current interests within a field. A study by Campbell and Newell (1973) lends support to the idea that much of the cutting edge of educational administration research is found in the dissertation, the reason being that "professors of educational administration engage in many activities, but they appear to have little time for, or inclination toward research" (p. 138).

Because of the lack of interest in research by those who traditionally do research in a discipline, in this case, professors of educational administration, the bulk of the research in this field is done at the doctoral level or by others who are not professors. For these reasons, dissertation research appears to be an important area in which to undertake the needed synthesis of current thought on the female educational administrator. The purpose of this chapter is to analyze the research that has been done on women in educational administration, the objectives being to identify the issues that have been treated, to examine the methodological perspective of the research, to determine the quality of the research, and to formulate a paradigm for future research.

METHOD AND RESULTS

Sample

The major unit of analysis for this inquiry is doctoral dissertations completed and abstracted from January 1973 through January 1979. These studies were located by using the usual formal and informal bibliographic procedures, and the major strategy was to systematically check volumes 33–39 of *Dissertation Abstracts International*. Titles of dissertations were sought in the index under the following headings: educational administration, female, feminine, feminism, feminist, sex, sexism, sex-role, sex role, sexuality, woman, and women. Any study that related to women administrators in any educational setting and at any level was selected. The final sample, which represents a population of all available dissertations abstracted between January 1973 and January 1979, consists of 114 studies.

Procedure

This study consists of two phases. Phase I centers on the following four questions:

1. What topics have been researched and by whom have they been studied?
2. What types of research designs are used in research on women in educational administration?
3. What is the quality of the research?
4. Are there relationships between the quality of the research, the issues addressed, and the researcher's background?

Phase II consists of the formulation of a paradigm for future research, the word *paradigm* being used to reflect its general meaning of example or pattern. In order that the four research questions might be answered, the 114 dissertations sampled were read in their entirety. A content analysis was performed on these dissertations to identify issues, trends, and methodological approaches in the research. The quality of the dissertations was then assessed through a blind review process by the researcher, using a 100-point instrument constructed from research guidelines offered by Borg and Gall (1979).

Topics Researched and by Whom

The research direction of the dissertations may be classified into six general categories: status; profiles; attitudes; barriers; leadership styles and effectiveness; structural determinants. The breakdown of these studies by number may be found in Table 1.1.

STATUS. Studies under "status" document the number of women in administrative positions in grades from kindergarten to twelve (K–12) and in higher education. The number of women employed was recorded, and the types of positions were investigated. Also covered in this category are the number of women in graduate departments of educational administration and the number of women not yet administrators who aspire to such positions.

PROFILES. Dissertations under "profiles" cover K–12 and higher education. They look at the personal histories of women in educational administration and they include demographic, personality, and professional information. The career paths of the woman administrator, including her feelings of satisfaction with her job, are also profiled. Sex differences in characteristics of male and female administrators were also researched. The characteristics of specific women who have been successful in the field, as well as biographical portraits of particular women administrators, give an in-depth look at women in administration.

TABLE 1.1

Distribution of All Dissertations by Category and Educational Level

Category	Educational level								Total
	K-12	Community college	University level	Other	K-12, community college	Community college, university	K-12, community college, university	K-12, university, other	
Status	4	0	3	0	0	0	0	1	8
Profiles	20	2	16	0	0	1	0	0	39
Attitudes	13	1	4	0	0	0	0	0	18
Barriers	20	1	5	0	0	2	0	0	28
Leadership styles and effectiveness	13	1	2	1	1	0	1	0	19
Structural determinants	1	0	1	0	0	0	0	0	2
Theory literature	0	0	0	0	0	0	0	0	0
Communication	0	0	0	0	0	0	0	0	0
Total	71	5	31	1	1	3	1	1	114

ATTITUDES. Attitudes toward women administrators are the major focus of this category. However, the attitudes of women administrators were also measured, as well as the attitudes of administrators, both female and male, toward the characteristics important if the woman administrator is to be successful. The attitudes of both male and female administrators toward legislation, particularly Title IX, are investigated. K–12 and higher education are the settings in which these studies are done.

BARRIERS. Research on barriers to women in administration may be broken into three categories: internal barriers, external barriers, and strategies for overcoming barriers. Each of these topics is explored in the dissertation research both in the settings of K–12 and in higher education. Internal barriers include aspects of socialization; personality; aspiration level; individual beliefs and attitudes; motivation; and self-image. External barriers researched were sex-role stereotyping, sex discrimination, lack of professional preparation, and family responsibilities. Methods for overcoming these barriers include general advice, sponsorship, role models, legislation, and education.

LEADERSHIP STYLE AND EFFECTIVENESS. These studies encompass K–12 and higher education settings as well as one research and development organization. They cover performance as perceived by subordinates, performance as perceived by superordinates, performance as perceived by self, leadership styles of female versus male administrators, and leadership styles identified as necessary for effective leadership.

STRUCTURAL DETERMINANTS. There are only two studies in which research on the structure of the organization is investigated. One, at the K–12 level, looks at the organizational climate and its relationship to leadership styles of males and females; the other investigates the place of women in the organizational structure of higher educational institutions.

Characteristics of Researchers,
Institutions, and Dissertations

As might be expected, the majority of researchers were female, and the majority of advisors male; 94% of all the dissertations were written by females, and 79% of all the major advisors were male. It is of interest to note that while *none* of the males who wrote dissertations on women administrators worked with women advisors, 78.5% of the females worked with male advisors. This probably reflects not so much the interest of male professors in work on women administrators, as the lack of female professors available to direct such work. It is also of interest to observe that men did not begin researching the topic of women administrators until 1976, well after the effort was begun by women. Research on women in educational administration, then, is done primarily by women but supervised by men. The feminist leaning or persuasion of the researcher was recorded after investigating the language of the dissertation, the acknowledgments, the vita, and personal statements made. Researchers who stated that they were feminists, who listed in their vitae their membership in women's rights organizations, who used nonsexist language, or who, in their dedications or acknowledgments, made pro-feminist statements were categorized as feminists. Feminists account for 53% of the researchers while nonfeminists account for 47%. None of the men were categorized as feminists while 56.1% of the women were so categorized. Additionally, 75% of those women at universities where there are women's studies programs were feminists.

About 30% of the dissertations were single efforts from one university. The remaining 70% of the dissertations, as can be seen in Table 1.2, originated from 30 universities, each represented by two or more dissertations on women in educational administration. Of the total number of universities, 44% were affiliated with the University Council of Educational Administration (UCEA) in 1979; 55% had women's studies programs at the time the dissertations were written; and 70% had women's studies programs in 1979 (our period covers January 1973–January 1979). It is interesting to note that a number of the institutions at which more than one doctoral dissertation was completed had both UCEA affiliation and women's studies programs. In 1979, of the total number of universities where more than one dissertation was written, 73.3% had women's studies programs, 43% were UCEA affiliated, and 43.3% were both UCEA affiliated and had a women's studies program. Of those with only one dissertation, 54% had women's studies programs in 1979, 42% were UCEA affiliated, and 34% were both UCEA affiliated and had a women's studies program in 1979. It would appear, then, that by promoting an awareness of women's issues on a campus, women's studies programs might influence the number of dissertations written on the subject of women in educational administration. UCEA affiliation seems to have little effect on the number of such dissertations.

The dissertations on women in educational administration are varied in orientation, as has been previously mentioned. Within the six

TABLE 1.2
Universities and Disciplinary Affiliations of Researchers Completing Dissertations
January 1973–1979

University	Educational administration	Other educational disciplines	Total
!*University of Michigan		6	6
! University of Southern California	6		6
!*Arizona State University	2	2	4
Brigham Young University	4		4
! University of Massachusetts	2	2	4
! University of California, Los Angeles	2	1	3
University of Miami	1	2	3
!*University of Minnesota	1	2	3
!*University of Pittsburgh	2	1	3
! Western Michigan University	3		3
!*Boston University		2	2
East Texas State University		2	2
Fordham University		2	2
!*Michigan State University	2		2
!*Northern Illinois University	1	1	2
St. Louis University	2		2
U.S. International University		2	2
! University of Colorado		2	2
!*University of Connecticut	1	1	2
!*University of Florida	2		2
University of Houston	2		2
! University of Illinois, Urbana-Champaign	1	1	2
! University of Northern Colorado	2		2
!*University of Oregon	2		2
! University of the Pacific		2	2
! University of South Carolina		2	2
University of Southern Mississippi	1	1	2
!*University of Tennessee	1	1	2
!*University of Wisconsin, Madison	2		2
!*Wayne State University		2	2
Auburn University	1		1
! Ball State University	1		1
Boston College		1	1
Catholic University of America		1	1
! C.U.N.Y., New York		1[a]	1
*Columbia University	1		1
Duke University		1	1
East Tennessee State University	1		1

TABLE 1.2
(*Continued*)

University	Educational administration	Other educational disciplines	Total
!*Indiana University		1	1
Marquette University		1	1
*New York University	1		1
North Texas State University	1		1
! Northwestern University	1		1
!*Oklahoma State University	1		1
!*Pennsylvania State University		1	1
!*Purdue University	1		1
*Rutgers, New Brunswick		1	1
! Rutgers, Newark		1	1
!*S.U.N.Y. at Albany		1	1
!*Temple University	1		1
University of Alabama	1		1
University of California, Riverside		1	1
University of Denver		1	1
! University of Georgia, Athens		1	1
!*University of Iowa	1		1
! University of Mississippi	1		1
!*University of Missouri, Columbia		1	1
! University of Nebraska, Lincoln	1		1
!*University of Oklahoma		1	1
University of South Dakota		1	1
University of Toledo		1	1
!*University of Utah	1		1
!*University of Virginia		1	1
Virginia Polytechnic	1		1
!*Washington State University		1	1
Total	58	56	114

[a] Department of Sociology.
Key: ! = Women's studies programs available in 1979.
 * = Institution affiliated with University Council of Educational Administrators (UCEA).

categories investigated, 37 separate variables were examined. While the length of the dissertations range from 58 to 1261 pages, the median number of pages is 170.5. Only 16% of the dissertations are organized according to the *Publications Manual of the American Psychological Association*, the style manual used in publications of the American Educational Research Association. Hypotheses were tested in 43% of the dissertations. Examining the distribution of hypotheses testing according to research issue, one finds that studies of leadership style and effective-

TABLE 1.3
Distribution of Dissertations by Source of Data

Source of data	Number of dissertations	Percentage of all dissertations
Faculty	14	12.3
Administrators	57	50.0
Students	2	1.8
Documents	7	6.1
Faculty and administrators	23	20.1
Administrators and school boards	4	3.5
Administrators and documents	3	2.6
Faculty, administrators, and school boards	2	1.8
Administrators, school boards, and students	1	.9
Faculty, administrators, and documents	1	.9
Total	114	100.0

ness more often test hypotheses than do studies concentrating on any of the other issues. Most of the dissertations use administrators as their primary data sources. However, faculty, students, and documents are also used with some regularity as can be seen in Table 1.3. The greatest number of studies were done at the K–12 level, the fewest at the community college level (see Table 1.1).

Types of Research Design Used in Research on Women in Educational Administration

Six strategies are used in the dissertation research. The majority of the studies, as can be seen in Table 1.4, are surveys; 86% of the re-

TABLE 1.4
Distribution of Dissertations by Research Strategy

Research strategy	Number of dissertations	Percentage of all dissertations
Survey	98	86.0
Experimental	5	4.0
Secondary analysis	2	1.5
Historical	4	4.0
Case study	1	1.0
Futures	2	1.5
Survey and historical	1	1.0
Survey and case study	1	1.0
Total	114	100.0

searchers used the survey strategy, five dissertations were experimental in nature, two were secondary analyses, four utilized historical strategies, and one was a case study. These findings are consistent with methodologies used generally in educational administration dissertations:

> Questionnaires are the most common data gathering procedure in graduate research on educational administration. . . . A few years ago one study concluded that perhaps 80 percent of all educational administration dissertations completed during the period 1960–1966 relied on this technique [Haller, 1979, p. 48].

Table 1.5 shows the different methods of data collection used to be consistent with Haller's findings of research methods used generally in such dissertations. Thirteen researchers used a combination of methods for seeking answers to their questions, and the most common combination was the use of a mailed paper and pencil questionnaire along with an interview schedule. Table 1.6 lists the numbers and percentages of cases according to data-analysis procedure. The most common procedures were the use of descriptive methods of frequency, percentages, and measures of central tendency. Other procedures employed were bivariate, inferential, and multivariate statistics. Bivariate statistics include all correlational methods. Inferential statistics are chi-square tests, *t* tests, and analysis of variance. Multivariate statistics include multiple regression, discriminant analysis, and factor analysis.

Quality of the Research

Application of the quality instrument provides explicit scores for eight research domains of interest: quality of the abstract, review of the literature, sampling plan, instrument, statistical analysis, overall re-

TABLE 1.5
Distribution of Dissertations by Data-Collection Method

Data-collection method	Number of dissertations	Percentage of all dissertations
Interview	3	3
Paper and pencil questionnaire by mail	76	67
Paper and pencil questionnaire by person	14	12
Unobtrusive	6	5
Other	2	2
More than one	13	11
Total	114	100.0

TABLE 1.6
Distribution of Dissertations by Data-Analysis Procedure

Procedure	Number of dissertations	Percentage of all dissertations
No statistical analysis used	4	3.5
Type I (frequencies, percentages, measures of central tendency)	43	37.7
Type II (bivariate statistics)	1	0.9
Type III (inferential statistics)	25	21.9
Type IV (multivariate statistics)	4	3.5
Types I & II	1	0.9
Types I & III	18	15.8
Types I & IV	1	0.9
Types II & III	4	3.5
Types II & IV	1	0.9
Types III & IV	5	4.4
Types I, II, & III	3	2.6
Types I, III, & IV	3	2.6
Types II, III, & IV	1	0.9
Total	114	100.0

search approach, sexist content, and contribution to the literature. Mean score values for each domain are given in Table 1.7. Each area is critiqued individually as follows:

ABSTRACT. The absence of a full discussion of the sample, the design, and the statistical analysis is characteristic of many of the abstracts. The problem statement and the findings are usually correctly and comprehensively stated.

REVIEW OF THE LITERATURE. The reviews of the literature do not take up methodologies and instruments. In general, the reviews tend to be too broad. Many researchers treat women as a subject area rather than as a population, and thus they review the literature on women in general, rather than on the topic at hand. Further, although there are a number of dissertations on the subject of women in educational administration from 1974 onward, findings from these dissertations are generally not included in reviews of literature used in dissertations done at a later date.

SAMPLING. Few researchers use probability samples when conducting research, and even fewer discuss their use of volunteer subjects.

TABLE 1.7
Quality of Research Scores

Category	Total possible score	Mean score	Standard deviation	Maximum value	Minimum value	Range
Abstract	15	11.08	1.96	15	6	9
Review of the literature	15	12.59	1.43	15	9	6
Sampling plan	15	10.81	2.33	15	5	10
Instrument	15	10.58	1.95	15	7	8
Statistical analysis	15	12.04	1.15	15	8	7
Overall research approach	15	10.48	1.61	15	7	8
Sexist content	9	7.55	1.65	9	3	6
Contribution to the literature	1	0.38	0.49	1	0	1
Total score	100	75.61	7.24	96	60	36

Additionally, very few researchers discuss the limitations of their sampling plans, the majority of which appear to consist of local convenience samples.

INSTRUMENTATION. The validity and reliability of the research instrument are often not determined, and many researchers do not pretest the instrument. Most researchers formulate their own questionnaire and do not look into other instruments that might be more appropriate as well as readily available. Nearly as many questionnaires as there are researchers can be found in the dissertation literature.

STATISTICAL ANALYSIS. The statistical analyses of the dissertations fail to measure practical significance in studies where tests of significance have been done. No study tested the practical significance of the findings. Practical significance as referenced here is best explained by McNamara and Gill:

> Two kinds of statistical tests of particular interest to researchers are those that test for the significance of *relationships* and those that test for the significance of *differences*. To determine whether there are significant differences among two or more groups, researchers frequently employ a single-classification analysis of variance. This set of statistical decision rules allows one to specify *directly* the statistical significance associated with the test of an experimental hypothesis of interest. Practical significance, on the other hand, depends on an accurate estimate of the strength of a statistical

association. The practical significance assessment usually follows the design employed in tests for the significance of relationships, and often begins by asking "How much of the variance in a criterion measure can be accounted for by a prediction measure?" [1978, p. 28].

OVERALL APPROACH. In general, the major drawback of these inquiries was the use of a questionnaire when another method for answering the question under consideration was appropriate. Thus, there is an overuse of the survey method in these dissertations. Another problem in the survey research was the failure of researchers to estimate nonrespondent bias. The absence of an interview guide and the failure to carry out practice interviews are major weaknesses in these dissertations. The concept of random selection was confused with random assignments in some of the experimental designs, and researchers did not take the limitations of the experimental design into account when generalizing. In the historical studies, secondary as opposed to primary sources were often used; and in case study research, the failure to confirm incidents with several sources was a significant limitation.

SEXIST CONTENT. When researchers used instruments already formulated, they often chose sexist instruments. The Leader Behavior Description Questionnaire (LBDQ) and the LBDQ-XII, for instance, are sexist both in theory and in construction. Using the male pronoun throughout and validated with men, these instruments have been used to judge the performance of female administrators. Very seldom were attempts made to adapt the instruments to the populations for which they were being used. Sexist language, in general, is the norm in these dissertations, the male pronoun being used frequently throughout the dissertations, even when referring to female administrators. One reason for the narrowness in language despite the healthy percentage of feminist researchers might be the reluctance of committees to approve of and support nonsexist language.

CONTRIBUTION TO THE LITERATURE. The first seven categories of quality evaluate methods. Evaluation of contribution explores the quality of the findings. A score of one has been given to each dissertation that contributes to the general knowledge base about women administrators. Dissertations were rated as contributing to the literature if they explored new topics, methodologies, or populations, or if they replicated an experimental study done previously. It was found that 71 studies, or 62.2%, do not contribute in any substantive way to the general knowledge of women administrators since they either repeated research that has been replicated a number of times or researched trivial problems that do not contribute in any meaningful way to the overall literature on the woman administrator.

Relationships between the Quality of the Research Design, the Issues Addressed, and the Researcher's Background

Univariate analysis of variance models have been used to test relationships between the quality of research scores and several dissertation-related variables (see Table 1.8). The results suggest that only three variables—the research issue, the feminist stance of the researcher, and the data-collection method—are significantly related to the quality of the dissertations. The strongest relationship was found with the feminist stance of the researcher, defined previously as including researchers' statements that they are feminists, listings in vitae of membership in women's rights organizations, the use of nonsexist language, and the use of profeminist statements in the dedications and acknowledgments. Specifically, feminists are more likely to be associated with higher scores for the quality of their research. The feminist stance of the researcher is significant beyond the .0001 probability level, and the practical significance of this relationship is moderately high since it accounts for over 22% of the variance. In research on women in educational administration, then, the feminist tends to be the better researcher. While less dramatic than the variable of feminist standing, research issue and data collection method account for approximately 9% and 10% of the variance,

TABLE 1.8
Relationship between Variables and Quality of Research

Variable	F Value	p Value	Eta squared
Research issue	2.117	0.0688	0.08925
Sex of researcher	0.031	0.8599	0.00028
Disciplinary affiliation	0.025	0.9749	0.00045
Degree received	1.322	0.2527	0.01166
UCEA affiliation	1.020	0.3146	0.00903
Women's studies at university	0.024	0.8781	0.00021
Women's studies at university in 1979	0.304	0.5822	0.00271
Feminist stance of researcher	32.100	0.00001	0.22276
APA style	0.857	0.3567	0.00759
Research strategy	0.996	0.4316	0.00529
Data-collection method	2.296	0.0502	0.09609
Hypotheses tested	0.545	0.4514	0.00485

NOTE: APA = American Psychological Association
UCEA = University Council of Educational Administrators

respectively. Specifically, higher quality studies were done on the issue of barriers to women in administration and with the use of unobtrusive measures and historical techniques.

DISCUSSION AND PARADIGM
FOR FUTURE RESEARCH

Analysis of the dissertations on women in educational administration is useful for a number of reasons. First, it allows us to identify the state of the art of research on women in educational administration from the standpoint of method and issue. (For a synthesis of the research findings on women in educational administration see Shakeshaft, 1979.) Secondly, it explains some of the major weaknesses of the research so that particular areas may be strengthened in future studies. Finally, an examination of what has and has not been undertaken in the research suggests a paradigm for future studies. The major observation that cries for discussion is the fact that the dissertations emerge from a framework primarily male defined. That is, the research presents men and the male model as the norm and women and the female model as a deviation from the norm. Such research reconstructs reality by trying to fit the female experience into the male mold. That the dissertations in this study are of this variety, is not unexpected. After all, the majority of people doing the research on educational administration have been trained by men, and they are working with committees composed primarily of men.

Educational administration as a discipline borrows heavily both from the social sciences (Culbertson *et al.*, 1973) and from organizational theory and research. Many observations that are believed to be true and the ways in which these truths are pursued are taken from the substance and methodologies of psychology, sociology, anthropology, and management, disciplines traditionally focused on men and male institutions, and on phenomena and areas in which men dominate (Acker & Van Houten, 1974; Weisskopf, 1978). Given this history, it is surprising that questions related to women were asked at all. However, once these questions have been asked it becomes important to examine from what perspective they spring. For instance, the research on leadership and effectiveness originates from a paradigm that is male and that attempts to determine whether women "measure up." The LBDQ, as discussed earlier, is sexist in content and seldom revised for a female population. Similarly, the work on aspiration level assumes that the desire to move from teaching into administration is somehow correct and that not to wish to make such a move is deviant behavior that must be corrected.

The male model, whether it be in leadership style or aspiration level, pervades the dissertations. Again, this is not surprising. Education generally has used questions that imply a male norm with women as deviants: "Why can't Johnny read?" not "Why can't Janie add?" and "Are women teachers and administrators feminizing our schools?" not "Are male administrators and teachers polarizing our schools and causing them to become violent places?" Beyond the fact that the male model is the norm in the dissertations, women are not investigated as populations but as topics of study, much as someone would research whales or hurricanes. As mentioned earlier, the reviews of the literature within the dissertations tend to cover any piece of literature that relates to women, whether or not it is pertinent to the subject being investigated.

One review of the literature on women school principals, for example, is more than 900 pages in length and covers topics as far afield as the history of the women's movement in England and early feminist literature. This practice illustrates how the subject of women is confounded, and it reinforces the idea that men are a population and women a deviant subject matter. Speaking for women, Slocum (1975) puts more succinctly the problems of bias in dissertations: "We are human beings studying other human beings, and we cannot leave ourselves out of the equation. We choose to ask certain questions and not others" (p. 37). In the dissertations under discussion here, the questions asked are primarily male questions. However, it is important to note that these studies have not been useless exercises for obtaining academic degrees. Information has been gathered on the woman administrator that has previously been absent from research. Because research in the past has usually focused on the male administrator and has not looked at the female at all, these studies are important. They have brought the woman administrator into the mainstream of educational research. But where do we go from here?

If the research on the woman administrator up to this point has come primarily from the male model, the next step should be to move in the direction of a female-defined research paradigm, as Anton (1979) has urged. In order to move beyond the present state of research, the following findings from the analysis of dissertation research will be used as a basis for the conceptualization of a new paradigm regarding research on women in educational administration:

1. Women do most of the research on the subject.
2. Feminists produce higher quality studies in the area than do nonfeminists.
3. The use of the survey method, the overwhelming approach to such research, does not yield high-quality results.

4. Qualitative and/or historical techniques result in high-quality studies on the subject.
5. The majority of the studies do not contribute to the substance of the literature on the subject.
6. Much of the research in this field is sexist.

Given this information, a paradigm for research on women in educational administration can be postulated, the first tenet of which includes an expansion of qualitative methods. Analysis of the dissertation literature supports the notion that qualitative methods, at this stage of the inquiry, might be more productive than quantitative methods. Not only are observational techniques more highly correlated with quality research, but also much of the research, from a quantitative perspective, fails to add anything meaningful to the pertinent literature. Qualitative research methods may be characterized by a sustained contact between the researcher and the subjects; they are built on direct experience, and they produce data that is descriptive of events, people, places, and conversations (Biklin, 1980). At this time, descriptive data are needed about women in positions of power and the accompanying isolation. Available information is not sufficient for formulating, let alone testing, theories. What is needed is for researchers to collect information so that theories can be developed to explain the slice of life involving women in educational administration.

A further dimension of this paradigm is that the research must grow out of the personal experiences, feelings, and needs of the researcher. It must explore the situation in order to understand and legitimize it as seen from the eyes of woman. Such research is a way of seeing the world without using a yardstick that has been the measure of men in the world. Eichler's definition of feminist research conceptualizes what is implied when we refer to the feminist perspective of the paradigm:

> I shall here consider such research [as] feminist that regards women as subjects rather than objects. [Such research] does not mean men as the norm and women as the deviation from the norm. Nor does it legitimate its concern with women in terms of some problems of a "higher order"; instead it reconstructs reality by starting from a female perspective which may or may not need to be modified as men are taken into consideration [1977, p. 410].

Since the present study indicates that it is the feminist who undertakes the highest quality research, a feminist perspective is an essential component in the paradigm for research on women in educational administration.

A fourth component of the paradigm is borrowed from a concept by Anton (1979), who says that authority for truth needs to be reinvested in the subject. That is, conclusions from the work on women in educational administration need to be taken back to the participants to see if they ring true. If the authority of knowledge is reinvested in the participant, it is more likely that the research effort will reflect a female consciousness and a female experience. From the point of view of the subject, it changes research from a passive undertaking, to an active one. Research then becomes an interactionist method for discovering truth. This incorporation of the participants' interpretations and the collaboration between researcher and participant are essential elements in the research paradigm. An additional feature of the paradigm is a reliance on the oral tradition rather than the written one, both in gathering the data and in reporting the results. An oral tradition is more flexible and allows for the sharing of information and the refining of conclusions before the truth is engraved forever on the tablet. An oral tradition moves from the concept of expert to that of sharer of information. It is dynamic rather than static.

The sixth and final element in the paradigm is the use of research as an instrument for social change. It is clear that in many of the dissertations, the purpose of the research was to effect change, and in this paradigm, that purpose is recognized and named. Given this paradigm, what might be the direction of research on women in educational administration? The following discussion analyzes previous research categories and new directions in light of this paradigm.

STATUS. The number of women administrators at all levels needs to be recorded systematically. This is essential information for practical and political purposes. Although not the proper domain of the dissertation, this information provides helpful data for policymaking decisions that would help women enter positions in educational administration.

PROFILES. Studies which profile the woman administrator are of passing interest, but they do not help build theory or lend insights into the ways women can be integrated into the management of schools. In the dissertations analyzed, the profiles were unnecessary bits of information within the context of the paradigm.

ORGANIZATIONAL BARRIERS. From a feminist perspective, the question of what keeps women out of a man's world might change to the question of what changes can be made in the male world to facilitate women. Taking the existing system and altering it is one feminist solution. The study of aspiration level, for instance, would change focus. No longer would it be asked why women teachers are not aspiring to be administrators; instead one would ask how the system could be changed so that women who entered teaching with the goal of teaching and not administering might nevertheless have some function in the decision-making processes of the schools. The male hierarchy, with its administrative specialization, is not the only model that will work. It is, however, the only model that has been tried on large-scale populations. Looking at other models of organization that have been tried in feminist enterprises, such as flattened hierarchies and cooperatives, might give clues to how schools can be managed so that the administrative functions are more compatible with women's interest in teaching. Rather than looking at how women can change their aspiration level to suit the organization, research under this paradigm would look at how the organization can change itself to fit the aspirations of women.

Organizational changes are not the only solutions under this paradigm. Strategies for change need to be evaluated at all levels, whether individual or organizational. Strategies that challenge barriers need to be tested and evaluated. One solution that feminists have offered for change is the establishment of organizations that bring together the institutions seeking women candidates for posts and the women candidates qualified for such posts. Such organizations provide training programs for women in educational administration. These programs have to be evaluated for their effectiveness and assessed on the basis of the kinds of changes that are occurring. Are they producing imitation men, or are they giving women the skills they need for entering the administration arena and for introducing feminine values into traditionally male organizations? Much of the research done thus far has looked for a single barrier, for one reason why women are not in administration, and oftentimes, the one reason given is the makeup of the woman herself. Causation is multifaceted rather than singular, and blaming the victim is not productive in taking down barriers and providing strategies whereby women can enter the field of administration.

ATTITUDES. By asking people how they feel about women administrators, one is condoning the acceptance of negative attitudes. One is, in effect, saying that it is not only acceptable but also worthy of a major research effort to investigate whether women are capable of being school administrators. The subtlety of the sexism in this approach to administrative research might become clearer if we were to reverse the trend and undertake studies on male qualifications for administrative positions. By dichotomizing the choice in attitudinal surveys, researchers are perpetuating the myth that women might not be acceptable administrators simply because they are women. Attitudinal surveys in the dissertations are based on a sexist foundation. The only worthwhile information that attitudinal surveys can gather has been gathered. We already know that there are some sexist and negative attitudes about women administrators among teachers, administrators, school board members, and the public, and we also know that these attitudes are not as widespread as we would be led to believe by those who would prefer it if women remained out of school administration. Under the paradigm, it is suggested that attitudinal surveys would only be appropriate if they are linked with interventionist techniques to change attitudes. This approach would move us from repetitive documentation to strategy for change.

LEADERSHIP STYLES AND EFFECTIVENESS. The majority of the studies on leadership styles and effectiveness have been done for the purposes of seeing if women measure up to men. Not much is known about women's leadership styles—how they treat subordinates and what effects their supervisory styles have on school processes, on violence in schools, and on learning. If studies are to be done on this topic, they need to be done without the specter of "measuring up." The ways in which women solve problems might be particular to women, and men might learn from them. New questions have to be asked. Because of their lack of physical prowess, whether supposed or real, do women have ways of diffusing violence that might be used by male as well as female school administrators? Given their preference for teaching, are women able to administer in ways that encourage learning? The woman administrator is still a mystery. Very little is known about how she deals with everyday situations. Observing women administrators at work might give some insight into how they manage and might produce valuable practical data from which theories of administration can be built.

STRUCTURAL EFFECTS. Women's relationships to organizational structures are still unknown. How women administer and function in certain organizational structures and modes and what the relationship is between an organization and the position women hold are as yet unanswered questions.

THEORY LITERATURE. The theories upon which many administrative strategies are based come from management and are postulated by men and not by women. Theory literature needs to be reread and challenged within the feminist context of the ways in which women behave.

Are the theories valid? Do women see people in terms of the various theories? Where do women fit on the managerial grid, if they do fit? The bulk of the theories taught in courses in educational administration have no room for women. They need to be rethought, questioned, challenged, and ultimately rewritten.

COMMUNICATIONS. Women's methods of communication can tell much about the ways in which they administer. Do they communicate directly or through memorandums? Do they communicate with all levels of the hierarchy or just with their immediate subordinates and superordinates? Studies of women's communication patterns might provide insights into the ways in which women manage.

Conclusion

Some suggestions have been given for ways to incorporate the proposed paradigm for research on women in educational administration into topic areas that have already begun to be explored in the literature. This is only a beginning, and one hopes that working from this paradigm will bring about new ways of looking at all questions as the researcher moves into the realm of women's experience. The next step might be studies of women's leadership styles in female-defined organizations and this might be followed by studies of feminist organizations and feminist solutions to problems in organizational structure. The possibilities are boundless once the leap has been made from the male-defined perspective to the female-defined perspective. It is time to take that leap.

REFERENCES

Acker, J., and Van Houten, D. R. (1974). "Differential Recruitment and Control: The Sex Structuring of Organizations." *Administrative Science Quarterly*, June, pp. 152–164.

Anton, J. (1979). *The Feminine Perspective in Educational Research*. Paper presented at the annual meeting of the American Educational Research Association. Research on Women and Education, Cleveland.

Biklin, S. (1980). *Qualitative Research and the Study of Social Change in Education*. Paper presented at the annual meeting of the American Education Research Association, Boston, April 11.

Borg, W. R., and Gall, M. D. (1979). *Educational Research: An introduction*, Longman, New York.

Campbell, R., and Newell, L. J. (1973). *A Study of Professors of Educational Administration*. University Council for Educational Administration, Columbus, Ohio.

Carlson, R. (1972). "Understanding Women: Implications for Personality Theory and Research." *Journal of Social Issues*, 28 (2):17–32.

Culbertson, J., Farquhar, R. H., Fogarty, B. M., and Shibles, M. R., (1973). *Social Science Content for Preparing Educational Leaders.* Merrill, Columbus, Ohio.

Daniels, A. K. (1975). *A Survey of Research Concerns on Women's Issues.* Association of American Colleges, Washington D.C.

Eichler, M. (1977). "Sociology of Feminist Research in Canada." *Signs,* 3 (2):409–422.

Haller, E. J. (1979). "Questionnaires and the Dissertation in Educational Administration." *Educational Administration Quarterly,* 15:47–66.

Haug, M. (1973). "Social Class Measurement and Women's Occupational Roles." *Social Force,* 52:86–88.

Lloyd, B. (1976). "Social Responsibility and Research on Sex Differences." In B. Lloyd and J. Archer, eds., *Exploring Sex Differences.* Academic Press, New York.

McNamara, J. F., and Gill, D. H. (1978). "Practical Significance in Vocational Education Research." *Journal of Vocational Education Research,* 3:27–48.

Moore, K. M., and Wollitzer, P. A. (1979). *"Recent Trends in Research on Academic Women: A Bibliographic Review and Analysis."* Paper presented at the American Educational Research Association, San Francisco.

Register, C. (1979). "Brief, A-mazing Movements: Dealing with Despair in the Women's Studies Classroom." *Women's Studies Newsletter,* pp. 7–10.

Shakeshaft, C. (1979). "Dissertation Research on Women in Educational Administration: A Synthesis of Findings and Paradigm for Future Research." Doctoral dissertation, Texas A. & M. University, College Station, Tex.

Slocum, S. (1975). "Woman the Gatherer:Male Bias in Anthropology." In R. Reiter, ed., *Towards an Anthropology of Women.* Monthly Review Press, New York.

Weisskopf, S. (1978). "Essay Reviews." *Harvard Educational Review,* 48 (2):269–278.

PART II

POLICIES AND PRACTICES

Chapter 2

SEX EQUITY IN EDUCATIONAL POLICIES AND PRACTICES

W. W. Charters, Jr.

Without question there are numerous conditions of sexual inequity in American schools and colleges, as well as a host of other conditions that may not be discriminatory per se but presumably have inequitable consequences for females. Two recent books have sought to summarize the empirical evidence regarding the range of sexual inequities for students and other adults who inhabit educational institutions (Pottker & Fishel, 1977; Stockard *et al.*, 1980; see also Deem, 1978, who addresses research from the British perspective). Inequity takes many forms, and investigators have found significant sexual differences in many areas. Such differences have been found in teacher–student interactions, classroom disciplinary practices, portrayals of males and females in curriculum materials and textbooks, and items in standardized tests. They have been found in conceptions held by guidance counselors concerning appropriate occupational roles for men and women, in referrals of students for special educational programs, in the restrictions of course offerings and the unavailability of courses for females, in the retention rates of students in colleges and graduate schools, and in the distribution of students in high school courses and college majors. Such differences have also been found in the areas of financial and other support for graduate study, in the rank and salary of university faculties, in the fringe benefits and other employment conditions of public school teachers and in their assignments, in the composition of school boards and other policymaking bodies, in the administrative hierarchies of public schools, and so on.

We assume in this book that most if not all of these conditions can be changed, that they are due in some degree to the manner in which schools and colleges are organized, administered, and operated. We readily acknowledge that the educational institution is just one of a variety of social forces and institutions that produce inequities in American society and that education's intricate linkages with other sectors of society not only limit the extent to which policies and practices can deliberately be altered, but they also seriously modify the ameliorating effects that might be realized from changes within the institution. However, we reject the view that the circumstances found in our schools and colleges are mere reflections of the society in which they are embedded and hence are unalterable except as the large context is changed. That view attributes an unproven homogeneity to the pressures of community and society and takes no account of the functional autonomy, however restricted it may be, of complex organizations.

DISCIPLINED INQUIRY

The central contention of this book is that systematic, disciplined inquiry into the causes of inequities in the educational system is a valuable complement to efforts to eradicate or reduce these inequities. Our understanding of how and why events occur in complex organizations comes from the social and behavioral sciences, and our understanding of how educational systems have reached the state they are in comes from historical scholarship, and in both cases our understanding is meager at best. Despite the reams of material investigating the reasons for racial discrimination and the attempts of social programs to relieve it for over 20 years, dependable knowledge is scarce regarding ameliorating courses of action. We are convinced, however, that accurate information offers a stronger base for intelligent action than do the half-truths and myths of conventional wisdom and that serious anaylsis of inequitable circumstances is better than thoughtless response.

In disciplined inquiry we emphasize the production of knowledge that will lead to enlightened decisions, directly or indirectly, regarding courses of action—even if it is no more than to encourage decision makers to reconsider a favored alternative that has a marginal probability of success. Disciplined inquiry is in the vein of what Cronbach and Suppes (1969) some years ago called decision-oriented inquiry, which today is often called policy analysis or, perhaps more narrowly, program evaluation. Such research seeks the greatest leverage for change and concerns itself with malleable conditions as well as with conditions that establish boundaries that limit malleability.

Values and Objectivity

Much has been written about the role of the investigator's values in research in the social sciences, specifically about the biases and blind spots attributable to male domination of the several social science disciplines. Many of the criticisms are well taken, and we harbor no belief that such research is value free. Facts do not "speak for themselves," for a fact is a fact only within some framework that gives it meaning. The investigator's values intrude on the research enterprise at three distinct levels, only one of which matters to us as we speak of objectivity. On a grand scale, science, including the social sciences, values the view that it is worthy to attain knowledge by reference to an external world of states and events. Research is just one of several alternative ways of knowing. On a less grand scale, researchers wittingly or unwittingly exercise their values in the selection and formulation of problems for investigation. While certain topics obtain grants, others go begging; while some theoretical formulations are popular, others are out of date. Certain topics are likely to call attention to political causes to which the investigator is dedicated, while others are denigrated as being problems in an "ivory tower."

We and the other authors of this book are by no means neutral about the dignity of the individual person, and we recognize those circumstances that place certain values ahead of others. At the technical level of research, objectivity must be vigorously honored, especially at those points in the research process where we are most likely to fool *ourselves*. If the purpose of inquiry is to learn about some aspect or function of the world or the society—to gain knowledge that can help guide efforts to change something for the better—it is clearly to our advantage to avoid self-deception. People easily see what they want or expect to see and have difficulty in changing beliefs in the face of contrary evidence. Such problems, to which the modern psychology of perception and cognition can attest, make researchers especially prone to believing in their own preconceptions. The trappings of the so-called scientific method have emerged through the years as techniques for protecting researchers from their own biases. The fussiness of researchers who have precise definitions of concepts is an effort to forestall the undetected drifting of words to fundamentally different meanings. This is an especially serious problem in the social sciences if there is no well-developed technical vocabulary and if reliance is placed on concepts used in everyday parlance.

To establish the reliability of observations and measures requires some assurance that two or more investigators looking at the same event will agree in their description of it, even though they might disagree on conclusions drawn about it. To achieve validity in observations and measures, an effort must be made to attract the attention of researchers to the possibility that they are not measuring what they assume they are measuring. In population sampling, certain techniques help protect the investigator from inaccurate generalizations about the population, generalizations that otherwise might arise when measuring a handy group of people, even if the group is large. The technicalities of research design are concerned with who is to be measured with respect to what; when and how often the measures will be taken; and what comparisons are to be made between the measures. The research design can protect investigators from well-known hazards in the interpretation of results. The use of inferential statistics keeps researchers from making something out of trends and differences in their data that might have occurred by chance.

The ideal stance for researchers with regard to the findings of an investigation is one of skepticism and disbelief. Ideally, researchers should seek every means possible to explain away or disconfirm the results. This process should start at the very beginning of a study, when the problem is formulated and measures are developed and plans are made for obtaining evidence. The stronger the study is in eliminating plausible alternative interpretations, the more confidence researchers can have in the conclusions. We speak of such methods as ideal; they are rarely realized in practice. Nevertheless, it is toward objectivity that a researcher strives; and objectivity is one of the standards against which the researcher is judged by colleagues.

RESEARCH CHARACTERISTICS

The bulk of research cited by Pottker and Fishel (1977), Deem (1978), Stockard et al. (1980), and other reviewers of the literature in education, including Shakeshaft in the preceding chapter on dissertations, attempts to document the circumstances in which discrimination and inequity confront women in educational institutions. Documentary investigation, a form of descriptive research sometimes referred to as the status study or the survey, is to be distinguished from the form of empirical study that examines and tests cause and effect relationships. Both forms have their advantages as well as pitfalls, but the empirical study is a kind of knowledge-producing inquiry that can guide and shape social action. Both forms are discussed in the sections that follow.

Descriptive Research

Descriptive research in our field entails a design for the collection of information that will characterize one or more aspects of educational settings at a given time and in a given place. Reports of research in this vein generally stress the presentation of frequency distributions, percentages, or means with regard to the variables being measured. Inequity or discrimination is demonstrated by comparisons that show differences between males and females on relevant variables. Further cross-tabulations in the report are presented only to furnish descriptive information in greater detail, not to to account for these differences, as would be the intent in a study of causal relations. One instance of descriptive research is that of Saario, Tittle, and Jacklin (1973). In their study of four basal reading series commonly in classroom use in the early 1970s, they counted the frequencies with which females and males (separately for children and adults) were depicted as engaging in various categories of behavior, such as aggression, nurturance, and negative statements about self. Frequency counts and percentages were given for 16 categories based on the 945 characters identified in stories chosen from the readers. The point of the study was to show differences between the depiction of males and the depiction of females in the readers.

In another such study, Fishel and Pottker (1974) counted the number of females and males found in various grades of civil service work in the United States Office of Education and in the National Institute of Education in 1974. They wished to demonstrate the rather regular decrease in the proportions of females as Government Service (GS) grade increased. Using statistical data for 1972, they made similar counts for positions in the policymaking hierarchies at the state and local school district levels. The descriptive research of Grant and Lind (1977) reported the percentage of females awarded bachelor's degrees in American colleges and universities in some 23 major fields of study during the 1974–1975 school year. Their point was to document the great disparity in the proportions of females in certain major fields—male graduates being greatly overrepresented in the physical sciences, engineering, law, and business management, and female graduates in fine arts, library science, home economics, and education.

While these investigators might have had fairly clear ideas about the reasons for these discrepancies, testing cause and effect relationships was not a part of their investigation. The purpose of their studies was straightforward documentation. Other forms of descriptive research may not entail comparisons between males and females in any statistical sense—for instance, when a sample of citizens is polled on their reactions to the appointment of a female as a superintendent of schools or on their opinions about sexually mixed high school classes in physical fitness and other athletic programs. Another example would be querying a sample of female graduate students in a university (by interview or questionnaire) regarding episodes of discrimination they have encountered in their graduate program.

The Functions of Descriptive Research

Descriptive studies gain their significance when the situation documented or measured by the researcher is compared with value judgments as to how the situation ought to be. More often than not, the norm or standard of judgment is implicit rather than explicit. The value judgments may be widely shared in a society or limited to special subgroups. The descriptions furnished through the research may be immediately and technically useful to administrators or policymakers, for example, if such research points out previously undetected circumstances in the administrator's particular jurisdiction that in the administrator's view need corrective action. Had Saario, Tittle, and Jackson found no differences in the frequency counts for males and females (see previous section), undoubtedly they would have concluded that the depiction of the sexes in the textbooks they examined were unbiased. This, however, is not what they found; rather, they found large differences in many of the categories in which counts were made. The unsettled question is how large a difference there must be, and in which categories, before a judgment of bias can be entered. Questions of judgment cannot be answered by empirical means. For example, when is parity reached in the distribution of females in the various civil service grades in the federal government? How large must the percentage of respondents be who oppose the appointment of a female superintendent in order to assert the existence of sex bias in the population?

The impact of descriptive studies lies, then, in the departure of the facts as they are measured against an ideal or outside standard, a standard outside the empirical research process itself. In the area of sex equity and affirmative action, that standard may be specified in state or federal legislation, in administrative regulations, or in court decisions. Often, however, standards are implicit, and the appeal for equity is made to the society based on their generally held values regarding equality. The social survey movement that has loomed so large in sociology in this century began with the so-called London survey conducted and reported by Charles Booth in 17 volumes between 1892 and 1897. The purpose of these volumes was "to describe the general conditions under which each class lives and to reveal the relationship which income has to poverty, misery, and depravity" (Jahoda, Deutch, & Cook, 1951, p. 48). The facts revealed by the survey were sufficiently disturbing to give impetus to economic and social reforms during that period. An important function of the descriptive study, as shown in Booth's survey, is to point out disquieting facts not previously known and to arouse public indignation to the point where social action becomes necessary. In the 1930s and 1940s in America a modification of the survey movement became popular—the self-survey. It was prominent in the field of education, and it was based on the observation that the findings and reports of experts often remained unattended and did not motivate anyone to alter the existing state of affairs. Underlying the self-survey was the assumption that if groups of citizens and school personnel were given the opportunity to define the issues to be studied, they would collect the required information, propose remedial action, and have a deeper interest in the survey findings and a stronger commitment to seeing the reforms enacted. It was presumed that the survey group would bring locally relevant values to bear on the findings.

Technical Considerations

Regarding the procedures of technical research, descriptive studies must deal with two central matters: population sampling and accuracy of information or measurement. In discussing descriptive studies as distinct from exploratory research, Selltiz, Wrightsman, and Cook speak to these issues.

> The research questions presuppose much prior knowledge of the problem to be investigated, as contrasted with the questions that form the basis for exploratory studies. Investigators must be able to define clearly what it is they want to measure and must find adequate methods for measuring it. In addition, they must be able to specify who is to be included in the definition of "a given community" or "a given population." In collecting evidence for a study of this sort, what is needed is not so much flexibility [as in exploratory studies] as a clear formulation of *what* and *who* is to be measured and techniques for valid and reliable measurements [1976, p. 102].

The necessary technical skills are not unduly difficult to learn, but they apparently require more rigorous application than often is given them, especially in dissertation research. In addition, it is centrally crucial that detailed descriptions of the population and sampling procedure and of the methods of observation and measurement be carefully and thoroughly presented in the technical report of the study. This is important for two reasons: First, the methods employed in a study are as much a part of the study's results as the numbers and percentages themselves; second, giving a full account of the measurement and sampling procedures of a study permits subsequent research to be built on previous studies, a point that will become apparent shortly. Self-discipline in conducting a descriptive study is especially important when the investigator has a vested interest in the outcome. (The same is true for research into causal relationships.) Researchers undertaking descriptive investigations often have mixed motives. On the one hand, they want to portray whatever inequities they find with sufficient vigor to arouse public indignation and social action; on the other, they want to describe the situation with sufficient objectivity and accuracy so that their findings cannot be readily dismissed as biased or, perhaps worse, so that they do not misguide remedial action.

Descriptive Studies through Time

A special class of descriptive research currently gaining in prominence consists of descriptions that are repeated periodically. Data collected in the decennial census of the United States population come readily to mind, and so do biennial surveys of education, those periodic surveys sponsored by the national associations of superintendents, principals, and teachers. Likewise, some national polling organizations from time to time repeat the same questions when investigating public opinion about schools. A relatively new development, initiated largely by demographers and other social scientists, is the design whereby sets of "social indicators" are measured at regular intervals, as is done with the economic indicators that have become so important in formulating budgetary and monetary policy at the federal level. (Two recent publications that bring together social scientists interested in models of social indicators with researchers concerned with issues of inequity and discrimination are of unusual value in this connection. See Alvarez & Lutterman, 1979, and U.S. Commission on Civil Rights, 1978.)

Gaining access to information that is relevant to a particular research interest can sometimes be tedious, and one is often surprised by the volumes of information collected seasonally by state and even local educational authorities. Repeated measures in a school district, state, or larger jurisdiction reveal trends, and trends can point to trouble spots. Trends invite speculation about and investigation into the factors that account for them. Declines in Scholastic Aptitude Test scores in recent years have led to a flurry of research studies attempting to explain this, and in the process, we have increased our understanding of the SAT scores and of the forces that determine their trends, whether up or down. In addition, repeated measures systematically collected regarding equity issues provide the opportunity to estimate the effectiveness of intervention strategies, allowing policymakers to contemplate alternative ways to remedy institutional discrimination.

Once again, care must be taken, both in collecting data through time and in interpreting figures obtained from published or unpublished institutional sources. Changes can occur in the manner of obtaining data, in the definition of categories, in the measures employed, and in the populations covered. The methodological changes give rise to variations that are misinterpreted as being substantive trends. We can illustrate this point by referring to the sharp decline in the percentage of female principals in the United States from 1928 (55%) to the present (under 20%) that has been cited time and again in the literature of sex equity in education (for example, see Pottker & Fishel, 1977, p. 290). Intervening percentages for 1948, 1958, 1968, and 1971 indicated that the downward trend was rather regular. Most of the figures came from surveys undertaken by the Department of Elementary Principals of the National Education Association. Changes of this magnitude struck us as implying monumental alterations in the social forces affecting the employment of principals and worthy of detailed investigation.

Close reading of the small print concerning the methods used in the surveys, however, revealed that as the years went by the surveys became progressively more inclusive of rural and small-town school districts. The 1928 percentage was based on a 27% return of questionnaires sent to superintendents of large cities in 17 states who were asked to distribute them to elementary principals representative of the city's schools. The later surveys were based on nearly complete responses from a sophisticated probability sample of districts in the United States with enrollments of 300 pupils or more. As the more recent surveys indicated, the percentage of female principals is a direct function of enrollment in the school district, and, presumably, of the "urbanness" of the district. In short, the apparent decline of female principals may have been, at least in part, the result of changes in the population of districts included in the tabulations. There is reason to believe that the drop in the percentage of female principals is not altogether artifactual; but our point is that an investigator collecting and using data through time has to be sensitive to the importance of reporting and reading methodological details lest he or she expend needless effort attempting to explain a phenomenon that does not exist.

Studies of Cause and Effect Relationships

More profound than the descriptive studies that point out the existence of inequities in particular domains of educational institutions are studies that attempt to explain why inequities exist. How did institutions get that way? What keeps the inequities there? Answers to these questions are an essential prelude to an understanding of how conditions might be changed. Properly developed empirical research into the causes that effected some phenomenon can give rise to the remedies needed in decision making. Cause and effect research goes beyond the demands of population coverage and measurement accuracy to the tricky area of inferring causal relationships from empirical data. The investigator has to master additional techniques, including those of re-search design, data analysis, and inferential statistics, and these are not readily learned through casual study or a course or two in research methods and statistics. That the great bulk of research in education is to be found in doctoral dissertations (as Shakeshaft noted in the preceding chapter) and that the dissertation is typically the first (and also the last) piece of research undertaken by the educational researcher (as others have pointed out) leaves us pessimistic concerning the sophistication of the knowledge on which our understanding of causal relationships in educational equity is founded. (For further commentary on dissertations about educational administration, see Haller, 1979.)

At this time, research on why inequities exist in the educational institution is scanty. Our belief is that the considerable research energy currently being expended on descriptive investigation can be harnessed to more productive ends. The observations we make in the remainder of this chapter may help put the research problems into perspective, and it is hoped that this will direct investigation toward the generation of information that is of greater relevance to policy.

Sorting the Variables

Empirical research that attempts to examine cause and effect re-lationships tries to establish a relationship (sometimes called concomitant variation or a correlation) between two or more variables as measured by the investigator. A variable refers to some attribute according to which things or units (e.g., individuals, classrooms, school districts, nations) can differ or vary. Variation may arise when one is comparing one unit with another and when one is examining the same unit through time. Fear of success, sex-role stereotyping, teacher gender, strength of teacher preference for male versus female administrators, the proportion of a university's budgetary support that is devoted to female athletic programs are all variables. More than a dozen additional variables con-cerned with sexual inequities in American schools and universities were listed at the outset of this chapter. In our definition, descriptive studies of an empirical nature measure and report on one or more such var-iables, but in an effort to establish cause and effect relationships, such studies stop short of examining the relationships with other variables.

The variables we have cited are not all of a piece. Some stand as conditions to be explained, such as the inequities in educational institutions, and causes are to be sought. In the context of research into cause and effect relationships, certain conditions serve as dependent variables and others as independent variables. An example of the latter are the conditions of the educational institution that are thought to give rise to inequities—conditions of educational policy or practice that are presumed responsible, at least in part, for certain unjust consequences. (In experimental studies, the independent variable is manipulated by the investigator.)

Consider, for instance, the bias in the portrayal of males and females in children's readers. If this is considered as a dependent variable, one can either attempt to trace the causal nexus that has brought the bias about or question the contribution of such readers to the emergence or reinforcement in young children of stereotypes regarding sexual roles. As another instance, consider the conceptions of guidance counselors regarding the "appropriate" vocations for males and females. One can raise the causal question of how such conceptions come about (with an eye, of course, to how they might be changed); or else the question can focus on the effects of counselors' advice in shaping the behavior of students who are choosing courses or vocations.

The distinction can be oversimplified, since studies might also examine both the antecedents and the consequences of a problematic condition, developing and testing a chain of cause and effect relationships; or a given variable can serve as the dependent variable in one study and as the independent variable in a second study, as suggested in our preceding illustrations. Nevertheless, the distinction is useful in analyzing existing research or in planning one's own research. Our own interest, reflected in part in this book, leans toward considering the inequitable conditions of the school or college as a dependent variable, asking how the policies and practices come about, and seeking the leverage points for effecting change. In taking inequities in the educational institution as the dependent variable, it is of the utmost importance to specify them precisely and measure them accurately.

A considerable advantage is sometimes realized if the investigator builds on the concepts and the measurement procedures of prior research in the domain. In reviewing the literature on a topic, one is constantly impressed by the differences in the way the same general variable is defined and measured. Such differences make it exceedingly difficult for research to be cumulative. In any event, ideally, it is essential to have clearly in mind in the form of an objective measure, precisely what the condition is that is to be changed, so that one is able to specify what "improvement" means. As researchers and specialists in the field of educational policy and management, we tend to sort the issues for study on another basis as well. We attend most closely to those forms of sexual discrimination or invidious bias over which the educational system has at least some modicum of control, leaving to others the task of tracing and understanding inequities that are deeply generic in the societal conditions under which we live.

The Principle of Multiple Causation

Events do not just happen; they are the results of other distinguishable events and conditions, and a number of them, at that. The principle of multiple causation is part of the epistemology underlying science, including social science. The choice of one kind of person rather than another to teach science in American high schools, for instance, is the result of many factors that can be identified and specified, at least theoretically. The lesson this holds for the novice researcher is that it is folly to expect to discover the one cause of any phenomenon. Another thing novice researchers often fail to appreciate is that no single study, no matter how carefully designed, can answer once and for all the questions it seeks to address. There may even be a "law" at work here, namely, the more grandiose the questions the investigator puts forth in a study, the lower the probability that the study will answer any of the questions. The researcher must recognize that empirical knowledge is built by making small accretions, especially of information that fills voids left by prior investigations. The dictum that the dissertation must be an original contribution to knowledge is often interpreted by doctoral students to mean that they should start out fresh as though nothing had ever been learned that could be relevant to the dissertation topic. The reverse is the case. The investigator must learn as much as possible from preceding studies and must be constantly cognizant of the questions these studies failed to answer; he or she must plan the research so that one or a few of these questions are the basis for tests.

Sources of Causal Explications

In seeking to understand through empirical research how particular forms of inequity have come about or what keeps them in place or how they can be changed, the investigator must begin with ideas. Where do ideas come from and what does one do with them? The second part of the question is easier to answer than the first. After one has the ideas, one forms them into postulations, or hypotheses, which say: If Idea X is truly a cause of Inequity Y, then we expect to see more of Inequity Y where X is present (or where there is more of X), and we would expect less of Inequity Y where X is absent (or where there is less of X), *ceteris paribus.* This last phase, meaning other things equal, is essential to every hypothesis; it is the way researchers acknowledge the principle of multiple causation and remind themselves to keep track of the other possible causes of Inequity Y and, insofar as possible, to hold them constant. To eliminate for the moment the possibility that Inequity Y was the consequence of some other factor than Idea X is basically what the technicalities of research design are all about, as we said earlier.

For research to proceed, it is necessary to conceive of a way to operationalize Idea X, that is, to develop a means for measuring its presence or absence or its magnitude, and to do the same for Inequity Y. In nonexperimental research it is also necessary to develop measures of the other potential causes of Inequity Y in order to hold them constant by statistical means or, perhaps, by limiting the study to cases that do not differ with respect to one or more of the other potential causes. Then the researcher must find a population or sample that varies with respect to the measure of Idea X and observe whether or not the sample varies as expected with respect to the measure of Inequity Y, using all the means at his or her disposal to eliminate plausible alternative explanations.

Ideas regarding the causes of inequities in schools and colleges arise from various sources. Rare is the investigator who does not have, at the very least, some rudimentary hunches about the causal circumstances. A hunch is the beginning of a hypothesis, assuming that it can be translated into a measurable phenomenon and that instances can be thought of (and located) that will vary with respect to the presence or absence or magnitude of that phenomenon. As the investigator begins to think analytically about potential causes, the ideas and hunches are likely to begin to spill out in an unsystematic jumble, and the problem becomes one of having too many ideas rather than too few. Under that circumstance, the task draws on the investigator's ability to distinguish between ideas that are merely different ways of phrasing the same condition and ideas that represent generically different conditions. Becoming familiar with existing research on the topic or on related topics can give a substantial boost to effective systematization and conceptualization.

The ideal situation is one in which the researcher can draw on an existing theory relevant to the problem at hand. To understand, for instance, how sex bias operates in the selection of high school principals, it would be useful to have available a larger theoretical framework relevant to the process of selecting administrators in American school districts. To understand how sexually biased curriculum materials come to be used in American classrooms, it would be profitable to have a firm grasp of theories regarding the production, marketing, and adoption processes of curriculum materials in general. (For a considered analysis of the production and distribution of curriculum materials, see Cronbach, 1955; Goldstein, 1978.) Unfortunately, theoretical frameworks attempting to account for events and conditions in the world of educational policy and practice are either primitive or absent altogether. Herein lies a challenge, however, to the researcher familiar with the educational setting. The product of his or her research undertaking may have its greatest utility not in the findings per se but in the conceptualization of the problem. To turn the matter around, in reviewing the literature on a topic, the researcher might well attend as much to the various formulations of the problem as to the empirical results.

There are still other sources for formulating ideas regarding causes. One source often overlooked is the descriptive study itself. While descriptive studies are ordinarily concerned with characterizing the modal, or typical case, it is not uncommon for them to identify deviant cases. For instance, while it may be true that the preponderance of American elementary school principals are male, the statistical tabulations may show that the disproportion is regularly less in urban school districts. To explain by citing the opinion held by teachers and selection committees that females are not capable school administrators, we would have to assume that such biases are weaker in cities than in small-town and rural areas. Is that plausible, or are there other causal explanations at work? The investigator who is concerned with seeking out causal patterns can sometimes test hunches by reading the statistical data closely, especially when the descriptive information is reported in detail. The lesson implied by this is that investigators should not be content with summaries in the text of descriptive research; they should look with a wondering eye at the tabular details in the appendices.

It hardly seems necessary to mention published reviews of the literature as a prime source of ideas, but the extent to which they are ignored is surprising. We refer here to critical reviews, where the reviewer goes beyond summarizing the findings of studies in the area and examines the concepts, measures, and methodology used to produce the findings. Especially useful are those reviews that attempt to bring conceptual order to the topical field. In some cases the theoretical framework developed by the reviewer to organize the studies under examination can be as useful as the substance of the research he or she reports.

While not concentrating exclusively on the school setting, the review of the literature on sex bias in counseling by Smith (1980) is a good illustration of an effort of a reviewer to analyze an issue according to its component parts. According to Smith, a number of studies indicated that clinicians in the field of counseling and psychotherapy held sexually biased views about the nature of women and about the appropriateness of certain behavior and norms for women. For the sexually biased concepts of clinicians to have deleterious effects on female clients, Smith points out, several intervening conditions must also be true. First, the clinician's judgments must reflect the female stereotypes in his or her thinking rather than the true characteristics of the client's problem. Second, the clinician must behave in ways that specifically express the biased judgments and must make recommendations based on the sexual stereotypes. Finally, the client must perceive the counselor's reactions and accept his or her recommendations, which then culminate in a negative effect. These intervening conditions formulated by Smith organized her review of the literature and allowed her to point to the places where additional research was necessary.

One reason that novice investigators ignore published reviews of the literature and find little prior research on their topic is that they define the problem for study too narrowly. A very small net is cast. For example, the novice will turn away from a literature search in dismay because he or she finds nothing about the effect of the sexual composition of teachers' bargaining teams in South Dakota school districts on the inclusion of maternity leave as an issue to be negotiated. Too narrow a definition of the problem under investigation has another serious consequence. The investigator is deprived of what could turn out to be an abundance of research and theoretical development on a problem that is generically similar. A case in point is how the concepts and theoretical developments from studying the impact of federal regulations against racial discrimination might be applied to studying the effects of federal or state regulations against sexual discrimination. The particulars of the two may differ in important ways, but the general elements of the causal models may be sufficiently similar so that the literature in the one area can feed into a study of the other area. The lesson here is that research on issues of sex equity in educational institutions can be informed by acquaintance with one or another of the disciplines of social science— and the possibilities range from economics and public administration to social psychology, political science, cultural anthropology, and American intellectual history. These disciplines provide the generic theoretical frameworks and models that allow the investigator to recognize the special case of a larger, well-formulated issue instead of seeing the problem as a narrow and unique issue.

Reasons as Causes

A rather common form of investigation in education and elsewhere in the social sciences is to ask people directly why they took or failed to take some particular action. The questioning may occur in interviewing sessions or through questionnaires, typically with a predefined checklist of alternatives. Reasons cited most frequently are then reported as the causes of the behavior. The pitfalls of this approach are fairly obvious. The investigator using this approach, in essence, turns the task of establishing causal relationships over to respondents in the study; causation becomes a popularity contest held among laypersons, and the investigator's role is simply to tally the votes. Using reasons as causes is not entirely without merit if the investigator takes an active part in closely analyzing the issue at hand, in formulating a model (or accounting scheme, as it is sometimes called), in phrasing the questions to illuminate various aspects of the model, and in carrying out the analysis of responses in a way that leads to meaningful interpretations.

An important research technology has developed through the years concerning the empirical analysis of action, beginning with the seminal article by Lazarsfeld (1935) on "The Art of Asking Why" and reaching its highpoint of development in Lazarsfeld and Rosenberg's volume, *The Language of Social Research* (1955, sec. 5). The reasons people give for their behavior do indeed amount to something, but it requires systematic and sophisticated planning to elicit meaningful reasons and interpret them in a productive way.

Multivariate Analysis of Data

While the situation appears to be changing, it is still often the case in research seeking to trace the causes of inequitable circumstances in education that investigators who have measured a number of potentially causative variables limit their procedure to an analysis of each variable one at a time. Such analysis is bivariate rather than multivariate. The procedure followed is to ask, is Idea $1X$ related to Inequity Y, is Idea $2X$ related to Inequity Y, is Idea $3X$ . . . , and so on. The bivariate form of analysis fails to take into account the *ceteris paribus* part of every hypothesis. If there are a multiplicity of causal conditions, as we assume there are, then it is important to determine whether or not Idea $1X$ is associated with Inequity Y independently of Idea $2X$, Idea $3X$, and so on. The situation seems to be changing, as we said, probably as a result of the growing familiarity of doctoral students and others with computer packages that make multivariate analysis no more difficult than bivariate analysis. The facilitation of data analysis, of course, has unfortunate side effects from time to time because an investigator may get carried away by the avenues of analysis that have opened up and mindlessly seek to relate everything in the study to everything else, ignoring both the logic of the study and the assumptions inherent in the statistical procedures.

An additional observation with respect to multivariate analysis is less widely known than the procedures. Typically, investigators end their search for concomitant variation when one or more variables is found to be associated with Inequity Y at a given level of statistical significance, say the .05 level. When the relationship remains significant against the challenges of alternative hypotheses, investigators are satisfied that their hunches have paid off. Another necessary consideration beyond statistical significance is the *magnitude* of the effect of the variable or variables on Inequity Y. A statistically significant relationship between two variables may be found even though, for all practical purposes, the relationship is trivial. The level of statistical significance is strongly affected by sample size, so that even the weakest relationship can achieve significance if the sample size is large enough. There are various ways of estimating the magnitude of a relationship among variables, even when it is not directly given, as it would be in a multiple regression coefficient (McNamara, 1978).

Malleable versus Immutable Variables

Much of the social science research on issues of sex equity in education and elsewhere ends on a somber note. The conclusions imply that sex inequities are deeply engrained in modern industrial society and that the causal texture is so intermingled with the immutable attributes of society that changes can only occur with radical alterations in society itself. To some degree that may be true, but such a conclusion may be a product of the manner in which social scientists formulate the problem. If the investigator sets out to find explanations for inequities that are conceived as static attributes, he or she is bound to find them. When the investigator tries to locate causes in terms of traits and states rather than in terms of acts and events, pessimism must surely follow. Matters of our world do undergo change, however, sometimes in unexpected and dissatisfying ways. One cannot hope to understand or explain change by reference to conditions that are immutable. If research is to be related to policy, investigators must formulate the causal nexus so that malleable attributes, subject to human intervention, are included in the set, and they must search out the points where leverage can be applied with the greatest potential for change.

SUBSEQUENT CHAPTERS ON POLICIES AND PRACTICES

The remaining chapters in Part II pertain to the observations we have made as their authors present the results of their research. Throughout our discussion we have spoken of sexual equity and inequity and companion terms as though their meanings were self-evident. We have not undertaken to define the central terms with which a researcher works, a key task required of the sophisticated investigator. In Chapter 3 Pamela Jacklin discusses the conceptual definition of sex equity within the framework of jurisprudence. It is abundantly clear in her presentation that the concept of sex equity has not stood still throughout the years; it has undergone development and change in the course of American legal history and is still in the process of unfolding. Empirical researchers will need to stay in touch with developments in the area of jurisprudence the better to construct theories and carry out research in their own areas of interest.

Schmuck and Wyant in their chapter report on the statewide interventions they and their associates undertook to redress the sex inequities existing in the ranks of school and school district administrators. They recognized that an important point of leverage for change lay not in trying to reduce the sex bias of officials responsible for employing administrators (school boards and superordinate administrators), but in inducing more females to apply for administrative positions in the first place. The noteworthy feature of their work insofar as the present book is concerned is that they systematically collected data to illuminate the intervention process and, more generally, the entire hiring process. While the relatively small number of cases with which they worked limited the generalizations they could draw, the study represents a form of policy-relevant investigation whereby alternative explanations of sexual asymmetry in the administrative hierarchy could be put to test.

The chapter by Hutchison concerning curriculum materials and the sex bias found in them points rather directly to the manner in which empirical research, descriptive and causal, can be used to elucidate policy decisions regarding strategies for reducing the effects of bias. Clearly, changes in the materials themselves are some distance in the future. What of the alternatives? Among the more interesting of the immediate interventions is the training of teachers to recognize the existing biases and to use them as object lessons in the classroom.

REFERENCES

Alvarez, R., and Lutterman, K. G., eds. (1979). *Discrimination in Organizations.* Jossey-Bass, San Francisco.

Cronbach, L. J., ed. (1955). *Text Materials in Modern Education.* University of Illinois, Urbana.

Cronbach, L. J., and Suppes, P. (1969). *Research for Tomorrow's Schools: Disciplined Inquiry for Education.* Macmillan, New York.

Deem, R. (1978). *Women and Schooling.* Routledge & Kegan Paul, London.

Fishel, A., and Pottker, J. (1974). "Women in Educational Governance: A Statistical Portrait." *Educational Researcher,* 3: 4–7.

Goldstein, P. (1978). *Changing the American Schoolbook.* Lexington Books, Lexington, Mass.

Grant, W. V., and Lind, C. G. (1977). *Digest of Educational Statistics,* 1976 Edition, National Center for Education Statistics, Department of HEW, Washington, D.C.

Haller, E. J. (1979). "Questionnaires and the Dissertation in Educational Administration." *Educational Administration Quarterly,* 15: 47–66.

Jahoda, M., Deutsch, M., and Cook, W. (1951). *Research Methods in Social Relations,* vol. 1. Dryden Press, New York.

Lazarsfeld, P. F. (1935). "The Art of Asking Why." *National Marketing Review,* 1: 26–38.

Lazarsfeld, P. F., and Rosenberg, M., eds. (1955). *The Language of Social Research.* Free Press, New York.

McNamara, J. F. (1978). "Practical Significance and Statistical Models." *Educational Administration Quarterly,* 14: 48–63.

Pottker, J., and Fishel, A., eds. (1977). *Sex Bias in the Schools.* Fairleigh Dickinson University Press, Cranbury, N.J.

Saario, T. N., Jacklin, C. N., and Tittle, C. K. (1973). "Sex Role Stereotyping in the Public Schools." *Harvard Educational Review,* 43: 386–416.

Selltiz, C., Wrightsman, L. S., and Cook, S. W. (1976). *Research Methods in Social Relations,* 3rd ed. Holt, Rinehart and Winston, New York.

Stockard, J., Schmuck, P. A., Kempner, K., Williams, P., Edson, S. K., and Smith, M. A. (1980). *Sex Equity in Education.* Academic Press, New York.

Smith, M. L. (1980). "Sex Bias in Counseling and Psychotherapy." *Psychological Bulletin,* 87: 392–407.

U.S. Commission on Civil Rights (1978). *Social Indicators of Equality for Minorities and Women.* Washington, D.C.

Chapter 3

THE CONCEPT OF SEX EQUITY IN JURISPRUDENCE

Pamela Jacklin

> The Constitution of these United States says that all *men* are created equal.
> It don't say nothing about women.
>
> Anonymous[1]

In the United States, as in no other society, the idea of equality became connected to the language of justice in an explicit and public manner (Pole, 1978, pp. 13, 14). Where an idea gains vitality, such as equality has in American thought, the restricted definitions of those in power are subject to challenge by the political demands of those who believe in the vision of true equality. The discrepancy between the public commitment to abstract equality and the reality of an unequal society serves as a constant reminder of unfinished business. Consequently, it is not surprising that nineteenth-century feminists seized upon the concept of equal rights for men and women and proclaimed it their goal. (For a history of American feminism, see Beard, 1946, and O'Neill, 1969.)

The first women's movement, active from about 1840 until 1920, generated the demand that the concept of sex equity be embodied in American law. Feminists recognized the law as a tool for implementing public policy. As a result, they first called upon the courts to proclaim a constitutional mandate of equal rights for women. Despite feminist efforts, the Supreme Court rejected the view that the Constitution re-

[1]Quoted in the introduction to Koch & Chizmar, 1976.

55

quired equal treatment of men and women. Instead, the Court responded by clearly articulating the public policy of romantic paternalism.

As a reaction to the hostility of the nation's courts, nineteenth-century feminists turned their efforts to political action, seeking reform through legislation and the constitutional amendment for women's suffrage. After feminists won the vote and other legislative reforms during the 1920s, public policy reflected a commitment to equal civil and political rights for men and women in limited areas, such as suffrage. Different legal treatment of women remained the rule, however, with the courts and legislatures protecting women's special status as the center of family life.

Public policy changed little until the 1970s. When the contemporary women's movement emerged in the 1960s and 1970s, it was accompanied by revitalized efforts to alter American public policy. Feminists again sought change through legislative effort, constitutional change, and judicial action. The result of these recent efforts is an evolving public policy favoring sex equity.[2]

This chapter focuses on the articulation of traditional and evolving American public policy by judges and legislators. First, we present the concept of sex equity as it was incorporated into American jurisprudence in the nineteenth and early twentieth centuries. Thereafter, recent efforts to alter public policy through legislative change and judicial action are addressed.

EARLY CONCEPTUALIZATIONS OF EQUITY

The Judicial View of Romantic Paternalism

During the nineteenth century and the first half of the twentieth century, judicial premises regarding equity were based on the view that

---

[2]The term *sex equity*, rather than *sexual equality*, increasingly is used by feminists to mean treatment that is fair to women both in form and in result. The evolution of the concept of equity is interesting. Equity is a particular type of Anglo-Saxon justice that developed separately from the English common law. The common law provided the fundamental basis for American jurisprudence and rests on the premise that the duty of courts is to apply rules of law or precedents established in earlier cases. Historically, the common law courts are hostile to change, including legislative change. In contrast, equity jurisprudence raised fairness above the application of strict rules of precedent. The development of equity permitted the application of mitigating principles to cases where the result under the common law would be unfair, thereby defeating substantial justice. Because equity placed fairness above traditional rules of law, the concept of equity is an appropriate intellectual construct for feminists who aim to improve the legal status of women and claim that our legal system has served as a vehicle of women's subjugation.

women were a discrete and separate legal class, and that by nature citizens are divided into the two great classes of men and women (*State of Oregon* v. *Baker*, 1907; legal citations for court cases are listed at the end of the chapter). Judges assumed that physiological, cultural, and sociological differences justified, even demanded, that females be treated differently from males. Even where enlightened principles of equality were heralded, courts routinely explained that equality did not mean uniform treatment for males and females. The United States Supreme Court commenting on a Massachusetts case in 1896 explained as follows:

> When this great principle [equality before the law] comes to be applied to the actual and various conditions of persons in society, it will not warrant the assertion that men and women are legally clothed with the same civil and political powers . . . but only that the rights of all, as they are settled and regulated by law, are equally entitled to the paternal consideration and protection of the law for their maintenance and security [*Plessy* v. *Ferguson*, 1896].

The essence of our public policy until the mid-twentieth century was to provide paternalistic protection for women as a class. Two images are distinguishable in the traditional view of women presented in court opinions, according to Gladys Kessler, an attorney in Washington, D.C. The first image is that of "woman on a pedestal." As the center of stability of family life and the transmitter of cultural values, women were to be looked up to and protected from the ugly and base aspects of life.[3] This pedestal position is exemplified by the language of Justice Bradley in his concurring opinion:

> The civil law, as well as nature herself, has always recognized a wide difference in the respective spheres and destinies of man and woman. Man is, or should be, woman's protector and defender. The natural and proper timidity and delicacy which belongs to the female sex evidently unfits it for many of the occupations of civil life. . . . The domestic sphere . . . properly belongs to the domain and functions of womanhood. . . . The paramount destiny and mission of woman are to fulfill the noble and benign offices of wife and mother. This is the law of the Creator. And the rules of civil society must be adapted to the general constitution of things [*Bradwell* v. *The State of Illinois*, 1872].

[3]During the nineteenth century, jurists and legislators often emphasized the moral superiority of women. Many early feminists accepted this view but rejected the notion that women should be relegated to the domestic sphere. Rather, they argued that because of their moral superiority, women were obligated to participate in public life. Ironically, the more the courts and leaders extolled the virtues of women, the more women believed in their own superiority. As a consequence, increasing numbers of women moved into the political sphere, demanding the vote in the belief that women could reform corrupt political systems.

The image of women on a pedestal is accompanied by the image of women as simple, childlike, and even stupid. Because they were unable to deal with the realities of the world, they were to be sheltered, and husbands and fathers generally acted as their legal representatives. According to the common law doctrine of coverture, summarized by Blackstone in his *Commentaries,* married women could not exercise legal rights independent of their husbands:

> By marriage, the husband and wife are one person in the law: that is, the very being or legal existence of the woman is suspended during marriage, or at least is incorporated and consolidated into that of the husband, under whose wing, protection, and cover, she performs everything [Sprague, 1897, p. 79].

Women often remained under the legal protection of their fathers until marriage, after which their husbands exercised all legal rights for them. Under the common law, most women were deemed legally incapable of entering into contracts on their own or of managing their property. It was necessary to pass legislation, such as the Married Woman's Property Acts, in order for women to be guaranteed of these civil rights.[4]

As a consequence of the public policy of paternalistic protection of women, American judges systematically rejected efforts by women activists to utilize the courts to obtain equality of treatment. The Supreme Court never heard a case dealing with sex equity until after the Civil War, and from the Civil War until the 1970s, it chose to hear only a handful of such cases. The Court's decisions systematically rebuked efforts to implement the principle of equal rights and responsibilities through judicial action during that time. Between 1870 and 1970, it decided as follows on cases involving women's rights:

1. It held that a state could absolutely prohibit women from practicing law (*Bradwell* v. *The State of Illinois,* 1872).

2. It held that while women were national citizens, they constituted a special class who had no inherent right to vote (*Minor* v. *Happersett,* 1875).

3. It held that the physical differences between men and women, as well as women's procreative function, demanded special protective legislation to regulate working conditions for females (*Muller* v. *Oregon,*

----

[4]New York enacted the first Married Women's Property Act in 1848. Much of the impetus for the early Property Acts came from fathers who feared that dishonest or impecunious sons-in-law would steal or squander their daughters' dowries or inheritances. Feminists later advocated Married Women's Property Acts and worked to modify the doctrine of coverture through legislative reform. See Sachs and Wilson, 1978, pp. 77-80.

1908). (At the same time, similar legislation regulating working conditions for all workers had been held an unconstitutional interference with the liberty to contract.)

4. It upheld a state law permitting only women who were the wives or daughters of male bar owners to be employed as bartenders on the grounds that "ownership of a bar by a barmaid's husband or father minimizes hazards that may confront a barmaid without such protecting oversight" (*Goesaert* v. *Cleary*, 1948).

5. It upheld a state law limiting jury service by women to volunteer registrants because of the special responsibilities of women as center of the home and family; it simultaneously required all males to be included on jury lists (*Hoyt* v. *State of Florida*, 1961).

6. It affirmed without substantive opinion the right of a state to maintain sex-segregated state colleges some 15 years after dual educational systems based on segregation by race had been held unconstitutional (*Williams* v. *McNair*, 1971).

Legislative Efforts as a Response to Judicial Hostility

Advocates of equity turned to the state legislatures during the late 1800s, after recognizing the hostility of the courts to their efforts to change public policy. (For an analysis of the interaction between the political and legal activities of feminists, see Wilson, 1977, p. 125 *et seq.*) Legislative enactments mitigated some of the harshest effects of the public policy of paternalistic protection for women. Although the Married Women's Property Acts did not abolish the law of coverture, they modified the common law so that it allowed wives to sell or bequeath their property more readily, to own and manage property separately from their husbands, and, eventually to control their separate earnings (see Sachs & Wilson, 1978, pp. 210–226). The Nineteenth Amendment, enacted after more than 70 years of struggle, granted women citizens the vote. Protective legislation—ostensibly designed to improve the working conditions of women by such means as imposing limits on hours and requiring rest periods—was enacted eagerly by reformers. However, none of these legislative measures altered the fundamental policy of viewing sex as an appropriate classification device to distinguish people's legal rights and responsibilities. The rights and obligations of citizens still differed for males and females.

Summary of the Early View

According to early American public policy, whether by judicial pronouncement or by legislative measures, women constituted a special category of citizens deserving protection rather than equality under the law. The traditional concept of equity absorbed the contradiction between the "call of equality" and the reality of a legally imposed sexual caste system (see Freeman, 1971, pp. 203–206). Equity, in this historical context, was the provision of legal protection for men, as a class, to permit them to fulfill their functions in the working world, in politics, and in the marketplace of ideas; the provision of legal protection for women permitted them to function as the center of family life and the transmitter of cultural values.

EVOLUTION OF THE CONCEPT OF EQUITY

Redefining Public Policy through Legislation

The 1960s

With the second wave of American feminism in the late 1960s came increased attention to the status of women under American law. Interestingly, two of the most significant legislative changes for American women were enacted prior to the formation and lobbying efforts of new feminist organizations. In 1963, women from the Women's Bureau of the Department of Labor, from traditional women's rights groups (such as Business and Professional Women), and union women campaigned for and won the passage of the Equal Pay Act. The intent of the act was to provide equal pay for equal work, but coverage was limited to blue-collar workers and other employees paid by the hour. One year later, the Civil Rights Act of 1964 was passed, legislation generally acknowledged as this nation's most comprehensive attempt since the Civil War to guarantee enjoyment of certain rights and privileges without regard to race, color, or national origin (citations to statutes are listed at the end of the chapter). Title VII of the 1964 Civil Rights Act prohibited employment discrimination. There was vigorous opposition to Title VII, particularly from southern senators. In what some commentators considered an attempt to defeat Title VII, it was amended to include a prohibition against sexual discrimination in employment. The Senate's debate over the inclusion of the amendment was brief and marked by levity (see Freeman, 1975, pp. 53–54), and Title VII was amended to include a prohibition against discrimination on the basis of sex.

Thus, the legislative cornerstone was laid for a new public policy concerning sex equity. In 1967, women's rights lobbyists convinced President Johnson to amend Executive Order 11246 to prohibit government contractors from discriminating in employing on the basis of sex. This success was followed by the growth of an informal women's lobby, led by women from the fields of education, other professions, and the unions. With the resurgence of the women's movement in the last half of the 1960s, increased attention was paid to sexual bias in the law. Feminist groups noted the lack of legal protection against sex discrimination in education, in housing, and in obtaining credit, among other areas, as well as the lack of enforcement of the recently passed Equal Pay Act, Title VII, and Executive Order 11246. The Equal Employment Opportunity Commission (EEOC), the agency established to enforce Title VII, openly acknowledged that it did not take its mandate to eliminate sex discrimination in employment seriously. The 1970s have witnessed the emergence of a public policy of sex equity that limits the use of gender as a justification for differing legal rights and responsibilities. However, it is clear that the policy of sex equity encompassed in American law today permits continued use of sex as a basis for legal classification in some circumstances. The idea that sexual equality also means the equal sharing of legal rights and responsibilities is not yet firmly embodied in American law. As a consequence, it is an open question as to whether equal rights for men and women ultimately will prevail in this nation. Nevertheless, as a result of heightened awareness of the inequitable treatment of American women under the law, many individuals and groups began lobbying for legal reform and enforcement of existing laws.

The 1970s

Women's rights advocates were making an impact on Congress by the early 1970s. The Ninety-second Congress passed considerably more women's rights legislation than all earlier congresses combined (Freeman, 1975, p. 202). During this time period, the focus of broad elements of the women's movement was on the proposed Equal Rights Amendment (ERA). On March 22, 1972, the Senate passed the ERA, as the House had earlier, and the Amendment was sent to the states for ratification. Representative Martha Griffiths, commenting on the significant legislative victory for women's rights advocates in 1972, stated that: "The ERA created a moral climate for reform. Once it was put through, everything else became logical" (Freeman, 1975, p. 222).

Significantly, the legislative campaign led by women's movement activists did not end with congressional passage of the ERA. Women's groups promoted other legislation in an attempt to establish a clear national policy favoring equal rights for women in employment, education, and other areas. The Equal Pay Act of 1963 was amended to cover administrative, professional, and managerial employees as well as hourly workers; Title VII of the 1964 Civil Rights Act was amended to give broader enforcement to the EEOC and to provide coverage for additional employees, including teachers, who had previously been exempted from the application of the law. Perhaps the most significant new legislative enactment of the Ninety-second Congress was Title IX of the Education Amendment of 1972.

Title IX

From 1970 until Title IX was passed, professional women and academicians worked supportively with members of Congress and their staffs to gain acceptance for the prohibition of sexual discrimination as part of an omnibus education act. The prototype of Title IX was first introduced by Congressman Edith Green from Oregon, chairperson of the House Special Subcommittee on Education. Several events focused Congressman Green's attention on the issue of sexual discrimination in education. The Women's Equity Action League (WEAL) had complained to the Department of Labor, which is charged with enforcing the executive order prohibiting sexual discrimination in employment by federal contractors, alleging massive discrimination by hundreds of colleges and universities. Moreover, a task force on women's rights and responsibilities, appointed by President Nixon, had issued a report documenting sexual bias in various areas and recommending specific legislative changes to eliminate such bias in education. In 1970, Green added a provision against sexual discrimination in her higher-education bill that would have amended Title VI of the 1964 Civil Rights Act to prohibit sexual discrimination in addition to discrimination because of race and national origin in federally assisted programs and activities.

During June and July of 1970, Green held hearings on sex discrimination in education (Discrimination Against Women, Hearings, 1970). Although the hearings were not well-attended nor well-publicized at the time, they resulted in the compilation and publication of overwhelming data regarding the problems of sex discrimination in education, and they provided the background for much subsequent legislative lobbying and debate on Title IX. After the hearings, Green's entire 1970 higher-education bill died in committee. Efforts to pass an omnibus education act continued in the session beginning in the fall of 1971. Green again introduced a higher-education bill that contained a provision against sexual discrimination. Her 1971 provision differed significantly in two respects. First, the 1971 proposal limited the prohibition of sexual discrimination to educational programs and activities, whereas the 1970 proposal involved all federally assisted programs and activities regardless of the nature of the program. Secondly, certain exceptions to the prohibition of discrimination in educational programs were added. The bill totally exempted educational institutions where the student body was substantially of one sex; it also provided a limited exemption for religious educational institutions and a transition period for schools that were then in the process of changing from a single-sex to a coed composition.

Green then determined that it was unwise to attempt to amend Title VI of the 1964 Civil Rights Act and instead proposed to her subcommittee that the sex-discrimination prohibition be included in an education act rather than an amendment to Title VI. Her higher-education bill passed the House and the Senate with a somewhat amended provision against sexual discrimination. The bill was signed by the president on June 23, 1972, and Title IX became the law of the land. In effect, Title IX prohibited certain types of sexual discrimination in federally aided educational programs and mandated change in the operation of virtually all of the public educational institutions in the United States and many of the private institutions as well. As a consequence, it is one of the most significant legislative reforms of our time.

Judicial Perspectives on Public Policy

As legislative enactments were changing public policy on sex equity, the courts in turn began to respond to the evidence of changed perceptions and values regarding women's roles. The development of a new public policy coincided with an increasing scrutiny by the courts of the historical treatment of women. The inferior legal status of American women, decried by early feminists more than a century before, became the focus of considerable concern for women's rights advocates, and the conclusion of male law professors (who in their own words "have never been radicalized, brutalized, politicized or otherwise leaned on by the establishment") was stated as follows in 1971:

> By and large, the performance of American judges in the area of sex discrimination can be succinctly described as ranging from poor to abominable.... Sexism, the making of unjustified (or at least unsupported) assumptions about individual capabilities, interests, goals and social roles solely on the basis of sex differences, is as easily discernible in contemporary judicial opinions as racism ever was [Johnstone & Knapp, 1971, p. 687].

This critique of the policy of romantic paternalism toward women, a concept that required protection, not equality, coincided with the Supreme Court's first tentative step toward the recognition of a public policy favoring sex equity. In 1971, the Court found unconstitutional an Idaho law that gave males a statutory preference over females in serving as administrators of estates (*Reed* v. *Reed*, 1971). (It was the first time that a state law had been found by a decision of the Court to discriminate unreasonably on the basis of sex.) In reaching this decision, the Court applied the Equal Protection Clause of the Fourteenth Amendment, which had been ratified in 1868.

Equal Protection

The Equal Protection Clause of the Fourteenth Amendment and the Due Process Clause of the Fifth Amendment guarantee equal protection under the laws to all persons. This means that the government (federal, state, and local) must protect the rights of all citizens equally. The essence of the protection offered to all citizens is a prohibition against arbitrary legal classifications that would unfairly discriminate against one class of people (although reasonable classifications are permitted).[5] Throughout our nation's history prior to *Reed* v. *Reed,* the Supreme Court had always held that legislative classifications based exclusively on sex were constitutional. As noted earlier, the nation's courts were in agreement that "by nature, citizens are divided into two great classes—men and women" (*Plessy* v. *Ferguson,* 1896). The judicial parameters of the modern notion of sex equity can best be established by examining the Court's treatment of the fundamental equal protection question: Is sex a reasonable basis for classification under the law, and if so, when?

In *Reed* v. *Reed,* the Court did not challenge the concept of dividing men and women into separate legal classes. Rather, for the first time, the Court indicated there is a *limitation* imposed by the idea of equal protection. The limitation on the division of each sex into separate legal classes with distinct rights and responsibilities is the prohibition of arbitrary choices by governmental action. In *Reed* v. *Reed,* the Court decided that where the division of persons into sexual classes is not necessary to accomplish the objective of the same law, the state cannot make gender-

[5]Reasonable legal classifications are permitted under the concept of equal protection. A reasonable classification is one wherein the nature of the classification or the basis for dividing people into separate legal classes is reasonably related to the object of the classification itself. For example, the legal system treats juveniles accused of a crime differently from the way it treats adults accused of a crime. Another example is the provision of special tax advantages for senior citizens who sell their homes, which enables seniors to retain their money for use during their retirement years. In both cases, two distinct legal classes are established; in the first case, there is the class of juveniles and that of adults; in the second, the class of senior citizens and all other citizens.

based distinctions but must treat similarly situated persons alike. A distinction based on sex was arbitrary in this instance because it was employed merely to save time and money for the state by avoiding judicial hearings as to who could most competently perform the job of administrator. Accordingly, the court found it was not fair to utilize a gender-based classification favoring males as administrators of estates. As a result, Idaho could not eliminate the necessity of conducting a hearing to decide whether the competing male or female applicant should be named the administrator of an estate by applying a discriminatory statute giving preference to males.

Feminists' hopes were raised in 1973 when four Supreme Court justices issued a plurality opinion in *Frontiero* v. *Richardson* (1973), arguing that legal classifications based upon sex are suspect, that such classifications must be scrutinized closely by the court, and that sexual classifications are permissible only in rare circumstances. The facts in *Frontiero* concerned a servicewoman who alleged she was unconstitutionally denied dependents' benefits for her husband who was not in the military. At that time, servicemen automatically received dependents' benefits for their wives, but servicewomen had to prove that they provided more than half of their husbands' support in order to be entitled to such benefits. The majority of the Court held that this rule unconstitutionally discriminated against women. However, feminist hopes that the Court would deem sex a suspect classification under the law, as it does with race and national origin, were thwarted by its subsequent decisions.

Supreme Court decisions following *Frontiero* v. *Richardson,* at times have created confusion and at times have seemed marked with ambivalence. Those who hoped the Court would provide a clear, consistent, and compelling jurisprudence that affords full legal rights for women have been disappointed. Although sex (or gender, as the courts now prefer to speak of it) is clearly a disfavored legal classification, there are circumstances in which it is applied to differentiate between the legal rights of men and women. On the one hand, as Justice Stevens states in *Craig* v. *Boren* (1976), "habit, rather than analysis, makes it seem acceptable and natural to distinguish between male and female." On the other hand, the series of decisions we report on indicate that the Supreme Court has not rejected sex or gender as being an impermissible classification in all instances. The issues that the Court has contended with are not simple ones. In any time of major jurisprudential transition, the crosscurrents of reform, of individual justice versus fairness for all, and of logical social reality compete with each other. Although the Court's decisions may be confusing, they permit us to observe the parameters placed on sex equity; there is no other way to understand the present public policy on the subject.

Judicial Parameters for Sexual Equality

In setting parameters or limitations on equal protection, the Court has addressed itself to three areas: false or overbroad generalizations about men and about women, the rights of an individual versus the rights of a class or group, and true generalizations about men and about women as a basis for legal classification.

False or Overly Broad Generalizations

The Court has rejected gender-based classifications where there is an untrue generalization about a sex. For example, in *Frontiero* v. *Richardson*, the Court described the generalization that all wives are dependent for their support upon their husbands as an archaic and overly broad generalization concerning the financial position of women. Likewise, in *Weinberger* v. *Wiesenfeld* (1975) and *Califano* v. *Goldfarb* (1977), the Court found unconstitutional those provisions of the Social Security system that denied survivor's benefits to the families of female wage earners. The Court has increasingly rejected "outdated misconceptions concerning the role of females in the home rather than in the 'market place and world of ideas' . . . as loosefitting characterizations" incapable of supporting sex-based distinctions under the law. This statement was made by the Court in the case of *Stanton* v. *Stanton* (1975), where the Court invalidated a Utah law that permitted parental support of females to be terminated at age 18 but required parental support of males until the age of 21. The Court rejected what it called "old notions" of male and female roles and noted that the female was no longer "destined solely for the home and bearing of the family."

Having rejected in *Stanton* v. *Stanton* the generalization that males need to be supported for a longer period of time in order to provide them with the education necessary to equip them to support their families, the Court found that gender is not a basis for distinctions regarding the age at which a child is entitled to support. Similarly, the Court found the generalization that a woman's role in the home justified an automatic exemption from jury service to be false. Therefore, in *Taylor* v. *Louisiana* (1975), the Court held that such an exemption unconstitutionally deprived an accused person's right to trial by a jury drawn from a fair cross-section of the community. The Court has also held that gender-based classifications are impermissible where gender is employed as an inaccurate proxy for other more germane bases of classification. Thus, in *Stanley* v. *Illinois* (1972), the Court overturned a state law that permitted the state to remove illegitimate children from their fathers' custody without a hearing but guaranteed mothers of illegitimate children a hearing before such removal. The Court reasoned as follows:

> In light of the weak congruence between gender and the characteristic or trait that gender purported to represent, it was necessary that the legislature choose either to realign their substantive laws in a gender-neutral fashion, or to adopt procedures for identifying those instances where the sex-centered generalization is actually contrary to fact.

Thus, the state could not treat male parents of illegitimate children (as a class) differently from the way female parents of illegitimate children (as a class) were treated in regard to parental custody of children.

Gender classification based on stereotypical notions about women and about men are invalidated, in some cases, even where the classification purportedly favors or protects women. In *Orr* v. *Orr* (1979), the Court struck down an Alabama law providing for alimony to be paid only to wives, saying: "The fact that the classification expressly discriminates against men rather than women does not protect it from scrutiny."[6] The Court rejected "sex as a proxy for need." Moreover, it concluded that even if sex were an accurate classifying tool to determine who generally needed spousal support, needy women would obtain such aid through individualized hearings. Thus, Alabama's purpose of helping needy spouses would be better served by focusing on the individual spouse's need for support, regardless of sex.

Decisions that Focus on the Group or on the Individual

The Supreme Court's concept of equity prohibits distrinctions based on sex or gender where generalizations about the roles or abilities of each sex are false or overbroad. One question that arises in this regard is how one judges whether a generalization based on sex is true or false. The issue, simply put, is whether one should look at the class (or the sex) as a whole or at each individual separately, to judge the truth of a generalization. This problem is best understood in an actual case. In the *City of Los Angeles* v. *Manhart* (1978), the Supreme Court faced a true

---

[6]But see *Kahn* v. *Shevin* (1974), where the Court upheld a Florida law providing a property tax exemption for widows but not widowers. Justice Douglas wrote the majority opinion, stating that "[w]e deal here with a state tax law reasonably designed to further the state policy of cushioning the financial impact of spousal loss upon the sex for which that loss imposes a disproportionately heavy burden."

generalization about women as a class: Women live longer than males on the average. The Court had to decide whether a valid generalization about women as a group could form the basis for a legal classification. The precise question posed by this case was whether a demonstrable difference between males' and females' life expectancy justifies requiring women employees to make higher contributions to a pension plan. In this case, the Court found that congressional policy precluded discriminating against individual females simply because they were members of a sexual class that as a group lived longer than males. "The basic policy of [Title VII 1964 Civil Rights Act] requires that we focus upon fairness to individuals rather than fairness to classes."

Under Title VII, Congress required that the individual be the focus for judging the truth or falsity of the premise on which a legal rule is based. While it is true that women do live longer than men, on the average, an individual woman may or may not live as long as any given individual male. There is no way of knowing in advance when, exactly, any individual male or female will die. A focus on the individual rather than all members of one sex, therefore, precludes the assessment of pension contributions on the basis of sex. Thus because any given woman may or may not live longer than any given man, Title VII requires that the sexes be treated in the same manner. Terming the "statutes' focus on the individual . . . unambiguous," the Court held in the *City of Los Angeles* v. *Manhart* that requiring higher pension contributions from women employees violated federal law. In this way, the Court defined the concept of equity in cases of employment discrimination as requiring the incorporation of the principle of individualism. Under Title VII, a generalization that is true about women as a group will not justify different treatment based on the sex of employees. (In certain employment decisions, sex can be a qualification.)[7]

The Court did not conclude that class distinctions based on sex were incompatible with the concept of equity. Instead, the Court intimated

---

[7]Employment decisions based upon true generalizations about women or men, such as the fact that men are stronger than women on the average, must be distinguished from those situations where sex is a bona fide occupational qualification (BFOQ) under Title VII. Sex is a BFOQ where only persons of one sex can perform a job successfully and, as a consequence, the employer may limit applications for the position to persons of that sex. For example, only males can qualify as sperm donors; therefore, the position of sperm donor can be limited to males only. Additionally, EEOC has permitted BFOQs where authenticity is required or where privacy rights might be seriously infringed. Consequently, an employer may limit applications for a leading woman in a play to females and applications for a men's shower-room attendant to males.

In *Dothard* v. *Rawlinson*, 433 US 321, 97 S Ct 2720, 53 L Ed 2d 786 (1977), the distinction between sex as a BFOQ and the use of a generalization to justify treating male employees that whether equity demanded that individuals be treated in the same way, without regard to their sex, or whether equity only required fairness as between men as a class and women as a class, was a question of policy. It was the legislature, not the Court in the *City of Los Angeles* v. *Manhart*, that properly determined this policy issue. Therefore, the Court proclaimed its deference to Congress on this question. Congress had decided that sexual classifications *in employment* were illegal, even where distinctions were based on real, not fictional, differences between men and women.

True Generalizations

Under Title VII, then, restrictions that prevent women from holding certain jobs because of the strength required to perform those jobs would be illegal. It may be true that men are stronger than women on the average, but a given individual female may be stronger than a given individual male. By focusing on the individual to ascertain the truth or falsity of the premise upon which the legal rule is based, one concludes that in employment it would be impermissible to make a sex-based distinction based on the premise that males have superior physical strength. In employment cases, the Court requires that generalizations be judged on an individual basis wherever possible and that classification based on sex be eliminated where an individual member of either sex could be penalized by true but overbroad generalization about his or her sex. Even where distinctions based on sex are real, on the average, the Congressional focus on individuals in employment legislation prevents a true generalization from justifying a sex-based class.

Congressional policy requires that the focus be put on fairness to an individual in employment discrimination cases; but what of those cases where Congressional policy is not clear or where there is no Congressional policy? In such cases, the Court is free to decide that equity requires only fairness between classes (or sexes) where distinction is based on a true generalization about women or about men as a group. Education is a prime example of a policy area where Congress has not determined conclusively what equity requires. Title IX does not prohibit

---

differently from female employees is blurred. The Court held that sex is BFOQ for contact positions in Alabama's prisons. Citing the "jungle atmosphere" of Alabama's prisons and the high percentage of sex offenders housed therein, the Court concluded that women guards would be likely to invite attacks. "The employee's very womanhood would thus directly undermine her capacity to provide the security that is the essence of a correctional counselor's responsibility." Justices Marshall and Brennan dissented, saying: "This rationale regrettably perpetuates one of the most insidious of the old myths about women—that women, wittingly or not, are sexual objects."

single-sex public schools at the elementary or secondary level, except for vocational schools. In the face of Congressional uncertainty, the Supreme Court responded by permitting "separate but equal" public academic high schools (*Vorschheimer* v. *School District* (1977)). On the other hand, where federally assisted schools are coeducational, Title IX regulations prohibit separate classes for different sexes, with very limited exceptions. For example, physical education classes, traditionally segregated on the basis of sex, must be integrated except for participation in contact sports. Yet, the Department of HEW has interpreted Title IX to permit sex-segregated athletic programs so long as those programs provide equal opportunity for male and female athletes. Clearly, the ambivalence about the meaning of sex equity is expressed through our public policy.

Summary of the Present Concept of Sex Equity

Gender remains an acceptable basis for legal classification in modern American jurisprudence. Where Congress explicitly requires equal treatment for both sexes, the Supreme Court implements Congressional policy. In areas where Congress is silent, such as on the appropriateness of single-sex public high schools, the Court's approach is more cautious. Despite the failure of the judiciary to articulate clearly the meaning of sex equity, significant gains have been made since 1970. As a rule, sexual classifications based on stereotypical notions about women are examined carefully and often rejected by our courts. Judicial opinions generally acknowledge that the jurisprudence of romantic paternalism found support more in myth than in reality. The 1970s have witnessed the emergence of a public policy of sex equity that limits the use of gender as a justification for differing legal rights and responsibilities. However, it is clear that the policy of sex equity encompassed in American law today permits continued use of sex as a basis for legal classification in some circumstances. The idea that sexual equality also means the equal sharing of legal rights and responsibilities is not yet firmly embodied in American law. As a consequence, it is an open question as to whether equal rights for men and women under the law ultimately will prevail in this nation.

STATUTES

1. Civil Rights Act, 42 USC § 2000(a) *et seq.* (1970);
   Title VII, 42 USC § 2000(e) (1970).
2. Equal Pay Act, 29 USC § 206(d) (1970).
3. Title IX, Education Admendment of 1972, 20 USC § 1681 *et seq.* (1975 supp.).

CASES

1. *Bradwell* v. *The State of Illinois,* 83 US (16 Wall) 130, 21 L Ed 442 (1872).
2. *Califano* v. *Goldfarb,* 430 US 199, 97 S Ct 1021, 51 L Ed 2d 270 (1977).
3. *City of Los Angeles, Dept. of Water* v. *Manhart,* 435 US 702, 98 S Ct 1370, 55 L Ed 2d 657 (1978).
4. *Craig* v. *Boren,* 429 US 190, 97 S Ct 451, 50 L Ed 2d 397 (1976).
5. *Frontiero* v. *Richardson,* 411 US 677, 93 S Ct 1764, 36 L Ed 2d 583 (1973).
6. *Goesaert* v. *Cleary,* 335 US 464, 69 S Ct 198, 93 L Ed 163 (1948).
7. *Hoyt* v. *State of Florida,* 368 US 57, 82 S Ct 159, 7 L Ed 2d 118 (1961).
8. *Kahn* v. *Shevin,* 416 US 351, 94 S Ct 1734, 40 L Ed 2d 189, 42 USLW 4591 (1974).
9. *Minor* v. *Happersett,* 88 US (21 Wall) 162, 22 L Ed 627 (1875).
10. *Muller* v. *Oregon,* 208 US 412, 28 S Ct 324, 52 L Ed 551 (1908).
11. *Orr* v. *Orr,* 440 US 268, 99 S Ct 1102, 59 L Ed 2d 306, 47 USLW 4224 (1979).
12. *Plessy* v. *Ferguson,* 163 US 537, 16 S Ct 1138, 41 L Ed 256 (1896).
13. *Reed* v. *Reed,* 404 US 71, 92 S Ct 251, 30 L Ed 2d 225 (1971).
14. *Stanley* v. *Illinois,* 405 US 645, 92 S Ct 1208, 31 L Ed 2d 551 (1972).
15. *Stanton* v. *Stanton,* 421 US 7, 95 S Ct 1373, 43 L Ed 2d 688 (1975).
16. *State of Oregon* v. *Baker,* 50 Or 381, 385, 92 P 1076 (1907), quoted in *State of Oregon* v. *Hunter,* 208 Or 282, 286, 300 P2d 455 (1956).
17. *Taylor* v. *Louisiana,* 419 US 522, 95 S Ct 692, 42 L Ed 2d 690 (1975).
18. *Vorchheimer* v. *School District of Philadelphia,* 532 F2d 880 (3rd Cir 1976) offered by an equally divided court, 430 US 703, 97 S Ct 1671, 51 L Ed 2d 750 (1977).
19. *Weinberger* v. *Wiesenfeld,* 420 US 636, 95 S Ct 1225, 43 L Ed 2d 514 (1975).
20. *Williams* v. *McNair,* 401 US 951, 91 S Ct 976, 28 L Ed 2d 235 (1971).

REFERENCES

Beard, M. (1946). *Women as a Force in History: A Study in Traditions and Realities.* MacMillan, New York, p. 148.

Bernard, J. (1971). *Women and the Public Interest.* Aldine, Chicago.

Buek, A., and Orleans, J. (1973). "Sex Discrimination—a Bar to a Democratic Education: Overview of Title IX of the Education Amendments of 1972." *Discrimination Against Women, Hearings on Section 805 of H.R. 16098, Hearings Before the House Special Subcommittee on Education of the Committee on Education and Labor,* 91st Congress, 2nd Session *(1970). Connecticut Law Review,* 6: 1.

Dye, T. R. (1972). Understanding Public Policy. Prentice-Hall, Englewood Cliffs, N.J.

Fishel, A., and Pottker, J. (1977). National Politics and Sex Discrimination in Education. Lexington Books, Lexington, Mass.

Freeman, J. (1971). "The Legal Basis of the Sexual Caste System." *Valparaiso Law Review,* 5: 203–206.

Freeman, J. (1975). The Politics of Women's Liberation. McKay, New York, 53–54.

Jacklin, P. (1977). "A Matter of Simple Justice: The Prohibition of Discrimination in Federally Assisted Programs—Title VI and Title IX." Northwest General Assistance Center, Portland State University, Oregon. Unpublished Paper.

Johnstone, J. D., Jr., and Knapp, C. L. (1971). "Sex Discrimination by Law: A Study in Judicial Prospective." *New York University Law Review,* 46: 687.

Koch, J. V., and Chizmar, J. F., Jr. (1976). *The Economics of Affirmative Action.* Lexington Books, Lexington, Mass.

O'Neill, W. (1969). *Everyone Was Brave: A History of Feminism in America.* Quadrangle, New York.

Pole, J. R. (1978). *The Pursuit of Equality in American History.* University of California Press, Berkeley, pp. 13–14.

Ripley, R. B., ed. (1966). *Public Policies and Their Politics,* Norton, New York.

Sachs, A., and Wilson, J. H. (1978). *Sexism and the Law: A Study of Male Beliefs and Legal Bias in Britain and the United States.* Martin Robinson, Oxford, England.

Smith, M. P. (1973). *Politics and Public Policy.* Random House, New York.

Sprague, W., ed. (1897). *Abridgment of Blackstone's Commentaries.* Courier, Ann Arbor, Michigan.

Wilson, J. H. (1977). "The Legal Status of Women in the Late Nineteenth and Early Twentieth Centuries." *Human Rights,* 6: 125.

Zeigler, H., and Johnson, K. F. (1972). *The Politics of Education in the States.* Irvington, New York.

Chapter 4

CLUES TO SEX BIAS IN THE SELECTION OF SCHOOL ADMINISTRATORS: A REPORT FROM THE OREGON NETWORK

Patricia A. Schmuck and Spencer H. Wyant

It is penny wise and pound foolish for a school to cut back on the time or effort invested in the selection of educators [Erickson & Shinn, 1977, preface].

Personnel decisions are the most important decisions made by local school districts. The manner in which local school agencies use their resources to educate young people depends in great part on the leadership provided by superintendents, principals, and other leaders. Yet there has been surprisingly little attention devoted to study of the processes by which educational administrators are recruited, selected, and hired. In this chapter we describe results of our research on those processes as part of the Sex Equity in Educational Leadership (SEEL) Project, which was funded by the Women's Educational Equity Act Program of the U.S. Office of Education from 1976 to 1979. Our results shed light on hiring processes used by local school districts, the pool of applicants for administrative vacancies, and how the interaction of applicants and processes affected women's opportunities to become school administrators.

HIRING ADMINISTRATIVE PERSONNEL

The process of hiring administrators has changed dramatically in this century. In earlier days leadership in public schools was seen as a

73

"calling, similar to that of church missionary." School boards chose leaders on the basis of their moral character and public charisma. The administrator was to be a "conductor of the pedagogical train," a person by whom the school system was "to be conducted into the great Union Station of this imperial nation" (Tyack, 1976). But today the expectations and requirements have changed. Educational leaders have become managerial functionaries. Requirements of charisma have changed to requirements of certification, and demands for a pure moral character have changed to demands for skill in policy implementation. Other changes have altered the processes of hiring administrators, such as consolidation of districts, governmental mandates to promote greater equity, and a greater number of people seeking fewer available positions.

There have been two significant results of these various changes. The first is that the hiring of school administrators has become a much more formal process. In the past, administrative positions were often given as rewards for competent teaching or as slots for incompetent people who were tenured. While those reasons for becoming an administrator still operate in some cases, today school districts generally use more competitive and objective procedures for screening and selecting candidates. That is true in part because administration is now considered a specialized field, requiring abilities and experience that cannot be gained simply from years of experience in teaching. The second result is that changes in the role of the administrator and in processes for hiring administrators have coincided with a dramatic decrease of women in managerial positions in public schools.

The increasing formality of the hiring process, however, is to some extent a superficial development. While school districts must comply with an increasing number of regulations about how they hire administrators, they also have considerable discretionary power that allows informal practices to continue as a powerful force in determining who will be hired.

On one hand, laws and regulations that impinge on the hiring process are increasing. The federal government's role has increased: regulations such as Title VII of the 1964 Civil Rights Act, Title IX of the Educational Admendments of 1972 (although some cases have disputed whether Congress intended employment to be covered by Title IX), and executive orders mandate equal employment opportunities. Many states have laws that supplement or even strengthen federal mandates. Many school districts, especially large ones, have formal policies promoting equity in hiring.

On the other hand, school districts have considerable discretionary power despite those formal mandates. That discretionary power derives from at least three sources. First, formal policies governing hiring practices usually are found only in larger, metropolitan school districts. Most school districts are fairly small, and their policies are often no more than *pro forma* statements filed in a policy manual. It is quite possible to observe the letter of the law while subverting its intent. For instance, in our research we found examples of hiring that we called midnight specials, in which a position would be opened at 10 P.M. and a person, who often was the only applicant, hired at midnight. While such a flagrant abuse of equal-opportunity hiring is not common practice, it does exist, and it is rare that a school district practicing such an abuse pays a penalty for doing so.

The second area of discretionary power regards job descriptions. The Equal Employment Opportunities Commission (the regulatory arm of Title VII) requires that job descriptions contain "bona fide" occupational requirements, meaning that the requirements must be related to the tasks assigned. But the fact is that often job descriptions for administrators are not very precise and require only a bare minimum, such as "must have administrative certificate." Thus it is difficult to monitor or prove discriminatory intent in the face of ill-defined job requirements.

Finally, affirmative action policies rarely are specific about procedures to redress past inequities. In Oregon in 1977–78, 71% of the school districts we studied had an affirmative action policy, although it was often no more than one paragraph copied from guidelines suggested by the state department of education. Only 40%, however, had specific goals for redressing past inequities, and only 25% had specific plans, including timetables, that indicated how they would proceed with future hiring. Further, affirmative action policies in many districts do not address, nor are they required to address, the underrepresentation of women in administrative ranks. For instance, in one small elementary school district with four white male administrators, the affirmative action policy stated: "Male staffing in the district is considerable less [sic] than the work force percentage of men in Oregon, in the category of certified and classified. [We will] seek qualified male applicants for primary teaching positions."

In short, despite an increase in formal laws and regulations affecting hiring, local school districts retain considerable discretion. We are dubious about the impact of laws and other formal policy regulations on women's underrepresentation in management. Although legislation and court rulings have altered the situation somewhat, it remains easy for school districts to avoid the letter and spirit of the law. We do not suggest that school districts always intentionally circumvent the law,

devise methods of superficial compliance, or actively seek to discriminate against women. Our purpose is to suggest that practice does not
change easily even when long-held traditions are in flagrant violation of
the law. Experience and tradition remain the rules of thumb by which
many school districts operate.

THE NEED FOR BASIC RESEARCH

Despite the importance of decisions regarding personnel, increasing
government intervention into hiring processes, and concerns expressed
by women's organizations and other groups about the need for equity,
virtually no basic descriptive research has been done on the recruitment,
screening, selection, and hiring of administrators in school districts. The
absence of research and a solid base of data became apparent to us when
we tried to develop a strategy to counteract what we believed to be
biases that worked to the advantage of men and to the disadvantage of
women in this field.

Our first step was to review what was already known, and in 1976
there was very little. There were some case descriptions of hiring (McIntyre, 1966), some studies on sponsors (Rose, 1969), and some studies
describing demographic characteristics of persons hired (NEA, 1968;
Carlson, 1972). No data, however, existed on the applicant pool from
which candidates were hired or on the processes used by districts to
screen and hire candidates. We therefore conducted our own research to
fill that information gap while simultaneously proceeding with an action
strategy based on our best hunches. This chapter focuses only on the
research; our action strategy is described in Schmuck, 1980b; Smith *et
al.*, 1980; Stockard, 1980; and Wyant and Schmuck, 1979.

We called our research arm of the SEEL project the Oregon Network. It provided documentation of the recruiting, screening, and hiring
for nearly every administrative position in Oregon's public schools during the 1977–1978 school year. We reviewed 335 administrative positions
and 3896 applications. (Thirty-five of those positions were filled by administrative transfers that involved no change of status or pay; they are
not included in our analyses.) It should also be noted that the number of
applications does not equal the number of people seeking positions;
most people applied for more than one job. Because we agreed to protect
the anonymity of individual applicants, we cannot say with certainty
how many women and how many men applied for jobs in that year. Our
best guess, based on information given us by people who listed themselves in our directory of candidates, is that perhaps 1000 men and 200

women were actively seeking administrative positions in Oregon during 1977–1978. Those figures, however, are very rough hunches.

Operations

Spencer Wyant was hired as coordinator of the Oregon Network to supervise the six field researchers assigned to different regions of the state. The field researchers' tasks were to establish contact with the administrator in charge of hiring in each district in their region and to introduce themselves and the project. Although all administrators had received a mailing about the project, only a few remembered it. District personnel were asked to notify field researchers when administrative vacancies occurred in their districts. Follow-up visits then were made to districts with vacancies. Field researchers documented each vacancy, processes of recruitment and selection, and characteristics of applicants. Researchers maintained mail and telephone contacts with their districts to keep track of vacancies. Finally, researchers returned to districts with vacancies to document final selection procedures and decisions when someone was hired.

The Research Questions

In this chapter we try to answer four basic questions about how school administrators were hired in Oregon in 1977–1978:

1. How was the hiring of women in 1977–1978 related to existing patterns of sex segregation in the educational work force in Oregon?
2. What conditions make it more likely or less likely that females will apply for administrative positions?
3. What selection processes make it more likely or less likely that a female will be hired for an administrative position?
4. What qualifications of applicants are related to their being hired?

We collected information to answer those questions in only one state, Oregon, and in only one year, 1977–1978. Therefore, we cannot say with certainty how our results might be applicable to other states and other years; obviously, additional research is needed to determine how well the results we found represent hiring practices in general. Still, we have no reason to believe that either the state or the year were absolutely unique, and so we think our results can provide important clues for other research and action efforts.

We studied a total of 3896 applications and 300 positions in 129 districts; that is an average of about 13 applicants per position. Of the total, 3153 (81%) were submitted by males and 743 (19%) by females. Of the persons hired that year, 65 (22%) were women and 233 (78%) were men. (We were unable to obtain data on two hirings, and 35 administrative transfers were eliminated from the statewide total of 335 vacancies.) The vacancies occurred in slightly more than one-third of the state's 350 school districts. Of the 129 districts with openings that year, 90 (70%) hired only men, while the other 39 hired at least one woman. About four-fifths of the vacancies (79%) were filled by people who had been administrators in their previous positions; thus 21% of those hired were new to administration. Sixty-one new jobs were created and filled that year, representing an increase of some 3% in the state's administrative ranks.

SEX SEGREGATION IN THE WORK FORCE OF SCHOOLS

We found that administrative positions in Oregon's public schools were segregated by sex: some jobs were apparently considered "men's work" while others were "women's work." Positions such as superintendent and high school principal were nearly always held by men. Other positions, such as elementary school principal or coordinator, were also dominated by men, although there were some women in those jobs. Differentiation by sex existed even when men and women had the same job title. For instance, many schools have more than one vice-principal; men generally held vice-principalships in charge of discipline, a "masculine" function, while women were more likely to be assigned responsibilities for curriculum, a "feminine" function.

Although the proportion of women hired in Oregon in 1977–1978 was almost double the proportion of women in the existing administrative work force, the greater numbers of women did not change the pattern of differentiation of positions by sex. Women were more likely to apply for positions traditionally considered appropriate for women than for positions usually held by men. For example, the percentage of women in the pool of applicants for superintendencies was much smaller than the percentage of women in the pool of applicants for positions as assistant principal, as shown in Table 4.1. Females were fairly highly represented in the applicant pools for subordinate line positions, such as assistant superintendent and assistant principal.

Table 4.2 further illustrates the pattern of segregation by sex.

TABLE 4.1
Percentages of Female Employees and Applicants in Administrative Positions

Position	Female employees 1975–1976	Female applicants 1977–1978	Females hired 1977–1978	Female employees 1978–1979
Superintendent	1.2	3.0	3.0	1.9
Assistant superintendent	1.3	13.0	0.0	0.0
Principal	6.7	14.0	13.0	8.4
Assistant principal	11.8	25.0	21.0	14.5
Director or supervisor	20.2	15.0	19.0	18.5

SOURCE: Adapted from Jean Stockard, *Sex Equity in Educational Leadership: An Analysis of a Planned Social Change Project,* Educational Development Center, Newton, Mass., 1980.

Women were hired more often in staff positions than in line positions, slightly more in central office as compared with building-level positions, in elementary schools more frequently than in secondary schools, and as subordinates more often than as superiors.

We also investigated the question of whether the sex of the incumbent in a position was related to the sex of the person hired for that job. With one exception, we found that women tended to replace women, and men tended to replace men. Of all administrative jobs in which the incumbent was a male, only 13% of the new employees were female. Yet of the positions in which the incumbent was a female, 45% of the new

TABLE 4.2
Percentage of Administrative Vacancies Filled by Females in Oregon, 1977–1978

Type of position	Percentage of vacancies filled by females
Line administrator	16.3
Staff administrator	41.5
Building administrator	19.6
Central office administrator	23.7
Secondary schools (including junior high schools)	14.1
Elementary schools (including middle schools)	25.3
Head of unit or building	13.8
Subordinate administrator	33.9
Principal	14.5
Assistant principal	22.4

SOURCE: Jean Stockard, *Sex Equity in Educational Leadership: An Analysis of a Planned Social Change Project,* Educational Development Center, Newton, Mass., 1980, p. 56.

employees were female (Stockard, 1980). Thus, while the proportion of women in the state's administrative work force increased, that increase was in positions traditionally thought to be women's work. In line positions such as superintendent, assistant superintendent, principal, and director or supervisor, the percentage of women hired in 1977–1978 was very nearly equal the percentage of women who already held jobs in those categories. In no case did the percentage of women hired represent an increase of more than 3% over the percentage of women already holding jobs in that category. The job categories in which there was a substantial increase in the representation of women were the lower-status staff and support positions. For the categories of assistant principal, coordinator or director of special projects, consultant or specialist, and administrative assistant, the representation of women increased by about 20%. In short, the increased proportion of women in the administrative work force was largely due to increases in what traditionally have been considered "feminine" positions, rather than the more important "masculine" line positions. That finding reinforces our previous observations that administrative jobs in schools are segregated by sex. The exception to that finding occurred in the case of the elementary school principal, a position in which women tended to replace men, and men tended to replace women, as shown in Table 4.3. Lacking more detailed data, we can only conjecture as to the cause. Since the number of positions was relatively small, we did not pursue the causes of this hiring practice with further analysis.

Women were more likely to be hired in newly created positions. Approximately one-fifth of the vacancies in Oregon in 1977–1978 were new positions, and women filled almost half of those positions. Nearly one-half of the 61 newly created jobs were staff positions; in contrast, only about 20% of the 1977–1978 vacancies for which there were incumbents were staff jobs. In general, in newly created positions, women were more likely to get the lower-status staff jobs (50%) than the higher-status line jobs (20%).

TABLE 4.3
**Female Elementary Principals Hired and Sex
of Incumbent**

	Females hired	
Sex of incumbent	%	Number
Male	72	30
Female	28	12

RECRUITMENT CONDITIONS

Thus far, we have presented aggregated data that portray the situation for the state as a whole. We now turn to an examination of the practices of local school districts and how those practices affected the chances of women aspiring to become administrators.

Most vacancies occurred in small school districts, but women's chances of being hired as an administrator were greater in large metropolitan districts. Some 60% of the districts offering jobs were in rural areas or in small towns of less than 5000 population. Although the six largest school districts in the state accounted for only 21% of the jobs offered, they accounted for 28% of the females hired. That finding is consistent with what is known about the location of female administrators; they are usually employed in large districts in metropolitan areas. Metropolitan areas offer more opportunities for women for at least three reasons. First, women with family responsibilities tend to be more placebound than are men with similar responsibilities. Second, larger districts usually have more administrative positions in support and staff areas, the jobs for which women tend to be hired. Third, large districts simply have more vacancies. Only 10% of the districts offering jobs had more than five vacancies, and they were all large districts in the state's major cities. Ninety percent of the districts with openings had five vacancies or less; of those districts, approximately half had only one job vacancy. Undoubtedly, the size and location of districts with vacancies affect women's chances of being hired as administrators. Accidents of size and geography are one factor that influence hiring patterns, as are the deliberate policies and practices of school districts. But because we could not control for size and location in our data, we have no way of assessing the relative impact of those various factors.

The Recruitment Process

Districts have several ways of locating candidates for vacant positions, which is the first step in hiring an administrator. We first discuss recruitment practices and then affirmative action policies. After that, we turn to an examination of the applicants for administrative vacancies and the people who were involved at various stages of the hiring process.

Informal recruiting practices persist. In some cases the superintendent or another administrator simply decides that he or she wants a certain person for the job and then appoints that person. One male principal we interviewed in a separate study told us, "One Sunday afternoon I got a phone call from the superintendent, and he asked if I'd like to try a new job. I said sure, why not? And I've been principal ever since." More commonly, however, positions are filled through some kind of competitive process. Eighty percent of the positions in Oregon in 1977–1978 were filled by an openly advertised competitive process. In fact, there seemed to be a standard procedure that was followed in almost every case. First, the position was advertised, inviting applications. The applications submitted were then screened and candidates were selected for interviews. A small group of finalists was recommended to the person or group having authority to make the job offer, and this person or group then made the decision. We did find a very few cases in which that procedure was not used. There were also isolated instances in which the school board took some unusual action or in which there appeared to be a discrepancy between the district's hiring policies and the way in which a particular hiring was conducted. There were, however, very few such cases, and our data did not allow us to analyze them with any thoroughness.

Advertising of administrative vacancies took several forms. Approximately 12% of the 1977–1978 openings were advertised only within the district, while 68% were advertised outside the district as well. Generally, line positions such as those of superintendent and principal, and positions requiring special knowledge and skills were widely advertised. Entry-level and lower-status jobs were not widely advertised. Forty percent of the positions of assistant principal and 80% of those of administrative assistant were filled by appointment or were advertised only within the hiring district. Some three-fourths of the vacancies were advertised in the state's university placement services, while slightly less than half were advertised in the state administrators' association listings.

When we looked at the positions of elementary school principal and secondary school assistant principal, we were somewhat surprised at the effect of the special efforts of the districts to recruit equitably. One way in which districts can promote equitable hiring is to make a special effort to seek female applicants by contacting women's organizations, for example. Not surprisingly, we discovered something of a disparity between what districts said they were doing and what happened in specific cases. When the field researchers asked in their initial interviews whether the district made any special effort of attract female and minority candidates, 30% of the districts said they did so; but when the field researchers tried to find out during follow-up interviews whether special efforts were made for the particular job in question, special efforts were found in only 12% of the vacancies. (The issue may be somewhat confounded by the way we asked the question, since we are unable to tell whether the special efforts were directed to women, to minorities, or to both.) In our analysis we used the more stringent criterion of actual practice. The special-effort factor appeared to make the employment of a woman more likely once a woman had applied; but it did not appear to make it more likely that a woman would apply in the first place. The results for the 58 analyzable vacancies for elementary school principals and secondary school assistant principals are shown in Table 4.4. The table shows that while the proportion of women in the applicant pool was not larger when special recruiting efforts were made, the proportion of women hired was definitely higher. Because of the small number of positions and applicants that we could analyze, and because of various methodological problems, we can only speculate on the significance of those findings. One factor may have to do with the size or location of districts, or it may be that districts that made special efforts in recruiting also attended more closely to considerations of equity during the selection of candidates from the applicant pool.

The way in which a position was filled apparently did not greatly affect a woman's chances of getting the job. Only for the position of director or supervisor did the statistical analysis comparing the number of males hired with the number of females hired yield a statistically significant difference. In that case, a male was much more likely to be chosen when the position was advertised outside the district. Looking at all positions at once, it was more likely that a woman would be hired when the position was filled by appointment or by advertising within the district than when the job was advertised outside the district. Women were hired for 30% of the positions for which people were appointed, for 29% of the jobs advertised in the district only, and for 18% of the positions advertised outside the district. The latter result is probably an artifact, however; positions advertised outside the district were usually superintendencies and principalships, while those filled

TABLE 4.4
Effects of Special Efforts in Recruiting

| | | Applicants | | | | |
	Sex	Number	%	Number hired	Chances in 100	Odds ratio
Special effort	Female	29	15.7	3	10.3	4.38
	Male	156		4	2.6	
No special effort or	Female	198	18.2	9	4.5	.96
data not available	Male	887		42	4.7	

from within were usually staff positions such as those of coordinator or administrative assistant. Within each category of recruiting process, the segregation of jobs by sex was a consistent pattern. For appointive positions, 90% of the males but only 43% of the females were named to line positions; for jobs advertised in the district, 80% of the males but only 55% of the females were hired for line positions; and for jobs advertised outside the district, 86% of the males but only 59% of the females were hired for line positions.

In summary, it appears that women were more likely to be hired for an administrative position when the job was appointive rather than when it was widely advertised. That finding, however, is probably due to the difference between the kinds of jobs that are appointive and those that are advertised rather than to an effect of the recruiting process itself. The stereotype of what is considered woman's work or man's work appears to be a more powerful predictor of a woman's chances of getting the job than does the way in which the position is filled. Special recruitment efforts appear to increase a woman's chances, but that effect is in the selection process rather than in the process of attracting more women to the applicant pool.

Affirmative Action Policies

School districts vary in their formal and informal commitments to provide equal opportunities and, of course, attitudes influence behavior to a degree. In a study attempting to evaluate the effects of Title IX, researchers found that the key variable in district compliance with the regulations was the prevailing attitudes expressed by the district (Miller and Associates, 1978). The school districts we studied varied in their written policies concerning affirmative action: 71% reported having a policy, 40% reported having a plan, and 25% reported having specific timetables to recruit and employ underrepresented groups. We do not have any useful information on the effects of affirmative action plans, goals, or policies upon hiring practices. The policy of many districts consists of no more than a short paragraph in the district's policy manual; Oregon districts are required to have at least that minimal statement in evidence before they can be approved by the state education department's compliance inspection teams.

The goals and plans for affirmative action collected by the field researchers varied widely. Some were elaborate documents that obviously represented a great deal of effort, while others were very sketchy. Our impression is that the thoroughness of a district's plan is probably closely related to its size: larger districts have more people and resources available for the task. Our experience, along with the conclusions of Miller and Associates in studying the effects of Title IX, leads us to view policy statements and written plans with some skepticism. It is one thing to adopt a policy or a plan; it is another thing to keep equity issues firmly in mind when recruiting and selecting candidates for administrative positions. (Additional information on the effect of affirmative action laws and policies on hiring practices will appear in a forthcoming study by Williams.)

SELECTION CONDITIONS

We now turn our attention from recruitment to selection and examine what happens to females once they are in the applicant pool. We examine three questions: Are females hired in proportion to their representation in the applicant pool? Is there a relationship between the existence of a district intern program and the hiring of females? Does the composition of screening and selection committees influence a female's chances for being hired?

Applicant Pool and People Hired

"Equity will be achieved in administration when the composition of the applicant pool is equitable" was a statement made in an earlier study (Schmuck, 1980a). The data from the Oregon Network provide an opportunity to support or refute that statement. Of course, a female must be among the applicants to become a finalist, but is a certain proportional representation of women applicants necessary for a woman to be a finalist? Women were hired for administrative positions in Oregon during 1977–1978 at a rate slightly higher than their representation in the applicant pool. Sixty-five women (22% of the people hired) got administrative jobs; yet the 743 applications from females for all vacancies represented 19% of the applicant pool. Further analysis, however, shows that women's chances differed from position to position. For example, for the position of superintendent, only one female (representing 3%) was in the applicant pool, and she was hired; yet for the position of assistant superintendent, females represented 13% of the applications, and none were hired. We were curious to find whether a relationship existed between the proportion of females in an applicant pool and the proportion of women hired.

In general, we found that there was not a consistent relationship between females' representation in the applicant pool and their chances of getting the job. Having a higher-than-average proportion of women in the applicant pool was not uniformly related to the proportion of women hired. As shown in Table 4.5, that relationship varied from position to position. To demonstrate the relationship another way, we calculated an odds ratio that expresses the chances a woman in the applicant pool had of being hired. A ratio greater than 1.00 means that a woman's chances are better than those of a man in the same applicant pool; a ratio of less than 1.00 means that her chances are lower than those of her male counterpart. The results are shown in Table 4.6. (The table only includes positions for which there were sufficient numbers to produce reliable results.) In general, females tended to have an edge over males, except in positions of assistant superintendent (which are excluded from Table 4.6 because no females were hired), and of high school principalships. Fifty-four women applied for positions of high school principal, and one was hired (2 chances in 100); 466 applications from males were received, and 31 men were hired (7 chances in 100). Women were at a decided disadvantage when competing for positions as secondary school principals.

The results are open to several interpretations. They may reflect a genuine effort on the part of districts to hire affirmatively from among candidates available in the applicant pool. Alternately, they may represent a continuation of stereotypes about man's work and woman's work, as shown in the higher odds ratios for women in the categories of elementary school principal, director or supervisor, and coordinator. We do not have sufficient data to confirm either of those speculations. One confounding factor is that women were not equally represented in all

TABLE 4.5
Percentage of Female Applications and Percentage of Females Hired

Position	Percentage		Percentage change from application to hiring
	Female applications	Females hired	
Superintendent	3	3	0
Assistant superintendent	13	0	−13
Principal	14	15	+1
Assistant principal	25	22	−3
Director or supervisor	15	24	+9
Coordinator	28	37	+9
Consultant or specialist	74	67	−7
Administrative assistant	26	39	+13
Other	26	50	+24
Total pool	19	22	+3

TABLE 4.6
Odds Ratio of Female Applications and Females Hired

Position[a]	Number of vacancies	Female applications (%)	Females hired (%)	Odds ratio
Superintendent	26	3.2	3.8	1.14
Principal	32	10.2	3.2	.26
Secondary	32	10.2	3.2	.26
Elementary	46	14.5	19.6	1.35
Assistant principal				
Secondary	34	16.5	17.6	.99
Director or supervisor	27	13.7	18.5	1.34
Coordinator	20	26.4	30.0	1.09

[a] Does not include positions filled by appointment, transfer, or promotion.

applicant pools throughout the state. The vast majority of applications from women were to districts in the western part of the state, which is by far the more populous area of Oregon. Very few applicants were to the rural districts scattered throughout the eastern part. Oregon is divided, socially and geographically, by the Cascade Mountains, which run the length of the state north to south. The western one-third of the state includes mountains and the densely populated Willamette Valley. The eastern two-thirds consists of high plains, desert, and farm country. In this eastern two-thirds of the state, only four women were hired. Applications from females represented only 11% of the total in that region, substantially lower than the statewide average of 19%. The four women hired represented only 6% of the total number hired, dramatically less than the statewide average of 22%. What does that mean in terms of hiring practices? For one thing, it means that women were somewhat selective in their job search, applying to districts in the western part of the state, which appear more likely to hire them. Our analyses of hiring practices, therefore, may be affected by the decisions of those women who were applicants as well as by the hiring practices of local school districts. It would appear that the prevailing pattern that designates some jobs as women's work and others as men's work is reinforced both by district's hiring practices and by women's decisions in applying for jobs.

Formal Administrative Training: Intern Programs

In this section we focus on those districts that developed special programs to create a pool of qualified applicants through the process of internship. All school districts use certain processes to train and groom their future administrators. In most districts, informal processes such as chairing committees, developing reports, making presentations, and assuming other leadership tasks, are the avenues by which people gain experience and exposure. Some school districts provide more formal structures for training administrators. Intern programs are a prime example of a school district's attempt to provide valuable experience and exposure to people within the district. In 1977–1978 six districts with formal intern programs in Oregon had a total of 48 administrative vacancies; five of those programs had been developed specifically to assist the entrance of women and minorities into the administrative ranks. We were curious as to whether those programs provided any advantages to female aspirants. The limited data from those districts do not show a positive relationship between the existence of a formal intern program and the hiring of a woman. In fact, the percentage of women hired in those districts (16%) was lower than the statewide average of 22%.

Out of the 48 vacancies in the six districts with intern programs, eight positions (16%) were filled by women, one was filled by a minority male, and 39 (84%) were filled by white males. Sixteen of those positions were filled by direct appointment. Four females and no minorities were appointed. (In this analysis, we included the 35 appointive positions that we excluded from other analyses because we believed appointments would reflect a district's full intent to increase women and minorities in administration.) Data for the six districts are shown in Table 4.7.

TABLE 4.7
Relationship between Formal Intern Programs and the Hiring of Administrators

Districts with intern programs	Number of administrative openings	Number of administrators hired			
		White male	White female	Minority male	Minority female
District 1	1	1	0	0	0
District 2	0	0	0	0	0
District 3	13	8[a]	5[b]	0	0
District 4	5	5	0	0	0
District 5	4	2	2	0	0
District 6	25	23[c]	1[d]	1	0
Total	48	39	8	1	0

[a] Two white males by appointment.
[b] Three white females by appointment.
[c] Ten white males by appointment.
[d] One white female by appointment.

The appointments of women were to two central office positions and two administrative assistant positions. All the white males were appointed to positions of principal or assistant principal, primarily at the high school level. It should be noted that District 3 was the only one that provided some evidence of sex equity in hiring; five white females and eight white males were hired. Four of the females in that district filled positions in the central office; one was a high school administrative assistant. Males filled principal and assistant principal roles as well as central office positions.

We pondered those negative findings. Perhaps many of those programs were recent and had not had a chance to fulfill their intent of actively recruiting women and minorities. Perhaps the districts felt they were relieved of their affirmative action obligation by providing a formal intern program that remained unconnected to their traditional hiring practices. Perhaps consideration for those positions depended on seniority, and white males were the senior members of the pool. The answers are unclear, although it is evident that the existence of a formal intern program in those six districts had no positive relationship to the hiring of women.

Selection Committees

People hire people. It is reasonable to think that the composition of committees that do screening and interviewing can affect female candidates' chances. For positions openly advertised and recruited, there appeared to be a very standard procedure, as we have mentioned. Paper applications were screened, interviews were conducted, a recommendation was made, and a top administrator or the school board offered the position to the final candidate. Usually those procedures were performed by male administrators; in many cases, however, they were performed by committees of teachers, board members, or other persons. Because of the way figures were reported to the field researchers and because data are missing on many of the vacancies studied, exact information on who was involved in the selection processes is not available. A general estimate may be obtained, however, by calculating the proportions of persons in various positions who were reported as being involved in the various steps of the selection process, including the proportions of males and females at each step. Administrators were most most heavily represented at the screening stage, being slightly more than half of the persons involved in that step. The figures in Table 4.8 give the percentages of people in different roles (and of males and females) reported as being involved in the three major stages of selection. It should be emphasized again that these figures are not very "hard," but the trends seem fairly definite.

If the numbers in Table 4.8 translate into influence, then administrators were most influential at the screening and interviewing stages, but less so at later stages. These figures must be read with two points in mind. First, it is probable that the strong showing of board members, especially in the "offering" stage, is a result of the fact that 12% of the positions studied were superintendencies. Board members are usually more involved in hirings for those positions than in hirings for other positions, and thus they may be overrepresented in the figures. Secondly, it was often reported that "the board" made the final decision to offer a position. Most boards were composed of five or seven members, and all were counted in the figures, although all may not have been actively involved. It is clear that women were much less represented in the "offering stage" than in earlier stages, and presumably they had less influence. Yet the relationship is not a simple one, and we have some reason to believe that the presence of at least one woman on the committee in earlier stages may not be helpful to the female candidate's chances. We examined the composition of screening, interviewing, and offering committees in connection with vacancies for elementary school principals and secondary school assistant principals, as shown in Table 4.9. The table includes those vacancies for which there was more than one applicant and at least one female applicant. Obviously, the odds ratio is zero when there are no females candidates.

It would appear from Table 4.9 that, except in the screening stage, a woman's chances are increased by the presence of at least one female on the committee. Screening is the stage in which letters of application and resumes are reviewed to select the persons to be interviewed. There are a number of points to be made about Table 4.9. The first is that there

TABLE 4.8
People Participating in the Selection Process

	Percentages participating		
	Screening stage	*Interviewing stage*	*Job offering stage*
Administrators	51	45	32
Teachers	18	16	3
Board members	19	28	64
Others	12	10	2
Males	75	74	82
Females	25	26	18

TABLE 4.9
Composition of Committees and Odds of Females Being Employed as Elementary School Principals and Secondary School Assistant Principals

Composition of Committee	Applicants	Number of applicants	Number hired	Chances in 100	Odds ratio
Screening					
At least one female member	Female	134	4	3.0	0.75
	Male	607	24	4.0	
No female members	Female	86	7	8.1	1.56
	Male	391	21	5.3	
Interviewing					
At least one female member	Female	127	6	4.7	1.18
	Male	621	25	4.0	
No female members	Female	93	5	5.4	1.11
	Male	411	20	4.9	
Job-offering					
At least one female member	Female	79	5	6.3	1.79
	Male	439	6	3.6	
No female members	Female	137	6	4.4	0.85
	Male	566	29	5.1	

seems to be a slight bias in favor of women; the odds ratios are generally higher than 1.00. (We will see a similar pattern in Table 4.10.) The second is that males dominated the responsible committees; about half of the committees had no female members at all. The analysis in Table 4.9 divides committees into those with no women, and those with at least one. Since some committees might have had only one female while others had several, we cannot say much about the difference made by the proportion of women on a responsible committee. Further, we do not have data on the positions of the women who served on those committees; the status of the female committee members may well have been an influence, but we cannot say what that might be. The analysis presented in Table 4.9 should be read with a great deal of caution because the data are sketchy and not totally reliable. Further, we are sure that other factors confound the results. Sex, age, race, ideology, and the group dynamics of committees all affect the selection process, but we cannot say in what way those factors operate.

Stages of the Hiring Process

Another question we asked was whether any particular stage of the hiring process seemed to be a critical juncture, in the sense that women were shunted out of the way. By calculating the percentages of women represented at the various stages, we were able to chart their progress from application to interview, finalist status, and hiring. Those results are shown in Table 4.10. It does not appear from Table 4.10 that there is one stage of the hiring process that is an identifiable barrier to women. That is, in no column are the percentages uniformly and significantly lower for all positions than the figures in the column to the left of it. In fact, females were generally hired in proportions greater than their representation in the applicant pools, except for the positions of assistant superintendent, assistant principal, and consultant or specialist. (The substantial difference for "other" positions should probably be ignored, since it is based on too few cases to yield stable results.) The figures may, however, reflect the results of stereotyping. The largest gains are in the positions of administrative assistant (+13), coordinator (+9), and director or supervisor (+9). Those are the traditional "female" positions. The small decline in the consultant or specialist category is probably due to the fact that three-fourths of the applicants were women; the decline is most likely a simple regression to the mean. The percentage of women hired was identical (or nearly so) to the proportion of their representation in the applicant pool for jobs as superintendent, principal, and assistant principal. The one really striking discrepancy is that for the position of assistant superintendent, for which no women were apparently even interviewed. But in that category only four people were hired, and we are reluctant to ascribe much of a pattern to the results. It may be that the position was not considered appropriate for a woman,

TABLE 4.10
Percentage of Female Applicants at Stages of the Hiring Process

Position	*Percentage of females*				*Percentage change from applying to being hired*
	Applying	*Being interviewed*	*As finalists*	*Being hired*	
Superintendent	3	2	1	3	0
Assistant superintendent	13	0	0	0	−13
Principal	14	19	17	15	+1
Assistant principal	25	23	26	22	−3
Director or supervisor	15	15	24	24	+9
Coordinator	28	41	45	37	+9
Consultant or specialist	74	51	60	67	−7
Administrative assistant	26	25	26	39	+13
Other	26	68	50	50	+24
Total pool	19	22	23	22	+3

or it may reflect judgments about the particular qualifications of the applicants for those four jobs.

QUALIFICATIONS OF APPLICANTS

Selection as an administrator is based, at least in part, on demonstrated ability to perform the duties required in the job description. For instance, one job description for a small school district listed qualifications for the superintendency such as: holder of or eligible for a superintendent's credential, successful experience as a classroom teacher along with administrative experience, strong management skills and the ability to motivate and innovate, ability to communicate effectively with staff and school community, ability to evaluate staff performance and institute personal development programs, and expertise in planning, fiscal responsibility, and program accountability. Of that list of qualifications, only two are directly and easily measurable: credentials and experience. All other qualifications are at best subjective evaluations of predicted performance. Upon what criteria do committees make their final choice? Experience is often the prime factor, and as has been pointed out in several sources, the criterion of experience becomes the "Catch-22" for women wanting to move into management. The results of our investigation of the factors of age and experience in administrative selection are reflected in Table 4.11. At each stage, with one minor exception, the persons who advanced from one stage to the next were older and had more teaching and administrative experience than persons who did not advance.

Experience seemed to be the telling factor that determined an aspirant's chances for advancement through the selection process, just as lack of experience was the reason most frequently cited for not advancing women. Experience was an increasingly important criterion for advancement; it was cited in 35% of the cases at the interview stage, 37% of the cases at the finalist stage, and 41% of the cases in selection of the

TABLE 4.11
Average Age and Years of Experience of Persons Advanced through the Hiring Process

Stage of selection	Average age	Average years of administrative experience	Average years of teaching experience
Candidates interviewed	38.1	4.3	7.8
Finalists considered	38.2	4.8	7.6
Persons hired	39.3	7.0	8.6

successful candidate, females' lack of experience and the fact that no women applied for a position were the major reasons for not advancing females.

SUMMARY

Women are underrepresented as leaders in a field in which the majority of professionals are women. It is obvious that sex is a factor in the preparation and selection of school administrators. In the Oregon Network, we set out to discover the barriers that existed in the processes of hiring the leaders of schools. We studied more than 300 vacancies in Oregon in 1977–1978 and how they were filled, and the nearly 3900 applications for those positions. We examined segregation by sex in the work force, recruiting procedures, intern programs, selection processes, the composition of selection committees, and the candidates' qualifications. We found segregation by sex. Women applied for and were hired for subordinate or staff positions more often than for line positions or for jobs as heads of districts or buildings. When the incumbent was a woman, a female was hired to replace her nearly half of the time, but a woman replaced a man only 13% of the time. For elementary school principalships, however, a woman was much more likely to replace a man than to replace another woman.

Large metropolitan districts were more likely than smaller districts to hire women. Most positions (80%) were openly advertised, especially in the case of superintendencies, principalships, and specialist positions requiring particular skills or knowledge. A district's special efforts to recruit women did not seem to increase the proportion of female applicants, but did make it more likely that a woman would be hired once she applied. Women were somewhat more likely to be hired if the position was filled by appointment or through recruitment from within the district than if the position was advertised outside the district. That result, however, seems to be largely because appointive positions and those recruited from within the district were generally lower-status positions. We found no positive relationship between the existence of a formal intern program and the hiring of females. Women were hired roughly in proportion to their presence in the applicant pool, but it depended on the position in question. Women had an edge in being hired, except for jobs as assistant superintendents and high school principals; their advantage was most pronounced in positions of director or supervisor, of coordinator, and of administrative assistant. No single stage of the hiring process (application, interview, finalist, or hiring) seemed to act uniformly as a barrier to female aspirants.

Experience seemed to be the key to being hired. At each stage, the people who advanced were older and had more teaching and administrative experience than those who did not. Experience was the criterion most frequently mentioned for advancing candidates while lack of experience (along with "no women applied") was the reason most frequently given for not hiring females. Those findings represent what we consider a preliminary investigation. Many findings are tentative, and some raise more questions than they answer. We have not discovered any systematic active process of discrimination against women at any particular stage; but the fact remains that segregation of administrative positions in schools by sex continues. Does that mean that there are pre-hiring barriers? Are the major barriers stereotypes about woman's work and man's work, and do those stereotypes prevent women from preparing and applying for administrative jobs and prevent male administrators from encouraging them? Indeed, the findings raise a series of questions about the characteristics of the districts with vacancies, the positions offered, the recruiting practices, the selection procedures, and the applicants that can be answered only with more information.

1. *Districts:* What are the effects of district size and setting? Are there "background effects" that impinge on policy decisions?

2. *Positions:* Why should there be such a strong tendency for females to replace males in elementary school principalships? More information is also needed on the duties of different assistant principalships to see if the responsibilities given to women are different from those given to men.

3. *Recruiting:* What is involved in the decision to appoint someone to a position without competition? How are such decisions made, and how do they affect women's chances? Why should special efforts to recruit women and minorities have little apparent effect on women's representation in the applicant pool, while at the same time they seem to increase a woman's chances of being hired after that stage? Why do the intern programs designed to recruit women appear to work against them?

4. *Selection:* Why should the presence of at least one woman on the screening committee apparently work against women's chances of making it past this first hurdle? More information is also needed on the composition of screening committees to specify the positions represented and the effects of different proportions of women on those committees. We did not investigate cases in which there seemed to be a discrepancy between policy and practice, and that is an issue that bears further examination.

5. *Applicants:* If experience is such an important criterion, what kinds of experience count in the minds of people who hire administrators?

Female applicants tend to have more classroom experience but less administrative experience than their male counterparts; what is the effect of that difference?

Implications

Serious consideration needs to be given to the implications of the findings of the Oregon Network for educational policy and practice. We are not convinced that the solution lies in new laws or further regulation, yet the need for action to correct the underrepresentation of women in educational administration is clear. By and large, we think the research strategy we used worked well. The field researchers were able to gather information that probably was unobtainable by surveys or other more impersonal forms of data collection. Yet there are changes we would make if we did it again. In some respects, our timing was unfortunate. The field researchers did not get into districts for initial interviews much before Thanksgiving. It would have been preferable to have had them ready to begin before the school year began so that they could have tracked the hiring process through an entire school year cycle. We also found that the time estimated for the job was insufficient. The six part-time field researchers were hired at one-third time for eight months, but we made several adjustments to increase that time.

The quality and completeness of the field researchers' reports varied widely. Tighter monitoring and feedback to them would have made them more aware of what information they provided to us was useful and what was not. Closer supervision also would have served to make the reports more uniform, since the variability among the field researchers' reports proved to be a major problem when the time came to compile and analyze the results. We collected some information that we ultimately did not need, and we also failed to collect some data that would have been valuable. In later stages of the project, we sometimes discovered that there were important questions we simply could not answer, in part because of the forms we used. Most of the questions on the forms required that the field researcher write short descriptions; those questions in many cases would have been better framed as checklists or multiple-choice options, which would have helped standardize the data.

The greatest need in future research is for an investigation over several years that can detect trends in time. We know that the year we studied was in some respects unusual: there were more vacancies during that year than in either the preceding or following year. Lacking data, however, we cannot say in precisely what ways that year may have been different from others. A longer-term investigation would yield more stable results. Further, we do not know to what extent our monitoring of the hiring practices affected the process itself. We rather doubt that districts hired more equitably simply because our field researchers were watching, but we have no information on that question.

People run schools, and personnel decisions are among the most important ones that school districts make. The initial investigation of the Oregon Network provides some clues about how the selection of administrators perpetuates biases and stereotypes of woman's work and man's work. Additional research is needed, however, to provide the firm answers on which to base policy decisions and strategies for making educational administration more equitable.

ACKNOWLEDGMENTS

We thank the field researchers, Jim Bernau, Sara Cogan, Bill Erdman, Norma (Bean) McFadden, Walter Shelby, and Joanne Stern for their dedication and ingenuity. We also thank Jean Stockard and W. W. Charters, Jr., for their assistance with the data analysis.

REFERENCES

Carlson, Richard O. (1972). *School Superintendent Careers and Performance*. Merrill, Columbus, Ohio.

Erickson, K., and Shinn, J. (1977). "Half Million-Dollar Decisions: The Recruitment and Selection of Educators." *Oregon School Study Council Bulletin*, vol. 20, no. 6, February.

McIntyre, K. E. (1966). *Selection of Educational Administrators*. University Council of Educational Administration, Austin, Tex.

Miller and Associates, Inc. (1978). *The Status of Title IX in Region X*. 711 Capitol Way, Olympia, Wash., October.

NEA (1968). *The Elementary School Principal in 1968: A Research Study*. National Education Association Department of Elementary School Principals, Washington, D.C.

Rose, R. L. (1969). *Career Sponsorship in the School Superintendency*. Unpublished doctoral dissertation, University of Oregon, Eugene.

Schmuck, P. (1980a). "Changing Women's Representation in School Management: A Systems Perspective." In *Women and Educational Leadership* S. Bicklen & M. Brannigan, eds. Lexington Books, Lexington, Mass.

Schmuck, P. A. (1980b). *Sex Equity in Educational Leadership: The Oregon Story*. Education Development Center, Newton, Mass.

Smith, M. A., Schmuck, P., Kalvelage, J., and Starling, C. (1980). *Sex Equity in Educational Leadership: Women Getting Together and Getting Ahead*. Education Development Center, Newton, Mass.

Stockard, J. (1980). *Sex Equity in Educational Leadership: An Analysis of a Planned Social Change Project*. Education Development Center, Newton, Mass.

Tyack, D. (1976). "Pilgrims Progress: Toward a Social History of the School Superintendency, 1860–1960." *History of Education Quarterly*, Fall, pp. 257–300.

Williams, P. (in preparation). *The Impact of Anti-Sex Discrimination Laws on the Employment of Oregon School Administrators*. Doctoral dissertation, University of Oregon, Eugene.

Wyant, S., and Schmuck, P. (1979). *The Oregon Network: A Research and Service Activity of the Sex Equity in Educational Leadership Project*. Paper presented to the American Educational Research Association, San Francisco, April.

Chapter 5

THE PROBLEM OF SEX BIAS
IN CURRICULUM MATERIALS

Barbara Hutchison

Sex bias and stereotyping in the content of textbooks and other instructional materials continue to stand in the way of full educational equity for women. The problem has been confronted by proponents of educational equity at the national, state, and local levels. This chapter discusses what has been done and what can be done by policymakers to eliminate such sex bias and thereby provide better educational opportunities for all students. In addition, the chapter describes the effects of such sex bias, the efforts that have been made by various groups, including textbook publishers, to eliminate or reduce it, and the strategies being implemented at national, state, and local levels. Suggestions are explored regarding the direction that educational agencies can take in addressing this problem, and regarding further study and research in this area.

Although instructional materials that perpetuate discrimination are still found in the majority of schools in this country, no federal law prohibits their use in the classroom. While Title IX of the Education Amendments of 1972 prohibits discrimination against any student or employee, male or female, of an educational agency or institution, Section 86.42 of the Title IX regulation specifically *exempts* texts and instructional materials from coverage (Education Amendments, 1972). The

The information presented in this chapter does not necessarily reflect the opinion of the Northwest Regional Educational Laboratory, and no endorsement should be inferred.

purpose of the exemption was to prevent possible conflict with the First Amendment, which guarantees freedom of expression. The preamble of the regulation does, however, acknowledge the significance of the issue at both the elementary and secondary school levels, and it encourages agencies and institutions to take action to eliminate sex bias in textbooks. Before discussing the ways in which educational policy can assist in combatting the effects of such sex bias, this chapter reviews the problem and the steps that have been taken to remedy it over a period of more than a decade.

A REVIEW OF THE ISSUES AND THE REMEDIES

Twelve years ago a textbook was considered the "single most important teaching tool," the focus of 75% of children's classwork and 90% of their homework (Black, 1967). By the time students graduate from high school, they have read at least 32,000 pages from textbooks (Komoski, 1975). A survey in 1975 of approximately 24,000 schools revealed that 90–95% of school time was either directly based on or structured around the use of textbooks and other instructional materials (Black, 1967). Based on these findings, it seems safe to assume that despite the emphasis in recent years on experiential and "hands-on" learning, textbooks will continue to play a vital role in providing the basis of a student's educational experience. In the early and middle grades, when these materials constitute much of a student's information about the world, their power to shape attitudes is particularly strong and direct. What a student sees, hears, and reads about people, via textbooks, films, tapes, records, and television programming, is in large part what he or she will acknowledge to be true. This influence is still strong in high school and, to a lesser degree, in college.

The role models presented in textbooks are very important in helping children identify with and learn from the curriculum. The influence of materials on a child's sense of self-worth depends on the extent to which the child identifies with the characters and situations presented as he or she becomes emotionally involved with them (Zimet, 1972). Besides transmitting knowledge about the world, school texts also affect a student's career interests and expectations, especially through the role models presented as appropriate for each sex. Interests and expectations, in turn, influence a student's level of achievement and career choice in later years. There is a significant body of information concerning sex bias in education and its effect on students (Weitzman & Rizzo, 1974). For girls as they "progress" through school, the research documents losses of intellectual potential (especially in math and science), of self-esteem, and of occupational aspirations (Frazer & Sadker, 1973). For boys, there is the pressure of unrealistic and stereotyped expectations. It has been found also that the longer children are exposed to a sexist program (of materials), the more their attitudes conform to stereotyped sex roles and the more these attitudes are retained over time. (Nilsen *et al.*, 1977).

By inference, the content of textbooks has the institutional stamp of approval. Moreover, textbooks often determine curriculum, since what is covered in a text is usually what ends up being taught, and what is left out of a text is usually not considered important to course content. Because textbooks and other instructional materials are critically important, they must be designed to avoid the perpetuation of sex bias. Rather they should foster for all people, regardless of their sex, a sense of personal worth and dignity and a respect for their abilities and rights.

However, according to studies reviewed by the United States Commission on Civil Rights, "Stereotyped portrayals of minorities, girls and women, and older people were still prevalent in textbooks in wide use during the 1970s" (U.S. Commission on Civil Rights, 1980). More than a decade of concern about the way females are portrayed in textbooks has revealed that girls and women are often depicted in stereotyped ways, demeaned, or omitted entirely. The negative impact on female students has prompted many groups to take action. The following examples are only a few of the attempts that have been made to mitigate the effects of sex bias in textbooks.

• The Council on Interracial Books for Children, a nonprofit organization founded by writers, librarians, teachers, and parents in 1966, promotes antiracist and antisexist children's literature and teaching materials. It publishes the *Bulletin,* which analyzes children's books and other learning materials for bias, operates the Resource Center for Educators, which publishes reference books, lesson plans, and audiovisual materials. It also conducts workshops for librarians, teachers, and parents.

• At its 1972 convention, the National Education Association (1972) released the following statement: "The National Education Association calls upon parents and all groups involved in public education to join in a nationwide effort to reduce the effects of sex-role stereotyping, the standardized mental pictures of male and female that permeate all of our lives."

• In 1972, a study entitled *Dick and Jane as Victims* was conducted and published by Women on Words and Images (1975). The study examined the discrepancies between the treatment of girls and the treatment of boys in school readers. In systematically reviewing 2760 stories from 14 publishers, the authors found that females were presented in school readers as dependent, passive, unable to take care of themselves, house-bound, and generally as victims and targets of ridicule. Since the first printing of this study, nationwide attention has been focused on the issue of sex-role stereotyping in children's readers.

• *Fair Textbooks: A Resource Guide* (U.S. Commission on Civil Rights, 1979) is a bibliography of more than 1500 resources, including materials that may lead to more equitable textbook treatment of Asian and Pacific Islanders, American Indians, Hispanics, Blacks, religious minorities, females, the handicapped, and the aging. One section of this resource guide lists the guidelines that textbook publishers have developed to help authors and illustrators avoid inequities when preparing new books. Another section lists pertinent state laws and procedures and guidelines that state departments of education have developed on the portrayal of minorities and women in textbooks.

• A few of the numerous organizations that have made significant contributions in the area of sex bias in education are the Clearinghouse on Women's Studies, The Feminist Press (1974); the National Organization of Women (1973); the Project on Equal Education Rights (1977); and the Resource Center on Sex Roles in Education (Weitzman & Rizzo, 1974).

In response to growing external pressures, textbook companies have developed formal policies reflected in their guidelines for authors and editors and aimed at reducing sex bias in textbooks. Since 1972, over 170 groups, including publishing companies, educational organizations, and associations, have responded by developing guidelines for their staffs. The growing consciousness of the industry is a result of both their concern with the current attitudes in the society and their awareness of the impact of instructional programs on young people's thinking. The Association of American Publishers made a statement on bias-free content, illustrations, and language in September 1976 (U.S. Commission on Civil Rights, 1979, p. 299).

> Individuals of all ages and ethnic groups have much to gain from the elimination of stereotypes [in content]. Bias-free educational materials more accurately represent reality, encourage tolerance for individual differences, and allow more freedom for children to discover and express their needs, interests and abilities.
>
> [Illustrations] may carry an even stronger message than the text they illustrate. Pictures may leave a lasting impression about the tone of a book. . . .

Bias-free language is language that includes all people and treats them with equal dignity and respect, whatever their race, sex, age, religion [and] national and ethnic origin. Bias-free language deals with people as individuals, not as members of stereotyped groups. . . . It is the language of equal opportunity.

Publishers have approached the issue in a variety of ways with differing degrees of specificity. For a complete list of the guidelines and efforts of publishers, the reader may wish to consult *Fair Textbooks: A Resource Guide* (U.S. Commission on Civil Rights, 1979).

Despite publishers' efforts, students continue to read the same stories with little or no changes in series after series. When one considers that there is an average time lapse of approximately 4 years between textbook editions, and couples this with the fact that state laws may only require new textbooks every 6 or 8 years, it becomes apparent how an entire generation of students can pass through schools using biased textbooks even after it is evident to many that these texts limit the potential for both girls and boys. While the guidelines of textbook publishers for the promotion of fair policies have not been completely successful, publishers should not be considered solely responsible, either for the existence of sex bias in textbooks or for its elimination. It is important that other educational agencies and institutions take action on this issue.

In order to document the changes being made in textbooks, Britton and Associates, an instructional materials analysis firm located in Corvallis, Oregon, is conducting a study comparing textbook material relating to sex, race, and career bias before and after guidelines were issued (Britton & Lumpkin, 1977). This ongoing effort, initiated in 1972, analyzes new textbook series as they are published. A total of 4330 stories from 19 reading and literature series were assessed for texts published between 1958 and 1970, and 3504 stories or chapters from 12 series were assessed for 1974–1976. The results of the comparison, shown in Table 5.1 indicate a 2% increase in major female characters, which is not statistically significant.[1] An unpublished study by Britton and Associates of four high school social studies texts, published between 1976 and 1979 and used in Oregon schools resulted in the data shown in Table 5.2. As can be seen, publishers' guidelines aimed at reducing sex bias have not significantly increased female representation, either as major characters or in a wide variety of careers, in new texts. Based on current

---

[1]Britton, G., and Lumpkin, M. (1977). *A Consumer's Guide to Sex, Race, and Career Bias in Public School Textbooks.* Britton and Associates, Corvallis, Oregon, p. 10.

TABLE 5.1[a]
Occurrence of Major Characters, All Races

	Males	Females	Inanimate, nonsexual, or neutral
Before guidelines	60%	14%	26%
After guidelines	61%	16%	23%

[a] Britton, G., and Lumpkin, M. (1977). *A Consumer's Guide to Sex, Race, and Career Bias in Public School Textbooks*. Britton and Associates, Corvallis, Oregon, pp. 9–11.

TABLE 5.2
Occurrence of Characters and Careers

	Males	Females	Males and females	Inanimate, nonsexual, or neutral
Major characters, all races	86%	0%	8%	6%
Careers, all races	70%	14%		16%

and projected labor statistics and demographics, the traditional female roles and occupations portrayed in texts do not realistically prepare women for careers that will enable them to become self-sufficient adults, something women in society are expecting to be able to do in increasing numbers. In addition, limiting roles and occupations on the basis of sex also prevents many males from realizing their fullest potential.

Another important aspect to this issue is the need for texts to portray males and females playing and working together as compatible equals. While both sexes can be shown as being competent, as possessing abilities, interests, and admirable traits that are not sex stereotyped, the data indicate that stories of this type are still rare. For instance, in the study of high school social studies texts, only 8%, or 4 out of 50 stories, portrayed both males and females as major characters in the same story.

Changing textbooks is a slow process. First of all, it is expensive, both to rewrite and to launch a new textbook series. A series is sometimes promoted as a new edition even though extensive changes have not been made. For a book or series to qualify as a new edition, copyright law only requires a 10% change, which may be made in the binding, by the addition of color plates or illustrations, by revising a teachers' guide, or by inserting a few pages on new careers for women.[2]

[2] Britton, G., and Lumpkin, M. (1977). *A Consumer's Guide to Sex, Race, and Career Bias in Public School Textbooks*. Britton and Associates, Corvallis, Oregon, p. 13.

In many so-called new series, the majority of the stories remain the same as in the old edition.

FEDERAL STRATEGIES

The Women's Education Equity Act (WEEA) was passed by Congress as part of the Special Projects Act of the Education Amendments of 1974 to combat sexism in education (see U.S. Department of HEW, 1974). This act, the result of growing national and local concern for equality of educational opportunities for all children, has authorized the support of and funded a wide range of educational activities targeted at eliminating sex bias in education. The National Advisory Council on Women's Educational Programs, also established by WEEA, addresses all federal policies and programs affecting all levels of women's education. This legislation is one way federal policy is influencing what happens at every level. Local WEEA programs, where the primary focus is on sex bias in educational materials and where the audience is the practitioner in the field, are being operated by a variety of groups across the country. As the Advisory Council states in its fourth *Annual Report* of 1978: "Practitioners in the field—the educators, not the theoreticians— ultimately will determine if and when educational equity becomes a reality" (National Advisory Council on Women's Educational Programs, 1979).

In Oregon, one such WEEA program, located at the Northwest Regional Educational Laboratory, is the Women's Educational Equity Program (formerly the Non-Sexist Curriculum Development Program). In an effort to help educators eliminate sex bias in educational materials and practices, this program has developed a model workshop series entitled BIAS (Building Instruction Around Sex-Equity) and predicated on certain assumptions:

1. Sexism is frequently an unconscious attitude. Sexist practices continue to exist because "that is how it has always been done."
2. In order to build a school's capacity to provide instruction that is not limited by sex bias, educators need to make a conscious effort to learn new skills for identifying and for compensating for the bias that exists both in materials and practices.
3. Since children are first and primarily socialized at home, any effort to increase educational equity in the schools also needs parental support.

To reach people primarily involved in a child's education, three separate workshops have been designed for testing materials (1) **with** elementary and secondary school staff, (2) with interested parents, and (3) with students in teacher-education programs. The content of these workshops is of interest.

INSERVICE WORKSHOP. This 12-hour workshop provides educators with skills in (*a*) identifying discrimination in educational settings; (*b*) analyzing school materials for sex bias; and (*c*) preparing sex-equity action plans supportive of equal opportunities for all students. These plans include ideas for restructuring and adding to the curriculum (such as with lesson plans) and ideas for interaction with students to help teachers instruct in a more equitable way and expand students' awareness of sex bias and its damaging effects. Participants are trained in the use of an objective instrument for measuring in textbooks and supplementary reading materials the degree of sex and race bias, including that in the depiction of careers. The sex and race of major characters and the number of careers assigned to men, women, and minorities are recorded by participants, who are then asked to generate criteria for judging the quality of female and minority representations.

PARENT WORKSHOP. The parent workshop's main purpose is to encourage and create an awareness of what is meant by sex equity and of how an equitable education may be hampered by biased materials and practices within the schools. Parents learn how to analyze materials for bias and are given materials describing activities they can do with their children to increase the children's awareness of sex bias and stereotyping in books and television presentations. Parents are also encouraged to identify ways they can support school efforts to provide an equitable education.

PRESERVICE WORKSHOP. The preservice workshop aims at improving the training of students in teacher education courses. Students are provided with the same skills as those outlined for teachers in the inservice workshop, that is (*a*) identifying discrimination in educational settings; (*b*) analyzing school materials for sex bias; and (*c*) preparing sex equity action plans supportive of equal opportunities for all students.

Other program activities are the development of inservice and parent trainer's manuals, an annotated bibliography of nonsexist supplementary books, and a guide to nonsexist teaching activities. The program's work, a 3-year effort, ending in 1981, needs to be carried on and further developed at the state and local levels. In other words, policy formulated at the national level needs to be incorporated into state and local policies on education.

STATE STRATEGIES

All fifty states have explicit constitutional provisions, numerous statutes, and administrative rules that establish specific responsibilities for the education of their citizenry. Although no state patently discriminates on the basis of sex in the specification of its curricular requirements, variations by state do occur as to what courses are required by all students and what requirements are left to the discretion of local school boards. For this reason, decisions about curriculum and materials become largely the prerogative of local authorities. Nonetheless, the state does have a responsibility to set a framework within which local authorities operate. Individual states have in many cases enacted their own laws protecting both students and employees against discrimination on the basis of age, handicap, national origin, race, marital status, religion, and sex. As suggested in the preamble to the Title IX regulation, some states have taken action to combat the effects of sex bias in instructional materials. The efforts of many individuals and groups over the last decade to counteract sex and race bias in educational materials have prompted many state and local districts to develop guidelines and regulations regarding the selection of materials.

The California State Department of Education (1978), for example, has directly addressed the issue of bias by including the following policy in their Education Code. "In order to encourage the individual development and self-esteem of each child, regardless of gender, instructional materials, when they portray people (or animals having identifiable human attributes), shall portray women and men, girls and boys, in a wide variety of occupational, emotional and behavioral situations, presenting both sexes in the full range of their human potential." In addition, California has developed guidelines to provide consistent, systematic standards for evaluating instructional materials proposed for use in their public schools to ensure compliance with their Education Code.

In Oregon a different approach to the evaluation of instructional materials is evident. It is one of 26 states that has an adoption committee for textbooks. The Oregon State Textbook Commission's adoption committees review textbooks on a regular basis, and local districts have the right to select textbooks from an approved multiple list or to ask for other books to be approved by the Commission. State Textbook Commission reviewers are given a suggested rating scale for use in the evaluation of textbooks. The rating scale measures both the quality and quantity of the female, male, and minority representation in the books to be evaluated (Oregon State Dept. of Educ., 1975–1981). Oregon law also addresses the issue of biased textbooks, and it states that "respect for all people, regardless of race, color, creed, national origin, age, sex or handicap, and their contributions to our history and system of government shall be reflected in the textbooks adopted by the State Board of Education" (Oregon Administrative Rules, 1976). The law also requires the provision of resources for supplements to material if textbooks or curricular materials are found to have a discriminatory impact on the basis of age, handicap, national origin, race, marital status, or sex [O.R.S. 659.150 and O.A.R. 581-21-046 (6)].

The trend in the adoption of educational materials by states is toward approving of multiple publications so that room is left for flexibility and local tastes. While the adoption of certain textbooks does not guarantee that the book will sell in local areas, nonadoption makes it less likely that it will sell. For a publisher, losing an adoption can mean losing sales in an entire state for five or six years. Publishers admit to spending a lot of time gearing their books to meet the guidelines of states.

There is wide variation in the extent of states' involvement in the textbook selection process. Educational Research Service, in Arlington, Virginia, surveyed 414 school districts in 33 states in 1976 to ascertain how instructional materials were selected (Bowler, 1978). Of the 414, 108 had no selection committees. The remaining 306 had selection committees, but over half of these committees had only an advisory role. (The final selection occurred elsewhere, e.g., with superintendents or school boards.) Of the 306 committees, in only ten cases were teachers alone responsible for the approval of school materials. Of the 414 school districts surveyed, 252 had general statements of selection criteria. Of the 306 districts with selection committees, 41 had no written evaluative criteria for selecting materials; and most had no evaluative criteria for testing the materials or verifying whether or not the materials do what the publishers claim they will do. In addition, the Educational Research Service and the Educational Products Information Exchange Institute (EPIE) have found the following:

- Of all the nation's school districts 45.8% grant no release time to teachers on selection committees.
- Nationwide, 45% of the classroom teachers have no role in choosing the instructional materials they are required to use.
- The typical teacher has never been trained (in college or on the job) to evaluate or select materials for use in the classroom.
- Over 50% of the people who do have a selection role spend less than 1 hour per year making their choices.

Such statistics demonstrate the lack of overall guidance that could and should be provided at the state level in the area of textbook selection.

Although local districts are, in general, responsible for identifying and rectifying weaknesses in instructional materials, states still need to take a more active role in providing bias-free textbooks in the classroom. Textbooks must be approved by state officials in most states; they are bought with state money; they are used in state schools attended under state mandate; and they are presented to students within the context of authority—the classroom.[3] For these reasons, the state has a responsibility. Support by state boards of education in the effort to eliminate bias is crucial in order for a philosophy to be articulated and policies to be formulated which can then be carried out at the local level. Members on the staff of a state department of education communicate extensively, formally and informally, with educators in all the public school districts of a state, and they maintain links with officials in other states and with the federal government. They have an opportunity to lead statewide efforts to achieve educational equity for all students. The participation of state departments of education is particularly essential to the success of any *systematic* effort to analyze instructional materials for bias. A state department of education can contribute by directly participating in decision making; by using its extensive channels of communication to inform educators about past inequities and present goals to rectify them; by providing examples of its own criteria for systematic analysis of instructional materials; and by providing technical assistance to staff experts at the local level.

LOCAL STRATEGIES

The responsibility for selecting instructional materials is an important responsibility and one which needs to be addressed in a consistent and systematic fashion at the local level. Local communities are in the best position to assess and respond to the educational needs of their students. Parents, librarians, educators, administrators, and publishers should be afforded access to available resources, and decisions about curricula and textbooks should reflect multi-ethnic, unbiased attitudes in the community. Local authorities can take steps to make sure that instructional materials do not promote sex bias and stereotyping. Criteria can be generated at the district level to aid in the selection of bias-free textbooks and supplementary materials. Classroom teachers, administrators, and other school personnel can be trained to identify

---

[3]Women on Words and Images (1975). *Dick and Jane as Victims: Sex Stereotyping in Children's Readers.* Women on Words and Images, Princeton, N.J., p. 41.

and compensate for biased materials and practices. Bias-free compensatory materials to supplement the core curriculum can be purchased.

Selection Criteria

Local school districts should have policies and procedures for evaluating textbooks and other instructional materials for sex bias. Selection criteria are invaluable when choosing new texts and supplementary materials but should also be used to review texts already in use, in which case, the review could include suggested methods of compensating for existing bias. Decisions about what can be done to compensate for existing bias and whether to discontinue use of particularly biased texts could become part of the guidelines. Instruments for evaluating textbooks can be used by parents, students, educators, librarians, selection committees, researchers, state and local administrators, and others concerned with bias in educational materials. Familiarity and practice with these tools can result in a greater understanding of the issues and in a more informed basis for decisions, for example, those regarding textbook selection and adoption. Many instruments vary in terms of how comprehensive they are as well as in their level of specificity. Some have a statistical basis for establishing their validity and/or reliability. For a comprehensive list of textbook evaluative instruments, the reader can refer to *Fair Textbooks: A Resource Guide* (U.S. Commission on Civil Rights, 1979, pp. 67–81).

Training and Guidelines

Because sex-biased textbooks continue to find their way into the classroom, it is important for individual teachers and administrators to have some tools for accurately assessing bias in existing classroom textbooks and supplementary materials. In this way they can make a conscious effort to compensate for bias when it does occur. In addition, teachers, through constructive use of biased materials, can teach their students about bias in textbooks, as well as give them the skills and tools necessary to "counteract the biased images they confront daily in the society around them" (Moore, 1978).

As mentioned earlier, practitioners in the field will ultimately determine if and when educational equity becomes a reality, and one way for educators to gain necessary skills is through inservice training programs. Policies supporting such inservice training need to be formulated and implemented by the district and carried out either by districts or local schools.

To help teachers develop new units of study, it would be helpful for a district to formulate guidelines that address considerations regarding quality as well as quantitative criteria for nonbiased materials. Some of the guidelines generated at a National Conference on Non-Sexist Early Childhood Education (George, 1978), while they were originally intended for publishers of educational materials and professional journals, have meaning for the classroom teacher who often develops curriculum. In addition, they could also be used to assess or modify existing materials. These guidelines ask questions such as the following:

- Do they reflect an accurate and broad view of the world?
- Do they emphasize positive role models for both girls and boys?
- Do they help children understand their *real* capabilities?
- Do they have accurate visuals?
- Do they reflect teaming-up relationships between girls and boys?

Purchase of Bias-Free Supplementary Materials

Clearly stated policies and procedures encouraging the purchase of supplementary materials already assessed for bias need to be formulated and implemented. There are many such materials now available through WEEA programs and other organizations to which teachers need access. *Fair Textbooks: A Resource Guide* (U.S. Commission on Civil Rights, 1979) devotes an entire section to this subject.

IMPLICATIONS FOR FURTHER STUDY AND RESEARCH

There is little argument that school texts and supplementary reading materials help students identify possible future lifestyles, careers, and goals and provide learners with role models. However, as mentioned earlier, numerous studies have indicated that, despite an increasing social awareness of sexism, publishers are still producing books that portray females in a limited number of roles and with very limited skills. These contribute to the narrow horizons of female students. Part of the reason for these less than adequate materials is that publishers and state and local school personnel do not have the proper tools for reviewing them. If instruments with empirically verified value were available, publishers could set standards for reviewers and editors, and educators who make policy and decisions could have criteria to apply to the review and purchase of educational materials.

Certain reasons have prevented this from happening. First, the guidelines established and accepted by the publishing companies may be little more than "declarations of human worth," with no systematic criteria for acceptable female representation (Britton and Lumpkin, 1977, p. 6). Second, few systematic analysis tools have been developed. Third, and most importantly, no validated measures have been found that enable the consumer (the educator, members of textbook commissions, etc.) to judge the quality of female representation in texts or in supplementary reading materials. The Women's Educational Equity Program at the Northwest Regional Educational Laboratory in Oregon conducted a computer search of the ERIC database for such instruments using the following structure: Stereotypes or Bias or Racism and Reading Materials Selection or Measurement or Media Selection or Library Material Selection or Evaluation of Computer Programs or Rating Scales or Content Analysis. This search yielded 151 possible programs or projects for review. Of these possibilities, none produced an instrument that both allowed the user to quantitatively measure female representation in materials and also included a validated qualitative measure for assessing the sex bias or stereotyping in written materials. A standardized, agreed upon, validated qualitative measure is crucial for reviewers who are trying to judge whether materials present suitable role models for female students—role models that are not primarily dependent, passive, incompetent, fearful, etc.

The development of such an instrument would affect two audiences of primary importance: first, educational policymakers charged with reviewing and selecting texts and supplementary reading materials and, secondly, publishers of educational materials. The availability of a standardized, easy-to-use instrument for examining materials for quality as well as for the ratio of male and female representation could have a widespread impact on educational practices in the classroom. Educators using this instrument could help eliminate the purchase and use of discriminatory materials. As a tool in the hands of educators, the instrument could be used to select materials that reinforce nonbiased instruction. Another potential user of such an instrument would be the classroom teacher, the person who can ultimately make educational equity a reality. Teachers who are forced to use biased materials for lack of acceptable alternatives have a double burden: They not only have to be conscious of instructing in a manner that is free from sex bias, but they also have to work with materials that promote exactly what they are trying to eliminate. Teachers need to be able to assess the materials they use in order to discover where bias may still exist and in order to determine how they are going to overcome it and provide bias-free educational opportunities for children.

SUMMARY

While deeply ingrained societal attitudes and habits cannot be changed overnight, policymakers must work toward eliminating prejudice in future generations. An effective step is for all those involved at local and state levels to take responsibility for what children read in school.

This chapter has described the effects of sex-biased materials on children and suggested policies and procedures that can be formulated and implemented at the federal, state, and local levels to eliminate such materials.

- Criteria need to be set in order to enable publishers, textbook reviewers, and educators to determine the quantitative and qualitative representation of both sexes in texts and other instructional materials.
- New and existing materials need to be analyzed, using established criteria, to determine whether bias still exists and how it can be rectified.
- Educators need training in ways to identify and compensate for bias in the materials they are currently using.

These suggested policy changes will increase the educational opportunities of all students. Studies show that nonstereotyped materials have the greatest impact on girls' attitudes and behavior. When exposed to egalitarian materials, girls' concepts of females and males, and of their respective roles in life, broaden, and their behavior changes. However, when teachers strongly reinforce nonsexist attitudes in the classroom, the thinking of both boys and girls becomes less stereotyped (Simpson, 1978). For the benefit of individuals as well as of society, it is necessary to eliminate inequities in educational materials.

REFERENCES

Black, H. (1967). *The American School Book.* Morrow, New York.

Bowler, M. (1978). "The Making of a Textbook." *Learning,* March.

Britton, G. and Lumpkin, M. (1977). *A Consumer's Guide to Sex, Race, and Career Bias in Public School Textbooks.* Britton and Associates, Corvallis, Oreg.

California State Department of Education (1978). *Guidelines for Evaluation of Instructional Materials with Respect to Social Content.* Prepared by Curriculum Frameworks and Instructional Materials Selection Unit. Sacramento, Calif., p. 3.

Clearinghouse on Women's Studies, The Feminist Press (1974). *Any Change in Sexist Texts?* Women's Studies Newsletter, II (3), Summer.

Education Amendments (1972). Title IX, Part C, Elementary and Secondary Education Act. Education Amendments of 1972, P. L. 92–318.

Frazier, N., and Sadker, M. (1973). *Sexism in School and Society.* Harper & Row, New York.

George, F. (1978). "Guidelines for the Development and Evaluation of Unbiased Educational Materials." Non-Sexist Child Development Project, Women's Action Alliance, New York.

Komoski, K. (1975). Untitled presentation for the National Institute of Education, November.

Moore, R. B. (1978). "Sexism in Textbooks," *The Social Studies*, May–June, p. 114.

National Advisory Council on Women's Educational Programs (1979). *Educational Equity: The Continuing Challenge*. Fourth Annual Report 1978. Washington, D.C., p. 12.

National Education Association (1972). *"Sexist Textbooks Must Go—NEA to End Stereotype Role." Oregon Journal*. United Press International, Washington, D.C., November 23, p. 1.

National Organization of Women, New York Chapter (1973). *Report on Sex Bias in Public Schools*, 3rd ed., 99pp.

Nilsen, A. P., Bosmajian, H., Gershuny, H. L., and Stanley, J. P., eds. (1977). "Sexism in Children's Books and Elementary Classroom Materials." *Sexism and Language*. National Council of Teachers of English, Urbana, Ill.

Oregon Administrative Rules (1976). Department of Education, Chapter 581, Division 11: Textbook Adoption.

Oregon State Department of Education (1975–81). *State Adopted Textbooks for Oregon Schools*. Circular No. 3, Language Arts. Salem, Oreg., pp. *vi–vii*.

Project on Equal Education Rights (1977). National Organization of Women Legal Defense and Education Fund. *Stalled at the Start: Government Action on Sex Bias in the Schools*, p. 162.

Simpson, C. J. (1978). "Educational Materials and Children's Sex-Role Concepts," *Language Arts*, 55 (2), February, p. 161.

U.S. Commission on Civil Rights (1979). *Fair Textbooks: A Resource Guide*. Clearinghouse Publication 61, Washington, D.C., December.

U.S. Commission on Civil Rights (1980). *Characters in Textbooks: A Review of the Literature*. Clearinghouse Publication 62, Washington, D.C., p. 12.

Weitzman, L. J., and Rizzo, D. (1974). "Images of Males and Females in Elementary School Textbooks in Five Subject Areas." *Biased Textbooks*. Resource Center on Sex Roles in Education, National Foundation for the Improvement of Education, Washington, D.C., pp. 7–46.

Women's Education Equity Act (1974). Special Projects Act of the Education Amendments of 1974 (P. L. 93-380).

Women on Words and Images (1975). *Dick and Jane as Victims: Sex Stereotyping in Children's Readers*. Women on Words and Images, Princeton, N.J.

Zimet, S. G. (1972). *What Children Read in School*. Grune & Stratton, New York.

PART III

THE STRUCTURE OF CAREERS IN EDUCATION

Chapter 6

THE SEX DIMENSION OF CAREERS IN EDUCATIONAL MANAGEMENT: OVERVIEW AND SYNTHESIS

Richard O. Carlson and Patricia A. Schmuck

The concept of "a career" has proved useful to understanding work organizations and the movement and fate of people in them. Yet the concept is not overwhelmingly clear, and the word *career* is employed in various ways, with distinctions betwen its everyday use and its scholarly use. In everyday usage it simply refers to one's line of work, or occupation. It is also used to refer to progress through a sequence of positions that form an occupation. For example, if someone has been promoted from director to vice president, her career is going well. The word may also refer to one's commitment to an occupation or activity. For example, someone is a *career* army officer. It is also used when describing a woman who has rejected her role of wife and mother; she is called a "career woman." In this chapter, our definition of career is based on certain truths about the work world. Careers are made up of jobs, and a job is the pairing of an individual and an organization; but merely holding a job or position does not constitute a career. A career involves holding a sequence of jobs. Thus, being a third-grade teacher in the same school all of one's working life does not constitute a career in our definition. Lortie describes the role of a teacher as being "career-less" (1975, p. 84). To have a career, the jobs one holds over a period of time must be in an orderly and logical sequence. In education, although women hold the

117

majority of jobs, it is primarily the men who have "careers." Thus, we use the word *career* in this chapter in a very specific sense.[1]

In a dynamic society, it is difficult for people to map out a career rigidly and accurately in advance. The future holds many uncertainties; and a career is a result of a series of decisions made jointly by organizations and an individual. Nevertheless, however vague one's concept of the future, and however pessimistically one anticipates a career, few members of the labor force in a society such as ours can avoid the emphasis on promotion, security, insurance, hope, and aspiration. Few can take a job without learning quickly from fellow workers whether the job is considered a dead-end and in what direction movement is likely to occur. Thus, to investigate the personal considerations brought to bear on career choices and the sex dimension in careers in educational management, we must investigate the structure of management careers in education.

We refer to the forces at work as "career contingencies," and they include the visibility of the occupation; its appropriateness; its plausability as a choice; the counsel, encouragement, and sponsorship involved; the opportunity to perform; the quality of performance; the recognition of performance; the motivation to fulfill formal requirements; the needed socialization; gaining entrance; and the sequence of positions. These factors constitute the contingencies for an orderly, timely career in policymaking and management. A claim is not made that this is an exhaustive list of all contingencies, which are seen, rather, as an array of possible factors for investigation. Nor are the contingencies listed all alike. Some are highly personal, and their meaning depends on the individual. Individuals bring something original to bear upon their careers—not all educators become superintendents and principals. The motivation to fulfill formal entry requirements is an individualistic contingency. The availability of immediate resources, such as encourage-

---

[1] The three criteria of movement, order, and logical sequence of jobs can be considered a male paradigm in that they do not account for all aspects of a person's life experience and they exclude much of the female population. Much of the unpaid work in sour society, such as fund raising, chairing volunteer committees, political activity, and other important social services, which are often part of women's experiences, have not been considered in this concept of a career. Also, this concept does not take into consideration the fact that one might well learn many of the skills required for a position without going through the various chains of the organizational hierarchy. For example, by learning such skills as public speaking, exercising fiscal judgements, political persuasion, organizational abilities, and various leadership skills in the many different realms of life, one would be prepared to perform a job as superintendent. We realize the limitations of our definition. Our purpose however, is not to elucidate such differences between men's work and women's work, but rather to understand the movement of people in administrative positions in education.

ment, counseling, and advice, are critical variables involved in personal career choices.

Career contingencies based on immediate personal factors are discussed in the first section of this chapter. Three of the other chapters in Part III illustrate these personal factors. In Susan Paddock's chapter she describes the results of a questionnaire she distributed nationally to women superintendents, associates, and high school principals in 1977. Sakre Edson reports the results of a survey questionnaire and follow-up interviews with female administrative aspirants in Oregon who had not yet achieved their career goal of becoming principal in 1979. Paddock's and Edson's chapters reflect the personal career contingencies of women who have "arrived" and women who are still pursuing an administrative position. Jovick offers a different vantage point for viewing the personal considerations involved in career choices. He investigated the relationship between the structure of the school and the career ambitions of teachers. He looked at the ambitions of teachers in multiple-unit schools, which provide greater career latitude than the two positions of principal and teacher found in conventional schools.

Certain contingencies are natural precursers of others (e.g., fulfilling formal requirements is a precurser to securing an entry-level position). In education one does not become a principal without having first been a teacher; one does not become a superintendent without having held certain other positions in the field. Administrative careers in education have a structure and a pattern, and we refer to the contingencies over which an individual has no control, or none to speak of, as structural contingencies. Entry-level positions and subsequent positions on the career ladder depend on vacancies, and an individual cannot will a vacancy into existence no matter how motivated he or she may be. Karen Gaertner aptly describes the structural patterns of administrative mobility in one state and clearly delineates the sequence of positions leading upward within the structure of positions in education or out of education.

PERSONAL CONTINGENCIES

A particular career is not simply a random selection from among millions of jobs; it develops from the sequence of possibilities presented at critical junctures. The three important personal contingencies are perceived opportunities, competence, and aspirations. The actual job market sets limits, of course; but a significant aspect of the shaping of a career is the structure of opportunities as *perceived* by the individual— that is, the job market as the individual believes it to be. Jobs must be visible, and that visibility constitutes opportunity. *Competence,* which alone is not sufficient for a career (Deutsch & Madow, 1961), can be measured in terms of what is perceived and what is demonstrated. The salience of a person's *aspirations* depends on the kinds of achievements that the individual feels are important and that thus govern the directions in which he or she will expend effort. The career itself, or a particular occupation or job within it, can be highly salient, but other values may be of equal or higher priority. The level of a person's aspirations is significantly related to the amount of effort the individual will devote to the things he or she values and to any measures that are made of levels of achievement satisfactory or otherwise. Both salience of aspiration and level of aspiration can change as a person goes through various phases of a career (Dill, Hilton, & Reitman, 1961). These personal contingencies must be met in order for one to pursue an orderly and timely career involving policymaking and management positions in education, and we can demonstrate how these personal contingencies operate for women.

Perceived Opportunities

An occupation must be available and visible before a person can willfully enter it. New Yorkers rarely become fig orchardists, and the Manasa Mauler, from rural America, is a rarity among prize fighters. While some occupations vary in visibility in terms of the density of their work force population, others are everywhere highly visible. Almost all American adults, for example, have spent a good deal of their lives observing teachers and, to a lesser extent, school administrators at work. Because these occupations are highly visible to all, neither men or women are advantaged or disadvantaged by the contingency of visibility regarding the occupation of school administrator. This equality between males and females is not true, however, when it comes to the plausibility and appropriateness of choosing to be a school administrator. For men, a decision to enter school administration is credible because there is evidence of the likely success of men who pursue this as a career. For women, the choice seems at best a plausible one; at first glance it may appear reasonable, but because of the relative lack of supporting evidence for the likely success of women in this field, it is not necessarily so reasonable. The overwhelming overrepresentation of men in school administration makes a woman's choice to enter the occupation only plausible. Women are therefore disadvantaged and men advantaged by the evidence when considering the credibility or plausibility of the choice (Schmuck, 1980; Ortez, 1980).

Women are likewise disadvantaged in choosing school administration when we consider the social appropriateness of a career choice in administration. If it appears to an aspirant that the skills, characteristics, and qualities of people who work with some success in the occupation are similar to her own, then the choice of that occupation will seem appropriate to the aspirant. Given the sparsity for women of what have come to be called role models or same-sex functionaries in the occupation, a woman aspirant's opportunities to study and compare their talents, skills, and abilities with her own is very limited. Without such opportunities one cannot be on a secure footing about the appropriateness of the choice of an occupation. The imbalance of male and female role models is a further disadvantage for women in meeting the contingencies related to positions of policymaking and management in education. The scarcity of women role models affects the contingencies of counsel, encouragement, and socialization, at least to the extent that women choose women as sources for these things. The same applies to presocialization, which is part of informal on-the-job training. The scarcity of role models also makes it difficult for women teachers to be assigned to school tasks that are administrative in nature because such tasks are almost invariably assigned to teachers by male vice principals and principals (administrators). To the extent that men predominate in those positions, and to the extent that they give men rather than women the opportunities to try their hand at administrative tasks, women are again handicapped in getting past the occupational contingencies.

Competence

Competence can be measured in two ways, as demonstrated competence and as perceived competence. Measures of *demonstrated* competence do not appreciably differ between populations of males and females (Maccoby & Jacklin, 1974); nor do studies of administrators indicate that sex is a factor in competent leadership (Meskin, 1974). Thus, there are no sexual differences with regard to demonstrated competence. Measures of *perceived* competence between men and women in administrative positions, however, illustrate some differences. Women see themselves as competently performing in their jobs. In fact, one of the few sexual differences reported by Gross and Trask (1976) is that women saw themselves as more competent in providing instructional leadership than their male counterparts. Females who have already assumed administrative positions and have had the opportunity to try their hand, demonstrate their competence and perceive of themselves as competent people.

Perceived competence has been clearly indicated as a personal contingency for women who do not already hold such positions. The literature on the psychology of women in general, and the literature with regard to women teachers has been fairly consistent: Women tend to devalue their competence with regard to leadership roles. Much of the research in this area has been prompted by Matina Horner's work on women's fear of success and the motive to avoid success (1972). Her ideas captured the imagination of many researchers, but some of the replication studies have been contradictory. Condry and Dyer (1976) reviewed many studies that followed Horner's original research, and they suggest that perceived competence is not a stable personality characteristic but dependent on the situation. However, women in a male sex-typed situation and men in a female sex-typed situation tend to question their competence. In education women may perceive of themselves as competent with regard to instructional matters, yet with regard to the male sex-typed role of administration believe themselves to be inferior. It is clear that perceived competence has clearly been a negative factor in the past for women educators with regard to the personal contingency involved in careers in administration. Edson's chapter on ambitions and opportunity will be particularly illuminating in this regard because she has documented the self-assessments of women who aspired to administrative positions in 1979. These women may represent a new cohort of aspirants who do not devalue their skills in the pattern of their older female colleagues.

Aspiration

Appropriate rewards for work and the level to which a person aspires are part of the contingency of aspiration. Certainly, for most women who aspire to and achieve administrative positions, extrinsic rewards, such as counsel, encouragement, and the active sponsorship of academic and educational communities have not been part of their experience. It will be interesting to note what difference the emerging women's support systems and networks will have on the levels to which women aspire (Kleiman, 1980). Intrinsic rewards must also be forthcoming in order for a person to aspire to higher levels. Paddock, in her chapter on career paths, presents some findings indicating that women who have achieved positions in administration do not aspire to attain what we often think of as the dominant positive rewards of a career, such as greater status and higher salary levels. In fact, some women indicated an antipathy for the concept of a career as a timely, orderly, vertical progression of positions. One female principal said, "Success is not measured in moving from job to job in a vertical continuum. . . . it is measured by the quality of any job held."

At this point it is unclear whether there is a difference between the reward factor in women's aspirations for higher levels and the reward factor of men. Nor is it clear whether age is related to the perception of rewards. How persistent is the new cohort of women aspiring to or already in entry-level positions as compared with their male counterparts and with older women who have already achieved high-level management positions? The three measures of personal career contingencies—perceived opportunities, competence, and aspiration are important in explaining the evident unequal representation of men and women in management.

STRUCTURAL CONTINGENCIES

Equally important to personal considerations in choosing a career of management in education are contingencies that exist within the profession itself. Structural contingencies, over which individual aspirants have no control, relate to career barriers, vacancies, the lengths of vacancy chains (described below), and the elimination of positions. The relationships between structural contingencies and orderly career opportunities are shown in Figure 6.1. Since it is obvious that vacancies are indispensable to orderly career opportunities, that movement from one position to another is possible only if a vacancy exists, that if there are no vacancies, there is no movement, no career progression, vacancies and vacancies alone permit career advancement. Usually vacancies arise from retirements, resignations, and the creation of new positions. However, when organizations are growing and adding new positions and at the same time experiencing high resignation rates, vacancies abound and orderly career opportunities are high. Gaertner, in her chapter, has provided systematic data from one state to show career patterns in terms of positional changes made by individuals. This analysis accounts for vacancies that permit career advancement.

Vacancies created by retirements and new positions have

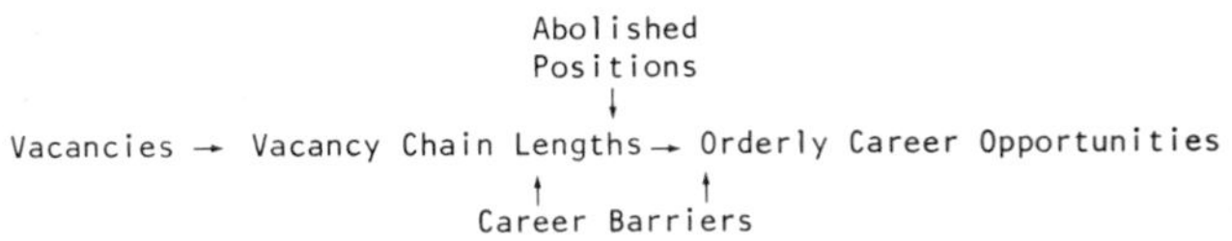

```
                      Abolished
                      Positions
                          ↓
Vacancies  →  Vacancy Chain Lengths →  Orderly Career Opportunities
                          ↑        ↑
                      Career Barriers
```

Fig. 6.1. Structural career contingencies.

"mobility" properties. That is, if Person 1 retires from Job A, Job A can then be said to be occupied by a vacancy. If Person 2 moves from Job B to Job A, the vacancy moves from Job A to Job B. In this manner vacancies move down the hierarchy while individuals move up the hierarchy. Ordinarily, once a vacancy enters a network of positions it moves, position by position, down the hierarchy from its point of entry to the lowest position in the hierarchy. The more positions it occupies as it moves, the more people advance in the hierarchy. Thus, long vacancy chains enhance orderly career opportunities, and short vacancy chains limit them.

The elimination of positions has an impact on the length of vacancy chains, which, in turn, affects orderly career opportunities. Whenever a position is vacated and then abolished, as often happens with higher-level positions, the vacancy leaves the network along with the position, permitting no one below that position to move up in the hierarchy because of the loss of the vacancy.

The length of a vacancy chain, a prime factor in determining orderly career opportunities, is influenced by the nature of the career barriers at work in an organization. Career barriers govern the movement of individuals from one position to the next higher position. Career barriers in educational organizations are almost invariably one of five types. One barrier involves assessment, either subjective or objective, of an individual's performance in office. This barrier holds back those who do not perform up to the standard and permits those who do to advance. A second barrier relates to the amount of formal education an individual has acquired. If it is not the designated amount, he or she does not advance. A third barrier involves seniority, which regulates upward movement by letting only those with the greatest seniority through. A fourth barrier has to do with experience. In general, this regulates movement by specifying a sequence of positions that one must hold and/or by prescribing a time period that must be spent in one position before one is eligible to move up to the next position. A fifth barrier involves personal attributes, however defined. One does not enter or advance beyond this barrier unless one has the "proper" personal attributes, which are locally defined. Such attributes are the target of regulations that fall under the category of equal employment opportunity.

The role of elementary school principal is a case in point. Elementary school principals rarely become superintendents. Gaertner's chapter shows that this position is most frequently related to the "exit" move. We might ask several questions regarding the lack of mobility from elementary principal to superintendent. Perhaps formal education is a barrier; many states require a different certificate for the two positions. Perhaps the experience provided in the role of elementary school principal does not provide the necessary on-the-job training to become a superintendent. Gaertner raises the question of whether the personal attribute of "femaleness" is the barrier that makes the linkage between these positions so tenuous. Gaertner does show, for example, that it is women, more often than men, that make the exit move from this position.

The five career barriers act on vacancy chains to alter the movement of vacancies and therefore influence the availability of opportunities for upward movement within a hierarchy of positions. The influence is of two types. Career barriers can cause a vacancy to be ejected prematurely from the network and can cause vacancies to leap over positions in their descent. Seniority barriers make networks impermeable, except at the lowest position. Education, experience, and performance-rating barriers can render a bounded set of positions permeable at positions above the lowest. When a bounded set of positions is permeable, vacancies can be prematurely ejected. If a vacancy in Position A is filled by someone from outside the network of positions, the vacancy leaves the network. It is prematurely ejected. It does not move down the hierarchy from the point of entry to the lowest position in the hierarchy, so the opportunity for career advancement for those in positions below Position A is lost.

Not only can education, experience, and performance-rating barriers cause vacancies to be prematurely ejected from the network, they can also cause vacancies to leap over positions in their otherwise orderly descent of the hierarchy. This is because education, experience, and performance-rating barriers only establish eligibility pools, and a member of the pool can leap over one or more positions if no position holder is in the eligibility pool. Position A could be filled by a person holding Position D because no one in Positions B and C has the prescribed education, experience, or performance rating. In that case the vacancy occupying Position A would move to position D, leaping over Positions B and C. The leaping over of positions by vacancies, permitted by the barriers of education, experience, and performance rating, but not by seniority, naturally shortens the length of the vacancy chain and reduces the number of orderly career opportunities.

Career barriers influence the movement of vacancies once they enter a bounded set of positions and therefore have an *indirect* impact on orderly career opportunities. However, career barriers can also have a *direct* impact on orderly career opportunities because with some career barriers an individual's competitive advantage will always peak to a maximum competitive advantage and with others an individual's competitive advantage will not peak. Seniority is a career barrier that provides for the peaking of an individual's competitive advantage. Under seniority rules each person eventually has seniority over all others in the position, so his or her turn for promotion eventually arrives. With education, experience, and performance ratings, however, unless these barriers are coupled with seniority, they do not allow for the peaking of an individual's competitive advantage. They restrict, however finely, the pool of the eligible, although they do not select the one person most eligible. They permit a person to gain advantage over those not in the pool, but they do not permit gaining within the pool.

Seniority guarantees advancement in time, while education, experience, and performance rating do not provide a guarantee. Formal education, culminating in a certificate or degree, is the barrier which is almost always used in connection with positions in educational policy and management. As has been shown, education, when used as a barrier, simply identifies a pool of eligible applicants. It restricts competition to those within the eligible pool. It does not identify the one person who is eligible. It does not permit an individual's competitive advantage to peak. It does not provide a guarantee that an individual's turn for a promotion will eventually arrive. As already mentioned, seniority does provide a guarantee that one's turn will someday come. It does not merely create a pool of eligible applicants, it identifies the one and only one eligible applicant. It does not restrict competition to those within the eligible pool; it eliminates competition.

Given this situation, it can be argued that inequity in policymaking and management positions in education would be eliminated if seniority were used either in place of or in addition to the education barrier as a means of regulating the movement of administrators to other positions and the movement of teachers to administrative posts. The use of seniority would achieve equality of opportunity—it would achieve what equal-employment opportunity rules and regulations have not. Even though the use of a seniority barrier would achieve equal opportunity in policymaking and management positions in education, the thought of its use is somewhat jarring. It would be a blow to our seemingly firm belief in competition. It would be a blow to our firm belief that employers are flawless in discriminating and making choices. It would be a blow to our belief that the efficiency and effectiveness of our schools is dependent upon some person or some group's ability to choose the right person for the right job at the right time. There is no evidence to prove the correctness of these beliefs. They are simply beliefs.

SUMMARY AND SUGGESTIONS
FOR FUTURE RESEARCH

There are many current attempts to change career contingencies as they disadvantage women's careers in education administration (Rosser, 1980; Schmuck, 1980; AASA, 1980). Most of these are direct action projects and do not have a basic-research component. If these attempts bear fruit and the field of education administration becomes more equally represented by women, we believe research on careers of administration in education will be especially intriguing. Historically, education has undergone a change in its sex composition; perhaps it will again. The first line of research we suggest is presented in the chapter by Tyack and Strober, who aptly point out that the sexual composition of adult professionals is related to larger social forces. Schools are, after all, an institution of the society they serve. Levi-Strauss pointed out that "only the study of historical developments permits the weighing and evaluation of the interrelationships among the components of current society" (1967, p. 13). The literature on educational careers tends too often to be microscopic rather than macroscopic; to emphasize individual psychology rather than broad sociological and historical content. We need to continue to relate women's place in the hierarchy of educational institutions to variables such as labor market demands and public ideology, and to organizational factors such as increased bureaucracy, control and certification.

If we use the historical variables discussed by Tyack and Strober as predictors and ask whether more women will be in the executive levels of school administration in the 1980s, our answer must be in the negative. Perhaps the only variable mentioned in their chapter that would lead to a positive answer is the shifting ideology concerning women's place in the society. Other variables, such as a declining economy and an increasing bureaucracy, would lead us to predict greater sexual segregation and stratification. Thus we need to view careers in education in the context of the larger society. We believe sufficient work has already been done regarding the similarities and differences between men and women who have arrived in administrative positions in education. Paddock, a contributor to Part III, and others have shown that women as a group, and men as a group have remarkably similar career paths. The intriguing question remains, of course: Why have so few women achieved such positions? We would predict that as more women move into administrative positions, they will continue to be similar to their male colleagues and will have achieved their position in similar ways.

March and March (1977) refer to "indistinguishable executives" in their study of superintendents. (Although their sample included 1528 individuals, they note that only 3 or 4 are not white males.) This does not mean that all executives are like each other, but that the system that matches organizations and individuals creates indistinguishability as an outcome. Thus, we would expect women who arrive in such positions to look very much like the men who occupy these roles. Indistinguishability among men is part of the current popular literature for women; they are encouraged to adopt and to adapt certain orientations that have worked for men in the past. Women are instructed on how to play the game and how to win in a man's world; on how to dress for success and how to "get yours" (Harrigan, 1977; Molloy, 1977; Pogrebin, 1975). One best-selling book, *The Managerial Woman*, tells women how to know themselves and how to decide if they really wish to compete for a career in a male-dominated system. It further instructs a woman about governing the "interaction between who she is" and her work environment (Hennig & Jardim, 1977).

By and large, this popular literature claims that "success" is a matter of effort, intelligence, and footwork; and it advises women to change the personal contingencies that have had negative consequences for women's representation in management. Some authors have presented the hope that women in management may be instrumental in making schools better. It certainly is a researchable question as to whether schools would be different institutions if more women were represented in leadership positions. We tend to think, however, that women will be indistinguishable from their male colleagues. Grambs (1976) said, and we agree: "Assuming that women do force schools to employ more women in administrative positions, the kind of women so employed, it is predicted, will be those who will accept the male model of how schools ought to be run. To the degree that this is true, we can then predict that having more women in school leadership will make no difference whatsoever in what happens in school" (p. 2). Clasby (1980) raises the question in another way: "Do women focus on gaining access to the existing system, or do they focus on changing systems which function unjustly for themselves and for others?" (p.2). The emphasis so far has been on gaining access to the system.

On the other hand, if women do gain access to the system, we need to look at whether certain career contingencies will change. For instance, much of the evidence cited here and elsewhere notes how women are disadvantaged by the informal network of men who encourage, sponsor, and mentor each other. Perhaps this barrier is being eliminated or perhaps compensatory systems are being created. Perhaps more men consciously think about providing such encouragement and help to women. Perhaps the creation of women's networks compensates for women's exclusion from the "old boys" networks which have fostered discrimination against women in the past (Kleiman, 1980). In fact, in our department of educational administration, the male graduate students complained because a continuous round of potlucks, rap sessions and social gatherings were provided for women but not for them. Networking and its subsequent encouragement and advice is an example of a compensatory feature added to a system that has worked to the disadvantage of women in the past.

As more women move into management roles we need also to investigate whether a dual career track develops. Will women move into certain positions and not others? Will women be randomly placed throughout all positions or will they continue to be segregated within certain positions? For instance, in Oregon in 1977–1978 more women were hired as administrators than in previous years. However, they tended to primarily hold positions as assistant principals and on central office staffs. Women in assistant-principal roles will be interesting to watch. The reason so few women are high school principals it has been argued, is that there are equally few women high school *vice* principals, the major pool from which high school principals are drawn. The high school vice principal's position is in the path of mobility; will this also be true for women, or will it tend to be an "exit" position, as is the elementary school principalship?

We need to investigate whether systems have an informal "lid," or quota, on the hiring of women in administrative positions. Some structural career contingency might be developed about the relative representation of men and women in a system. Certain token positions for women would be evidence of a dual career system. There is a story about a school district where an elementary school and a junior high school shared the same grounds. There were four administrators, two principals, two vice principals, who were all women. It was referred to as the matriarchy, and when an opening occurred for a vice principal, there was a concerted effort to hire a male. Perhaps it is believed that the system can tolerate the inclusion of only some or a certain number of females in leadership roles.

REFERENCES

AASA (1980) *Project Aware*. Effie Jones, American Association of School Administrators, Arlington, Va.

Clasby, M. (1980). "A Value Dilemma in Equality for Women:A Reflective Essay." *UCEA Review,* vol. XXI, no. 1, Winter.

Condry, J., and Dyer, S. (1976). "Fear of Success: Attribution of Cause to the Victim," *Journal of Social Issues,* vol. 32, no. 3, pp. 63–83.

Deutsch, K. W., and Madow, W. G. (1961). "A Note on the Appearance of Wisdom in Large Bureaucratic Organizations." *Behavioral Science,* 6:72–78.

Dill, W. R., Hilton, T., and Reitman, W. (1961). *The New Managers.* Prentice-Hall, Englewood Cliffs, N.J.

Grambs, J. D. (1976). "Women and Administration:Confrontation or Accomodation." *Theory Into Practice,* vol. XV, no. 4, pp. 293–300.

Gross, N., and Trask, A. (1976). *The Sex Factor in the Management of Schools.* Wiley, New York.

Harrigan, B. L. (1977). *Games Mother Never Taught You.* Warner Books, New York.

Hennig, M., and Jardim, A. (1977). *The Managerial Woman.* Doubleday (Anchor Press) Garden City, N.Y., p. 159.

Horner, M. (1972). "Toward an Understanding of Achievement-Related Conflicts in Women." *Journal of Social Issues,* vol. 28, no. 2, pp. 157–176.

Kleiman, C. (1980). *Women's Networks.* Lippincott (Crowell), New York.

Levi-Strauss, C. (1967). *Structural Anthropology.* Doubleday, Garden City, N.Y.

Lortie, D. C. (1975). *Schoolteacher.* University of Chicago Press.

Maccoby, E., and Jacklin, C. N. (1974). *The Psychology of Sex Differences.* Basic Books, New York.

March, J. C., and March, J. H. (1977). "Almost Random Careers:The Wisconsin School Superintendency, 1940–1972." *Administrative Science Quarterly,* September, no. 22, pp. 377–409.

Meskin, J. (1974). "The Performance of Women School Administrators—a Review of the Literature." *Administrator's Notebook,* vol. 23, no. 1.

Molloy, J. T. (1977). *The Woman's Dress for Success Book.* Follett, Chicago.

Ortez, F. (1980). *Career Change and Mobility for Minorities and Women School Administrators.* American Educational Research Association, Boston, Mass.

Pogrebin, L. (1975). *Getting Yours.* Avon Books, New York.

Rosser, P. (1980). "Women Fight 'Old Boys' for School Administrator Job." *Learning,* March, pp. 31–34.

Schmuck, P. A. (1980). *SEEL:The Oregon Story,* Education Development Center, Newton, Mass.

Chapter 7

JOBS AND GENDER: A HISTORY OF THE STRUCTURING OF EDUCATIONAL EMPLOYMENT BY SEX

David B. Tyack and Myra H. Strober

QUESTIONS FROM HISTORY

In this exploratory study we ask: How and why did women enter public school teaching? Why did men remain in public education as teachers in the upper grades and as managers even after elementary teaching became almost a female monopoly? What impact did the sexual composition of teaching have on the occupation and on the school as a social organization? How much has sexual asymmetry changed since 1940, and what are the prospects for the future? We raise the questions in this way because we believe that gender is one of the fundamental organizing principles in society, as important a category for analysis as class or race or age. To know the sex of a typical child, past or present, is already to know much about how that person has access to power, prestige, and opportunity and to know much about how she or he would be shaped by cultural norms of behavior.

We subscribe neither to the genetic determinism of some sociobiologists nor to the voluntaristic optimism of some social psychologists who think that the differences between men and women result from "roles" that can be changed like a script in a play by reforming

The larger study of which this chapter forms a part was supported by the National Institute of Education. The authors, and not the Institute, are, of course, responsible for the views expressed here.

131

early socialization or by training women to be more assertive. We see the structuring of society by gender as something more tractable than genes and more resistant to reform than roles. We see differentiation by sex as deeply embedded in the history of male and female participation in the economy, in changes in cultural norms for women's behavior, in the development of the family, and in the evolution of other social organizations, such as schools. (For a perceptive discussion of how gender structures society, see Kelly-Gadol, 1976).

The structuring of society by gender is so pervasive—cutting across divisions of class, race, and age—that its effects have often been taken for granted or deliberately slighted by those who stood to benefit from existing arrangements. In recent years, however, many scholars have attempted to reconceptualize American history by examining the role of gender. Labor economists have asked how and why women have been and are still segregated to a large degree in the work force and why they, like blacks, have tended over time to earn only about three-fifths of the wages of white males. They have explored why the demand for women in sex-labeled jobs has increased and how employers have dipped at critical junctures into different segments of the massive reserve pool of workers represented by women, both single and married. (For a discussion of the feminization of teaching, see Strober & Best, 1979; Oppenheimer, 1968 and 1970; for several analyses of occupational segregation by sex, see Blaxall & Reagan, 1976.) Social historians and sociologists have been disputing the traditional separation in scholarly study of the family and the workplace, and they have insisted that women's work in the market economy must be linked to changes in the family, in demography, and in the life cycle, not treated as though it existed in a separate world (Kanter, 1977; Tilly & Scott, 1978).

Cultural historians have shown how the nineteenth-century doctrine of domesticity drew boundaries around a "woman's sphere" and justified limited female participation in work and public life outside the family. Such cultural belief systems help explain the connections between family and women's work and the configurations of opportunity and exclusion in employment for women (Cott, 1977; Sklar, 1973; Harris, 1978). Although artifacts of society at particular times and places, these beliefs and behavior patterns carried great authority, for, as Goffman (1979) writes, "gender, in close connection with age grade, lays down more, perhaps, than class or other social divisions an understanding of what our ultimate nature ought to be and how and where this nature ought to be exhibited" (1979, p. 8).

We are currently engaged in a large study designed to examine the structuring of employment by sex in public education, focusing especially on the years from 1840 to 1980. We have drawn on the work of economists, sociologists and historians in an attempt to achieve an interdisciplinary understanding of this phenomenon. We seek to link together into an integrated argument four major factors: labor supply and demand forces, cultural values, organizational changes, and changes in the family. We see these influences not as single parsimonious explanations, nor as competing hypotheses, but as interpretations that nest, like Chinese cups, one within another. In this chapter we suggest an argument that seeks to integrate these different explanations.

It would be easy to conclude that it was somehow inevitable that public school teaching became largely women's work while males continued to manage the enterprise; but we reject the practice of taking this for granted. During the colonial period, men dominated the teaching profession in public institutions. (The definition of public, it should be pointed out, was far more comprehensive than at present, including many institutions that today would be called private.) Well into the twentieth century, in certain other nations, Prussia, for example, men continued to dominate in teaching at all levels. Beginning in the urbanized northeast United States, women teachers started to become a majority in public schools in the middle decades of the nineteenth century. By 1870, when national statistics were available for the first time, about 60% of the teachers nationwide were female. The percentage of women slowly increased to 70% in 1900 and then to a peak of 86% in 1920. Thereafter the percentage of men increased gradually, accelerating during the Depression of the 1930s but dropping again during World War II. Since World II, the proportion of women in public school teaching has dropped; in 1978, they constituted about two-thirds of all public school teachers (Woody, 1974, pp. 496–500). Thus, there has been considerable fluctuation in the sexual composition of the teaching force.

These nationwide figures mask important regional and rural–urban variations. In 1870, for example, men teachers were still a majority in 26 states. Urban Washington, D.C., had a teaching force that was 92% female, while adjacent Virginia had women in only 35% of its teaching positions. In 1880, in California as a whole, women constituted 66% of all public school personnel (including principals), but in San Francisco 92%. Another source of variability in sexual composition was the level at which teachers taught; women tended to monopolize the primary grades, while men appeared most frequently in the upper grades and the high schools. (The two major sources of statistics on teachers by sex are the annual and biennial reports of the U.S. Commissioner of Education and decennial Census reports. For concise discussion of Census data on teachers, see Folger & Nam, 1967.)

Thus we see the composition of teaching by sex not as some ineluctable and unilinear evolution, but as a set of historical puzzles. How and why did women enter public school teaching in the nineteenth century? What were the sources of the variability in the sex ratio? Why did men persist as teachers even though they cost more to hire than women did? And why did men continue nearly to monopolize key administrative positions? Why did the proportion of males increase after World War II at all levels of the system? As the composition of educational employment by sex has changed and changed again, what has been the impact on the occupation and on the school as a social organization? What effects has gender had on the development of professional associations? In this essay we suggest some tentative answers to these questions.

Historical Analysis of the Labor Market

We begin with an examination of the macro forces of supply and demand in the labor market for teachers and concurrent changes in cultural values affecting the employment of women as teachers. Throughout most periods of American history there has been a strong demand for teachers. This has resulted from a combination of factors: a large increase in the absolute numbers of children and youth of school age; a rise in the percentage of pupils enrolled and of their average daily attendance; steady extensions of the length of the school term; very high turnover of teachers, especially in rural areas; and an overall decrease in class size. Until well into the twentieth century the people who hired teachers did not set high educational standards; they typically required that instructors be literate and reasonably well versed in the three R's, of certified moral character (as determined by community standards and often attested to by letters of reference), of native birth, and generally possessing middle-class appearance and habits. Save for a few positions in the cities, normally occupied by males, employers only sought people who were willing to accept low wages (U.S. Bureau of the Census, 1900; Ellsbree, 1939).

Where could such a labor force be found? In an economy characterized by abundant land in the west, expanding commercial and industrial opportunities in cities, and careers opening up in the professions, mature males could generally find employment in occupations that paid more than teaching and offered much greater long-term advancement. Young men, especially during the winter in rural communities, would sometimes be interested in teaching for a short term, generally as a stepping stone to something else. College students working their way through school or farmers' sons, for example, might find even low pay attractive for a few weeks' work. We shall explore these and the other motivations of male teachers later in this chapter.

Although the wage scale for teaching was often on a level with that of the casual laborers who dug the canals and built the railroads, school board members did not usually want to dip down into the social structure to hire mature men of lower status, such as Irish Catholic immigrants in New England, for example. They wanted to pay proletarian wages and still keep teaching a white-collar occupation. Where could school boards turn to acquire staffs for the burgeoning common schools of the 1840s and the 1850s? One place to look was among the growing reserve labor-pool of literate, middle-class, single young women (Beecher, 1846).

From the beginning of American history women had always taught young children. Sometimes, they taught only in their own families and sometimes in "dame schools," in which married or single women conducted small classes in homes to teach the ABCs to boys and girls of about 7 years old and younger. Through a long and complex process, females gained access first as students and then as teachers to tax-supported or private schools held ouside the home. By the end of the eighteenth century young women began to be hired to teach little children during the summer term of the one-room schools near their homes. The transition from the dame school held in the home to the one-room school was a slight step, but a significant one. The "cellular" character of American elementary education, in which a single teacher instructs a group of children in the three R's all day within the walls of a single room, continues to reflect something of its early origins. The one-room school resembled in some ways the family farm. As girls gained access to formal schooling, the literacy of women rose rapidly from the late colonial period to the mid-nineteenth century, especially in the north. This created a population of young women qualified by education and moral character to serve as school teachers (Woody, 1974, chaps. 3–6; Bernard & Vinovskis, 1977; Vinovskis & Bernard, 1978. For the concept of the "cellular" classroom, see Lortie, 1975).

Emma Willard, Catharine Beecher, Mary Lyon, and other pioneers in women's education publicized a rationale for training young women specifically as teachers and for hiring them to replace men. Using arguments that were later voiced by common school crusaders such as Horace Mann and Henry Barnard, they claimed that women were *by nature* and God's design the ideal teachers of little children: nurturant, patient, able to understand young minds, and exemplary in their moral influence on the rising generation. To these promoters, teaching served the millennial dream of a Protestant, republican society, one in which women teachers could be the missionaries of civilization. Recognizing how powerful the "cult of true womanhood" was, they did not promote the idea that women should be teachers *instead* of being mothers. Rather, they argued that teaching prepared women to be better mothers and that it was but a step from the parental home to the schoolhouse and then back again to the conjugal home as wife and mother. Endorsing the notion of a special sphere for women, the pioneer educators enlarged the domestic sphere to include the school and thereby helped to create a market for the graduates of their seminaries. Besides, as they were quick to add, women were considerably cheaper to hire than were men (Sklar, 1973; Land, 1977; Scott, 1979; Melder, 1979).

While public and private schools were opening their doors to female students and teachers, and as spokespeople were developing a rationale for employing women, concurrent changes in the family economy in New England and in the life cycle of young women further promoted the feminization of teaching. In the years following the American Revolution, daughters in farm families were adding cash income to the family economy in variety of ways. At home they were beginning to do piece work—braiding straw hats, sewing uppers of shoes, spinning cloth, and the like—for commercial capitalists who provided raw materials and paid families for finished goods. When cotton-mill owners sought young women to work as operators, daughters of farmers went to towns on the Merrimac River and worked and lived together in supervised boarding houses. Some worked as domestics in other people's houses, and increasing numbers worked as teachers, often alternating mill work with instructing in country schools. They were excluded from most other jobs, which were reserved for men (Cott, 1977, chaps. 1, 3; Dublin, 1979, chap. 1).

Teaching was thus only one way in which young women were beginning to take part in the market economy. They were also working for cash in the putting-out system of mercantile capitalism and working directly for wages in a nascent industrial society. As Allmendinger and Dublin have shown, teaching and factory work enabled young women to contribute to the family economy and to achieve some economic independence while awaiting marriage—or indeed, to be self-supporting in case they remained single (Dublin, 1979, chap. 3; Allmendinger, 1979) It is not accidental that school teaching first became feminized in the northeast, where industrial capitalism first began its take-off into sustained growth. The factory system replaced certain portions of traditional household work, thereby lessening the need for the domestic services of daughters, and women began to work for wages outside the home. (Katz, 1968; Woody, 1974, chap. 10; for a comparison with Canada, see Prentice, 1975).

Thus far the reasoning seems uncomplicated. Women were hired because there was high demand for literate and moral teachers at cheap prices, because teaching came to be seen as a legitimate part of a woman's sphere, and because women would work for lower wages than men's. By this reasoning one might expect that over time public school teachers would have become 100% women or that men would have been hired only if they agreed to serve at the same wages as those paid to women. Neither of these came to pass, however. Based on quantitative studies we are conducting using statistics reported by states for 1850 and by the U.S. Commissioner of Education beginning in 1870, we can make the following observations: Men did remain in teaching, and within any particular labor market they received higher salaries than those paid to women. Indeed, the story becomes more complex the closer one looks at it. Women teachers in city systems generally earned more per month than men in rural school systems. States that spent the most per pupil for schools typically had the largest ratio of women teachers. (In 1870 the zero-order correlation between expenditures per pupil and the percentage of female teachers, by state, was .67.)

It is by no means clear what the causal direction is, if any, between this association of high costs and feminization. The most telling variable is the *gap* between male and female salaries, not the absolute values; where the gap was greatest in the female–male salary ratio, one found the largest percentage of women teachers. One place to start unraveling this complex story is to ask where the male teachers were. During the latter nineteenth century they constituted about 30% of all public school teachers. Male teachers appeared in the largest numbers in rural schools, where salaries were low, school terms short, professional requirements meager, and the gap in female–male salaries the smallest— in short, where they cost the least to hire. The regions that had the largest percentage of males, the south and southwest, were the most backward in educational development (Blodgett, 1900).

THE ORGANIZATION OF RURAL AND URBAN SCHOOLS

To understand the variability in the sexual composition of the labor force in teaching, it is essential to shift to a different kind of analysis, to ask how and why urban and rural school districts tended to operate as different labor markets, each split by gender. We thus turn to the organizational character of urban and rural schools and their relation to their surrounding communities, aware that in the century from 1870 to 1970 there was a gradual convergence between schools in cities and countryside and a lagged regional drift toward greater standardization. Stinchcombe (1965) has observed that institutions continue to reflect the organizational structure they displayed at the time of their founding. Construction crafts such as carpentry or bricklaying, for example, which are very old, tend to˙ be organized quite differently from modern production-line factories. So it was with rural and urban schools. The country school reflected in its structure and functioning the freehold family farms that typically constituted its environment.

Until the twentieth century, few rural teachers had more than an elementary school education. Teachers were typically local young people in their late teens or early twenties, often selected by school trustees from among their own relatives. Teachers' wages were often seen as the spoils of trustees' offices, a way to recoup taxes for the family income. (For the flavor of such schools, see Eggleston, 1965). In the schools a young man or woman perhaps a trustee's brother or sister supervised a small number of children (often no more than ten) of different ages drawn from the immediate neighborhood. Roles in the school were more familial than bureaucratic and organization was flexible. The older children were expected to help the younger ones while the teacher supervised recitations. Often parents and other patrons gathered to hear what the children had learned or to witness a spelling bee. In many parts of the country, teachers went house to house to "board 'round," eating and sleeping at the homes of the parents of the pupils (Tyack, 1974).

Throughout most of the nineteenth century, the rural school was the modal public school. In 1880 over 77% of all Americans lived in rural areas; yet only about 47% of the public school funds were spent on rural schools (Solmon, 1970). Except in the heavily urbanized states, the rural schools were open generally less than half as many days as the city schools. As late as 1919, Nebraska school law required districts of fewer than 20 pupils to be open only 4 months, whereas districts with over 75 students had to be in session for 9 months (University of Nebraska, 1919). Even short rural school years were often divided into two or three separate terms, and often employing different teachers. Typically, the school calendar was designed to match the need for the labor of children, and teachers, on the farms. The hiring of a teacher in these rural areas approximated a free competitive market in which it was probably typical for school trustees to hire a hand to work on the farm and a young woman to serve as a house helper. Trustees wanted to economize and to get the most productivity for the least amount of money. Often, when state funds ran out after a few weeks, parents chipped in for private tuition so the teacher could be paid for a longer term. A county superintendent in Georgia said that patrons paid a teacher according to their assessment of the merit of the teacher, "just as a person might be employed by a private individual" (NEA, 1905, p. 125).

Under such conditions of an open market, in which entry requirements were low, trustees bargained with women and men for their services. Cost was clearly a very important factor in the trustees' decisions about whom to hire, and also an important factor was their preconception about sex-linked abilities. Where school terms were split into summer and winter sessions, trustees commonly hired women as appropriate teachers to work with young children in the summer months. During the winter term, however, when older boys entered the school in large numbers (for rural schools tended to have a wide age range in enrollment), trustees often preferred men as teachers because they considered them better disciplinarians and more competent for teaching male youth. They were willing to pay a small salary premium to obtain the services of male teachers. Over time, however, as women showed that they could succeed in teaching older children, and as fewer men began to apply (for reasons we shall examine), women gradually replaced men in country schools. During much of the nineteenth century, in certain rural sectors of the country, teaching in the winter term in country schools was not a completely sex-labeled occupation (Johnson, 1904).

For what reasons did both men and women want to enter this labor market? Young women, having few alternative occupations, could work either in their own or neighbors' homes. Unlike young men, they could not migrate so easily to cities or to new land opening up in the west, for custom dictated that they live in established families. For young women awaiting marriage, teaching in a farm economy, where such jobs were rare, was an attractive opportunity to earn cash. When daughters lived at home, their income was a welcome addition to the family economy, and it sometimes permitted them to accumulate a dowry. In addition, it was a respectable occupation that gave a woman a certain visibility as a possible marriage partner and an opportunity for sociability in lonely dispersed settlements. The marriageable school marm became a staple of American fiction, particularly in Westerns. (One rich source of data on the lives and motives of teachers is the set of autobiographies and biographies of pioneer teachers commissioned by the teachers' sorority Delta Kappa Gamma in many states.)

Men, by contrast, had more opportunities to move away from farm communities and to perform alternative rural work, such as lumbering, trapping, and construction during seasons of light agricultural work; but teaching a short term in a country school had an appeal for males as well as for females. It was one of the very few nonmanual jobs available; it provided cash income, and it was a useful stepping stone for a person eager to establish himself in the community. If a young man wanted to get started as a minister, politician, shopkeeper, or lawyer, a position as schoolmaster gave him visibility. He could also easily combine teaching in a winter term with farming his own homestead the rest of the year. The job required almost no preparation, took only a few weeks out of the year, and had low opportunity costs (or foregone earnings.) (Kirkpatrick, 1917). When rural school terms lengthened and were combined into a continuous year and when standards for certification rose, women began to replace men as teachers. Rural wages in teaching did not rise substantially, and even for a full-year teaching term of 6 to 8 months, the salary was barely sufficient to support one person, much less a family.

The pay for teaching was still attractive to a woman living at home or inexpensively as boarder in a farm family; but for a man, the long school term and the higher entry costs (new laws required certification or attendance at teachers' institutes) were greater barriers. A man was no longer willing to teach a few weeks for cash and then pursue another job as his primary occupation because interrupting other activities to attend a summer teachers' institute or to bone up for a county examination seemed not worth the effort if measured against alternative uses of his time and money. In Wisconsin in 1902, rural teachers estimated the direct costs of institutes, books, and other professionally related expenses to be almost equal to one month's salary (NEA, 1905). As the school term lengthened and professional requirements increased in Nebraska, the percentage of male teachers dropped from a majority in 1870 to only about 12% in 1910. By 1920 there were only eight states where the percentage of male teachers was more than 20% and only one had more than 30%; these were predominantly rural states where the terms were relatively short and where bureaucratic controls were scanty (Committee of Graduate School of Education, 1919).

In effect, the longer terms and increased standards for entry turned teaching into a "para-profession," as Morain (1977) observed in his study of the feminization of teaching in rural Iowa. A little "professionalization" of this sort drove men out of teaching, for it increased the opportunity costs without resulting in commensurate increases in pay. By contrast, the professionalization of more lucrative and prestigious fields, such as medicine or law, which included the upgrading of training programs and licensing requirements, tended to drive women out of those occupations, sometimes by the deliberate setting of quotas in male-dominated graduate schools (Morain, 1977).

Early Employment in Urban Schools

While technically a part of the same "common school system" as the rural schools, urban public schools were quite different structurally, and they constituted in many respects a different labor market. The school year in the city was often twice as long as that in poor and sparsely settled rural areas. In 1880, for example, in 32 of the 38 states, urban schools were open over 180 days, and in 25 states more than 190 days, as compared with the nationwide average of 130 days. In that same year, cities spent $12.62 per capita on education, as compared with only $3.28 in rural areas. According to Solmon (1970), the lost potential earnings of pupils in the city were vastly greater than those of rural youth since the long school term and different employment patterns in urban economies meant that it was not so easy to do seasonal work as it was on the farm. Salaries for teaching were typically two to three times higher in cities, and because of the long term, it was normally the teacher's only occupation. Although there was some individual bargaining with school board members or the superintendent over wages, it became more and more common for cities to set uniform salary schedules for men and women at the different levels of the system (sometimes by grade of certificate and by years of experience).

Generally, city teachers were considerably older, better educated, and more experienced than teachers in the country, and a large proportion of them had attended a city normal school. Most important, for our purposes, was a strong emerging sexual pattern of employment in city schools whereby women outnumbered men by about ten to one and taught in the lower grades, while men worked in the higher grades and as managers (Coffman, 1911; Blodgett, 1900, pp. 134–140; NEA, 1905, pp. 10–45). The segregation of women into the lower rungs of urban school bureaucracies was not simply and only an unplanned result of inevitable economic and cultural forces, although those larger forces obviously played an important part. Such segregation was also the result of a deliberate policy adopted at the birth of the very important organizational invention, the graded school.

From the beginnings of the graded school, which many trace to the Quincy School in Boston in 1847, its promoters argued that women should be teachers while men should be retained as principals and superintendents. They used the familiar arguments about women's superior understanding of small children and their cheaper wages but added to these the claim that women would also be more willing to follow the direction of their superiors. It was no easy matter to bureaucratize older urban schools, which had typically been a somewhat miscellaneous collection of classrooms presided over by fairly autonomous masters and mistresses. Male teachers, especially, resisted being told what to do, as Horace Mann found when he criticized the Boston schoolmasters. This can be contrasted with the situation in the patriarchal society of mid-nineteenth century America, when it was expected that women teachers would follow the lead of male supervisors (Tyack, 1974, pp. 59–65).

In its early forms, the graded school was predicated on a specified curriculum broken down by age levels and taught by teachers who were carefully supervised. Children were taught step by step and advanced when they passed the examination for their grade level. Many of the architects of the new order in urban schools pointed to the new factories as a partial model for this new-style school. The superintendent was male and the principal was usually male in small systems, though often female in larger ones headed by a male superintendent. The head administrator was to ensure discipline in the system, thereby alleviating concern about whether women could control the older boys. Where women were hired as principals in urban systems, they typically worked in primary schools, where they supervised only women. The parts of the system were to be fitted together with machinelike precision. As normal classes in the city high schools proliferated, they trained young women in precisely the techniques and knowledge they needed as teachers (Philbrick, 1885).

The segregation of women in the lower grades of city schools that were supervised by male managers foreshadowed similar developments toward the end of the nineteenth century in other complex public and private institutions involving nurses in hospitals, workers in libraries, clerical staffs in big businesses, and saleswomen in large stores. These jobs were higher in status than proletarian factory work; They required that workers have respectable demeanor and (with the possible exception of saleswomen) sturdy cognitive skills; They demanded little prejob training; they linked well with what were thought to be distinctively female interests and abilities; and they could be adapted to the relatively high turnover that results from women marrying because a stable cadre of male career administrators and professionals could remain securely in command (Rothman, 1979).

Advancement and Positions of Power

It was partly to solve the problems of continuity of control in an occupation chiefly populated by young and transient women that educators insisted that male teachers and administrators be retained in the city systems. In fact, however, male as well as female teachers showed high turnover rates, and some women made urban teaching a lifelong career. But the stereotype that men were permanent members of the work force and women only temporary led school boards to an assumption about managerial training costs. They assumed that they could decrease their overall management training costs (mainly the costs of having inexperienced managers) by hiring only men for the top jobs. In most urban systems it was expected or required that women employees resign when they married. (Even after 1940, when married women were hired to help alleviate the teacher shortage, they customarily left the occupation when raising children. See Peters, 1934; Folger & Nam, 1967.)

Men in urban systems, on the other hand, had clear-cut career ladders that led into administration. They were expected to work full-time throughout their careers and to be ambitious for advancement, and thus they could demonstrate their loyalty and visibility. Marriage for men was not a source of difficult role conflicts between home demands and work; in fact it was practically a contingency for advancement. This is evidenced by the fact that male superintendents of schools have almost all been married, whereas the small contingent of prominent woman administrators have typically been single, widowed, or divorced (Tyack, 1976). Males with careers in education also had important advantages in linking the schools to the community. Because of men's higher status in the culture and their access to all-male community organizations, they could interact more easily than women with male power-wielders, socially and politically. Thus, in educational enterprises, where goals and measures of achievement are often diffuse and hard to assess, the society was reassured by having leaders whose social characteristics were of high repute.

It is not surprising, therefore, that superintendents were almost all male, middle-aged, white, Protestant, and experienced in education. This gave public schools a higher social credit rating. Within the system, the same status characteristics also gave them an advantage in controlling their young female subordinates, the teachers. Very few male teachers remained long in education; but for those who did, career ladders opened up in the urban schools (Lortie, 1975; Tyack, 1976).

Educational associations also provided an important forum for male leaders, a place in which they could establish regional and even national reputations. A number of the educational associations founded in the middle of the nineteenth century, such as the National Education Association (NEA), barred women at first. Some, such as Phi Delta Kappa, remained all-male until very recent years. Founded in 1857, the NEA did not have a woman president until 1910, and it did not elect a woman classroom teacher as president until 1928. State education associations had much the same record of male dominance, even though women far outnumbered the men. A large proportion of the men who led both the state and national associations were school administrators. (For an exploration of the role of such inner networks in associations of educators and other professionals, see Gilb, 1966.)

One way in which these male bosses blurred the real lines of power, both in the educational associations and in the school systems they administered, was by appealing to an ideology that supposedly linked leaders and led. In the mid-nineteenth century the dominant ideology envisioned an evangelical Protestant mission to educate the youth of the republic. We join forces, men and women, leaders and led, in a common cause, the leaders of education associations argued, and women imbued with this evangelical conception of their task would join an educational movement led by men in much the same spirit in which they would join a Methodist church run by a male minister. Later, such ideology slowly shifted to a diffuse philosophy about "professionalism," which decreed: We are all professionals together, from superintendent to first-grade teacher. Whether religious or professional, such ideologies masked the actual relationships between those with power and those without it (Tyack & Hansot, forthcoming).

Sometimes, however, important splits developed in the ranks of teachers' organizations along the potential divide of gender. From their earliest days, educational organizations debated whether men and women teachers should receive equal pay for equal work. Typically, they decided piously that they should, but then ignored the actual disparities (Ellsbree, 1939, pp. 159, 167). It was only when city women in the early twentieth century formed their own sexually segregated organizations to push for equal pay that men retaliated with ungallant zeal. Reversing the valence of the earlier stereotype of a woman as nurturant and mother-teacher, men complained that women teachers "feminized" the boys. Indeed, perhaps feeling vulnerable as scattered males in a crowd of women, male leaders often stressed their "masculine" qualities, especially their ability to conquer bullying boys in rural schools—a common theme in the autobiographies of male educators. As managers in education, men at the turn of the twentieth century often turned to business or the military for models for their work, just as their early predecessors had turned to the ministry for inspiration (Strachan, 1910).

Some women in urban schools formed militant all-female associations to push for equal pay, higher salaries, pensions, and other material benefits. Urban school teaching was one of the best jobs open to women. It provided higher than average pay among jobs in the "professional" category of women's work, as well as steady employment and a respectable calling. But the pay and benefits were still scaled to the needs of young single women, not to those of persons who wanted to make teaching a lifelong and self-supporting career. In addition, militant teachers in places like Chicago fought for their autonomy in the classroom, and they fought against centralization of decision making in male managers. In the journals and records of these leaders can be found an eloquent sense of the common cause of women career teachers, a stifling sense of powerlessness they often experienced as schools became increasingly bureaucratized (Haley, 1904, pp. 145–152).

Restrictive Supervision

The effects of the feminization of teaching can be traced not only in the bureaucratization of urban schools and the politics of professional associations; they are also obvious in the subordination of teachers to narrow standards of propriety imposed by local communities, especially in small-town America. Had mature men constituted a majority of the teaching profession, it is hard to imagine that school patrons would have insisted on such tight supervision of the morals and mores of teachers as they did in the case of young women. Old-time rules governing the behavior of teachers now sound like humor from *Mad Magazine*. As Waller has shown, such constraints were part and parcel of the notion that schools should be "museums of virtue" and that their keepers should be paragons who exemplified "those moral principles which the majority more or less frankly disavow for themselves but want others to practice; they are ideals for the helpless, ideals for children and for teachers" (Waller, 1965, p. 34).

It was the unmarried woman teacher, caught in a web of restrictive cultural expectations, who was most helpless to resist. Within the cellular classroom and their restricted social space outside, shielded by a patriarchal superintendent, women teachers were expected to exemplify and preach abstinence, while community males smoked and drank, expected to create the impression that teachers reproduced by "budding," while seeing their sisters and brothers produce families by other means. Although less strictly held to moral account than women, men teachers were also restricted—by the female Victorian stereotypes at their job. Behaving much as ministers might, men teachers sometimes sought "to escape the stereotype [by becoming] breezy, virile 'he-men'" (Waller,

1965, p. 421). Community supervision of the behavior of teachers, both in and out of the classroom, was more stringent in smaller communites than in pluralistic big cities, of course; and in both types of settings, teachers have gained considerably more autonomy than they had half a century ago.

POST-WORLD WAR II CHANGES

There have been important gender-related changes in educational employment since 1940, even though elementary school teaching has remained largely a woman's job. These new developments, as with earlier changes, have been responses to supply and demand forces, shifting cultural values, organizational changes, and changes in the family. Of particular importance have been the new acceptability of employment for married women, changing configurations in educational institutions, and the increasing militance and power of educators themselves, including new roles for teacher associations. Most of the years since 1940 witnessed an intense demand for teachers, at first because of the war and then because of increased enrollments caused by the great bulge of pupils following the "baby boom" and the greatly increased retention of students in the high schools. The decline in births during the Depression of the 1930s, coupled with a high demand for both male and female workers in the largely prosperous generation following World War II, produced a labor shortage in the group that had been the most common source of teachers in the past—single young women.

The vast expansion of enrollments in higher education, fueled by the G.I. Bill, produced a much larger proportion of college graduates than in any earlier generation of youth (Ferriss, 1969). At the same time, institutional changes in public education created different patterns of employment, which attracted more men into teaching. The number of one-room schools plummeted from over 130,000 in 1940 to fewer than 1,000 in 1980; and the number of high school teachers more than tripled to over a million. The urban and suburban sector of education expanded rapidly, and the complexity of its functions and hierarchy increased, thereby creating multiple career ladders. Despite the shortage of teachers, educational associations lobbied for higher educational qualifications and helped to win greater pay for teachers. In the 1960s and 1970s teachers' unions and associations became more militant, winning important power in collective bargaining in most states (Cole, 1969; Rosenthal, 1969).

These intersecting changes helped alter the characteristics of female teachers. By 1960 women teachers were no longer young, unmarried, and minimally educated, as they had traditionally been. The median age had become 44; the average term of service, 14.2 years. About 70% had had four years of college, and only 29% were single. Their income of over $4000 was well above the median for women professionals, and it had increased in real dollars by over one-third during the 1950s. What happened in a number of other sex-labeled fields during these years, for example in secretarial work, happened also in education. Public school employers retained married women as teachers and also dipped into the very large reserve labor pool of married women who had formerly taught. A large percentage of women teachers had dropped out temporarily when their children were young, but they reentered the occupation at this time, creating a bi-modal age distribution among female teachers (Folger & Nam, 1967).

The number of male teachers increased markedly in both elementary and secondary schools during the postwar years. The largest absolute gain was in the high schools, where the number grew from 103,293 in 1945–1946 to 542,000 in 1978, a percentage growth of the total number of from 35.7% to 54%. Men also entered the elementary schools and their numbers reached 203,000, a percentage increase of from 6.4% to 17%. By 1978, almost 34% of all teachers, elementary and secondary combined, were men. This striking increase in male teachers resulted from several forces. In the 1950s, there had been a concerted drive to attract more men into the secondary schools, the sector which was growing the fastest. The G.I. Bill had provided opportunities for a college education for lower-middle-class men, the traditional pool from which male teachers were recruited; and the rapid increase in the number of new administrative positions provided a carrot to aspiring young men (Ziegler, 1967).

Men practically monopolized the most prestigious positions, those of high school principal and superintendent, as they typically did in the past; and in most other positions, including elementary principalships, they registered steady gains as well. Male administrators had slightly higher levels of education than women, but they were younger and had less experience. Most men did not enter public school classrooms planning to remain there throughout their careers. They sought either to move into administration or to seek other work outside. As long as school systems continued their volcanic growth in the 1950s and 1960s, career ladders were abundant for the minority of ambitious men who stayed continuously in the profession. For women, however, the competing demands of family, especially the need to tend young children, interrupted their careers, and few planned to compete for administrative positions. The earlier cultural belief that woman's place was in the home was modified to allow married women to teach; but powerful stereotypes and institutional sexism still persisted (Clement, 1975).

Not all men, and much less all women, saw their advancement in the profession as requiring stepping into administration. During the 1960s and 1970s teacher militants changed the character of educational associations, splitting teachers away from the administrators who had long held the upper hand, demanding higher pay, more control over working conditions, and other forms of power for teachers. Studies by the American Federation of Teachers and the NEA indicate that there was an important dimension of gender in this militance. In both studies men took the lead in mobilizing teachers, especially in urban junior high schools. Alienated by demeaning regulations, convinced that their pay and status were incommensurate with the opportunities available elsewhere to men of comparable education and experience, these leaders articulated grievances, attracted other dissidents, and used techniques of organization borrowed from other unions and from the civil rights movement in order to press their case on administrators and school boards. The continuing teacher shortage, together with strong tenure provisions, gave teachers greater protection in their new-found posture of resistance. Teacher organizations also became strong in local, state, and national politics (Cole, 1969; Rosenthal, 1969).

CONCLUSIONS

Conditions continue to change. Excessive enrollments in teacher education programs and declining numbers of students in public schools have produced teacher surpluses and layoffs in many parts of the country. Many teacher leaders who were once aggressive are now on the defensive as jobs are eliminated and as citizens cut taxes. Ironically, now that the women's movement has begun to make educators more aware of the nature of institutional sexism, for example, in the grossly unequal distribution of managerial jobs, the enterprise of public education is not expanding but declining (Lyman & Speizer, 1980).

This chapter examined how gender has affected teaching and administration as occupations. We explored this historically, partly in the hope that we might illuminate the structuring of opportunity by sex and hence help set policies that will produce greater equity, however clouded the overall outlines of the future in education. We close this brief exposition of our argument with a comment on our point of view toward studying the experience of women. In women's history in recent years there have been several approaches. One has lamented the exclusion of women from the writing of mainstream history and has attempted to remedy that oversight by talking about heroines who were there along with the heroes. This "contributory" approach, popular now in high school textbooks, is better than nothing, but it is generally not very analytic. More interesting, but partly flawed, is another approach that portrays women as victims, usually of the actions and beliefs of men. This takes a step toward understanding the structure of sexism, but it tends to downplay the attitudes and agency of the women themselves and may present a rather wooden interpretation of patriarchy and inequality.

Ralph Waldo Emerson's much-admired aunt, Mary Moody Emerson, who managed to educate herself and those around her magnificently amid the press of household toil, once wrote in her diary: "There is a secret pleasure in bending to circumstances while superior to them" (Woody, 1974, p. 135). Many women who were apparent "victims of circumstance" constructed lives of great dignity. A number of recent scholars whose work we admire have reached beyond heroines and victims to a woman-centered history that seeks to explore the relationships that have existed between women—how they supported one another, how they gave meaning to their lives, how they attempted to change their lives. This seems to us a fruitful approach, provided one keeps in mind the particular institutions and the broader social structure within which these relationships take shape. (For a review of historical studies of the American woman, see Sicherman, 1975).

We accept all three approaches as partially useful. Women teachers *did* contribute enormously to public education, and some were genuine culture heroes. Women teachers *were* victims—having been paid tiny wages, channeled by prim cultural values, and denied access to advancement in the system. Women teachers, especially in the seminaries and in city teachers' associations, *did* create bonds of sisterhood and *did* act collectively in some of the most impressive forms of militance that women achieved. But what we wish to stress in this study is the *structuring of society*, by sex, and particularly in the public school system, within which both women and men teachers systematically plied their craft and lived their lives. We hope that a clearer understanding of the roots and dynamics of gender inequality in educational employment will hasten its demise.

ACKNOWLEDGMENTS

We wish to thank our research assistants, Suzanne Greenberg, Audri Gordon Lanford, Theodore Mitchell, and Katherine Poss, for their collaboration on this project. We are also grateful to Grant Vance for providing figures from a forthcoming study by the National Center for Educational Statistics.

REFERENCES

Allmendinger, D. (1979). "Mt. Holyoke Students Encounter the Need for Life-Planning, 1837–1850." *History of Education Quarterly*, 18 (Spring):27–31.
Beecher, C. (1846). *The Evils Suffered by American Women and American Children: The Causes and the Remedy*. Harper & Row, New York.
Bernard, R., and Vinovskis, M. (1977). "The Female School Teacher in Ante-Bellum Massachusetts." *Journal of Social History*, 10 (Spring):332–345.
Blaxall, M., and Reagan, B., eds. (1976). *Women and the Workplace: The Implications of Occupational Segregation*. University of Chicago Press (especially Blau, F. D., and Jusenius, C. L. "Economists' Approaches to Sex Segmentation in the Labor Market: An Appraisal," pp. 181–200, and Strober, M. H. "Toward Dimorphics: A Summary Statement to the Conference on Occupational Segregation," pp. 293–302).
Blodgett, J. (1900). *Report on Education in the United States at the Eleventh Census: 1890*.
Clement, J. (1975). *Sex Bias in School Administration*. Integrated Education, Evanston, Ill.
Coffman, L. (1911). *The Social Composition of the Teaching Population*. Teachers College, Columbia University, New York.
Cole, S. (1969). *The Unionization of Teachers: A Case Study of the UFT*. Praeger, New York.
Cott, N. F. (1977). *The Bonds of Womanhood: 'Women's Sphere' in New England, 1780–1835*. Yale University Press, New Haven.
Dublin, T. (1979). *Women at Work: The Transformation of Work and Community in Lowell, Massachusetts, 1826–1860*. Columbia University Press, New York.
Eggleston, E. (1871). *The Hoosier Schoolmaster*. Hill & Wang, New York, 1965.
Ellsbree, W. (1939). *The American Teacher: Evolution of a Profession in a Democracy*. American Book Company, New York, chaps. 16, 21.
Ferriss, A. (1969). *Indicators of Trends in American Education*. Russell Sage Foundation, New York, chap. 2.
Folger, J. K., and Nam, C. B. (1967). *Education of the American Population*, 1960 Census Monograph. Government Printing Office, Washington, D.C., chap. 3.
Gilb, C. (1966). *Hidden Hierarchies: The Professions and Government*. Harper & Row, New York.
Goffman, E. (1979). *Gender Advertisements*. Harper & Row, New York.
Haley, M. (1904). "Why Teachers Should Organize." *NEA Addresses and Proceedings*. 43rd Annual Meeting of the National Association of Education. Winona, Minn.
Harris, B. J. (1978). *Beyond Her Sphere: Women and the Professions in American History*. Greenwood Press, Westport, Conn.
Johnson, C. (1904). *Old Time Schools and School Books*. Dover, New York, 1963.
Kanter, R. M. (1977). *Work and Family in the United States: A Critical Review and Agenda for Research and Policy*. Russell Sage Foundation, New York.

Katz, M. (1968). *The Irony of Early School Reform: Educational Innovation in Mid-Nineteenth Century Massachusetts.* Harvard University Press, Cambridge, pp. 56–58.

Kelly-Gadol, J. (1976). "The Social Relation of the Sexes: Methodological Implications of Women's History." *Signs,* 1 (Summer):809–823.

Kirkpatrick, M. (1917). *The Rural School from Within.* Lippincott, Philadelphia.

Lande, D. (1977). *Angels and Amazons: Women Teaching in Nineteenth Century Massachusetts.* Senior honors thesis in Sociology, Harvard University.

Lortie, D. (1975). *Schoolteacher: A Sociological Study.* University of Chicago Press.

Lyman, K. D., and Speizer, J. J. (1980). "Advancing in School Administration: A Pilot Project for Women." *Harvard Educational Review,* 50 (February):25–35.

Melder, K. (1979). *Training Women Teachers: Private Experiments.* American Educational Research Association paper.

Morain, T. (1977). *The Entry of Women into the School Teacher Profession in Nineteenth Century Iowa.* Unpublished paper, Iowa State University.

NEA (1905). *Report on the Committee on Salaries, Tenure, and Pensions of Public School Teachers of the United States.* National Education Association, Winona, Minn.

Oppenheimer, V. K. (1968). "The Sex-Labeling of Jobs." *Industrial Relations,* 3 (May):224–228.

Oppenheimer, V. K. (1970). *The Female Labor Force in the United States: Demographic Factors Governing Growth and Changing Composition.* Institute of International Studies, University of California, Berkeley.

Peters, D. W. (1934). *The Status of the Married Woman Teacher.* Bureau of Publications, Teachers College, Columbia University, New York.

Prentice, A. (1975). "The Feminization of Teaching in British North America, 1845–1875." *Histoire Sociale/Social History,* (May):50–75.

Philbrick, J. (1885). *City School Systems in the United States.* U.S. Bureau of Education, Circular of Information 1. Government Printing Office, Washington, D.C.

Rosenthal, A. (1969). *Pedagogues and Power,* Syracuse University Press.

Rothman, S. (1979). *Woman's Proper Place: A History of Changing Ideals and Practices, 1870 to the Present.* Basic Books, New York, chap. 1.

Scott, A. F. (1979). "The Ever Widening Circle: The Diffusion of Feminist Values from the Troy Female Seminary, 1822–1872." *History of Education Quarterly,* 18 (Spring):3–25.

Sicherman, B. (1975). "American History." *Signs* 1 (Winter):461–485.

Sklar, K. K. (1973). *Catharine Beecher: A Study in American Domesticity.* Yale University Press, New Haven.

Solmon, L. (1970). "Estimates of the Costs of Schooling in 1880 and 1890." *Explorations in Economic History,* Supp. 7 (4):575.

Stinchcombe, A. (1965). "Social Structure and Organizations. In *Handbook of Organizations* (J. March, ed.) Rand McNally, Skokie, Ill. pp. 142–91.

Strachan, G. (1910). *Equal Pay for Equal Work: The Story of the Struggle for Justice Being Made by the Women Teachers of the City of New York.* B. F. Buck, New York.

Strober, M., and Best, L. (1979). "The Female/Male Salary Differential in Public Schools: Some Lessons from San Francisco, 1879." *Economic Inquiry,* 17 (April):218–236.

Tilly, L. A., and Scott, J. W. (1978). *Women, Work and Family.* Holt, Rinehart and Winston, New York.

Tyack, D. (1974). *The One Best System: A History of American Urban Education,* Harvard University Press, Cambridge.

Tyack, D. (1976). "Pilgrim's Progress: Toward a Social History of the Superintendency." *History of Education Quarterly* 32 (Fall):263–267.

Tyack, D., and Hansot, E. (forthcoming). "From Social Movement to Professional Management." *American Journal of Education.*

University of Nebraska (1919). Committee of Graduate School of Education. *Rural Teachers.* U.S. Bureau of Education, Bulletin 20. Government Printing Office, Washington, D.C., p. 16.

University of Nebraska (1919). Committee of Graduate School of Education. *Rural Teachers.* Government Printing Office, Washington, D. C., p. 23.

U.S. Bureau of the Census (1900). *Census Statistics on Teachers.* Bulletin 23, 12th Census. Government Printing Office, Washington, D.C., pp. 9, 17.

Vinovskis, M., and Bernard, R. (1978). "Beyond Catharine Beecher: Female Education in the Antebellum Period." *Signs* 3 (Summer):856–869.

Waller, W. (1965). *The Sociology of Teaching.* Wiley, New York.

Woody, T. (1929). *A History of Women's Education in the United States,* vol. I. Octagon Books, New York, 1974.

Ziegler, H. (1967). *The Political Life of the American Teacher.* Prentice-Hall, Englewood Cliffs, N.J.

Chapter 8
AMBITIONS AND THE OPPORTUNITY FOR PROFESSIONALS IN THE ELEMENTARY SCHOOL

Thomas D. Jovick

Although the role of elementary school teachers is the same, whether one is a man or a woman, there are some obvious differences between men teachers and women teachers with regard to career advancement. For men teachers, careers tend to advance in the hierarchial structure of education, whereas for women, teaching tends to be the terminal point in their careers. This is true despite the fact that the majority of teachers in elementary schools are women (Stockard, 1980). One common explanation given by researchers and theorists is that there are sex-related differences in the contingencies of life; differences in expectations about personal lives, the career of teaching and career aspirations, and differences in motivations and experiences. Other researchers and theorists point to the discriminary patterns in preparatory, recruiting, and selection processes that have prevented women from acquiring positions in the upper levels of educational organizations (Stockard, 1980; Schmuck, 1980). This chapter examines the influence of certain organizational variables. Indications are that both the governance and the work structures in schools play important roles in teachers' motivation because these structures enhance or restrict a person's opportunities to acquire the rewards that cause people to aspire to high levels of engagement and morale in teaching. The theories of Kanter (1977), Cohen (1973), and Lortie (1964) allege that schools can provide such opportunities by making certain building-wide changes in the systems of authority and work that affect teachers. While these

153

theories pertained to opportunities for both sexes, this chapter examines whether certain changes in a school's work and governance systems affect women teachers in the ways Cohen and Kanter claim. The content of this chapter is twofold: it is a replication of a theory about elementary school teachers that was proposed and empirically tested by Cohen, and it is a test of a portion of a competing theory from Kanter's work with corporations. Cohen and Kanter attempted to characterize the relationship between changes in a school's structure and the level of women teachers' ambition to work and career satisfactions. After summarizing the work of Lortie and Kanter and reexamining some of Cohen's data on open-space and self-contained schools, this chapter then analyzes more recently collected data from a longitudinal research study of multiple-unit and conventional elementary schools.

SUMMARY OF RESEARCH BY LORTIE, KANTER, HERZBERG, AND COHEN

Lortie (1975) emphasized that finding opportunities for professional growth is a major problem for the long-term teacher because the teaching occupation is "career-less." In the areas of formal authority, prestige, and work, no successive status positions exist within a school by which teachers can gauge their progress and professional growth. In corporations, on the other hand, such positions do exist; they represent stages of professional advancement, and normally, a variety of rewards and privileges come with each stage. These stages in a person's career are important for an organization because they foster the occurrence of cycles of effort, achievement, and renewed ambition; the cycles, in turn, generate within a person an identification with, and a future stake in, the particular occupation and a satisfaction with it as a career. The absence of such stages within the teaching profession results in a lack of correlation between the efforts of teachers and the rewards they can expect. The school organization only marginally and haphazardly fosters one's exceptional efforts, one's renewed ambition in teaching activities, or one's satisfaction with teaching as a career.

Empirical and theoretical research into people's attitudes about their jobs has pointed to the importance of certain rewards in enhancing morale and performance in an organization (Locke, 1976). The more important of these rewards—what Lortie calls psychic rewards, what Herzberg *et al.* (1959) call motivators, and what other researchers call intrinsic rewards—are professional growth and development, responsibility, challenge, recognition, and achievement. This same body of research identified another set of other rewards which, although important, hold far less encompassing implications for the individual and the organization. These are what Lortie calls extrinsic and ancillary rewards and Herzberg calls hygienic work factors, and they involve the extent to which circumstances such as the working conditions, the pay, the fairness and number of rules and regulations, the availability of resources, and one's relationships with superiors and peers hinder or facilitate the accomplishment of one's work tasks. Throughout the rest of this chapter they will be called extrinsic rewards.

If Kanter is correct in *Men and Women of the Corporation* (1977), when school administrators wish to build staff morale and foster ambitious involvement with work, they must provide opportunities for teachers to obtain intrinsic rewards. To rephrase Herzberg's original contention, extrinsic rewards are not nearly as important because, when they are unsatisfactory or deficient, intrinsic rewards can minimize their deleterious effects on morale. Based on Kanter's reasoning about workers' behavior in organizations, teachers would be reluctant to engage in any instructional activities, beyond the expected minimum standard of participation, in schools that offer few opportunities for acquiring intrinsic rewards. Such a discrepancy between the required effort and the ensuing reward is simply too great, and the rewards do not warrant long-term ambitious efforts. When opportunities for intrinsic rewards are few, depressed levels of satisfaction with teaching as a career result because the work does not adequately provide for the realization of meaningful values over a long enough period of time.

Kanter alleges that the most pervasive and influential force in obtaining intrinsic rewards is the "opportunity structure," or the way an organization fashions a number of components of the workers' situation so as to affect his or her chances of acquiring such rewards on the job. In the schools, the opportunity structure involves the extent to which the network of governance, instructional tasks, and communication allow for professional growth and development, increased responsibility and influence, recognition, and achievement, and the extraordinary use of teaching skills and knowledge. Kanter concludes that in order to eliminate the barriers that prevent a person from receiving intrinsic rewards and to remedy the debilitating attitudes and behaviors that result when barriers exist, the organization must institute a change in its internal structure.

Cohen's study, *Open Space Schools: The Opportunity to Become Ambitious* (1973), is particularly relevant here because some of her ideas about women teachers in elementary schools tie in with Kanter's analysis of behavior in organizations. Cohen's research stresses the important relation between the opportunity structure of the school and the work-related ambitions and career satisfactions of women elementary school teachers. Cohen characterized the conventionally organized elementary school as deficient in opportunities whereby women teachers can acquire intrinsic and extrinsic rewards. She focused her investigation on intrinsic rewards because of their implication for the teachers' career satisfaction and work ambition, or what she called professional ambition. She attributed the unfavorable circumstances to two structural characteristics. One is the architectural structure of most conventional schools, typically an egg-crate organization of classroom cells. This structure results in the isolation of teachers; it prevents any observation of other teachers' techniques (good and bad), and it prevents collaborative planning and involvement in school-wide and classroom instructional activities. The other structural characteristic Cohen identified is the authority structure, which usually places decisions about such matters as scheduling and the assignment of children into the hands of the principal, while it places decisions about instructional activities for a group of children into the hands of a single teacher. Teachers do not typically participate in school-wide decisions, nor do they tend to collaborate much about their own classroom activities.

Together, the architectural and authority structures in the conventional elementary school constitute an overall arrangement that restricts opportunity. It limits teachers' opportunities to acquire psychic rewards and to demonstrate skills and achievements. Cohen reasoned that by making certain internal alterations in structure throughout an organization to allow for greater collaboration and interaction among teachers and to afford them greater influence, schools could make psychic rewards more accessible. She studied open-space schools because their structure represented such a significant departure from the work and authority structures found in conventionally organized schools. Architecturally, the design of the open-space schools eliminates the traditional interior walls that keep the sounds and activities of one teaching area separated from those of another. Most open-space schools contain large rooms to accommodate anywhere from two to nine teachers and their classes. These teams of teachers acquire the power to decide collectively upon the course of instruction for the children assigned to them as a group. The schools provide regular meeting times so that each team can collaborate and plan programs and curriculum.

These structural differences result in changes in the nature and frequency of communication about classroom and school-wide matters among teachers, more so within teams than between teams. Because of the interaction networks of teachers, there are more opportunities to demonstrate expertise, receive praise and recognition, exert influence, and exchange ideas and techniques. The open-spaced architecture itself necessarily increases the visibility of each teacher's instructional activities. This provides a basis for teachers' discussions and evaluations of one another's teaching techniques. To Cohen, a major difference in the open-spaced school was the increase in opportunities for teachers to acquire greater intrinsic rewards. There was also an increase in opportunities to obtain some ancillary and extrinsic rewards, with the exception of pay increases and promotions. Cohen's original hypothesis about the relationships among opportunity structure, ambition in teaching, and career satisfaction differed in an important way from Kanter's theory because their concepts of the nature of ambition were different. They did agree on the basic ingredients of the ambition construct, however.

Cohen carefully distinguished between "vertical" and professional ambitions. Teachers with high vertical ambition wished to move out of teaching as a career and into the hierarchy of management. Those with high professional ambition wished to become more involved in teaching and instructional activities in the school. Professional ambition was a key concept for Cohen, reflecting a willingness to go beyond the ordinary demands of teaching while remaining in the occupation. Professional ambition includes Kanter's crucial concept of commitment, whereby an individual remains in an organization and works with a high level of involvement, concern, and attachment to the job. Kanter saw commitment as a necessary ingredient in high-quality performance and high morale. She treated ambition and commitment as the psychological disposition of a person, which were readily amenable to change. The best way for an organization to build and maintain high ambition and commitment would be for it to increase the opportunities for individuals to acquire psychic rewards at work. Her work suggests that teachers would respond to a restricted opportunity structure by lowering their expectations for psychic rewards to fit in the availability of such rewards. This would lead to a reduced commitment to teaching. However, because teachers find their lowered expectations for rewards fulfilled in such situations, the level of career satisfaction would not necessarily be lower.

In contrast to Kanter, Cohen has conceptualized ambition to be much like a relatively stable personality trait. Those who report high ambition seek out opportunities for professional growth and development at work. Those with low ambition do not. She contended that the opportunity structure must match the level of ambition of the individual, especially of the more ambitious individuals. According to Cohen, changing the opportunity structure would not alter a person's commitment or ambition; nor would it affect the career satisfaction of the less ambitious because the career already matches their professional ambitions. What would be affected, however, are the career satisfactions of the more ambitious and their psychic rewards. More ambitious teachers would experience a higher level of career satisfaction in schools that provide greater opportunities; for those who already seek psychic rewards such alterations in the structure of a school increase the chances to acquire such rewards, and if these people take advantage of the opportunities, they will increase their career satisfaction.

Because of this fundamental difference in their conceptualizations of ambition, Kanter and Cohen hypothesized competing models to describe the relationships among opportunity structure, ambition, and career satisfaction. In the model Cohen proposes, the nature of the interaction between ambition and career satisfaction depends on whether a school's structure fosters few or many opportunities. Although she failed to detail the expected level of satisfaction for those low in ambition, she implies that it is at least average or above. Figure 8.1 depicts the expected realtionships. We can compare this with the predictions of Kanter's model, where an enriched opportunity structure would raise the level of career satisfaction for all teachers, not just the ambitious ones, and raise the level of ambition as well.

Reanalysis of the Cohen Data

To measure work ambition, Cohen questioned teachers on several points: their desire for more frequent opportunities to help young teachers develop classroom skills; whether they could see themselves leading workshops on teaching techniques; whether they wanted to demonstrate their personal teaching styles and techniques to other teachers; and whether they felt competent to make supervisory evalua-

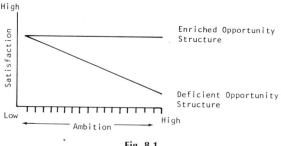

Fig. 8.1

tions of other teachers. The average score over all of the questions resulted in an ambition score that ranged from a low of "1" to a high of "6." The questionnaire for career satisfaction consisted of five items that as a group tapped feelings of general satisfaction with teaching as a career. The questions asked teachers the extent to which they were satisfied with their present job and with teaching as an occupation; whether they would take a job in a field other than education that provided an opportunity for close contact with adults and children; and whether they would choose teaching as a career if they could make a choice now. Possible scores ranged from a low of "5" to a high of "22." The original Cohen data consisted of a three-way contingency table with the ambition and career-satisfaction scales trichotomized into categories of high, medium, and low. Cohen's interpretation of the data relied on visual inspection of the percentage differences in the cells of the table.

In this reanalysis of Cohen's data a log-linear analysis of frequency data was used according to methods developed by Goodman (1970), Kullback (1974), and others for multidimensional contingency tables.

This procedure provided a statistical test of the data in Cohen's contingency table to determine whether her theory or Kanter's theory suitably described the relationships among opportunity structure, ambition, and satisfaction. A complex set of calculations produce a set of expected cell frequencies for each theory, which is then compared with the actual frequencies by means of a Chi-square test. The higher the probability level and the lower the value of the "information statistic, the better the fit."

The analysis indicated that Kanter's theory was more parsimonious and showed a better fit than Cohen's theory. Indeed, it was also the best-fitting model out of a number of other more parsimonious models. (The Chi-square probability level was .71 for an information statistic of 2.10 with 4 degrees of freedom). Cohen's interpretation of her own data was not substantiated by the formal statistical analysis.

THE MITT STUDY

Other data from a longitudinal research project called Management Implications of Team Teaching (MITT) offered the chance to test both Cohen's and Kanter's theories using more powerful statistical procedures. The MITT project was a 2½-year field study that compared the multiple-unit staff organizations in one group of elementary schools with the conventional staff organizations in a matched set of schools. The nature of the variables and the research design in this study provided data that were conceptually relevant to Cohen's formulations and that allowed a more extensive examination of the variety of relationships she postulated. After two years T5 their correlation was evidence that all three measures constituted a "package" of readily apparent effects.

For this reason T5 data was used as the focus of the following analyses. Data from T1, the first data-collection point in the spring of 1974, served to test for changes that occurred in both types of schools both before and after the schools organized multiunits.

Analyses of the MITT Data

If the interaction Cohen originally proposed really existed, the correlation between ambition and satisfaction would be positive in the multiunit schools and inverse in the conventional schools. Using a Fisher-Z transformation, the equality of these correlations was tested. Merely upon inspection one sees that the expected differences do not exist because both correlations are positive; the question left to be answered is whether they differ in magnitude. At T5, the correlations were .19 for multiunit schools ($N=185$) and .15 for conventional schools ($N=178$), both significantly greater than zero ($p=.05$). The Fisher-Z test yielded a nonsignificant T of .39. Thus the MITT data did not support Cohen's original hypothesis that the relationship between ambition and satisfaction would be different depending upon the opportunity structure. In testing Kanter's theory, which specifies that the difference between the organizations of the schools affects both ambition and satisfaction and completely accounts for the correlation between ambition and satisfaction, the first thing of interest is whether multiunit and conventional schools differed in their levels of ambition and career satisfaction at T5. The t tests in Table 8.1 show no evidence for such differences. The women teachers in both types of schools reported the same levels of

TABLE 8.1
Differences between Multiunit and Conventional Schools in Level of Ambition and Career Satisfaction at T5

	Level of ambition		Career satisfaction	
	Multiunit	*Conventional*	*Multiunit*	*Conventional*
Mean	3.12	3.01	18.03	18.46
SD	1.06	.82	3.43	3.09
N	191	181	188	181
t		1.05		−1.20

ambition and satisfaction. The researchers in the MITT study administered the same ambition and career-satisfaction questionnaires that Cohen had used in her study. Teachers in 27 schools received questionnaires and were interviewed every 6 months for 2½ years ending in the spring of 1976. The faculties of 14 innovative schools were organized into multiple units or teams in the fall of 1974, two years before the final data were collected. These 14 schools are called multiunit schools because their formal managerial structure followed the "multiunit" school model that had been developed by Klausmeir and others at the Wisconsin Research and Development Center for Cognitive Learning.

The matched controls—13 schools from the same districts in which the multiunit schools were located—had no multiunit features during the course of the MITT investigation. Their managerial structures reflected the lack of differentiation typical of the conventional elementary school; that is, the instructional staff was responsible for students in their own classrooms, and the principal was responsible for the supervision of teachers and for managerial decisions. In contrast to the Cohen schools, the two sets of schools in the MITT project were distinguished solely on the basis of their formal organizational structure, that is, by the presence or absence of formal teaching units. No school was of the open-space type. The stipulation of what constituted a team was more rigid than in the Cohen study, even to the point of eliminating schools from the study if they were partially organized or had started to organize according to the unit structure and then dropped it. (For the final report of the project, which presents the characteristics of the sample in greater detail, see Packard *et al.*, 1978.)

Alterations in the Opportunity Structure in Multiunit Schools

The formation of teaching units in the multiunit schools produce major changes in the work and governance systems and thereby eliminate at least two barriers to the teacher's opportunity to exert influence. Teachers who belong to teaching teams and share responsibility for the instruction of a group of students must communicate and collaborate about professional matters, and this provides opportunities to exert influence about classroom matters, at least among team members. Although teachers do not work in a single, large, open space, as in Cohen's open-space schools, the chances for communication and visibility abound. In addition, the teaching faculty in the school accepts the responsibility for collegial decision making on an expanded range of instruction-related issues, and this alteration of the authority structure also increases the opportunity for teachers to exert influence both on those within their team and also on other faculty members.

By the final data-collection point (Time 5, or T5) in the spring of 1976, the work and governance system in the MITT multiunit schools had changed to what Lortie called a horizontal-collegial form (Packard *et al.*, 1978). Collegial groups increased their exclusive decision-making powers in the school. The incidence of teachers' collaborative instruction of students within and across subject areas also increased, as did frequency of their communication about school-wide and classroom matters. Another change was that most communication was limited to that between members of the teams. The frequency of communication, the degree of collegial decision making, and the level of interdependence in instruction correlated quite substantially with each other, and the authors contend that theoretically, the structural change in schools that adopted multiunits affects all teachers in the school; but realistically, it may be the more seasoned teachers who take advantage of the opportunities it provides. Were this latter true, the teachers who remained in the multiunit schools should show greater ambition and satisfaction than those who remained in the conventional schools. An analysis of the mean differences in ambition and career satisfaction at T5 showed no such differences (Table 8.2), while the reanalysis of Cohen's frequency data supports Kanter's arguments that such structural alterations affect both ambition and career satisfaction. Analysis of the MITT data gives no support to the theories of either Cohen or Kanter, but the lack of support found in the MITT data suggests that the school-wide structural changes within the multiunit schools may have altered opportunities for some but not for others. Were this true, the analysis of mean scores for satisfaction and ambition would not have detected the differences within multiunit schools on individuals who held more advantageous access to opportunities than others.

TABLE 8.2
Differences between Multiunit and Conventional Schools in Level of Ambition and Career Satisfaction at T5 for the T1–T5 Cohort

	Level of ambition		Career satisfaction	
	Multiunit	*Conventional*	*Multiunit*	*Conventional*
Mean	3.11	3.04	17.75	18.55
SD	1.09	.86	3.69	3.07
N	104	112	102	112
t		−.50		1.73

As part of the structural innovation, faculties in the multiunit schools created a formal position of authority for regular classroom teachers within each teaching team. This was the role of team leader, and it conferred on its incumbents the advantage of increased opportunities. The role constituted a "middle-management" type of addition to the formal authority structure of the school, although the incumbent neither held the position permanently (typically, leaders were changed yearly) nor possessed a career-advancement link to another authority position within or outside the school. Each team leader acquired a legitimate power base in the school simply by assuming the role and officially served on school-wide instructional cabinets together with the principal and other team leaders. Each leader coordinated activities and handled affairs that the team as a group did not not manage.

Cohen and Kanter believe that those who hold such a formal position of authority in an organization also have greater opportunities to acquire power on an informal basis and greater opportunities to control their own access to both psychic and extrinsic rewards on the job. This is because the formal-authority role attaches a measure of status to the incumbent and opens channels to greater responsibility and privileged communication with superordinates. In comparison to individuals in lower-status positions in the same organization, those in positions of authority tend to report greater ambition and morale at work. According to the reasoning of Cohen and Kanter, women who become team leaders should be in a better position than other women teachers to acquire rewards and to develop a power base for informal influence. The team-leader position was a structural alteration that allegedly changed the chances for its occupants to obtain psychic and extrinsic rewards. The positioning of the team-leader's role in the formal work and authority structures increases the leader's opportunities for communication about school-wide and instructional issues—with other leaders and the principal at one level and with teachers in his or her own team at another level. Theoretically, team leaders' more extensive and frequent involvement with affairs important to the faculty will raise the faculty's estimate of leaders' influence, bring leaders greater rewards, boost their ambition, and elevate their satisfaction with teaching as a career.

Kanter's theory adds a qualifying note concerning ambition: when individuals lack the opportunities that those in better positions in the same organization have, they will tend to lower the level of their ambition and commitment and seek rewards outside of work. Her reasoning suggests that the ambition level of those who do not become team leaders will become lower as that of the leaders becomes higher. Because this chapter deals exclusively with women teachers, the data in Table 8.3 are

TABLE 8.3
Number of Teachers Who Became Team Leaders by T5

	Males	Females	
Leaders	7	38	$X^2 = 2.5$, $df = 1$
Nonleaders	16	185	

presented to demonstrate that males did not have an advantage over females in their access to the team-leader positions. The proportions of men and women who moved into the role were essentially the same and suggest that women certainly received the opportunities associated with being a team leader.

By T5, two schools had dropped their teams and some schools had consolidated a number of their teams. This resulted in a drop in the total number of teams from 64 at T2 to 45 at T5. The X^2 analyses of the same relationships at T2, T3, and T4 show the same statistically nonsignificant results (Chi-square values were less than 2.5).

The comparison between team leaders and nonleaders uses only the T1–T5 cohort of women teachers because they are the ones who had been exposed to the innovation for the same length of time. Table 8.4 presents the comparison for ambition and career satisfaction at T5. The results indicate that women who became team leaders by T5 reported greater ambition for teaching and greater career satisfaction than did nonleaders. The formal distinction between team leaders and nonleaders explained 3% of the variance in career satisfaction and 11% in ambition. Similar *t*-tests for the same cohort on the T1 data also show significant differences favoring those who became team leaders by T5, and they indicate that some of the differences between those who became

TABLE 8.4
T Tests Comparing T1–T5 Cohort of Team Leaders and
Nonleaders at T5 on Ambition and Career Satisfaction

	Ambition		Career satisfaction	
	Leaders	Nonleaders	Leaders	Nonleaders
Mean	3.71	2.87	18.90	17.30
SD	1.16	.96	2.98	3.86
N	30	74	29	73
t	3.78[a]		2.00[a]	

[a] Statistically significant at @ = .05.

TABLE 8.5
T1 and T5 Means for the T1–T5 Cohort for Team Leaders and Nonleaders on Ambition and Career Satisfaction

	T1	T5
Ambition		
Leaders	3.64	3.71
Nonleaders	3.15	2.87
Career satisfaction		
Leaders	19.68	18.90
Nonleaders	17.74	17.30

team leaders by T5 and those who did not existed prior to acquisition of the team-leader position. To depict the change, Table 8.5 presents the T1 and T5 means for both these variables. The trend in the means for ambition supports Kanter's expectation that those in positions with allegedly greater opportunities for rewards will increase their ambition levels whereas those in less opportune positions will lower theirs.

However, a regression analysis indicated the increase for leaders and decrease for nonleaders occurred by chance (interaction not statistically significant with $F = 1.56$, $df = 1/99$, and therefore could be ignored as unimportant. The results in Table 8.6 indicate that women who became team leaders showed substantially greater ambition than those who did not become team leaders, and that this difference was not due

TABLE 8.6
Influence of Team-Leader Position on Ambition at T5 [a]

Independent variable	Increment in R^2	Beta	F_{Beta}
Ambition, T1	.44	.61	69.9[d]
Leader position[b]	.05[c]	.23	10.2[d]

[a] The regression analysis without the interaction is the same as the analysis of covariance. Kenny (1975) recommends analysis of covariance to compare differences between groups that were formed on the basis of characteristics of individuals. In the multiunit schools, principals and sometimes team members selected team leaders on the basis of unspecified individual characteristics; teachers did not select themselves to be leaders. For the analysis, ambition was assumed to be an individual difference correlated with the selection criteria.

[b] Coded: 1 = team leader, 0 = nonleader.

[c] Statistically significant increment at alpha = .05, df, = 1/98.

[d] Statistically significant at alpha = .05, df = 1/98.

to the fact that the women who became team leaders had higher ambition from the start. The analysis suggests that by altering the authority structure among regular classroom teachers, educational planners can boost the ambition of those who acquire authority. Those left out of such a role will not necessarily reduce their ambition for teaching. The regression analysis for career satisfaction indicated that the drop in satisfaction between T1 and T5 was greater for team leaders than for nonleaders (interaction statistically significant with $F = 4.17$, $df = 1/94$ and explains a 2% increment in the variance). The decreases for both the team leaders and the nonleaders are unexplainable.

DISCUSSION

Analyses of the MITT data offered no evidence to support either Kanter's or Cohen's predictions that major alterations in the governance and work structures would affect the ambition and career satisfaction of women elementary teachers. Furthermore, MITT evidence contradicted the re-analysis of Cohen's data, which showed that women in open-space schools reported greater ambition and career satisfaction than women in self-contained schools. However, a number of related analyses of the MITT data suggest that the changes in the multiunit schools may not have fulfilled Kanter's expectations for what constitutes a meaningful alteration in the opportunity structure of the schools. The final report of the study (Packard *et al.*, 1978) indicated that several changes in the governance and work structures were scattered or minor. Additional analyses in Packard *et al.* indicate that the women teachers in the multiunit schools showed no greater involvement in their school's system of acquiring influence and no greater acquisition of intrinsic and extrinsic rewards than did those in the conventional schools.

In addition, some of the optional curricular and instructional innovations that accompanied the alteration in the multiunit schools tended to favor adherence to objectives and a standardization of work. Special evaluation tools, behavioral objectives, student regrouping, and specially developed curricular materials were used, and these would tend to limit choices in methods of instruction and foster routinization—phenomena characteristic of conventional schools.

Analyses that include both men and women in the multiunit schools (Packard *et al.*, 1978) showed that the increased scope of team leaders' responsibilities and involvement did not produce a dramatic change in the status of their influence or prestige. Although those who became team leaders tended to report a greater sense of influence over school-wide affairs, their acquisition of the position only marginally increased their informal political influence in the school. Interestingly, the increased participation of team leaders in "upper-echelon" communications with principals and other team leaders about classroom and school-wide issues did not materialize; team leaders did not monopolize the communication channels to principals or other team leaders. This is consistent with Lortie's (1964) prediction that team leaders and nonleaders would form equal and collaborative relationships in their work rather than develop differences based on rank. He claimed that the faculty would tend to preserve the norm, whereby teachers expect their colleagues to treat them as equals, and in a nonintervening yet friendly way. The role of team leader would emerge as one of "leader in teaching" and carry no implication of supervisory authority over other teachers in the team. He hesitated to predict what differences would emerge between team leaders' and nonleaders' ambition, morale, and access to rewards; but his analysis suggests either that there would not be any such difference or that they would be much less dramatic than those predicted by Cohen's and Kanter's theories.

REFERENCES

Campbell, D. T., and Stanley, J. C. (1966). *Experimental and Quasi-Experimental Designs for Research*. Rand McNally, Chicago.

Cohen, E. G. (1973). "Open-Space Schools: The Opportunity to Become Ambitious." *Sociology of Education*, 46:143–161.

Cronbach, L. J., and Furby, L. (1970). "How Should We Measure 'Change'—or Should We?" *Psychological Bulletin*, 74(1):68–80.

Goodman, L. A. (1970). "The Multivariate Analysis of Qualitative Data: Interactions Among Multiple Classifications." *Journal of the American Statistical Association*, 65:226–256.

Herzberg, F., Mausner, B., and Snyderman, B. (1959). *The Motivation to Work*. Wiley, New York.

Kanter, R. M. (1977). *Men and Women of the Corporation*, Basic Books, New York.

Kenny, D. A. (1975). "A Quasi-Experimental Approach to Assessing Treatment Effects in the Nonequivalent Control Group Design." *Psychological Bulletin*, 82(3):345–362.

Kullback, S. (1974). "The Information in Contingency Tables: Technical Report." *National Technical Information Service* (AD-785 599/2GA).

Locke, E. A. (1976). "The Nature and Causes of Job Satisfaction." In *Handbook of Industrial and Organizational Psychology* (M. D. Dunnette, ed.) Rand McNally, Chicago.

Lortie, D. (1964). "The Teacher and Team Teaching: Suggestions for Long-Range Research." In *Team Teaching* (J. Shaplin and H. F. Olds, Jr., eds.) Harper & Row, New York.

Lortie, D. (1975). *Schoolteacher*. University of Chicago Press.

McNamara, J. F. (1978). "Practical Significance and Statistical Models." *Educational Administration Quarterly*, 14(1):48–63.

McNemar, Q. (1962). *Psychological Statistics*, 3rd ed. Wiley, New York.

Packard, J. S., Charters, W. W., and Duckworth, K. E., with Jovick, T. D. (1978). *Management Implications of Team Teaching: Final Report*. Center for Educational Policy and Management, University of Oregon.

Schmuck, P. (1980). *Sex Equity in Educational Leadership: The Oregon Story*. Education Development Center, Newton, Mass.

Stockard, J., Schmuck, P. A., Williams, P., and Kempner, K. (1980). *Sex Equity in Education*. Academic Press, New York.

Chapter 9

"IF THEY CAN, I CAN": WOMEN ASPIRANTS TO ADMINISTRATIVE POSITIONS IN PUBLIC SCHOOLS

Sakre K. Edson

INTRODUCTION

Kathy

Kathy has just helped to coordinate a statewide administration confer-ence. She has returned to her hotel room to change into a navy blue skirt and blazer—clothing she calls her "interviewing outfit." The interview occurs here because she cannot imagine another free moment in the days ahead. She leaves shortly with her family to take a new job in another state. As she talks about managing schools and about making them better places for children, the fatigue drops away and her eyes begin to sparkle. She sums up: "You just can't give up. It's terrible to get calls all the time saying, 'Well, kid, you missed again!' But if you're *that* sensitive, you shouldn't be in administration anyway. If you can't take the crap, you'd better not be in the game. Because it's still pretty rough out there."

Marilyn

Frustrated is the main word in Marilyn's vocabulary. She is in her mid-fifties, and most of her life she has lived and worked as an educator in a small, coastal district. She is perpetually in motion as she talks about the three years spent interviewing for a higher position in administration. Her last words on the interview are: "I'm sorry, but these male administrators are just jocks! They don't know anything about public relations or faculties or curriculum. And *kids?* You never hear them mention kids! That's why I want to be an administrator. Even if I never get a position, just once I'd like to work for a competent building administrator. Let me know if you hear of one, will you?"

Leslie

"I know I was the first black a lot of my students were associated with. The only blacks most of these kids see are on television—killing someone or being a pimp." Leslie's first five years in education were as a junior high

169

teacher and a high school coach in a rural area. She is now getting another level of experience as a primary teacher in the suburbs, and she feels she is ready to be an administrator. She is aware of the obvious spotlight she works under as a minority female. "When I become an administrator, I can guarantee you they will be waiting and watching for me to flop. I imagine it happens to any woman administrator. They're just waiting so they can turn and tell you, 'I told you they can't handle the pressure, the responsibility.' I will probably go home many nights torn up inside; but they'll never see it at my job—I mean, they'll never see me shed a tear or break under pressure. I might do it in the privacy of my home, but *they* won't see me do it—no way!"

Rachel
    Rachel, a vice-principal, is the first woman building administrator to be hired in her region in years. On the wall is a student-made poster stating: "A woman has to be twice as good." But Rachel does not talk about feminism, she talks about humor. "When I interviewed for this job, somebody asked me how I'd get along with a younger man as principal. I said, 'Well, so far I don't have trouble with younger men!' And they laughed." She goes on to add: "At my job I don't do my thinking as a woman, I do it as a person. I'm not a conformist, so I don't lead the kind of life that is more acceptable in this community. Most people are married, and I haven't been married for years. I raised all my children alone. I am outspoken; I go to the pub when I like. A lot of people appreciate me for the person I am. I guess you could say I have a healthy ego. I've learned that you spend most of your life at your job, and you'd better by happy doing it."

What do these four women have in common? All actively seek their first principalship. Although a body of research exists on women's limited representation in administration (Lesser, 1978; Paddock, 1977) and on the barriers they face in the field (Schmuck, 1975; Beck, 1978), little information exists about females actively pursuing administrative positions in public schools. Most studies focus on women who *lack* the desire to gain employment in administration (Krchniak, 1978; Oller [Edson], 1979a; Dias, 1975; Weber *et al.*, 1980). This research generally examines two groups of women: first, female educators already qualified for administrative work who do not aspire to administration; and second, female students taking educational administration classes who may or may not pursue administrative career goals.

Studies of qualified female educators who do not go into administration work suggest that most of them simply do not want to—even when they hold certificates or have had prior experience in the field (Mansergh, 1976; McMillan, 1975; Krchniak, 1978; Newman, 1980; Weber *et al.*, 1980). Krchniak, found women very inactive regarding the pursuit of administrative goals, and Weber *et al.*, concluded that many were not even considering such career goals (1980, p. 4). The women teachers in Newman's study felt that administrative work was not "worth the hassle" (1980, p. 515). Those in Mansergh's study felt that there were too many odds against their ever gaining such positions: "Many teachers have seen how difficult it is for a woman to obtain an administrative position and have stopped trying to do so" (1976, p. 5).

Concerning the female students in educational administration classes (McCarthy *et al.*, 1979; Reynolds, 1979; Oller [Edson], 1979*a, b*, and 1978), no one disputes that people taking such classes have an interest in the subject, but it would be erroneous to conclude that these students will necessarily pursue administrative careers. Recent studies suggest that doctoral students often do not use their degrees as springboards to school administration, but instead get nonadministrative positions in the field of education, working, for example, as consultants, researchers, and in government service. Indeed, the certification students rather than the doctoral students in education administration are probably more representative of the typical aspirant. Many of the studies of women doctoral students like the studies of qualified women teachers, indicate that these women lack the desire to pursue school administration as a career.

Although informative, these two bodies of research fail to provide much insight about women who *do* wish to become school administrators. The study that I present in this chapter is unique because it focuses on women who have acknowledged their active pursuit of the position of a principalship. It becomes increasingly critical for educational researchers and practitioners to study these committed women aspirants in view of the great influx of women into the labor market (Stromberg & Harkness, 1978; Glazer & Waehrer, 1977) and into programs of educational administration (Silver & Spuck, 1978), and in view of the increasing numbers of women exhibiting high aspiration levels in connection with administrative work (Dias, 1975, p. 128) and the growth of programs encouraging women to seek administrative positions (such as those funded by the Women's Educational Equity Act [WEEA] from the U.S. Office of Education).

Description of the Study

The study in this chapter defines female aspirants as individuals who indicate a desire to attain a position within the administrative hierarchy of the public schools and who also *actively pursue* their aims in at least one of four ways: by taking certification classes; by enrolling in a doctoral program in educational administration; by working in an entry-level administrative position, such as a vice-principalship; and by applying and interviewing for administrative posts. To find candidates to participate in the two-part study I communicated with four groups of women in the state of Oregon in 1979 who were working toward a first principalship: women in certification programs at the two state universities offering certification for principals, women at the same two universities engaged in doctoral programs in educational administration, women participants in the 1978 Oregon Women in Educational Administration Conference[1], and women listed in the Directory of Administrative Candidates of the Oregon Network.[2] All the women selected for this study viewed themselves as active aspirants and were striving to attain their desired career goals by one or more of the four ways mentioned above.

After 400 names of possible candidates were obtained, each person was sent a questionnaire on which 116 respondents actually indicated that they were actively pursuing a principalship as one of their career goals. Following the collection of quantifiable data on these 116 respondents, 21 of these women were chosen for in-depth interviews about their career experiences to date. These 21 women, selected on the basis of demographic characteristics such as age, race, marital status, and years of experience in teaching and in administration, represented the broad range of women within the state who aspire to principalships. The completed study as presented here is divided into three sections. First, a composite picture of the "typical" female aspirant in the state of Oregon is presented, and the composite data are compared with the characteristics reported in a national study of women who already hold administrative positions. Second, the barriers the female aspirants reportedly experienced in their search for administrative careers are discussed. Finally, an examination is made of the motivational forces that led the aspirants to consider a principalship and to persist in their efforts to attain that position.

A PORTRAIT OF FEMALE ASPIRANTS

Typical people do not exist. Nevertheless, a composite portrait of women who pursue a principalship can highlight general characteristics that may bring into question certain fixed perceptions that we continue

[1]The Oregon Women in Educational Administration (OWEA) is a statewide support group for women in education, both aspirants and current officeholders. Originally conceived and funded through the Sex Equity Project (a WEEA grant) the organization now runs at the grassroots level on volunteer time and money.

[2]The Oregon Network was a clearinghouse for employers offering administrative positions and for females and males seeking such jobs. Originally part of the Sex Equity Project, it is now operated, in part, under the supervision of OWEA.

to have about women and educational administration. After discussing how women in Oregon pursue administrative careers, I will describe the typical female aspirant in Oregon and compare this aspirant with women already holding administrative positions as they are described in a nationwide study by Paddock in 1977.

How Women Pursue Administrative Careers

The aspirants in this study pursued their goal of obtaining a principalship in a number of ways, and Table 9.1 details four methods they used. A majority of them chose to take certification classes or work in actual administrative positions, and as the figures indicate, women are actively trying to gain the administrative credentials and experience they are so often told they lack. The low numbers of women choosing doctoral programs suggest that earlier studies focusing on doctoral students as representative of female aspirants in administration may not be as illustrative as once thought (McCarthy *et al.*, 1979; Reynolds, 1979; Oller [Edson], 1978, 1979*b*). This small percentage of women cannot be attributed to an overall decline in the numbers of women enrolled in such programs in administration because recent studies document an increase in the numbers of female doctoral students in administrative programs, both across the nation (Silver & Spuck, 1978) and in the state of Oregon (Oller [Edson], 1978).

The Typical Aspirant

For this description of the female Oregon aspirant the traits and background factors are presented along with the percentages of women who answered similarly. The typical aspirant was 38 years old (the range

TABLE 9.1
Methods Women Use in Aspiring to Educational Administration[a]

Method	Usage rates[b] (%)
Working on certification	66
Working in entry-level positions	50
Applying and interviewing for jobs[c]	40
Working on doctorate in educational administration	9
Still in the planning stage	3

[a] $n = 116$.

[b] Percentages do not total 100% because some respondents indicated more than one method.

[c] Of the 33 women applying and interviewing, 44% were at the elementary level, 31% at the secondary level, and 25% at either level.

was from 25 to 57 years old). She was Caucasian (97%), and grew up in a medium-sized town (27%). During her childhood, her mother had a high school education (32%), while her father's educational level was typically somewhat lower. The aspirant's mother kept house (67%), while her father owned a small business (18%), was a skilled craftsperson (16%), or was an unskilled or semiskilled worker (12%). She viewed her family as solidly middle class (53%). Unlike females in previous studies, the Oregon female aspirant did not fit the pattern of being the oldest or only child in the family (Paddock, 1977; Hennig & Jardim, 1977).

In her adult life, the Oregon aspirant considered herself middle class (53%) or upper middle class (41%), perhaps reflecting her marital situation. She was a married woman (53% for the first, 16% for the second time). Her husband was either a certified public school employee (20%), a professional person (11%), or an executive manager (16%). She had two school age children (53%) and lived in the state's largest city. Her educational background and preparation for administration included a master's degree from an Oregon institution (97%). She was certified to teach (9 years of experience at the elementary or secondary level) and also had administrative certification (63%) and a principal's endorsement (42%). She had 3.6 years of administrative experience (chairperson, coordinator, or director). She worked as a teacher (29%) or as a preline administrator (28%), in addition to keeping house (25%). She was taking classes (36%) at a city university (71%) for administrative certification (71%).

Oregon Aspirants Compared with Secondary Principals in a Nationwide Study

Although Paddock's national study of women administrators included superintendents and assistant superintendents, she also presented information on secondary-level principals (1977). Table 9.2 compares the typical female Oregon aspirant with the typical female secondary principal described by Paddock. As seen in the table, the characteristics of Oregon aspirants varied only slightly from those of the principals. Information about the age at which Paddock's subjects believed themselves to be *active* administrative aspirants is limited, but Oregon women appear to aspire at a young age. Aspirants were more likely to be Caucasian and married, and in comparison with all the administrators in Paddock's study, including superintendents and assistant superintendents, they were not likely to be the first or only children in their families (44% of Paddock's women versus only 32% of the Oregon women).

TABLE 9.2
Characteristics of Women in Educational Administration

	Oregon aspirants, 1979[a] (%)	National secondary principals, 1977[b] (%)
Age	38 years old	47 years old
Caucasian race	97	79
Small town-rural background	43	46
Professional parent(s)	19	18
Protestant religion	43	45
Republican affiliation	30	26
Currently married	69	60

[a] $n = 116$.
[b] $n = 97$.

Their children were more often younger; 46% of Paddock's women had children over 18 years old, while Oregon women usually had children in the 13-to 17-year-old range. It still remains to be seen whether aspirants, and therefore possibly tomorrow's female principals, are aspiring at a younger age or whether these younger aspirants will drop out before reaching their administrative goals.

Comparisons between the formal qualifications reveal that women aspirants in Oregon varied from the national norm. Nearly all the respondents in Oregon (97%) had master's degrees, whereas the women administrators had often terminated their formal studies with a bachelor's degree. As compared with women in the earlier study, aspirants today more nearly approximate the educational levels of male administrators. Women are often found lacking in administrative credentials when compared with their male peers (Schmuck, 1976). In the Oregon study, however, women aspirants often had their certificates for administrative work (63%) and their principal's endorsements (42%). Aspirants were very aware of the importance of formal schooling in furthering their careers. Those who did not have certification in hand were often working on ways to obtain the necessary credentials, because they knew women were thought to be unprepared in this area. In several of the interviews, aspirants underlined their concerns about schooling. For example, a woman just hired for a principalship said: "I started working at my new job and went back to night school. I'm kind of a goal-oriented person, so I didn't want to dillydally around. I just went straight through and finished and got all the credentials. I have everything I need. The worst thing I could think of was to be a new principal and also have to go to night school the first year." Advice from another newly hired vice principal was similar: "I think it is critical to get your education out of the way. I think my strongest asset is that I have all the education for a standard credential. So I can go anywhere—from here to Timbuktu."

In addition to certification teaching experience is also required for administrative work. Paddock reported that women administrators had taught for an average of 9 to 10 years, and men usually only for 7. Women in the Oregon study already had 8 to 9 years of teaching experience. Compared with the women in the earlier study, more Oregon women apparently elected to stay in the job market while raising their families. Only a few of the aspirants were currently in administration (28%). By the time the rest become administrators, they may have accumulated more teaching experience than either female or male administrators presently have. Another area where women usually lack the necessary qualifications is in actual administrative experience. While Oregon aspirants had numerous years of teaching experience, a large percentage (76%) also indicated experience at one or more positions that precede principalships. The administrative experience at each level, from internships to teaching-principalships, and the average amount of experience in each are shown in Table 9.3.

The figures indicate that although women who want to be principals have more experience than previously thought, much of it still tends to center at the support level rather than in line positions. Many aspirants try to overcome this deficiency, as one newly hired department chairperson explained: "I give myself 2 to 3 years in this position. During that time, I hope to accumulate a doctorate with three years of administrative experience and the added years of teaching. I could then

TABLE 9.3
Administrative Experiences of Women Aspirants

Position	Aspirants in study[a]		Average number of years in position
	%[b]	Number	
Administrative assistant or intern	9	11	3.1
Specialist, coordinator, chairperson, supervisor, and/or dean	35	41	3.8
Director	15	17	1.3
Vice principal	16	18	2.5
Teaching principal	1	1	1.0

[a] $n = 116$.
[b] Percentages do not total 100% because some respondents indicated experience at several levels.

go to almost anyone for a job. . . . There shouldn't be too many excuses after that for not hiring me." For those still struggling to gain the necessary prerequisite experience, frustration is common. As expressed by a teacher in a conversation with an administrator, "How can I get the necessary experience if you're not willing to give it to me?" This sort of situation is common to many of the women aspirants.

BARRIERS TO CAREER PROGRESS

Although many aspirants were actively preparing themselves for managerial careers, 71% of the total number believed certain barriers were a hindrance to the attainment of their goals. Table 9.4 describes these barriers and their relative importance as reported by the aspirants. Traditional female barriers, such as family responsibilites and lack of confidence, rank low in the frequency with which they were cited. The two barriers most frequently cited were lack of experience and discrimination. Upon closer examination, we can see that the two are bound together for the following reasons. Women do believe that however regrettably, females are discriminated against in pursuing administrat-

TABLE 9.4
Barriers to Advancement in Educational Administration

	Aspirants reporting barriers[b]	
Barrier	%[a]	Number
Lack of experience	56	46
Perceived discrimination in the field	55	45
Family responsibilities	38	31
Inability to relocate for career	33	27
Lack of certification	27	21
Unsureness of self and own skills	18	15
Lack of finances to continue training	17	14
Not hearing about openings	17	14
Not hearing about openings in own expertise	12	10
Lack of encouragement from colleagues	10	8
Thinking current job too good to change	6	5
Lack of encouragement from family	4	3

[a] Percentages do not total 100% because some respondents indicated more than one barrier.
[b] $n = 82$.

ive careers; and they are repeatedly told in interviews that they cannot be hired because they lack experience, a problem they invariably refer to when discussing instances of discrimination. At the same time, they feel they are not given the opportunity to gain the necessary experience because females are not generally seen as appropriate candidates for administrative jobs. This is a vicious circle. As noted earlier, the experience women lack is in the area of line or building positions, for as we have seen, many women already have support-level experience.

Some aspirants felt that inexperienced men were often selected for their potential, whereas women were required to have already demonstrated their competence. One woman aspirant recalled her interview for a principalship as follows: "The only thing against me was that I didn't have any experience; and I began to think that that was the way it was going to be everywhere. Who's going to give you the experience? Who's going to trust you?" Fortunately, she later found a district that was willing to give her that experience, and she was hired as a principal.

The vast majority of Oregon women (80%) believed they need to be far more qualified than men if they are ever to attain management positions. In spite of their experience with budgets, discipline, and coaching, many women in the study continued to experience difficulties in getting hired. One newly hired principal said, "Women have to be very good and work twice as hard." Believing they have to have unique qualifications to get a position, female aspirants consistently use terms such as *earn* and *prove* in connection with their attempts to get administrative jobs. This often weighs heavily on aspirants and some begin to believe that even superior experience is not enough. One woman determinedly said, "It's very difficult for women to get hired. My qualifications would have to be a lot higher. I would have to have my Ph.D. I'm firmly convinced of it." A remarkable statement for a woman with a master's degree and 11 years of teaching and administrative experience; and many others echoed these same sentiments.

The Oregon women clearly saw administration as a male domain (99%) and most believed that few women actually got hired (85%). Again and again in the interviews, women noted that few females, if any, presently hold administrative positions in their districts. One reported as follows:

> There is one woman who went from a counseling position to an elementary principalship. I do not have a role model in our immediate area, and I think that that's the really important part of having women in administration. It's important to have men and women doing a variety of things that traditionally they have not been doing. Children can then see men teaching first grade and women as principals.

Discrimination in the hiring process was clearly seen (69%). One woman who discussed an interview said that she had had the backing of the superintendent and the community but that the committee wouldn't hire her. Later she found out why. "I talked to a minister who was on the committee at a social gathering, and he said, 'Gee, you had all of the qualifications, but I'll be honest with you: I couldn't go with a woman.'" A recently hired female said:

> I still feel strongly that there is definitely some dicrimination in job hiring, and I can't say it in just words. It's just feelings I have inside of me. . . after I've been interviewed. Any woman who goes through 8 hours of an interview like I did, when the men were only there half a day, realize that it's always going to be harder for women until it's more open.

Other aspirants reported similarly harrowing interview experiences. One woman was interviewed by 20 people (many of them school board members) as she uncomfortably sat at a primary-school table and chair. Another discouraging recollection came from a woman who had coached and taught health and physical education for 10 years: "As soon as I walked into the board room, I knew I didn't have a chance because on the board were six men. It was a farming community. It was a traditional school and they were looking for an athletic director; and just by their body language when I walked in, I felt discouraged, as though something was wrong with me."

Clearly many women aspirants were searching for reasons—any reasons they could find—to explain why they could not get hired even though they had the necessary credentials and experience to qualify for many of the positions in administration. They often described the discrimination in terms of their race, age, or sex, as in the comments of an older black woman who felt she would be a good principal: "A few years ago in this district they were also saying that no qualified blacks were applying, and I was living right here and applying every year. Maybe school boards and principals would like to think of me as invisible, but I'm not. I want them to accept the fact that I am very visible." While some aspirants stress race, others think that their age, whether too young or too old, is the barrier to advancing their careers. One recently hired department chairperson and teacher expressed frustration at gaining experience because of the constant questions she is asked about her youthfulness. She hypothesized: "I often think if I were dumpy and short-haired, if I wore glasses, and were old and had wrinkles that I wouldn't get those same questions in interviews. My problem hasn't been as much the feminine issue as the age problem. There are several young men aspiring, and that doesn't seem to be their problem."

Of those that feared they were getting too old to get hired, one respondent, recently hired as a principal, recalled: "I ended last year feeling depressed that it was going to take me a long time, and I was wondering: Are they going to be concerned about fifty? Fifty's just a number. In my mind I'm not fifty. But sometimes they look at the age and they'll say they've got to look for someone younger." Although the women cited issues such as race, age, and experience, the issue of their gender was clearly paramount. When they sought experience, their sex became a factor; when they sought jobs, the lack of experience was brought up. These women were not militant; but because they had adequate qualifications for at least entry-level positions, they often felt frustrated. Even though some women searched for other reasons for not getting hired, the interviews and questionnaires told the same story: As in Paddock's conclusions with working administrators, the main hurdle for female aspirants in administration was their gender.

MOTIVATIONAL FACTORS FOR FEMALE ASPIRANTS

In spite of the numerous barriers in the experiences that female aspirants report, they remain surprisingly committed and motivated to succeed in their desire to become principals. However, without some knowledge of the factors that initially motivated these women to pursue administrative careers, it remains difficult to assess either the real or imagined importance of these barriers. Studies that examine the barriers only tend to portray women aspirants as passive victims of an unfair and unjust system of public school administration. These studies both obfuscate the many complex ways in which women aspirants actively respond to the barriers they perceive and also fail to provide any insight into why many women continue to persist in seeking administrative positions. In questionnaires and interviews, women aspirants described numerous reasons for pursuing a principalship. Some indicated that their own personal motivations prompted them to seek an administrative career; others reported that they were motivated by family, peers, and superiors. Most indicated that a combination of internal and external motivations led them to aspire to administration. Table 9.5 summarizes their responses.

The vast majority of the female aspirants (87%) spoke of their personal desire for professional growth and the challenges administration would be likely to bring to their lives. These women did not report either a fear of success or a motive to avoid success, as has been noted in earlier studies (Horner, 1972; Condry & Dyer, 1976; Cherry & Deaux, 1978).

TABLE 9.5
Factors Motivating Women to Aspire in Educational Administration

Motivational factor	Aspirants[b]	
	%[a]	Number
Desire for professional growth and challenges	87	99
Projection of self as good administrator	83	94
Encouragement by boss (administrator)	57	65
Encouragement by peers (co-workers)	57	65
Desire to do something for students	54	62
Desire for better salary of administrator	51	58
Desire to be influential	47	55
Encouragement by family	46	52
Desire to move out of current situation[c]	40	45
Desire for prestige of administrator	25	28
Desire to be role model for others	25	28
Need for better career as result of change in life	16	18
No personal desire or need, just "fell into it"	10	11

[a] Percentages do not total 100% because several responses were indicated by each respondent.

[b] $n = 114$.

[c] Nearly three-quarters were teachers.

Rather, they clearly articulated their aspirations and gave positive assessments of their own skills and their ability to understand and deal with problems facing public education. Many aspirants (83%) indicated that their personal assessments of themselves and their skills led them to pursue an administrative career. One vice principal affirmed: "Administration gave me an opportunity to exert myself in the sort of leadership fashion that I have always liked. I like working with people, so I feel this role is better suited to me than being in the classroom, where I was more limited and didn't have as much opportunity."

Another woman simply stated: "I like a challenge. It's just an intriguing type of thing—administration." Such strong personal motivation does not necessarily surface only after long teaching careers, as one woman aspirant suggested: "I have always felt that I am competent to be in the leader role. There is just no way I would sit back and teach year after year after year. That was something I decided after my first year of teaching. There was just something else I was going to do, and that something is to become an administrator." Often women aspirants were motivated by what they saw as poor administration on the part of current administrators, both male and female. Some specifically mentioned male administrators and the lack of confidence they had in the work men do in managing public schools. One woman who only recently decided she wanted to be a principal explained:

> I see some of the male members of our staff playing the political game, beating a path down to the principal's office and not really pulling their weight as far as plain good old hard work is concerned. It makes me mad; it irks me. I think, by golly, if they are going to aspire to be administrators, I just better see to it that I do too. Because I *know* I could do a better job than they can.

Informants in the study often expressed their concern about the quality of administration and the effect it was having on the students in public schools. Aspirants wanted to be administrators because they sincerely desired to help children (54%). A recently hired vice principal spoke of her previous job as a counselor: "Counseling is such one-on-one, band-aid kind of an approach that after 6 years I decided I wanted to be in a position to make policy and to be more instrumental in creating a positive climate in schools." Although many women decided to aspire to a principalship because of their own personal choices and assessments, others were prompted in their career goals by external agents, such as getting encouragement from their bosses (57%), peers (57%), or family (46%).

Because of its importance, encouragement from administrators deserves specific attention. One aspirant described such encouragement: "After teaching 6 years, the principal in the mid-high came to me one day and said, "You get along well with kids. How would you like to be a couselor-dean?' I enjoyed the work very much and found out I was learning a lot about running the school in the process. I then became very interested in running the school." Another vice principal described how her superintendent prompted her to apply for the position she currently holds. "My superintendent saw it. He has always been very supportive. He called me and said there was this job, so I applied." This means of encouragement, called "mentoring," is critical for succeeding in many fields. Hennig and Jardim (1977) established that many successful business women had male bosses who were their supporters, their teachers, and their strength in the company.

In educational administration such mentors can be equally crucial in the motivation of aspirants, male or female, to get into the field. Just over half of the Oregon women (56%) indicated that such a person, usually a male principal, had played this role and guided them. Those who had a mentor valued the relationship highly. One woman went to a male superintendent when she got offered a vice principalship: "It's kind of neat to have somebody to go to for a perspective on these other districts. If you can find yourself a friend who is somewhat knowledge-able of a place or two, it will give you a little more perspective on whether or not you'd like to go there." Likewise, a newly hired vice principal said: "The vice principal at the school where I was a counselor was al-ways really encouraging to me, and I probably learned more about ad-ministration from him than I ever did from any of the classes. Just talking to him, helped me go through the budgeting and auditing processes. It really did me a lot of good."

That some women aspirants do not have such a mentor relationship may be a major deterrent to their further advancement in administra-tion. Two older aspirants who have not yet been successful in gaining a principalship did not have such a person to look out for their career interests. One mused, "I just thought everyone knew I was looking. Maybe that's not enough." If having a mentor relationship is indeed critical to administrative employment, far more research must be done on why so many women lack them. In summary, women in this study were not inactive or undesirous of administrative positions as earlier studies indicated. They were strongly motivated by their self-assessed skills and by the inadequate administration they saw going on in schools. If these women lack anything, they lack the necessary mentor needed by administrative aspirants to gain entry into the field.

CONCLUSION

The women in this study were determined to succeed. They be-lieved they had the experience, the credentials, and the motivation necessary to become tomorrow's principals. One woman explained her determination: "I have a zest for life that I have always been grateful for. I believe if I keep persisting, I'll succeed. One friend of mine applied for a job and was so disappointed when she didn't get it. Yes, I've felt like that, but I've come beyond it. Now I'm over that hurdle and I'm really trying again." Getting beyond the hurdle requires thinking thoroughly about themselves, about the field of administration, and about their own ability to battle the discrimination in the field. These women were not passive in the face of this discrimination, as was so often depicted in earlier studies. Many of them are aware that their gender alone will probably have a negative effect on hiring committees; but they continue to take the steps necessary to reach the goals they have set for them-selves. The women actively asked questions during job interviews. They have learned to handle, in their own unique ways, the sexist com-ments and situations they meet day-to-day.

The aspirants also sought advice from interviewers when they didn't get hired, so that the next interview will go that much better. They let people know they felt ready to move into administration, and they sought mentors who could aid them in that process. In short, they understood the odds against them, but they refused to be turned back. "I *know* I can do it," one woman exclaimed. "It's going to be a lot of hard work, but I know I can do it!" They trusted their abilities and qualifications for administration and they believed in their own intelligence to overcome the obstacles. One theme dominates all others: their confidence in their ability to do the job, and to do it better. Ultimately, this is what moves them forward. As one aspirant related: "When I decided to go for this job, I looked around at the kind of principals there were. I thought, Lord, I can do it at least as well as they're doing it! If they can, *I* can." Eager, experienced, and committed women are aspiring to careers in the field of educational adminstration. No matter what difficulties administration may hold for them, women are determined above all else that administration is what they want. As one woman concluded:

> I'm nobody's walking-around dummy. I know what I want; I know how to do it. Just let me do it.

REFERENCES

Beck, H. N. (1978). *Attitudes toward Women Held by California School District Board Members, Superintendents, and Personnel Directors Including a Review of the Historical, Psychological, and Sociological Foundations.* Unpublished doctoral dissertation, University of the Pacific, Stockton, California.

Carlson, R. O. (1972). *School Superintendents: Careers and Performance.* Merrill, Columbus, Ohio.

Cherry, F., and Deaux, K. (1978). "Fear of Success versus Fear of Gender-Inappropriate Behavior." *Sex Roles*, 4:1.

Condry, J., and Dyer, S. (1976). "Fear of Success: Attribution of Cause to the Victim." *Journal of Social Issues*, 32:2.

Diaz, S. L. (1975). *A Study of Personal, Perceptual, and Motivational Factors Influencial in Predicting the Aspiration Level of Women and Men toward the Administrative Roles in Education.* Unpublished doctoral dissertation, Boston University.

Glazer, N., and Waehrer, H. Y., eds. (1977). *Woman in a Man-Made World.* Rand McNally, Chicago.

Hennig, M., and Jardim, A. (1977). *The Managerial Woman.* Simon & Schuster, New York.

Horner, M. A. (1972). "Toward an Understanding of Achievement-Related Conflicts in Women." *Journal of Social Issues*, 28:2.

Krchniak, S. P. (1978). *Variables Associated with Low Incidence of Women in School Administration: Toward Empirical Understandings.* Paper prepared for the Annual Meeting of the American Educational Research Association, Toronto, Canada, March.

Lesser, P. (1978). *The Participation of Women in Public School Administration*. Paper prepared for the Annual Meeting of the American Educational Research Association, Toronto, Canada, March.

Mansergh, G. (1976). "Attitudes of Teachers toward Women School Administrators and the Aspirations of Teachers for Administrative Positions in the State of Minnesota." *Catalyst for Change*, 5:3.

McCarthy, M. M., Kuh, G. D., and Beckman, J. M. (1979). "Characteristic and Attitudes of Doctoral Students in Educational Administration." *Phi Delta Kappan*, vol. 61.

McMillan, M. R. (1975). "Leadership Aspirations of Perspective Teachers—a Comparison of Men and Women." *Journal of Teacher Education*, 26:4.

Newman, K. K. (1980). "Stages of an Unstaged Occupation." *Educational Leadership*, 37:6.

Oller (Edson), S. K. (1978). "Female Doctoral Students in Educational Administration: Who Are They?" *Sex Equity in Educational Report*, vol. 7.

Oller (Edson), S. K. (1979a). "Female Graduates in Educational Administration: Myths and Realities." *Sex Equity in Educational Leadership Report*, vol. 10.

Oller (Edson), S. K. (1979b). *Differential Experiences of Male and Female Aspirants in Public School Administration: A Closer Look at Perceptions within the Field*. Paper presented at the Annual Meeting of the American Educational Research Association, San Francisco, April.

Paddock, S. (1977). *Career Paths of Women Administrators*. Unpublished doctoral dissertation, University of Oregon, Eugene.

Reynolds, B. (1979). *An Analysis of Patterns of Administrative Career Aspirations Among Graduate Students in Colleges of Education*. Unpublished doctoral dissertation, Wayne State University, Detroit.

Schmuck, P. A. (1975). *Sex Differentiation in Public School Administration—Wanted: More Women*. National Council of Administrative Women in Education, North Arlington, Virginia.

Schmuck, P. A. (1976). "The Spirit of Title IX: Men's Work and Women's Work in Oregon Public Schools." *Oregon School Study Council Bulletin*, 20:2.

Silver, P. F., and Spuck, D. W., eds. (1978). *Preparatory Programs for Educational Administrators in the United States*. The University Council for Educational Administration, Columbus, Ohio.

Stromberg, A. H., and Harkess, S. (1978). *Women Working*. Mayfield Publishing, Palo Alto, California.

Weber, M. B., Feldman, J. R., and Poling, E. C. (1980). *A Study of Factors Affecting Career Aspirations of Women Teachers and Educational Administrators*. Paper presented at the Annual Meeting of the American Educational Research Association, Boston, April.

Chapter 10

MALE AND FEMALE CAREER PATHS IN SCHOOL ADMINISTRATION

Susan C. Paddock

The career paths and attitudes of school administrators, especially of superintendents, have been fairly well documented (Carlson, 1972; Hemphill *et al.*, 1965; Knezevich, 1971), and descriptions exist of their normative aspects. Most of these studies have focused on men, which is understandable since the overwhelming majority of school administrators in the United States are men; however, the assumption about careers and occupational socialization has been that men's careers provide the norm and women's careers are the exception. Less than 20% of all elementary principals, less than 2% of all secondary principals, and less than 1% of all district superintendents are women (NEA, 1973). Beyond these numbers, however, little is known about who the women are, how they came to have careers in administration, how they view those careers, and if there are differences between their career paths and those of male school administrators.

Description of the Study

The study in this chapter was undertaken in order to learn more about women superintendents, assistant or associate superintendents, and high school principals in the United States; and an attempt was made to determine whether such male and female differences exist in the attributes and the career paths which women and men administrators have followed.

In 1977 a questionnaire was mailed to all women in the United States who were identified as holding one of the three positions just noted. The questionnaire was a composite of two questionnaires developed and validated by the National Association of Secondary School Principals and the American Association of School Administrators in studies of their members (Carlson, 1972; Gross & Trask, 1976; Hemphill, 1965; Knezevich, 1971; Rose, 1967). These questionnaires were used so that comparisons could be made between women in this study and the predominantly male respondents in previous studies of secondary school principals and superintendents. Of the 619 individuals who were identified as women administrators in the specified positions, 42 returned their questionnaires unanswered with the indication that they had been misidentified as to position. Of the 512 assumed to be correctly identified as to sex and position, 260, or 51%, returned usable questionnaires. (This assumes that all individuals who did not return the questionnaires (49%) were women holding one of the identified positions; in fact, the sample may actually represent more than 51% of all women administrators.)

Respondents sending in usable returns from all geographic regions included 42 superintendents (44.2% of the 93 identified), 118 assistant or associate superintendents (52.9% of the 212 identified), and 97 secondary principals (34.2% of the 284 identified). The return rate from principals was disappointingly low; nevertheless, the data on their questionnaires were used in the study since the demographic features of this female sample closely resembled those of a previous study of female high school principals (Baron, 1977). The responses were analyzed using descriptive statistics, simple cross-tabulations, and chi-squares. Three basic categories relating to careers were investigated—informal career contingencies, career patterns, and attitudes toward careers. Contingencies are factors that appear to be important in the hiring of school administrators. The three categories were investigated in relation to women, and comparisons were made between men and women in all categories.

Present Status of Women Administrators

The women administrators in our 1977 study had been in their positions, on the average, for four and a half years. Almost half of the female superintendents (45.2%) were in their first or second year in that position. The latest national statistics on men and women superintendents are for 1974–1975. We cannot be sure whether the women in our study will raise the 0.01% female representation of that year because current national statistics on the total number of men and women are not available. Optimism prompts us to suggest, however, that women's representation is increasing. One woman respondent said: "The era in which I decided to seek administrative positions has evidenced the importance of time in seeking advanced positions. Affirmative action and Title IX [E.S.E.A. of 1972] are relevant to my. . . appointment." Another said, "It is gratifying to know how many more opportunities are now available to competent women."

Most respondents worked in unified K–12 school districts (kindergarten through twelfth grade). Over half of the superintendents (56.1%) worked in elementary school districts located in rural or small-town areas. The isolation that must accompany positions in these areas was reflected in one woman's answer when we asked, "To whom do you directly report?" Her answer: "To God." The assistant superintendents and high school principals more often worked in suburban or urban school districts, and the principals served in schools comparable to those of male principals. To be sure, the absolute number of women in the high school principalship was limited, but the fact that they served in different kinds and sizes of high schools indicated that they are unlike women superintendents, who served primarily in small school districts.

CAREER CONTINGENCIES

Although being hired for an administrative position depends on formal qualifications and standards determined at the state level, it may also depend on informal factors not closely related to an evaluation of one's present or potential performance. It may be inferred that career contingencies are operating when, for example, educational administrators are "disproportionately middle aged, native born, male, married, white Protestants from nonurban backgrounds" (March, 1976); that is, when selected attributes occur more frequently among position incumbents than would be expected for the population in general.

Clearly, women do not fit the stereotype of the white middle-class *male* administrator. In our study we wanted to determine if they were like male administrators in ways other than gender; that is, whether factors of religion, race, and background appeared to influence their appointment to positions as well. The heterogeneity of the respondents indicates, however, that career contigencies are *not* operative for women, as evidenced in Table 10.1 where we see certain attributes that appear to be career contingencies—for example, being white, Protestant, and from a rural background—are indeed not contingencies for women. That is, women administrators reflect these national attributes, while men administrators are distinctly atypical. This suggests that once maleness is no longer an attribute, other career contingencies lose their po-

TABLE 10.1
Possible Career Contingencies

	Principals		Superintendents		*Likelihood as career contingency*
Attribute	Women	Men[a]	Women	Men[b]	
Mean age	46.8	45.0	49.0	48.1	Yes
Caucasian (white)	78.9%	96.0%	100.0%	100.0%	Yes for super-intendents
Small-town rural background	46.9%	NA	66.7%	86.1%	No
Parent in a profession	16.7%	NA	14.3%	11.0%	No
Protestant	45.4%	NA	57.1%	87.0%	No
Republican	25.5%	NA	26.8%	37.0%	No
Now married	59.8%	92.0%	61.0%	100.0%	No

NOTE: NA = not available.
[a] From R. O. Carlson, *School Superintendents: Careers and Performance.* Merrill, Columbus, Ohio, 1972.
[b] From S. J. Knezevich, *The American School Superintendent: An AASA Research Study.* American Association of School Administrators, Washington, D.C., 1971.

tency. Thus gender may be the most difficult career contingency to overcome in educational administration at this time. Once women surmount this barrier, the other attributes may no longer carry weight as necessary preconditions for employment. Beyond these data, however, the one attribute that effectively discriminates against women as administrators is marriage.

Women in our sample included 21.4% who were never married, 51.1% who were married for the first time, 9.8% who were remarried, 9% who were divorced, and 8.3% who were widowed. While these figures for women correspond to national averages for working women (Kievet, 1972), they are far below the comparable figures for men administrators. In Carlson's study (1972) of male superintendents, none of them were in the category of never married; 97.6% were married for the first time, 2.4% were remarried, and none were divorced or widowed. Our study and others indicate that marriage is clearly a career contingency that operates differently depending on whether you are a man or a woman. Gross and Trask's study (1976) for example, showed that there was a strong disposition against hiring a married woman as superintendent. Male school administrators are expected to be married; but for women, marriage is at best a double bind. Indeed, there seems to be a "Catch 22" element for women seeking an administrative post: a married woman is expected to show primary allegiance to her family, and an unmarried woman is often considered a threat or an invader (Carlson, 1976; Epstein, 1970). In either case, a woman is sometimes thought to have "personal problems" that would prevent her from functioning effectively as an administrator.

The divided role of professional and homemaker is one of the biggest barriers to women's career development. It was mentioned by women respondents more frequently than any other barrier, and it arises repeatedly in literature on the working woman (Epstein, 1970; Howe, 1975; and Theodore, 1971). As Howe (1975) notes, the "career system is shaped by and for the man with a family who is family-free." The problem of the working woman who is a wife and mother is generally seen as her own personal problem. She must choose between a few prepackaged options, and the result of having to make this choice is, as Howe says, "structured strain, caused by a combination of an over-demanding set of role obligations, lack of consensus as to the hierarchy of obligations, and the clash of obligations from home and occupational statuses."

The women in our study used their own words to translate this concept of home and family responsibilities into career barriers. One woman wrote: "The barriers were cultural expectations I accepted—the need to concentrate efforts in the early years of marriage on promoting my husband's career." Another woman described a primary barrier to her career as "my own feeling that I needed to give primary attention to my family until the youngest was in school." She said, "This took 17 years out of my professional activities." A principal with two preschoolers wrote, "I am in a higher position than my present life-style can accommodate," and a superintendent, "I sometimes wonder whether it is all worth it."

Some of the obligations and conflicts attached to a woman's role may have been alleviated for our respondents because most mothers had older children, who do not require as must time and energy. Over 46% had children over the age of 18, and many had only high schoolers at home. Nevertheless, women did experience role conflict in their home and career responsibilities. One principal summed up what many others had written, "We are not being fair to young women by telling them that they can do what homemakers do and have a career besides. It is a physical impossibility."

PATTERNS

Careers are affected by the jointly held expectations of those who control or speak for the organizations that employ administrators. These expectations are evident in recruitment, sponsorship, promotion, and succession practices—and, thus, in the career patterns of individuals who intend to climb the organizational career ladder. Qualified individuals who understand and meet institutional expectations are usually able to move more quickly into higher positions. Almost all studies of careers have looked at men's careers as being the norm. Women's careers have generally been thought to be the exception. In our study, women's career patterns in educational administration were compared to men's in order to determine the extent to which women's careers fit the male norm in professional preparation, experience, and mobility.

Professional Preparation

Although obtaining an advanced degree may not be necessary for entry into an administrative position, graduate study of some sort is usually a prerequisite for remaining in that job. Almost all states have certification requirements for administrators, and most states insist on at least a master's degree (Kane, 1976).

Data show that there is a difference between women administrators' and men administrators' academic training for administration. Significantly more women than men (19% versus 2%) terminate their studies with a bachelor's degree. In addition, more than twice as many men as women have their highest degree as a specialist in educational supervision and administration (male principals, 47%; female principals, 25.8%; male superintendents, 16.3%; no female superintendents). However, at the other end of the continuum, significantly more women superintendents than men superintendents (33% versus 12.5%) have obtained doctorates.

When women earned advanced degrees, they did so later in their administrative careers. There is no information on men principals, but we know that men superintendents completed their master's degrees at an average age of 31.8 years (Knezevich, 1971). For women superintendents, the corresponding age is 33.8 years. Other studies indicate that men administrators begin their advanced studies as a kind of preservice preparatory training, while women seek advanced training as in-service training after moving into an administrative position. Training for administration thus appears to serve a different purpose for women than it does for men. For men, it is a tool needed in order to obtain a position. For women it enables them both to retain a position and to improve their performance in a position already attained.

Experience: The Career Ladder

With rare exceptions, all administrators began their careers in the classroom, and experience became the first rung in their administrative career ladders (see Table 10.2). Both men and women administrators had considerable experience as teachers, but the women in our study spent more time as teachers than did their male counterparts. Most men had 7 or less years of teaching experience, most women had 9 or 10. The differences are especially notable for superintendents; while 52% of the women had 10 years or more of teaching experience, only 23% of the men did. Because of the longer classroom time for women, they entered administration at a later age than men and had a shorter career, or abbreviated career ladder, in administration.

In our study, women entered teaching earlier than men, but their teaching careers were often discontinuous. Furthermore, they were older when they decided to enter administration and to seek advanced degrees. Most did not decide to seek an administrative or supervisory position until they were over age 31, and they received the position when they were over 32. Men superintendents and principals, on the other hand, began their administrative careers at about age 30 (Hemphill, 1965). Carlson (1972) suggests that men generally decide to seek administrative positions in their mid to late twenties, and that they achieve sought-after positions about 3 to 4 years after deciding to seek

TABLE 10.2

Mean Ages of Women and Men Superintendents at Milestones in Their Graduate Study and Professional Experience[a]

Women superintendents	Age	Men superintendents
Mean age of women super- intendent respondents[b]	49	
	48	Mean age of all
Completed doctorate or completed specialist's degree	40	superintendents[c]
Started specialist's program	38	
Started doctorate program	37	
	36	Completed specialist degree
Completed master's degree or started master's program	33	Completed doctorate
	32	Started doctorate program
Received first administrative position	31	Completed master's program
	30	Received first administrative or supervisory position
	29	Started master's program
	24	Entered education as teacher
Entered education as teacher	21	

[a] From S. J. Knezevich, *The American School Superintendent: An AASA Research Study.* American Association of School Administrators, Washington, D.C., 1971.

[b] 1977 statistics.

[c] 1969–1970 statistics.

them. Schmuck (1975) notes that in seeking administrative positions, men more frequently persevere in the same district until they are successful.

Career Discontinuities

A career may be interrupted, or discontinuous. If this happens, one's ascent up the career ladder is slower. Most studies indicate that men rarely interrupted their educational careers to work in other jobs. When it did happen it almost always occurred during their teaching rather than their administrative years, and it often involved military service (Hemphill, 1965). The story for women is quite different. Not including short-term marternity leaves, but including longer-term homemaking and child rearing jobs (albeit unpaid), almost one-half (49.1%) of all women administrators in our study interrupted their careers in education after receiving their bachelor's degree; and of these, almost half interrupted administrative as opposed to teaching careers. The reason most frequently given for career discontinuities was bearing and rearing children. While service in the military is considered valuable experience for men, being a homemaker is not usually thought of as adding to the skills and talents women need for administrative jobs. Thus, women who interrupt their careers do not spend the intervening time in what school boards and selection committees consider useful or relevant experience.

Staff and Line Positions

Carlson (1972) described the typical career pattern of a public school superintendent as relatively short and as a sequence from principalship to assistant superintendency to superintendency. Schmuck (1975) suggested that the career pattern of women administrators may be quite different from men's since women hold many staff positions between their tenure of customary line positions. However, the women in our study, who were top line administrators, did not have career patterns that differed greatly from those of men. Contrary to what popular belief dictates, not all the women administrators in our study held staff positions before becoming line administrators. (This might have been partly because they worked in small districts.) Only about one-half (54.1%) of the study's respondents reported having held staff positions, and about half of these reported positions that were in guidance or curriculum, areas that lend themselves to movement into line positions. The figures for women principals and superintendents compared favorably with the numbers of men principals and superintendents who have held staff positions (Hemphill, 1965). Assistant superintendents were more likely to have held staff positions than were other women administrators; 71.6% of the superintendents as compared with 39.4% of the principals had held staff positions, usually as consultants or supervisors. This may indicate the assistant superintendency as a quasi staff position.

Geographic Mobility

While both men and women administrators are relatively immobile, women appear to be more immobile than men. Of the women in our study, 94% had been an administrator in only one state, and 72% in only one district. In addition, less than half were willing to move to new districts and only 28% were willing to move to new states. By comparison, Carlson's research (1972) indicated that among male superintendents, 65% were willing to relocate. The women in our study who had worked in more than one district, however, were significantly more willing to move than were women who had served in only one district. The women who did not want to move cited family ties and responsibilities as the primary reason. Limited mobility may also be related to career attitudes, which are explored in the following section.

Time Factors

The career patterns of women in this study were little different from those of men. The careers of both were relatively short. One-quarter of all women superintendents moved from teaching to a principalship to a superintendency and 18.7% moved directly from teaching to a principal-superintendency, or to a superintendency in a small district. The shortest career path was that of a woman who reported that she became a superintendent "when I began to teach my one-room school." Further, it is clear that a woman's movement into and through an administrative career depends to a great extent on timing. "It seems," wrote one woman, "that I often was at the right place at the right time and advanced through these quirks rather than by deliberate preplanning." Although our women respondents tended to spend more time as teachers and their careers were more discontinuous and they were older at the time of their first administrative assignments, once in administration work, they demonstrated career patterns that were similar to men's. The organization of the school appeared to be a strong force in shaping one's career, regardless of one's gender.

Attitudes

People can view their careers by looking at how far they have come or at how far they have to go. It is somewhat similar to looking at a bottle half filled with liquid. Is the bottle half full or half empty? Careers can be anchored in the past, or downward, and in the future, or upward. If one emphasizes past accomplishments then one is downward-anchored; if one emphasizes future placements, one is upward-anchored. Rose (1967) suggested that most educational administrators (80% of superintendents, all of whom were male) are downward-anchored; they do not emphasize their future careers but rather how far they have come. Understandably, older men are more likely to be downward-anchored. By contrast, 43.6% of the women superintendents and over half of all the women administrators in our study could be typified as upward-anchored, a division that is also true for careers in other professions (Carlson, 1972). Surprisingly, career anchorage is not related to womens' ages, perhaps because women enter administrative positions later or have a longer life expectancy.

Somewhat surprisingly, women's career anchorage points were not related to their aspiration levels. Although a downward-anchored woman in our study might have aspired to a superintendency or a state-level position, that is, a higher position, she was still most impressed by what she had already accomplished. We would not expect this situation among men administrators because their aspiration levels are related to their career anchorage points (Rose, 1967). There was also no clear relation between women's career anchorage points and indexes of success, such as status and salary level. In fact, many women who emphasized their future careers did not necessarily have clear career goals in terms of the positions they wished to hold. Job characteristics were more important than position title. One principal said, "I determined my career in terms of flexibility and access to things I like to do." For her, future career choices would be based on the same variables. A superintendent stated, "I only want to work with kids and people."

Most women did not use standard definitions of success and the career choices thereby implied. "Success is not measured in moving from job to job in a vertical continuum," said a principal, "but rather... it is measured by the quality of any job held." Another principal agreed: "Success represents ending up in a job one really likes and finds personally challenging and fulfilling, [a job in which one] and does well." Women's definitions of the key to success were good working relationships and "doing a job which is interesting and challenging."

Previous studies demonstrated that male school administrators generally were satisfied with their jobs and careers (Carlson, 1972; Hemphill, 1965). The women in our study also appeared to be highly satisfied. Women principals indicated a higher satisfaction than men principals had in previous studies: 80% of the women said they would choose the same career as compared with 63% of the men in earlier studies (Hemphill, 1965). We can only guess why these women were somewhat more satisfied. Perhaps along with lower aspirations women have lower expectations for job and career satisfaction. Having "made it" in a man's world, they expect little more than what they already have and are thus well satisfied with both job and career. Perhaps dissatisfied women, particularly those who are married, have more freedom to leave an unsatisfactory position because society accepts and supports the idea that women can depend on their spouses' salaries but does not extent such acceptance to men. These explanations were not verified by this study.

CONCLUSIONS

It appears that women administrators generally have career paths that are similar to those of their male colleagues. The variations from the male norm—for example, women's later entry age and their career discontinuities—illustrate that career patterns and attitudes are a reflection of the interaction between institutional and individual pressures. The contingencies that institutions place on certain careers, the patterns of recruitment, sponsorship, and promotion, and the barriers that are informally or formally erected influence the direction of careers. Patterns of socialization and conflicts in role performance influence careers from another and sometimes opposing direction. The interaction of these forces affects both career patterns and career attitudes. Thus, a variety of influences, rather than any one variable, affect careers in any institution.

What this study has attempted to do is to look at the *results* of those interactions. In so doing, the study has found that women's careers are remarkably similar to men's, a testimony to the strength of the educational institution in forming and reforming careers. What remains for study is a close examination of the influences and interactions themselves, so that the dynamics of any individual's career in educational administration can be better understood.

REFERENCES

Baron, E., (1977). *The Status of Women Senior High School Principals in the United States.* Unpublished doctoral dissertation, Boston College.

Carlson, J. M. (1976). "Current Attitudes toward Women and Men Who Never Marry." In *New Research on Women and Sex Roles.* (D. McGuigan, ed.) Center for Continuing Education of Women, University of Michigan, Ann Arbor.

Carlson, R. O. (1972). *School Superintendents: Careers and Performance.* Merrill, Columbus, Ohio.

Epstein, C. F. (1970). *Women's Place.* University of California Press, Berkeley.

Gross, N., and Trask, A. E. (1976). *The Sex Factor and the Management of Schools.* Wiley, New York.

Hemphill, J., Richards, J. M., and Peterson, R. E. (1965). *Report on the Senior High Principalship.* National Association of Secondary School Principals, Washington, D.C.

Howe, F. (ed). (1975). *Women and the Power to Change.* McGraw-Hill, New York.

Kane, R. (1976). *Sex Discrimination in Education: A Study of Employment Practices Affecting Professional Personnel,* vol. 1. National Center for Educational Statistics, Department of HEW, Washington, D.C.

Knezevich, S. J. (1971). *The American School Superintendent: An AASA Research Study.* American Association of School Administrators, Washington, D.C.

Kievet, M. B. (1972). *Review and Synthesis of Research on Women in the World of Work.* ERIC Clearinghouse on Vocational and Technical Education, Ohio State University, Columbus.

March, J. S. (1976). *American Pre-Collegiate Educational Administration: A Short Analysis.* Unpublished paper, Stanford University, Calif.

NEA (1973). *Research Action Notes.* National Education Association Resource Center on Sex Roles in Education, Washington, D.C.

Rose, R. L. (1967). *Career-Bound; Place-Bound: An Attitude Study of the Superintendency.* Center for the Advanced Study of Educational Administration, University of Oregon, Eugene.

Schmuck, P. A. (1975). *Sex Differentiation in Public School Administration.* National Council of Administrative Women in Education, Arlington, Va.

Theodore, A. (ed). (1971). *The Professional Woman.* Schekman, Cambridge, Mass.

Chapter 11

ADMINISTRATIVE CAREERS IN PUBLIC SCHOOL ORGANIZATIONS

Karen N. Gaertner

The purpose of the research reported in this chapter was to define, identify, and describe the career patterns found in public school administration. The concept of careers in an organization as a phenomenon of the organization has been in the literature at least since Weber's discussions of bureaucracy; and though some good theoretical work was done during the 1950s (e.g., Becker & Strauss, 1956; Martin & Strauss, 1959), empirical investigation that captures the substantive richness of the theories is lacking. Early empirical work was largely in the form of case studies and participant observations (for good examples, see Dalton, 1959; Janowitz, 1960). This type of research was valuable in identifying some of the characteristics of careers in organizations (the difference between general and specialist's careers, the use of staff positions for poor performers, and the cumulative nature of training and socialization); but the research was plagued by the limitations of the methodology employed.

Later work that was done in the area demonstrated methodological sophistication, but it had little relationship to the more substantive issues raised by the previous authors (Vroom & MacCrimmon, 1968; White, 1969; Gillespie, Leininger, & Kahalas, 1976). This wave of research tended to use stochastic process models to predict future num-

An earlier version of this chapter was presented as a paper at the 1978 annual meeting of the American Sociological Association, September 4–8, San Francisco, California.

199

bers of people in positions based on known probabilities of mobility between positions. These are valuable tools for human resource planners, but they hardly capture or test the substance of careers in organizations. In the area of public school administration, most studies of careers were either confined to large urban school districts (Brown, 1972) or focused on a single position, usually the superintendency (Carlson, 1961; March & March, 1977). Because of this relatively narrow perspective much of the process of mobility was lost—we again lose the forest for the trees.

In the context of these gaps in research, the study in this chapter was undertaken with two goals in mind; to identify the career patterns in an entire administrative hierarchy and to do so in a way that bridges the gap between theory and methodology. We define the state school system as the focal organization and seek to identify and describe patterns of movement within the system. This definition is appropriate, first, because so much of the variability in the system of public education is accounted for by state and federal regulations and practices and second, because movement between districts in the state is enhanced if not encouraged by statewide tenure and benefit policies. District boundaries are very permeable, and district administrative action is likely to show consistency, just as managerial action in partly autonomous subunits of a manufacturing firm would be likely to reflect the policy of the parent company.

Our concern is with careers as a phenomenon of the organization and as patterns of mobility between positions that is controlled by the organization. Glaser (1968) suggested that the primary problems an organization must confront with respect to employees are turnover, job succession, and training. We would add one's motivation to participate and to produce to this list, and go on to suggest that a career in an organization is defined at least in part by the patterns devised by organizations to solve these problems. In other words, the career is designed to train the employee to hold future positions and to motivate the employee to continue working in expectation of future status increments (Martin & Strauss, 1959; Sofer, 1970; McFarland, 1968). Patterns of mobility tend to take the form of sequentially ordered and related positions such that each position provides the experiences deemed necessary for adequate performance in subsequent positions (Thompson, 1967; Becker & Strauss, 1956). Thus, the flow of people through an organization may be characterized as a relatively continuous process of socialization and training that enables the organization to maintain a sufficiently prepared supply of employees for its needs (McFarland, 1968; Vetter, 1967; Levenson, 1961; Becker & Strauss, 1956; Friedman, 1969; Martin & Strauss, 1959; Sofer, 1970).

Careers in organizations consist of several types of positions, each contributing to the viability of the pattern. Each pattern has a small number of entry positions that describe the minimal level of competence, the prior socialization and training, required for entrance to the pattern. Career patterns also have plateau positions that serve as outlets for relatively poor performers, and exit positions from which people leave the career path and the organization. Exit positions define the ceiling of the career and facilitate the formulation of realistic expectations by career incumbents regarding their future prospects. Career patterns are also marked by one or more "assessment positions" in which performance can be more objectively evaluated. A person's performance in such a position largely determines his or her future career pattern. Martin and Strauss (1959), who described assessment positions as "nodes" from which several paths emerge, noted that the skills required to perform well in such positions tend to be those that are required at higher levels in the organization. Thus, these assessment positions allow the incumbent to develop skills and allow the organization to observe performance more closely and objectively, both of which increase the probability that capable people will be promoted to positions of greater responsibility.

METHOD AND RESULTS

Our task in this research was to identify and describe career patterns in public school administration. Using Goodman's log-linear effect parameters, we identified pairs of positions that shared a disproportionately large number of incumbents. These positions, when ordered by the direction of movement, define certain career patterns. Once connections between positions have been established we describe the patterns in terms of the constituent positions and position incumbents.

Data

The data used in this study are from the state of Michigan, where between 1968 and 1973 extensive records were kept concerning the public school districts ($N = 520$) and the people employed therein. The data are of three types. The first and most important data concern job histories for the 5-year period for all state public school employees except clerical and janitorial personnel. This data set includes information on exployees' present district of employment, current position, salary, highest educational degree, race, sex, and age. The second data set, collected by the district, concerns characteristics of the school system in the district, including such variables as enrollment, student achievement, qualifications of professional staff, pupil–teacher ratio, and type and amount of financial resources. The last data set, derived from 1970 census data aggregated to the district level, provides measures of population characteristics, such as size of the largest city, education of the adult population, and family income. The job histories will be used to identify career patterns, and the other two data sets will aid in the description of these career patterns.

Analysis

We identify career patterns in terms of positional changes made by individuals. A position change is defined as a change in the assigned position code between any two years, excluding missing data. For example, if a person was present in Years 1, 2, and 4 and missing during Year 3, and if the position assignment codes are identical for the three years for which we have data, no change is counted. If the position in Year 1 is different from the position in Years 2 and 4, one move is recorded. If the position assignments are different in all three years, two moves are recorded. We have arbitrarily defined entrance and exit moves as two or more consecutive years of no information for the person.

Given this method of counting moves, we constructed a transition matrix with cell entries representing the number of people moving from Position A to Position B during the 5-year period, and diagonal cell entries representing the number of people who did not change positions at any time during the period. Using this table as raw data, we then calculated Goodman's effect parameters for each cell (description follows). These effect parameters indicate the extent to which there is more (or less) movement between any pair of positions than would be expected, given the marginal distributions of sending and receiving positions. The pattern of effect parameters identifies career patterns, or heavily travelled routes between positions.

Log-Linear Effect Parameters

Normally in contingency table analysis one is concerned with relationships between variables. One usually seeks a single statistic that describes the relationship between two or more variables in a contingency table. In the case of dichotomous variables, Goodman's log-linear effect parameters do precisely the same thing. The benefit of the Goodman system, however, is in its generalizability to polytimous variables. The investigator need not worry about the ordinallity of a variable because Goodman's effect parameters allow the assessment of category to category relationships. Several articles by Goodman (1970, 1971,

1972*a*, 1972*b*) and others (Davis, 1972; Reynolds, 1977) described these techniques. Our summary of the relevant procedures draws primarily from the work of Davis.

The method is analogous to analysis of variance. We can think of a cell in a two-variable table as having four component parts that add up to the cell frequency: (1) a contribution from the sheer size of the table; (2) the appropriate row effect; (3) the appropriate column effect; and (4) the "interaction" between the appropriate row and column categories. In Goodman's system, the table total component, *MU*, is the geometric mean of the cell frequencies. In logarithmic terms it is the mean of the logs of the cell frequencies. (Rather than jump back and forth between cell frequencies and logs of cell frequencies, we discuss the method in terms of logarithms only.) A row effect is the mean of the logs of the cell frequencies in that row minus *MU*; a column effect is, similarly, the mean of the logs of the cell frequencies in that column minus *MU*; and the interaction effect is the log of the focal cell frequency less the row, column, and *MU* effects. In a three-by-three table, the following calculations would generate an effect parameter for the top left hand (1,1) cell.

$$MU = \frac{(g_{11} + g_{12} + g_{13} + g_{21} + g_{22} + g_{23} + g_{31} + g_{32} + g_{33})}{9}$$

where g_{ij} is the log of the ij^{th} cell frequency,

$$r_1 = \frac{(g_{11} + g_{12} + g_{13})}{3} - MU$$

$$c_1 = \frac{(g_{11} + g_{21} + g_{31})}{3} - MU$$

$$\lambda_{11} = g_{11} - (r_1 + c_1 + MU).$$

Lambda (λ_{11}) is the unstandardized effect parameter. To standardize the parameter so that it may be compared to others, one simply divides by the standard error of the parameter. Goodman gives the variance of the effect parameter as

$$S^2 = \sum \frac{a^2}{f},$$

where *a* is the value by which each cell in the table is weighted in calculating the effect parameter, and *f* is each cell frequency. To derive the weights (the *a*'s), one simply substitutes the original equations for *MU*, r_1, and c_1 into the equation given for lambda. In our three-by-three example the weights are 4/9 for cell (1,1), 2/9 for the other row and column cells (1,2; 1,3; 2,1; 3,1), and 1/9 for the remaining four cells. The standardized effect parameters may be interpreted as Z scores.

For this analysis the 25 positions in the administrative hierarchy in the public school districts were collapsed to 9 positions. The criteria for collapsing were substantive similarity of positions and minimal mobility between positions to be grouped together. The resulting 9 positions, the average number of position incumbents during any one year, and the average salary associated with that position are given in Table 11.1.

Discussion

Table 11.2 shows the raw data on mobility between positions from which career patterns were identified. Two regularities in these data are immediately apparent. The first is that over the 5-year period, public school administrators were relatively immobile. A majority of adminis-trators did not change positions (64.8%). This is consistent with the findings of other studies relative to mobility rates among public school administrators (Brown, 1972; Carlson, 1961). If we remember that this table excludes persons who moved between administrative and teaching positions during the period, these data suggest that public school administrators have fairly stable positions, changing on the aver-age every 15 years or so. Note further that these data mask movement between districts, for a given position. This type of movement occurred infrequently. There were 138 such interdistrict, intraposition moves, or 3.4% of the total number of people who did not change positions. Analysis of these interdistrict, intraposition moves identified no sys-

| | | TABLE 11.1 | |
| | | Positions in Administrative Hierarchy | |

Code	Position	Average number of position incumbents	Average salary
1	Superintendent	420	$20,108
2	Assistant superintendent	201	20,172
3	Administrative specialist[a]	436	18,311
4	Administrator of instruction	183	18,741
5	Secondary school principal	825	16,741
6	Elementary school principal	1728	15,730
7	Assistant principal, secondary	692	15,533
8	Assistant principal, elementary	267	15,132
9	Instructional or curricular supervisor[b]	980	14,769

[a] Includes administrators of business, plant and facilities, employed personnel, and special education.
[b] Includes consultants, coordinators, and supervisors of subject areas and school levels.

TABLE 11.2
Raw Data on Mobility between Positions

		Position 2										
		1	2	3	4	5	6	7	8	9	Exit	Total
Position 1	1	347	13	7	2	7	11	0	0	2	83	472
	2	34	114	23	5	5	8	2	0	3	36	230
	3	14	26	277	14	11	27	6	3	15	99	492
	4	13	24	12	94	12	9	8	1	14	45	232
	5	40	18	17	10	605	31	32	1	12	126	892
	6	7	21	14	16	32	1463	16	5	16	288	1878
	7	5	8	9	1	160	40	380	4	15	97	719
	8	0	0	3	3	5	93	12	168	1	42	327
	9	1	12	17	33	7	22	71	10	568	212	953
	Total	461	236	379	178	844	1704	527	192	646	1028	6195

tematic patterns of district characteristics between which these moves occurred. It was thus concluded that this type of mobility plays a negligible role in the development and maintenance of career patterns in public school administration.

The second regularity observed in Table 11.2 relates to the rather high proportion of moves that involve an exit. Overall, we observe 2179 intraposition moves, 1028 or 47.2% of which are exits. We see, for example, that people beginning as administrative specialists (Code 3) are more likely to leave the system ($N = 99$) than to move to another position within the system. There are two exceptions to this trend; movement out of the assistant elementary principal position (Code 8) and movement out of the assistant secondary principal position (Code 6). In both cases more people moved to the appropriate principal position than exited.

Table 11.3 gives the standardized effect parameters for the frequencies presented in Table 11.2 (these parameters may be thought of as Z scores). The parameters indicate "connectedness" between positions, controlling for marginal distributions. A positive value suggests more than the expected level of movement between two positions, while a negative value suggests less than the expected level. To simplify interpretation, we have taken all the significant positive effects and summarized them and their relationships with each other in Figure 11.1. Because Table 11.3 clearly indicates direction of movement, we have drawn Figure 11.1 with this direction and with some notion of hierarchical level imbedded in the pattern. Put more simply, Figure 11.1 represents the identified administrative career patterns in our data set (the

TABLE 11.3

Standardized Effect Parameters for Mobility between Positions

Position 2

	1	2	3	4	5	6	7	8	9	Exit
1	15.208^a	2.205^b	$-.027$	$-.982$	$-.677$	-1.133	-2.179^b	-1.014	-1.430	3.020^a
2	6.002^a	11.050^a	3.617^a	$.039$	-2.031^b	-2.739^a	-2.021^b	-1.216	-1.452	-1.701
3	$-.131$	1.472	18.215^a	$.545$	-3.330^a	-2.937^a	-2.749^a	$-.602$	$-.148$	-1.598
4	$.911$	2.438^a	$-.694$	12.526^a	-1.593	-4.312^a	-1.041	-1.094	-1.036	-3.660^a
5	3.098^a	$-.977$	-2.044^b	-1.438	20.017^a	-3.575^a	1.497	-1.999^b	-1.799	-1.627
6	-3.094^a	$-.982$	-3.309^a	$-.440$	-1.247	27.130^a	-1.673	$-.542$	-1.441	4.568^a
7	-2.427^b	-2.234^b	-2.705^a	-3.118^a	11.198^a	$-.700$	14.949^a	$-.012$	$.018$	-1.255
8	-1.979^b	-2.172^b	-1.474	$-.300$	-1.213	7.539^a	2.226^b	14.200^a	-1.799	$.305$
9	-3.747^b	-2.154^b	-1.954	3.449^a	-4.824^a	-4.732^a	5.318^a	1.577	19.558^a	2.629^a

Position 1

[a] $p < .01$, two-tailed test.
[b] $p < .05$, two-tailed test.

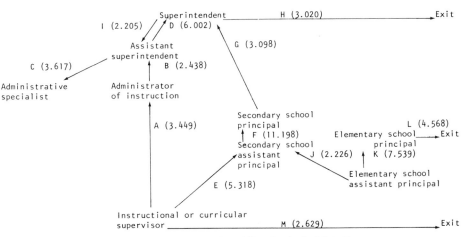

Fig. 11.1. Career patterns in public school administration.

number in parentheses on each path is the effect for the path from Table 11.3).

There are three patterns of mobility identified by the data. The first leads to the superintendency, Paths A, B, and D. This may be thought of as a specialist's career pattern in instruction and in central office administration. The second pattern is via Paths E, F, and G to the superintendency, a pattern through school unit or teaching supervision. The third pattern is only weakly connected to the superintendency via Path J. Its more realistic peak is elementary school principal (Path K). (We discuss each of these patterns in more detail after noting a few other general characteristics of the patterns.) As suggested above, there are two ceiling positions indicated by the data, those of the superintendent and the elementary school principal. Clearly the routes to the former position occupy more hierarchical levels and represent greater remunerative rewards for the persons traveling through them than does the route to elementary school principal. The larger career patterns also show two plateau or demotion moves, Paths I and C.

There are also three exit positions, or positions from which exits are significantly more likely to occur than expected. These exit positions are the two ceiling positions of superintendent and elementary principal, and the lowest level administrative position of instructional or curricular supervisor. Note that these are not exits to teaching but rather exits to outside the public school system. A full analysis of mobility between teaching and administration is beyond the scope of this chapter. For our present purposes it is sufficient to note that there is considerable movement from teaching into both elementary administrative positions, the secondary assistant principal's and the instructional or curricular supervisor's.

Finally, we observe what appear to be two assessment positions, the lowest position (instructional or curricular supervisor) and the assistant superintendency. The former is the first administrative position for many moving through these patterns. It represents a substantive break in job content, and as seen in Figure 11.1, has many paths leading from it, including a strong connection to an exit move. The second assessment position may be thought of as a testing ground for the superintendency. Poor performers from this position are not dismissed. Rather, they are "plateaued," or demoted (Path C). There are possibly two paths leading from the assistant superintendency to the superintendency, one between districts traveled by adequate performers and one within a single district traveled by superior performers.

THREE PATTERNS OF ADVANCEMENT

Instruction and Central-Office Administration

The route following Paths A, B, and D, begins with a position requiring the development of specialist's skills needed for the primary mission of a public school system, which is to educate the preadult population. This position is often but not always combined with teaching, and it involves supervision of the content of education, not the action of teaching. It is an assessment position from which people move in several directions. It is also the position from which people return to teaching most often (data not shown). This suggests that incumbency may be temporary by design, allowing "mismatches" to be remedied without the usual problems associated with demotion. This position may also be a plateau for some people. The effect parameter for stationariness in this position is the third highest in Table 11.3 ($Z = 19.558$, cell 9,9), indicating a strong tendency for people not to move out of the position. Additional evidence for the dual function postulated for this position derives from the characteristics of people who exit the system from this position (Path M). These people are significantly less educated and significantly older, they get paid significantly less and are significantly more likely to be females than are instructional or curricular supervisors as a whole. Those who move upward to administrator of instruction, by contrast, do not differ from their source group in any way save salary. Movers are paid more, on the average, than the source group as a whole.

The next position in the career pattern is that of administrator of instruction. This position is the first central office administrative position in the career path. The specialists at lower levels often combine their responsibilities for coordination or supervisory administration with classroom teaching. The administrator of instruction, however, is not involved with classroom teaching, but is solely occupied with administrative responsibilities. Thus, movement between the two positions often represents a complete break from teaching and a commitment to administration. This move also represents the largest difference in average salary between adjacent positions ($14,769 versus $18,741), further reflecting the qualitative difference in positions. The administrator of instruction position builds upon the training and experience generated in the lower-level supervisory position. It is the position that represents total removal from the activity of teaching, focusing instead on the development of administrative skills that will be valuable at higher levels in the organization.

As we look at those who move from administrator of instruction to assistant superintendent (Path B) we find that the only significant difference between movers and all position incumbents is salary, the movers making an average of $20,858. Interestingly, the movers have an average age of 42 while the average administrator of instruction is 45. Though this difference does not allow us to reject the null hypothesis that there are no differences in age ($t = -1.932$, 23 degrees of freedom, $.05 < p < .1$), the difference is suggestive of the age grading in career paths to which Becker and Strauss (1956) and others referred. That is, not only are career paths characterized by a sequence of positions through which persons move, they are also characterized by age gradings that constrain the range of possible moves open to incumbents such that career paths do not become "blocked." There is a similar tendency with respect to sex. The people who move from administrator of instruction to assistant superintendent are 95.8% male, while the pool from which those movers are drawn is but 80.2% male. This difference does not allow us to reject the null hypothesis of no difference, ($Z = 1.918$, $.05 < p < .1$), though it is consistent with the trend for higher-level positions to be predominantly male.

Hughes (1945) argued that persons with inappropriate "auxiliary" characteristics tend not to hold visible and central discretionary positions in organizations. Given the large number of women teachers in public school education it would be difficult to argue that women would be inappropriate curriculum supervisors or instructional supervisors. However, for positions that involve policymaking at higher levels (the domain of men across many populations), femaleness probably becomes an inappropriate auxiliary characteristic if for no other reason than that the people with whom the assistant superintendent interacts are much less likely to be classroom teachers and are more likely to be administrators and managers in many types of organizations, most of whom will be males. Thus we observe what appears to be a trend toward filtering in higher-level positions, or the tendency for these positions to become predominantly male.

Qualitatively the move from administrator of instruction to assistant superintendent represents another level of generalization and a broadening of skills. By now the person moving into the assistant's position has had experience (and presumably developed some expertise) in instructional administration. Movement into the assistant superintendency allows people to extend their range of competencies by dealing with a variety of administrative matters, often acting as the superintendent in his or her absence. We have identified two significant paths out of the assistant superintendent's position traveled by administrators, the path to the top position (Path D) and the demotion or lateral path to administrative specialist (Path C). People who travel the latter route are not significantly different from the average assistant superintendent in any respect, though there is some tendency for them to be older and less well paid. Compared to those who move via Path D to the superintendency, they are somewhat older, but otherwise not different from their more successful counterparts (average ages are 44 and 48, $t = 1.896$, *d.f.* $= 49$, $p = .06$).

As others have suggested (Goffman, 1952; McFarland, 1968) "plateauing" and demotion tend to be cloaked in ambiguity to make the move more acceptable to the person experiencing the status change. Thus, we would not expect to see large differences in salary when comparing upward movers to lateral or downward movers at this level in the hierarchy, though given more data we would expect to see a slower rate of increase in salary for the less successful administrator. It may also be argued that any filtering with respect to ascribed or "auxiliary" characteristics that may take place with movement through the career path has already taken place by the time persons reach the assistant superintendent's level (assistant superintendents are 96% male and 93.1% white); thus any differences between people following different routes at this level must be minor.

Up to this point, movement through this career pattern is almost exclusively intradistrict. Of the 80 moves represented by Paths A, B, and C, 76 (95%) are within predominantly large urban districts. However, 11 of the 34 moves from assistant superintendent to superintendent are between districts. This phenomenon suggests a possible difference between intra- and inter-district moves. Those who move between districts are likely to have moved to a smaller, less urban, less complex, poorer district where student achievement is lower (though the differences are not statistically significant); this suggests that larger districts may serve in a training capacity, keeping the best performers and sending moderately good performers to districts in which the superintendency may not be as demanding.

Finally, we consider the moves out of the superintendency. The people who leave the school system from the superintendency (Path H) are significantly older and less well paid than the average superintendent, suggesting retirement and/or poor performance; but there are no differences between those who leave the system and those who experience a lateral move or demotion to the assistant superintendent's position (Path I). Given the relatively high average age of persons traveling Path I (53), we cannot argue that this move is for broadening or training purposes. About 70% of these moves take place within relatively large but otherwise average districts, suggesting a terminal lateral move. The other 30% that involved interdistrict movement show no differences between the sending and the receiving districts, which further supports the argument that this is not a broadening or training move.

Secondary-School Supervision

The route to the top of school district administration through supervision of the instructional process in the school begins with the same position as did the first path, but the path is to secondary school assistant principal, then to secondary school principal, and from there to the superintendency. The lower-level moves of this career pattern are most likely to occur in large districts for reasons already stated. Interestingly the first path in this career is followed almost exclusively by highly educated young males, many of whom are nonwhite. Over 83% of those following Path E are males, and almost 40% are nonwhite. (The total sample is 79.6% male and 91.2% white.) Over 97% have a master's degree or better, while the sample proportion was 89.7%.

It would appear that this move provides the primary route into public administration for nonwhites, and though the receiving position is not nearly as nonwhite as the path into it (because of numerous white teachers moving directly into the assistant principal position), the position is still significantly more likely to be occupied by a nonwhite than we would expect. Given that this type of movement is most likely to occur in large urban school districts with a relatively large proportion of minority students, we would argue that this finding represents an attempt to match the race of the assistant principal with the race of the majority of students in the school.

The next move in this career path is from assistant secondary school principal to secondary school principal. As noted before, the assistant's position is disproportionately filled with nonwhites. It is also a very young and male position, much more than the previous position, and a relatively highly educated position, 91.9% of the incumbents having a master's degree or more. Compared to all assistant secondary principals, those who move from assistant to principal are more likely to be male, less likely to be white, and likely to make more money. Again, we see this path as the route of upward mobility for nonwhites and not as a route for women. The movers are similar to the pool of all assistant principals in age and education. This move is also most likely in large urban school districts.

Because of movement directly from teaching into the position of secondary principal in smaller districts, the position does not reflect the racial composition of those who have moved into it through the identified career path. The position is 94.6% white, significantly more white than the population of administrators. Similarly, the position is also almost entirely male (96.4%) and almost all incumbents have an advanced degree. The characteristics of the position incumbents are very similar to those of superintendents; thus, any filtering that might occur based on "auxiliary" characteristics has been accomplished at this point. Those who move into the superintendency from this position are not different from the pool as a whole. Though movement through the lower ranks is a very real possibility for nonwhites, the route to the very top all but excludes nonwhites.

The qualitative justification for this sequence of positions is easily understood. The secondary school principal's job involves many of the same tasks as the superintendent's. The principal often supervises curriculum, always supervises the teaching staff, must deal with parents and interested others, and usually plays a significant role in budgeting and budget management. Thus incumbency in the position is seen as adequate preparation for the superintendency, as the skills mastered in the principal's office are relevant for performance in the superintendent's office, particularly in smaller districts. When this type of move also involves a change in district (as was the case about 25% of the time), the sending districts tend to be larger and more complex than the receiving districts. In other words, the position of secondary school principal in large, complex school districts provides good training experiences for persons moving to the top position in smaller, less complex districts. When the move takes place within a district, it is also more likely to occur in small, rural, relatively poor districts, suggesting a specification by size of district in the type of experience deemed appropriate for incumbency in the highest-level position.

The Path through Elementary Schools

The career path that does not lead to the superintendency, at least not very directly, begins with the position of assistant principal in an elementary school and primarily moves to the position of elementary school principal (Path K), though there is some chance for persons to move from elementary school assistant principal to secondary school assistant principal (Path J). Elementary school principal represents the top position in the career pattern. There are no connections between this position and others in the school districts, but there is a very strong "connection" with an exit move. The most obvious fact about the incumbents of positions in this career path is that they are disproportionately likely to be women. Almost 44% of all elementary school assistant principals are women, and over 28% of all elementary school principals are women. (The entire sample is about 20% female.)

The exception to this trend, if it may be called an exception, is the proportion women in the third position, that of secondary school assistant principal. In many respects this position is not best thought of as "part" of the elementary education career path. Rather, it is more accurately characterized as the door through which a few persons travel from one career path to the others. The secondary school principal position is disproportionately male, and in this data set, movement into that position from the elementary school assistant principal position is entirely male, occurring within large urban districts. We also find a relatively large proportion of nonwhites in parts of this career pattern, not unlike in our previous results. Movement through the assistant elementary school principal position to the elementary school principal position is more likely to occur in large urban school districts, while movement directly from teaching into the principal position is most likely to occur in smaller, more rural districts—largely because the assistant position does not exist in smaller districts.

We have noted that the elementary school principal position is a terminal position in this short career path. This conclusion stems from the following conditions: (1) there are no significant connections leading out of this position to any other position in the system; (2) there is a very strong connection between this position and an exit move (the exit effect parameter = 4.568 from Table 11.3); and (3) this position shows more stationariness than any other position in the system (diagonal effect parameter = 27.130 from Table 11.3). The people who left the system from this position during the period of time studied were rather different from the average position incumbent. They were much more likely to be female (47.6% of the leavers were female, while only 28.2% of the position incumbents were female); they were less likely to have a master's degree (only 79.9% as compared with 88.6% of all elementary principals); they were considerably older on the average than their peers (54 versus 45); and they got paid significantly less. These groups, like those who left the system from the superintendency, are likely to be retiring from a rather lengthy career in public school education.

One might ask why we find such a strong separation between elementary school principal and the superintendency when we found such a strong connection between secondary school principal and the superintendency. There are several explanations for this observed difference: The task requirements of elementary school principals are not as complex; there are smaller numbers of students, parents, and staff members; and there is a less differentiated staff and a less complex curriculum to supervise. Moreover, as a large proportion of elementary school principals and teachers are female, one might speculate that this position does not connect to the top for reasons that have to do with factors not related to tasks, such as discrimination based on gender on the part of the position incumbents. Given what we do know about the task requirements of the two positions, it is certainly reasonable to assume that the position of elementary school principal does not prepare the incumbent for a promotion to superintendent nearly as well as the position of secondary school principal.

SUMMARY AND CONCLUSIONS

We have identified three different sets of positions within the administrative hierarchy that are connected to each other through a kind of pairing as measured by the flow of people between positions. These patterns contain many of the characteristics predicted, perhaps the most important of which is the assessment position. The data revealed two such positions, one at the entrance to the long career patterns and one near the top. Assessment positions do not necessarily provide for objective evaluation of the position incumbent. The more important characteristic of these positions is that they provide visibility for a variety of people. They can also fit into the notion of sponsorship in an administrative hierarchy. Position incumbents can become candidates for sponsorship by higher-level people based on performance and visibility in the position. Similarly, people being sponsored can be given access to assessment positions so that their sponsor can "show them off" or help them become familiar to those who at some point might have control over the fate of the protegé. These positions, critical factors in understanding the mobility process in organizations and in understanding access to opportunity, certainly require more study.

The mobility patterns identified also showed a filtering phenomenon with respect to race, sex, and educational attainment as hierarchical level increased, though the precise form of the phenomenon varied by pattern and characteristic. This stratification process parallels that found in the larger society. Though the data were not appropriate for studying the determinants of this stratification process, it is probably the case that the same kinds of mechanisms that operate in the larger social system also operate within the school districts. That is, the process is a combination of skill and ability differentials, differential opportunity structures for different classes of people, and different aspirations on the part of the individuals. Insofar as stratification and mobility in the larger system are in part defined by the combination of organizational stratification and mobility processes, it can be argued that changes in social stratification will be first observed in smaller-scale systems, such as work organizations, before they become apparent in society.

There are several "next steps" from this sort of research. First, characteristics of specific positions and people moving through them over some period of time need to be investigated further. This is especially true for assessment positions and plateau positions. Assessment positions theoretically control movement through career paths, so the opportunity structure around those positions would seem to be a critical factor in understanding promotability and career development for individuals within any administrative hierarchy. Plateau positions, and their incumbents, represent perhaps the greatest challenge for those concerned with personnel policy and administration. Plateau positions are often filled with people who are deemed to be beyond further growth and development, people who may have peaked or begun a decline in terms of competency or who for some reason are no longer motivated to perform well. Plateau positions often reinforce these problems. They are often sterile, routine, "no-growth" positions. These position incumbents are usually within 10 to 15 years of retirement, have often put in many good years with the organization, and are people toward whom the organization may feel some loyalty. The challenge for organizations is to continue to provide a structure within which these people can perform well and grow and develop in ways that may be different from those avenues pursued in the past but nevertheless valuable for both the organization and the individual. The process of "plateauing," while necessary, can be very dysfunctional. The challenge for organizations is to make this process less dysfunctional for all concerned.

Another set of next steps for this research is one that views these findings as establishing a context within which understanding of individual development needs and mobility patterns can be developed. The usual study of careers in organizations centers around *individual* issues and variables, not structures. This research is pioneering in the sense that it takes seriously the establishment of an understanding of structures, and it therefore provides a more well-defined context within which the more traditional issues of career development can be explored. This research has demonstrated that patterns of interposition mobility in an entire administrative hierarchy can be identified empirically from a relatively constrained set of job histories. Certainly a comparison between the identified career patterns and a sample of longer job histories is necessary in order to lend validity to the findings, particularly with respect to the context within which positions are more or less closely connected. Some evidence (Carlson, 1961) suggests that mobility connected with a change in superintendents is not as regularized as mobility without a superintendency change. When a new superintendent is appointed, particularly from outside the district, an increase in the observed rate of movement between administrative positions is likely to occur, as is an increase in the number of high-level administrators. This is usually attributed to the need for superintendents to "clean-out" the old guard and establish their own administration. Thus a study of changes in mobility patterns in the presence of a change in the superintendency is another important next step in this research.

Despite the constraints imposed by the data, this type of analysis is valuable for understanding the mobility and stratification processes in administrative hierarchies. Knowing what positions have "trained" current position incumbents can help administrators understand the strengths and weaknesses of others with whom they work. Planning for future mobility and the evaluation of lower-level administrators for future positions can also be facilitated with this knowledge.

REFERENCES

Becker, H. S., and Strauss, A. (1956). "Careers, Personality, and Adult Socialization." *American Journal of Sociology*, 62: 253–263.
Brown, D. J. (1972). *Organizational Mobility of Educational Administrators*. Unpublished doctoral dissertation, University of Chicago.

Carlson, R. O. (1961). "Succession and Performance among School Superintendents." *Administrative Science Quarterly*, 6: 210–227.

Clements, R. V. (1958). *Managers: A Study of Their Careers in Industry.* Allen and Unwin, London.

Dalton, M. (1959). *Men Who Manage.* Wiley, New York.

Davis, J. A. (1972). *The Goodman Log-Linear System for Assessing Effects in Multivariate Contingency Tables.* National Opinion Research Center Lithograph, Chicago.

Friedman, A. (1969). *The Leaders of National and International Labor Unions.* Unpublished doctoral dissertation, University of Chicago.

Gillespie, J. F., Leininger, W. E., and Kahalas, H. (1976). "A Human Resource Planning and Valuation Model." *Academy of Management Journal*, 19: 650–656.

Glaser, B. G. (1968). *Organizational Careers.* Aldine, Chicago.

Goffman, E. (1952). "On Cooling the Mark Out: Some Aspects of Adaptation to Failure." *Psychiatry.* 15: 451–463.

Goodman, L. A. (1970). "The Multivariate Analysis of Qualitative Data: Interactions among Multiple Classifications." *Journal of the American Statistical Association*, 65: 226–256.

Goodman, L. A. (1971). The Analysis of Multidimensional Contingency Tables: Stepwise Procedures and Direct Estimation Methods for Building Models for Multiple Classifications. *Technometrics*, 13: 33–61.

Goodman, L. A. (1972a). "A Modified Multiple Regression Approach to the Analysis of Dichotomous Variables." *American Sociological Review*, 37: 28–46.

Goodman, L. A. (1972b). "A General Model for the Analysis of Surveys." *American Journal of Sociology*, 77: 1035–1086.

Hughes, E. C. (1945). "Dilemmas and Contradictions of Status." *American Journal of Sociology*, 50: 353–359.

Janowitz, M. (1960). *The Professional Soldier.* Free Press, New York.

Levenson, B. (1961). "Bureaucratic Succession." In *Complex Organizations: A Sociological Reader* (A. Etzioni, ed.). Holt, Rinehart and Winston, New York, pp. 362–375.

March, J. C., and March, J. G. (1977). "Almost Random Careers: The Wisconsin School Superintendency, 1940–1972." *Administrative Science Quarterly*, 22: 377–409.

Martin, N. H., and Strauss, A. L. (1959). "Patterns of Mobility within Industrial Organization." In *Industrial Man* (W. L. Warner and N. H. Martin, eds.). Harper & Row, New York, pp. 85–101.

McFarland, D. E. (1968). *Personnel Management: Theory and Practice.* Macmillan, New York.

Meader, H. D. (1970). "Evolution of Career Paths." In *Manpower and Planning,* Industrial Relations Monograph 31. Industrial Relations Counselors, Inc., New York.

Reynolds, H. T. (1977). "Some Comments on the Causal Analysis of Surveys with Log-Linear Models." *American Journal of Sociology*, 83: 127–143.

Sofer, C. (1970). *Men in Mid-Career.* Cambridge University Press, New York.

Thompson, J. D. (1967). *Organizations in Action.* McGraw-Hill, New York.

Van Riper, P. P., and Unwalla, D. B. (1965). "Military Careers at the Executive Level." *Administrative Science Quarterly*, 9: 421–436.

Vetter, E. W. (1967). *Manpower Planning for High Talent Personnel.* Bureau of Industrial Relations, Graduate School of Business Administration, University of Michigan, Ann Arbor, chaps. 2, 3, 4.

Vroom, V. H., and MacCrimmon, K. R. (1968). "Toward a Stochastic Model of Managerial Careers." *Administrative Science Quarterly*, 13: 26–46.

White, H. C. (1969). "Control and Evolution of Aggregate Personnel: Flows of Men and Jobs." Administrative Science Quarterly, 14: 4–11.

PART IV

SCHOOL ORGANIZATION

Chapter 12

THE SEX DIMENSION OF SCHOOL ORGANIZATION: OVERVIEW AND SYNTHESIS

Patricia A. Schmuck

In the United States during the nineteenth century, in the days of schoolmasters, some educators argued that women would make better school teachers than men because they were purer and had milder manners and would set a better example for children (Woody, 1929). It was also argued that schools would become more efficient because women could take directives better than men. Besides all this, there was an economic advantage: women were paid lower wages than men. In spite of the inevitable opposition to such ideas, the feminization of the teaching force became a reality. In addition, from that time through the early part of the twentieth century, many women became principals of elementary schools. Arguments in favor and opposed to women as school teachers were based on a belief in intrinsic sexual characteristics. Ideas related to how the presence of females would somehow change the nature of the classroom and the school were not well explicated, but that was understandable; at the time, ideas about behavior and organizations were not complex.

Since then, social scientists and educational researchers have become more sophisticated, and ideas about behavior in social contexts have found their way into college classrooms. Training now includes an understanding of the complex social psychology of behavior. As life became more centered in organizations during the twentieth century,

221

more researchers attended to the dynamics of small groups and to the impact of organizations on behavior. Despite the increasing sophistication of knowledge about behavior, however, theory and research about the sex variable in educational institutions remained undeveloped. The presence or absence of female leadership in education was no more understood than it had been in the nineteenth century. Women participants in education were ignored in studies of educational administration, and no one questioned how an organization that was segregated and stratified by sex would influence participants' behavior. The fact that women were ignored as educational practitioners is understandable. Most of the research on schools concentrated on the roles of educational leaders, and they were primarily men. While most of this research was being conducted, the number of women among elementary school principals was diminishing. The few women in these roles were excluded from research samples, and the data aggregated so that sexual distinctions were not made.

Only during the last decade has attention been devoted to the statistical variable of sex. Perhaps one of the strongest accusations of the scholars who attacked the motives of the research community was made by Weisskopf. She said, "The natural and social sciences have out of self-interest, hubris, and ignorance, participated in the systematic oppression of women" (1978, p. 267). Others have shown how the experiences of women have been distorted or misrepresented in the reporting of research (Weskott, 1980); some have illustrated how previous research conclusions must be reinterpreted in the light of our knowledge about the sexual segregation and stratification in organizations (Acker & Van Houton, 1974). A thorough accounting of school organizations was provided by Lortie in *Schoolteacher* (1975). He pointed out that placement by sex in the educational work force is based on socially accepted sexual stereotypes that differentiate between a woman's place and a man's place, but he treated sex stereotypes as cultural givens rather than as manipulable variables. While he explained how sexual factors influence recruitment, socialization, and the allocation of rewards, he did not question or attempt to answer why this should be the case.

This chapter synthesizes past research and describes the contributions of the other chapters in Part IV. The authors in subsequent chapters provide examples of how to correct previous research problems. This chapter discusses differences between male and female educational leaders and the influence of organizational structures on participants' behavior. It concludes with suggestions for future research in these two areas.

COMPARISONS BETWEEN MALE AND FEMALE
EDUCATIONAL LEADERS

Researchers with a psychological perspective have tried to explain the behavior of educational leaders by investigating the relationship of psychological variables to the performance of administrators. Early theories about traits attempted to isolate demographic or personality characteristics that would predict successful educational leaders. Research oriented more toward social psychology focused on the interaction of superordinates and subordinates (leaders and followers) rather than on the traits of leaders, taking into account the complex relationships that can occur. Most of these interactional studies were conducted within schools and concentrated on relationships between principals and teachers (Gross & Herriott, 1965).

Two important publications in the 1970s directed attention to the sex variable in the performance of administrators—a review by Meskin (1974) of five studies comparing male and female elementary school principals and the first significant text on sexual differences in educational leadership, *The Sex Factor and the Management of Schools* by Gross and Trask (1976). The textbook was based on data from questionnaires and interviews concerning the leadership and performance of male and female principals in 189 elementary schools located in cities with populations exceeding 50,000. (The original study included all levels, but only in the elementary schools were there enough female principals to allow a comparison.) According to the authors, their study was a response to the criticism that "most studies of organizations have ignored the fact that their members have a gender" (p. 225). Although their study had been completed and published earlier (in *Staff Leadership in the Public Schools,* Gross & Herriot, 1965), their study on the sex factor remained only a technical report in the United States Office of Education for over a decade. The 1976 text was primarily a response to demands for such information from people in "public education, university, and government circles and in the women's movement for equal rights"; it was a timely and important contribution and a bench mark for other studies.

Three chapters in Part IV follow the example of Gross and Trask and compare women and men in positions of leadership in education. Gilbertson's chapter reports on her careful observations of teachers' interactions with two male and two female elementary school principals. In the chapter by Charters and Jovick, their study of the relationships between elementary school principals and teachers uses various instruments in 29 schools. The chapter by Pitner reports on observations of three female superintendents and compares this research with her earlier research on three male superintendents (Pitner, 1979). The prevalent conclusion in these studies of sex-related differences in the behavior of organizational leaders is that gender, like most of the demographic variables and personality characteristics that have been investigated, is not a basis for predictions or for powerful explanations of performance. Charters and Jovick write, "It is not hard to imagine a multiplicity of factors, both personalistic and situational, that shape a manager's style, and if the sex plays any part at all, its effects are overwhelmed by other determinants."

These conclusions are consistent with the findings of Maccoby and Jacklin (1974) who analyzed over 1600 studies on the subject and concluded that sex appears to be correlated with behavior only on measures of visual–spatial ability and aggression. The research findings are ambiguous at best about important personality characteristics such as dependency, timidity, anxiety, competitiveness, dominance, nurturance, and fear; they do not support the hypothesis that sex is a useful predictor for individual behavior. In a comprehensive review of the literature on leadership, Stodgill (1974) also concluded that demographic and personality variables do not predict differences in leadership behavior, and the chapters in Part IV support his conclusion. However, although the sex of the educational leaders does not appear to be related to differences in their behavior as administrators and although various findings show that biological sex alone does not significantly influence such behavior, it does appear that the social and political implications surrounding the variable of sex are important in how leaders carry out their defined functions. Consistent and perplexing findings indicate male and female differences in the interaction of administrators with others. Two such findings are discussed in the next two sections. The first is that among elementary school principals, females tend to have more influence with their teachers than males have. The second is Pitner's finding that in spite of the apparent lack of differences between the behavior of male and female superintendents, differences exist in the ways they carry out their roles in relation to the community. Related to this is the finding that superintendents tend to communicate more with members of the community who are the same sex as themselves.

Influence

Two arguments lead to the prediction that women will have less ability than men to influence others. One theory (Unger, 1978) posits that being male in a male-dominated society carries more status, and thus males have more potential for being influential in personal relations. The other (Johnson, 1976) argues that because of the stereotypes of society regarding sexual roles, women are expected to exert influence in indirect ways, for example, by manipulation and cajoling, whereas men are expected to exert power directly, for example, by persuading and commanding. According to this argument, females are socialized to influence in indirect ways, and men in direct ways. (For a full review of the literature on power, see Denmark, Tangri, & McCandless, 1978.) Because of their lower female status and because of the way they have been socialized, we would expect female elementary school principals to have less influence over their teachers than their male counterparts have; but empirical data show just the reverse.

The studies presented in the chapters in Part IV, along with research by Gross and Trask, indicate that as seen by teachers, elementary school principals who were female appeared to have more power than those who were male in the extent to which they influenced school affairs, for example, in determining grading standards and establishing regulations. This was true even when the effects of school size were removed (see the chapter by Charters & Jovick). Along with these views of teachers, the studies also reveal that the female principals themselves thought they exerted more supervisory control over teachers than did their male counterparts; and their relationships with teachers were seen to be even stronger when femaleness was combined with more years of experience in the elementary school. In addition, they more often expected that there would be conformity to their educational standards by teachers in the classroom and that they would be informed about teacher–parent communications, findings supported by Koboyashi (1974).

The point of reporting such perplexing findings is to illustrate the difficulty of studying gender as an independent variable; since it most likely interacts with other variables to produce complex results and is less likely to manifest clear-cut major effects, it can only be studied as one of several factors that may account for administrators' behavior. Differences in the ability to be influential remain intriguing and raise certain questions. Are women who have survived sexually biased hiring practices more competent than their male counterparts? Are women who achieve leadership positions in education more motivated to acquire and wield power than comparable men are? Does the world of the elementary school with its all-female teachers create one set of dynamics when the principal is female and a different set when the principal is male? Would we see the same picture in a high school, where most of the teachers are male? The answers are not clear, but the findings regarding females' greater ability to influence teachers in the elementary school are worth pursuing.

Role Performance

Pitner's chapter comparing three male and three female superintendents supports the general finding that gender is not significantly correlated to differences in administrators' behavior. She found that all superintendents, regardless of sex, had to supervise schools, provide leadership, engage in activities to promote public support of the schools, communicate with the press, and meet with a variety of people. Nevertheless, one interesting finding showed that male superintendents tended to communicate more with male groups, such as the Elks, the Rotary, and the Lions Clubs, and female superintendents more with female groups, such as the predominantly female Parent–Teacher Association (PTA). Many questions arise with regard to this finding. Is this a pattern in school districts beyond the six documented by Pitner? Does it have implications for school operations? For passing budgets? For the level of community support? Superintendents link the school and the community, an important function, and this study raises the question of how their sex may make a difference in their performance in the area of community relations.

THE INFLUENCE OF ORGANIZATIONS ON INDIVIDUALS

In examining how the structure of organizations influences the behavior of people within them, attention is focused on (1) the segregation of men and women into different positions and (2) the status hierarchy whereby positions are arrayed.

Power and Opportunity

Although no study of power and opportunity has been conducted within educational organizations, two studies are worthy of note. Acker and Van Houton (1974) reexamined the findings of earlier organizational studies and criticized these studies for ignoring the fact that superordinates (bosses) were males while subordinates (workers) were females. They suggested that predictable differences in power, the giving and taking of orders, were multiplied as a result:

> Sex structuring in organizations . . . consists of differentiation of female and male jobs, a hierarchical ordering of those jobs so that males are higher than females and are not expected to take orders from females. As a result, males generally have more power in organizations than females; we call this the sex power differential. . . . It may be that sex power differentials have a more profound effect in some cases than [do other] organizational variables [pp. 152, 163].

They went on to explain that the processes of decision making, socialization, and control in organizations cannot be adequately understood without accounting for the relative positions of women and men in an organization's hierarchies.

Another noteworthy investigation was carried out by Kanter (1977). In her documentation of the impact of sex in the organizational hierarchy of the INDSCO corporation, she pointed out that position was a powerful determinant of behavior and that segregation put women into positions with fewer opportunities and less power, reserving positions with more opportunities and more power for men. This was confirmed by interviews with 25 female presidents and vice presidents of nationally recognized firms as reported by Hennig and Jardim (1977). Kanter found in another study (1976) that "bosses get bitchy" regardless of their sex when they occupy positions that are relatively restricted as to power and opportunity. Her overall conclusion was that behavioral responses are "set in motion by the way large hierarchical organizations are structured" (1976, p. 163), and she argued that the work place should be restructured so that women and men are equally represented in positions that provide for power and opportunities.

Women who occupy such positions are in the minority. They remain as "tokens" and are treated differently from the way men in comparable positions are treated. Miller, Labovitz, and Fry (1978) found that women in high-status positions received fewer communications, had less influence over peers and subordinates, and were generally more isolated than their male counterparts. Hagen and Kahn (1975) found that such women suffered unpleasant consequences for demonstrating their competence more often than men did. Fennell and her colleagues at the Center for Research on Women used the concept of legitimation to explain behavioral difference in small groups and to derive implications for larger organizations (1978). They argued that woman fail to succeed in leadership positions not because they are incompetent, but because their authority is not supported by their male colleagues and because their subordinates are more likely to accept instructions from men. Finigan (1979) looked at groups in which one sex or the other was the numerical minority and found that members of the minority contributed less while the majority dominated the group. Clearly, the sexual composition of groups contributes to observed differences between women's and men's behavior in organizations.

The Concept of Opportunity and Power in School Organizations

Kanter (1977) argued that the structure of hierarchical opportunities discriminates between men and women. Although getting in and getting ahead are challenges for all educational administrators, the evidence shows that males have greater access to coveted positions (Schmuck, 1976, 1981; Stockard, 1981). In the past women had opportunities to become elementary school principals; but the declining numbers of women in this position suggest that these opportunities have also become more limited. One explanation for the underrepresentation of women as school administrators involves men's propensity to "protect" women. Because the work is thought to be "easier," female elementary school principals are more often assigned to smaller schools in communities with higher socioeconomic status (Pharis & Zakariya, 1979). Even in staff positions when men and women have similar jobs, women are protected from the "tough" tasks. As one woman reported: "I had to prepare a report for the school board meeting, and a man presented the report. I [had] told him that I would do it because we all knew a lot of flack would come out of it. But he did it and got all the flack we knew would come. Protection is nice, but on the other hand. . ." (Schmuck, 1976, p. 99).

While protection may arise from altruistic motives, it nevertheless perpetuates unequal opportunities for those seeking entrance and promotions in educational administration. Stockard and Johnson, in their chapter in Part IV, explain how protection is a bind for women, and they trace its probable causes to certain male motivations and the institutional arrangements that reinforce them. Specifically, males are shown to be unsure of their identity and of the "appropriate way to behave." They feel constrained to set themselves apart from women and to devalue what women do because they have greater problems than females in developing their sexual identity during their early associations with the female caretaker, the mother. By placing women in "easy" situations men actually protect themselves from being confronted by evidence that women can do "tough" jobs. All of this serves to perpetuate inequality (see also Stockard & Johnson, 1979).

In another chapter, Wheatley points out that while the opportunities in schools are characterized as "the chance to grow better at one's craft, to become an expert, and to gain status and recognition for that," women have few opportunities because of the bind of protection, and thus the negative female stereotypes are reinforced. That is, women are characterized by male administrators as unable to handle tough situations, too emotional, unable to be decisive, and unable to see the total picture because they do not have the opportunity to display behavior showing that they do not need protection. Data from Gilbertson in one chapter and from Charter and Jovick in another provide an example of such differences in opportunities to become administrators. The fact that elementary school principals, regardless of sex, interacted more with male teachers than with female teachers regarding the functioning of schools suggests the existence of a "grooming process" in which male teachers have a greater opportunity than female teachers have to grapple with larger school issues. Wheatley characterizes such differentiated interaction as an opportunity shortage for women. She distinguishes between people who are "moving" and those who are "stuck."

In the studies reported here, male teachers are more involved than female teachers in discussions about organizational problems in the school, and consequently, male teachers gain more experience regarding administrative concerns. This may illustrate how the belief arises that men have more influence by virtue of their being male; that is, how principals, regardless of their sex, come to believe that male teachers have more influence than female teachers have. Although sexual discrimination in preparation for administrative work has been discussed as one of the barriers facing women's entrance into administration (Schmuck, 1981), there has been little substantive data to demonstrate the subtle, sexually based interactions between those beginning an administrative career and those in a position to assist them. We need to understand these better.

SUGGESTIONS FOR FUTURE RESEARCH

Shakeshaft, in the first chapter in this book, suggests eight different areas for future research on sexual differentiation in educational administration. Regarding the effects of a sexually segregated and stratified institution on the behavior of participants, Shakeshaft writes, "Women's relationships to organizational structure are still unknown. Questions of how women administer under certain organizational structures, how women function in various organizational modes, and the relationship of the organization to the positions women hold all need answering." The following pages elaborate on Shakeshaft's idea and also present suggestions for future research in the two areas already discussed— comparisons between male and female leaders and the social and sexual context.

Research on Comparisons of Male and Female Leaders

All the chapters in Part IV treat men and women as if they differed only by virtue of their biology. Sherman and Denmark (1978) and Unger (1978) have pointed out the confusion between the variable of biological sex, which means persons composed of XX chromosomes or XY chromosomes, and sex role, or gender, which means the social roles associated with XX persons and XY persons. An example of work conducted in regard to sex-role orientation is that of Bem (1978). From controlled laboratory experiments using a self-assessment checklist consisting of adjectives based on stereotypes of masculine and feminine traits, Bem observed behavioral differences among persons receiving different scores on "masculine" and "feminine" dimensions. (For other measures of sex-role orientation, see Spence & Helmreich, 1979, and the special issues of *Sex Roles: A Journal of Research*, December, 1979, which is devoted to such instruments and measurement problems.) In particular, Bem's findings highlight differences between androgynous individuals (those who score above the mean on both dimensions), individuals oriented toward the same sex ("masculine" males and "feminine" females), and individuals oriented toward the other sex ("feminine" males and "masculine" females).

The findings indicate that a variable of sex-role orientation may obtain a more fruitful line of inquiry than does a biological variable. Bem showed that androgynous subjects displayed a high level of independence and nurturance and that such males and females looked very much alike. A variety of behaviors were available to them, and they were able to be both tough and tender. In addition, the findings showed that males behaved as expected when distinguished by their sex orientation:

> Consider first the androgynous male. He performs spectacularly. He shuns no behavior just because our culture happens to label it as female, and his competence crosses both the instrumental and the expressive domains. Thus, he stands firm with his opinion, he cuddles kittens and bounces babies, and he has a sympathetic ear for someone in distress. . . . In contrast, the feminine male is low in the instrumental domain and the masculine male is low in the expressive domain (Bem, 1978, p. 77).

Perhaps most significantly, the behavior of women did not conform to the predictions made based on their sexual orientation. Masculine females, on the one hand, were virtually indistinguishable from androgynous individuals; they exhibited both instrumentally independent and expressively nurturant behaviors. Feminine females, on the other hand, exhibited neither instrumental nor expressive behaviors; they seemed to be the most restricted people in all categories.

Measures of sex-role orientation have not been applied to school settings. Moreover, such scales are fraught with measurement problems that complicate analysis (Silvern & Ryan, 1979). However, the point here is that findings about sex-role orientations have involved the social definitions of maleness and femaleness, and this has complicated the issue that was previously treated as the simple problem of sorting individuals according to their biology. Consider Bem's research in light of the findings about the greater influence of female elementary school principals as compared with the influence of their male counterparts. Such women would perhaps be classified as androgynous or as masculine females (high in independence and high in nurturance). According to Bem's findings, we would not expect to see feminine females in leadership roles. Predictions concerning the sex-role orientation of male elementary school principals are less certain. One might expect that a male working with young children and primarily female teachers would be androgynous (high in independence and nurturance) or would be a feminine male (low in independence and high in nurturance).

Studies of elementary school principals may be comparing women who are androgynous or masculine to men who are androgynous, feminine, or perhaps masculine. While biology may not distinguish differences in performance, perhaps one's accomodation to a socially defined sex-role does. There is impressive evidence to suggest that biological sex alone is not correlated with differences in administrative performance. This is not to say, however, that we should ignore the sexual dimension as a research variable. We need to expand our view to move from a focus on biology and focus more on the social meaning of maleness and femaleness in educational leadership settings.

Research on the Social and Sexual Context

Leadership is an interactional process between superordinates and subordinates. Leadership, from this point of view, involves more than investigating the behavior of leaders; it also involves looking at the behavior and expectations of those being led. Evidence has already been presented that women who have achieved high-status positions in male-dominated institutions are not treated in the same way as their male colleagues are treated. Presumably, this is the case because the way women behave in these situations is contrary to social expectations. Studies of elementary school female principals do not back up the research assertions that women have less power, influence, and communication with their subordinates than their male colleagues have, and perhaps this is because the context of the elementary school is primarily female. Women leaders in educational situations where there are primarily male subordinates have not often been subjects for study.

Questions abound: How do women leaders fare in contexts that are primarily male? Pitner showed little difference between the administrative behavior of male and female superintendents except for the tendency to relate to community groups that were the same sex as themselves, but she observed leaders' behavior, not the behavior of subordinates. Finigans' research on small groups indicated that the sex ratio of the group influences the behavior of the minorities; minority members did not assume leadership over majority members. What happens to women who are a minority in a superintendent's cabinet? Fennell's work on legitimation suggests that subordinates are less likely to accept directions from a female than from a male and that the male-dominated authority structure is less likely to back up the authority of a female. While this does not appear to be true in the elementary school, we need to expand our research to other and primarily male educational contexts, such as those of the high school and of district offices. Do women high school principals get the backing of the central office and of their teachers just as men high school principals do? Professor Higgins, of *Pygmalion* fame, asked the question, "Why can't a woman be more like a man?" The answer is, because while some women behave like some men behave, in a society with sex-prescribed roles, women are still treated differently.

Schools provide a unique setting in which to study the meaning of maleness and femaleness in our society. Schools remain relatively simple organizational structures compared to those of business and industry. Schools also serve equal numbers of males and females in the society. In addition, schools have the historical distinction of being one of the few professions available to women. I strongly urge continued applications of new perspectives that account for the sexual dimension in educational research. There are many things we do not know. We need clearly explicated hypotheses about the roles of men and women in the society, and we need to test these hypotheses in carefully devised research. Research should not be used, as it has been used in the past, to buttress and fortify arguments about the appropriate place of women and men.

The purpose of educational research should be to raise questions that have not been asked before.

ACKNOWLEDGMENT

I appreciate the assistance of Jane Arends, Chris Keys, and Richard Schmuck, all of whom made helpful comments on an earlier draft of this chapter.

REFERENCES

Acker, J., and Van Houton, D. (1974). "Differential Recruitment and Control: The Sex Structuring of Organizations." *Administrative Science Quarterly*, 19:152–162.

Bem, Sandra. (1978). "Beyond Androgyny: Some Presumptuous Prescriptions for a Liberated Sexual Identity." In *The Psychology of Women: Future Directions in Research* (J. Sherman and F. Denmark, eds.) Psychological Dimensions, Inc., New York.

Denmark, F., Tangri, S. S., and McCandless, S. (1978). "Affiliation, Achievement, and Power: A New Look." In *The Psychology of Women: Future Directions in Research* (J. Sherman and F. Denmark, eds.). Psychological Dimensions, Inc., New York.

Fennell, M. L., Barchas, P., Cohen, E., McMahon, A., and Hildebrand, P. (1978). "An Alternative Perspective on Sex Differences in Organizational Settings: The Process of Legitimation." *Sex Roles*, 4(4): 589–604.

Finigan, M. (1979). *The Influence of Sex Ratio on Group Processes in Small Professional Work Groups*. Unpublished doctoral dissertation, University of Oregon.

Gross, N., and Herriot, R. (1965). *Staff Leadership in Public Schools*. Wiley, New York.

Gross, N., and Trask, A. (1976). *The Sex Factor and the Management of Schools*. Wiley, New York.

Hagan, R., and Kahn, A. (1975). "Discrimination against Competent Women." *Journal of Applied Social Psychology*, pp. 362–376.

Hennig, M., and Jardim, A. (1977). *The Managerial Woman*. Anchor Press, New York.

Johnson, P. (1976). "Women and Power: Toward a Theory of Effectiveness." *The Journal of Social Issues*, 32 (3): 99–110.

Kanter, R. M. (1976). "Why Bosses Get Bitchy." *Psychology Today*, 9: 56–59.

Kanter, R. M. (1977). *Men and Women of the Corporation*. Basic Books, New York.

Koboyashi, K. A. (1974). *Comparison of Organizational Climate of Schools Administered by Female and Male Elementary Principals*. Unpublished doctoral dissertation, University of the Pacific, Stockton, California Dissertation Abstracts, 35, pp. 129–130A.

Lortie, D. (1975). *Schoolteacher*. University of Chicago Press.

Maccoby, E., and Jacklin, C. (1974). *The Psychology of Sex Differences*. Stanford University Press, Calif.

Meskin, J. (1974). "The Performance of Women School Administrators—A Review of the Literature." *Administrator's Notebook*, 23: 1.

Miller, J., Labovitz, S., and Fry, L. (1978). "Inequities in the Organizational Experiences of Women and Men." *Social Forces*, 54:365–381.

Pharis, W., and Zakariya, S. B. (1979). *The Elementary Principalship in 1978: A Research Study*. National Association of Elementary School Principals, Arlington, Va.

Pitner, N. J. (1979). *So Go the Days of Their Lives: A Descriptive Study of the Superintendency.* Oregon School Study Council, University of Oregon.

Schmuck, P. (1976). *Sex Differentiation in Public School Administration.* National Council of Administrative Women in Education, Arlington, Va.

Schmuck, P. (1981). *Sex Equity in Educational Leadership: The Oregon Story.* Education Development Center, Newton, Mass.

Sherman, J., and Denmark, F., eds. (1978). *The Psychology of Women: Future Directions in Research.* Psychology Dimension, Inc., New York.

Silvern, L., and Ryan, V. (1979). "Self-Rated Adjustment and Sex-Typing on the Bem Sex-Role Inventory: Is Masculinity the Primary Predictor of Adjustment?" *Sex Roles: A Journal of Research,* December.

Spence, J., and Helmreich, R. (1979). "On Assessing 'Androgyny'." *Sex Roles,* 5(6):721–738.

Stockard, J. (1981). *Sex Equity in Educational Leadership: An Analysis of a Planned Social Change Project.* Education Development Center, Newton, Mass.

Stockard, J., and Johnson, M. (1979). "The Social Origins of Male Dominance." *Sex Roles: A Journal of Research,* 5(2): 119–218.

Stodgill, R. (1974). *Handbook of Leadership: A Survey of Theory and Research.* Free Press, New York.

Unger, R. K. (1978). "The Politics of Gender: A Review of Relevant Literature." In *The Psychology of Women: Future Directions in Research* (J. Sherman and F. Denmark, eds.) Psychology Dimensions, Inc., New York.

Weskott, M. (1979). "Feminist Criticism of the Social Sciences." *Harvard Educational Review,* 49(1):422–430.

Weisskopf, S. (1978). "Sexism, Inequality, and Education." *Harvard Educational Review,* 48(2):267–278.

Williams, K., Parks, B., and Finley, C. J. (1977). *Measures of Educational Equity for Women: A Research Monograph.* American Institute for Research, Palo Alto, Calif.

Woody, T. (1929). *A History of Women's Education in the United States.* The Science Press, New York.

Chapter 13

THE SOURCES AND DYNAMICS OF SEXUAL INEQUALITY IN THE PROFESSION OF EDUCATION

Jean Stockard and Miriam Johnson

Our analysis of sexual inequality in the profession of education is set in the broader context of sexual inequality as a worldwide phenomenon. Those who contend that male dominance is a universal cultural phenomenon usually base their argument on the biological differences between men and women, and they tend to conclude that this state of affairs is thus inevitable. While we do not discount the influence of biology, we see male dominance essentially as a social phenomenon, and we believe that although it is ubiquitous, it is not inevitable.

Male dominance is deeply embedded both in social institutions and in individuals' psyches, and understanding why this is so can help us guard against being overly optimistic about ending sexual inequality and discrimination by legal prohibitions alone. Understanding why male dominance runs so deep also alerts us to the possibility of its reappearance under a new guise after measures to remove certain inequities have supposedly been successful.

In previous writings we documented the existence of male dominance, and we explored its tendency to be perpetuated in the motivational systems of individuals and in institutional arrangements and everyday decisions and interactions (Stockard & Johnson, 1979, 1980; Stockard *et al.*, 1976). In this chapter we apply this analysis specifically to sexual segregation and sexual stratification in the profession of education. After documenting the existence of cross-cultural sexual stratification and its occurrence in the United States today, we briefly

235

outline the mutually reinforcing factors that tend to perpetuate it. With this background we describe how these factors operate, specifically with regard to sexual inequality in the education profession. Finally, we discuss the implications of this analysis for social change.

AN OVERVIEW OF MALE DOMINANCE

Although varying in the degree of emphasis placed on sexual differences, all societies have had a sex-based division of labor. This sexual division of labor undoubtedly was promoted by differing biological contributions to reproduction by men and women, and especially women's ability to bear children and lactate. In no society has childcare been the primary responsibility of men, and conversely, warfare and hunting have never been the primary responsibility of women. Perhaps this latter fact is related to the superior strength of men; the notion that hunting and warfare are difficult for nursing mothers; or the likelihood that males are reproductively more expendable than females. However, beyond the assignment of hunting and warfare to men and childcare to women, societies have varied remarkably in the roles they have considered appropriate for men and those seen as appropriate for women. In some societies women carry the heavy loads, while in others men do. In some societies men grow one type of potato and women another, while still yet in other societies, women do the trading and men are the dancers. This variability suggests that the sex-based division of labor cannot be explained by biological factors alone.

However, more important for us is the fact that the social roles that have been assigned to men and women not only are different, but also they are differentially evaluated and rewarded. In all societies the activities and positions that are considered to be the most important, that are accorded the highest prestige in that society, tend to be defined as especially (if not exclusively) appropriate for men. Moreover, in all societies positions of highest authority, such as membership in the tribal council or important religious groups, tend to be the special province of men. This is not to say that women cannot or do not exercise power, but that they usually do so individually and/or informally. Women as a group are not accorded formal authority greater than that of men. It is these phenomena to which we refer when we use the term "male dominance"—the cultural disposition to accord formal authority and prestige to males.

For something like 99% of human history, people lived in hunting and gathering societies, where labor was divided on a sexual basis, women doing the gathering and men the hunting. Probably through the elaboration of women's gathering activities, horticulture developed; and with the domestication of animals and the invention of the plow, societies based on agriculture came into being. With each technological advance, societies became more complex; and within each stage of development a division of labor persisted where the activities that were considered most important were assigned to males. With the advent of industrialization, the division of labor became far more complex, and many more jobs developed. In contrast to the situation in less advanced societies, however, the vast majority of the jobs created by industrial and postindustrial societies do not depend on any sexually differentiated biological capacity, such as strength and reproductive capabilities. In addition, most industrialized nations, both capitalist and socialist, have written the principle of equal opportunity into law.

In the United States, equal opportunity to obtain jobs may not be denied on the basis of race, color, creed, or sex. In other words, status is to be achieved, not ascribed, and we like to think that the high or low incomes people receive are based on the skills and responsibilities demanded by their jobs. This is the principle of equal pay for equal work; the job and the performance are paid for, not the person. From the foregoing it would appear that the stage has been set for the end of sexual inequality in the occupational world; but in point of fact, in spite of these laws, jobs continue to be disproportionately occupied, so extremely that for the sexes to be represented in the various occupations in the same proportions in which they are represented in the labor force as a whole, fully two-thirds of all employed men and women would have to change jobs (Gross, 1968, p. 202). In general, women workers are much more concentrated in just a few occupations; half of all of them are employed in only 21 of the 150 job categories listed by the United States census, while half of all working men are employed in 65 job categories. Thus, in spite of the belief in the principle that all jobs should be open to both sexes, which has now been enacted into law, men and women are in fact distributed very unequally among jobs.

Moreover, the remuneration for those jobs in which women predominate is less. Among all full-time employees in the United States, women earn less than two-thirds of what men earn. Basically the principle of equal pay for equal work has been subverted because when women hold similar jobs that pay less, it is difficult to prove that the work they are doing is comparable. In fact, however, when occupations are matched according to categories of educational training and skills required, those jobs in each category that are held predominantly by women turn out to pay less (Stevenson, 1975). Even within given occupational categories, the posts that are less prestigious and pay less are filled by women. In retail sales, for example, men generally sell cars and large appliances, and women usually sell clothing and small kitchen goods. In recent years, the wage gap between women and men has remained as large as ever, and it is in fact growing larger. As more women enter the labor market, the majority take jobs considered "appropriate" for women, for example, jobs as secretaries and nurses, and these continue to pay far less than do typical masculine jobs, such as those of plumbers and electricians.

Thus, in spite of laws prohibiting discrimination in hiring and promoting employees, sexual inequality persists. The immediate reason for this is the persistent differentiation between women's jobs and men's jobs, which makes it easier to continue to pay men more highly. In some industrialized countries, especially in those with socialist governments, the overall differentiations in wages have been sharply reduced, and this has thereby also reduced the differences between men's and women's wages. However, even in these societies, jobs continue to be separated into male and female categories, and those in which women predominate tend to pay less.

THE BASIS FOR MOTIVATIONS, INSTITUTIONAL ARRANGEMENTS, AND EVERYDAY INTERACTIONS

Sexual inequality and segregation appear to be resistant to current government policies; and they persist because they involve very basic human motives. These motives are not innate; they emerge from and are perpetuated by deeply embedded and universal social arrangements. To analyze the basis of male dominance, we must consider the interplay of motivations, social institutions, and everyday interactions in the perpetuation of sexual inequalities.

MOTIVATION. Psychoanalytic thought from its early days to the present has considered the motivational basis of male dominance. One trend in such thinking suggests that because of women's responsibility for the early care of children, females have less of a problem in forming a definition of themselves as females than males have in forming a definition of themselves as males. To an infant of either sex its female caretaker is the very powerful person on whom it is almost totally dependent, and this simple fact has implications for the differences between females' and males' development. Both sexes begin life in a symbiotic relationship with the mother in which they are to some extent merged with her. This likeness to mother may create dependency problems for the female child, but it does not present an identification problem because the mother is the same sex. A boy, on the other hand, must not only become independent of the mother, but he must also identify with a male figure, and it is not likely that as an infant he has had much contact with a male. The core of a males' gender identity is therefore not likely to be so firmly masculine as females' is to be feminine. This sets the stage for the formation of a reaction in males against femininity itself. The boy gains independence and identity by rejecting that which is feminine. He tends to define masculinity as that which is not feminine, and he sets masculinity over femininity as the desirable state. This desirability of masculinity, the prestige that accrues to masculinity, then becomes a force motivating males to become masculine while at the same time motivating them to denigrate femininity in themselves and in the biological sex which embodies it. Males' problems in achieving a masculine identity play into, and perhaps can account for males' sensitivity to being called feminine (a sissy, a fag, a girl) and their apparent need to separate themselves from women in a male peer group. Females, on the other hand, because they are of the same sex as their primary caretaker do not need to denigrate men in order to establish their sense of being female. This analysis suggests that if men as well as women were to be involved in early childcare, males' psychic need to separate themselves from and devalue women, as well as male dominance itself, might be lessened.

INSTITUTIONAL ARRANGEMENTS. To isolate a motive for male dominance is only part of the picture because the motive derives from *institutional arrangements* that promote women's rather than men's mothering and directly perpetuate sexual inequality. In our society, the relationship that exists between the family and the economy reinforces the motivation in men to dominate and devalue women; and at the same time this relationship reflects or embodies this domination. For example, the breadwinner's role has become a key factor in the definition of masculinity. This has the effect of making the role of caretaker more exclusively one for women and decreases the likelihood that fathers can serve as identification objects for their male infants, since their main task is seen as one of providing economically. This lack of opportunity for identification increases the young male's tendency to overreact against women and things feminine. In addition, the assignment of women to mothering and related activities in the home directly reinforces employers' beliefs that women will not devote themselves wholeheartedly to their outside jobs, and it contributes to the idea that women lack the requisite commitment for highly responsible jobs. Coser and Rokoff (1974) have argued that even though many so-called women's jobs (such as that of elementary school teacher) actually require great responsibility and professional dedication, the societal expectation that women will neglect their jobs for their families is used to justify considering the women who have these jobs easily replaceable, which in turn is used to justify the low pay attached to the job. The low pay helps to perpetuate a woman's greater commitment to the home and a husband's absence from it. There is little economic incentive for a husband to share in the care of children or take his wife's place when his outside job pays so much more than hers does.

EVERYDAY INTERACTIONS.   Sociologists who call themselves symbolic interactionists correctly stress that in the last analysis, people are not affected by social institutions; they are affected by other people. *Social institution* is merely a term for summarizing the patterns or regularities in human behavior, and such patterns are concretely realized by individual decisions in our everyday interactions. In day-to-day conversations, the separation of roles into sexual categories and female devaluation are symbolically communicated. Men's greater power in the society is communicated through their speech patterns, their body language, their job titles; and both women and men interpret these communications of greater power and respond to them. Generally, women are constrained not to challenge sexual segregation and their own devaluation. Since they often find themselves in situations where being promoted or being fired depends on a male boss, this is not surprising. Similarly, men are not likely to challenge other men who are enforcing role segregation and women's devaluation because this might make their own masculinity questionable. Challenges to the system from both females and males are therefore relatively rare, and the absence of challenge contributes to the perpetuation of the status quo in everyday life.

SUMMARY.   Male dominance is embedded in institutionalized patterns concretely enforced by individual decisions in everyday interactions; and these patterns are sustained by motives generated in the institutionalized practices that assign differing male and female roles during child care. While it is possible to analyze male dominance by considering motives, social institutions, and everyday interactions separately, it must be recognized that the three support each other.

SEGREGATION AND DEVALUATION IN TEACHING AND EDUCATIONAL ADMINISTRATION

In the field of education there are few exceptions to the foregoing generalizations regarding male attitudes. Processes of segregation and the devaluation of women are readily apparent; even though education has been a predominantly female profession for many years. While women predominate as elementary school teachers and librarians, and are about equally represented with men in secondary teaching and counseling, they are much less often found in educational administration. In secondary schools, men and women tend to teach different subjects, women concentrating in the humanities, men in the sciences and to some extent in the social sciences. In school administration there is also strong sex segregation. Women are much more often found in the staff positions in central offices than in the line positions of superintendent and principal, which have the greatest authority (Schmuck, 1980b). The sexual segregation in the field of education often results in men being paid more than women. Administrators are paid much more than teachers, and line administrators earn more than those in staff positions.

Secondary school teachers more often have advanced degrees and thus are higher on the pay scale than elementary school teachers. Secondary school teachers also usually have more opportunities for supplementary income from after-school duties and thus often earn more than elementary school teachers do, even when both have attained the same level of educational preparedness. Within secondary schools, men may earn more than women from after-school duties, such as coaching boys' teams, because it is assumed that their responsibilities are greater. It has often been argued that these differences reflect differences between males' and females' aspirations. For instance, among college students majoring in education, women more often aspire to elementary school teaching and men to secondary school teaching. A study comparing prospective male and female teachers who planned to pursue their careers continuously found that the men were more likely to contemplate accepting administrative responsibilities, at least for the more responsible and high-level positions, and more likely to plan to pursue activities leading to these. However, this study of college students found no sexual differences in the willingness to accept a position as vice principal (McMillan, 1975).

Studies in the 1970s (Mansergh, 1976; Matheny, 1973; and Timmons, 1973) found no differences between women and men teachers' administrative aspirations, even though earlier studies found that women teachers were less likely to plan to obtain an administrative post someday (Barter, 1959, cited by Van Mier, 1975). Evidence does suggest, however, that while men often plan their move into administration several years before it occurs, women may not think much about being an administrator until the opportunity arises (Paddock, 1977; also see Cobbley, 1970; Zimmerman, 1971; and Scriven, 1973; all cited by Fishel & Pottker, 1975). A good deal of evidence indicates that even if women aspired to administrative positions, their chances of being hired would not be especially great. Studies of the attitudes of school superintendents and school board members, those who make hiring decisions, indicate that "there is strong bias against appointing women to administrative positions" (Fishel & Pottker, 1975, p. 114, citing Barter, 1959; Warwick, 1967; Cobbley, 1970; Taylor, 1971; Matheny, 1973; LaBarthe, 1973; Longstreth, 1973; Neidig, 1973).

Evidence also suggests that encouragement to seek administrative positions is an important spur to such actions. Women are apparently encouraged less than men are to seek administrative jobs (Fishel & Pottker, 1975, citing Jenkins, 1966; Warwick, 1967; Taylor, 1971; Matheny, 1973); and women who do become administrators often point to the importance of encouragement by their supervisors in their actually attaining the positions (Paddock, 1977; Fishel & Pottker, 1975; citing Cobbley, 1970; Zimmerman, 1971; Scriven, 1973). Once women do attain administrative positions, there is no guarantee that their co-workers or superiors will be supportive. A study of five different work organizations (including a public school system) found that women who held more responsible positions, such as those in administration, had more uncomfortable experiences in the work organization than men or other women and that women with higher positions in the bureaucratic structure were more likely than were similarly placed men to risk "losing friendship and respect, influence, and access to information" (Miller, Labovitz, & Fry, 1975, p. 378).

In the picture that is drawn of the profession of education, women tend to predominate overall but men hold the more powerful, prestigious, and well-paying positions. Women may not aspire to these positions as often as men, but they are not encouraged to do so, and they may face active opposition from officials who do the hiring and from co-workers when they do have such aspirations and when they actually attain typically male posts. What can account for this situation? Can it be changed?

THE EFFECT OF INSTITUTIONALIZED PATTERNS, EVERYDAY INTERACTIONS, AND INDIVIDUAL MOTIVATIONS IN MAINTAINING SEXUAL INEQUALITY

Institutional Patterns

Sexual segregation in education and the elevation of males as administrators over female teachers were documented as early as the late nineteenth century. As school organizations increased in size and complexity, and as the bureaucratic form of school organizations became more common, men tended to be hired as administrators to manage large numbers of women teachers. Tyack (1974, pp. 61–62) reports that from 1870 to 1920, a time of rapid centralization of schools, the proportion of women teachers grew from 59% to 86%. The one-room school house with the teacher as the ultimate authority was replaced, at first in cities and later in unified districts, by large bureaucratic organizations. Women teachers were hired, but they worked under the supervision of men administrators in this new more business-like organization of the school.

This pattern of sexual stratification was especially noticeable in urban areas, which more often had large schools. A study by the National Education Association of 467 urban elementary schools in 1905 found that only 2% of the teachers but 38% of the principals were men. In the high schools, 38% of the teachers and 98% of the principals were men. Pay differentials in that era paralleled the differences found today between the pay of administrators and the pay of teachers; but before the era of equal pay regulations, there were even larger differences between women's and men's pay. Not only were men elementary school teachers paid much more than women elementary school teachers, but they were paid more than women high school teachers and even more than women principals! (See Tyack, 1974, p. 62; Kalvelage, 1978; Schmuck, 1980b.)

Education is similar to other typically female occupations, such as social work, nursing, and library work, in that the administrative component is overwhelmingly male. In addition, there is evidence that as the administrative component of these fields grew (as occurred in the late nineteenth century with education), men were more likely to enter the area (Grimm & Stern, 1974; Grimm, 1978). Because the more highly valued jobs throughout all areas of the society tend to go to males, when more prestigious positions open within a field it would be expected that these better paid positions would be given to men rather than to women. This may be especially true if men have few other occupational choices (compare O'Connor, 1977). Perhaps then, one reason that the proportion of women elementary school principals declined from the 1930s to the 1970s (see Pottker & Fishel, 1977) is a combination of two factors: more elementary school principalships were available, and men with a college education had fewer job options in other areas.

Current hiring practices also tend to perpetuate patterns of sex segregation that are already present. A study of the hiring of school administrators in Oregon in the 1977–1978 school year found that, although men were generally preferred, women had a greater chance of being hired in a post if a woman had held the position previously or if it were a new position. Men were hired more often if a man had previously held the position. In other words, if previous tradition defined the position as suitable for a woman or if there were no past practice on which to rely, the chances for a woman to be hired were somewhat greater (Stockard, 1980).

Everyday Interactions

Ultimately, of course, the institutional patterns we are describing are perpetuated by individuals' actions and decisions. Individual people eventually decide who will or will not be hired, and individual people set salary schedules. Individuals also decide whether or not to seek or prepare for a certain job. Thus, everyday interactions and decisions perpetuate patterns of sex segregation and the devaluation of women. Both men and women are involved in these actions, which become mutually reinforcing. Men are disposed to maintain sex segregation and to devalue women's contributions. Men hold powerful positions in education, and their decisions can perpetuate segregation and devaluation. Women at the same time interpret men's expectations, actions, and power and make decisions that take these into account.

Tyack (1974, pp. 62–63) describes how the actions and decisions of individual commissioners of education and other powerful male educators in the late nineteenth and early twentieth centuries were aimed toward recruiting men as managers in education and maintaining sex stratification in the profession. For instance, in Philadelphia, women once became common in the assistant principal slots that had been stepping stones to principals' positions. Tyack reports that "confronted with this threat to male supremacy, the Philadelphia schools created a 'School of Pedagogy' limited to men and adopted a rule that only men would be hired in the two top grades of the boys' grammar schools." These individual decisions helped develop and maintain patterns that ensured the maintenance of sex stratification in education.

Expectations that there should be sex segregation within education have also been documented in more recent history. As mentioned earlier, officials who do the hiring (who are generally men) often do not approve of or support womens' being administrators. Nor are teachers, especially males, likely to support the idea of women as administrators, unless they have worked with a woman administrator previously (Fishel & Pottker, 1975, citing Matheny, 1973; Neidig, 1973; NEA, 1973; Linton, 1974; Barter, 1959; Warwick, 1967). Interestingly enough, men teachers who have been administrators hold the least favorable attitudes toward women administrators (Mansergh, 1976), probably because they are the ones whose past or potential jobs would be most threatened by aspiring women administrators.

These expectations are then reflected in actions. Male administrators do not appear to encourage women to pursue administrative careers of their own (Fishel & Pottker, 1975, pp. 113–114, citing Jenkins, 1966; Warwick, 1967; Taylor, 1971; Matheny, 1973); undoubtedly male administrators believe that administration is for men but not for women. Moreover, when women do become administrators, they may face negative reactions from co-workers and from other administrators (Miller, Labovitz, & Fry, 1975). If our analysis of sexual stratification as an interconnected system of motives, institutionalized patterns, and everyday interactions is correct, then change is likely to occur only when positive actions are taken to break up the system. In the long run, inequality is perpetuated not just by a lack of encouragement to women or by negative reactions to them as administrators, but by the absence of affirmative actions in the hiring of women. Men usually hold the gatekeeping positions in the profession of education, and they have the power to act upon their beliefs and attitudes and to continue the patterns of sexual segregation in hiring.

For instance, it was predominantly men who made the hiring decisions in Oregon studied in 1977–1978, and men were usually preferred for administrative slots. All men have to do to perpetuate the system that works against women is to act on male assumptions about women's motivations and aspirations. They do not have to be deliberate in their attempts to keep women out and in their intentions to keep all the power for themselves in order for women to be excluded. In fact, probably few men now are so deliberate in their actions. In addition, their actions are reinforced when women who interpret male expectations and actions make decisions that also perpetuate sexual segregation and their own devaluation. As noted above, women aspire less often than men, at least to the higher-level administrative positions. This appears to be true even among those with suitable training. Although one-third of all the doctorates in education are given to women, statistics from the Oregon State Department of Education show that in 1976-1977, only 14% of the people with doctoral degrees who were employed in the state's schools were women. There has been a strong tendency for women with doctoral degrees in administration to enter areas other than the public schools, for example to do research and work with educational service districts (see Edson, 1979).

Moreover, when women do aspire to administration, they tend to aspire to sexually typed areas and to have somewhat lower ultimate goals. Data gathered in 1978 (Stockard, 1980) from a sample of women and men listed in a directory of aspirants to administrative positions showed that the men (many of whom had already attained administrative positions) more often aspired to the top-line positions of superintendent, assistant superintendent, and principal, while the women more often aspired to the staff positions of assistant principal, director or supervisor, coordinator, consultant, and to other administrative assistant posts. (Compare the tendency of women who are ordained ministers not to have regular congregations and parishes but to fill other staff positions, such as that of director of religious education; see Neal, 1979.) Estler reported 1968 data on the percentages of men and women administrators who saw their current jobs as their final occupational goals: 79% of the women compared with 50% of the men principals, and 41% of the women compared with 8% of the men assistant principals (1975, p. 375, citing NAESP, 1970, p. 16). Other reports cited by Estler show that in a sample of people who did not see the principalship as their final goal, 27% of the men but only 2% of the women aspired to the superintendency, and 25% of the women but 18% of the men aspired to the position of supervisor or director of elementary education—typical staff positions (Estler, 1975, p. 375, citing NEA, 1968, p. 17).

Women who do attain administrative positions sometimes define their work as being suitable for women, a tactic that is probably useful in stemming any criticisms from male co-workers (Epstein, 1970; Kanter, 1975; Stockard & Johnson, 1980, pp. 14-16). Among elementary school principals, women sometimes emphasize the nurturant and maternal aspects of the job and men the business-like procedures and relations with the community. It may well be true that women do have special skills in establishing emotionally based social relationships. Studies of the behavior of women and men school administrators indicate that women are especially skilled in areas that are often culturally typed as being feminine, such as their greater concern with the social and emotional development of students (Gross & Trask, 1976) and their greater awareness of the potential problems of students (Hoyle, 1969). We are not suggesting that in order to become equal women must become more like men. Rather the argument is that so long as men are dominant, these special skills of women will tend to be seen as "lesser" simply because they are characteristic of women (compare Johnson *et al.*, 1976).

Women in positions of power might demonstrate a different style of administration, and this difference may be difficult to characterize. Research by Finigan (1979) regarding small work groups outside the field of education suggested that the masculine leadership style included more attempts to dominate and more actions that work against group cohesiveness. Other studies showed that female administrators were more likely to hold leadership positions in schools that were closely knit (Morsink, 1968, cited by Fishel & Pottker, 1975); and women principals were shown to have better communication with their teachers (Wiles & Grobman, 1955, cited by Fishel & Pottker, 1975; see also Meskin, 1974). These possible salutary effects of women's leadership will remain largely untested so long as the cycle of sex segregation and the devaluation of the work women do are perpetuated. Because men are generally more powerful, women are not usually in a position to challenge their actions; and when women make decisions based on their own perceptions of reality, they often help perpetuate the status quo.

Individual Motivations

Although males' and females' styles in interaction and leadership may differ, there is little evidence of sufficiently distinctive sexually differentiated skills to make any one type of work in education more suitable for one sex than the other. Actually, both male and female types of skills are needed in most jobs. Why then, in a society that claims to be dedicated to equality of opportunity, to fairness, and to rationality, does sex segregation persist? We have suggested that it is partially due to the absence of positive action. Why is it so difficult to take positive action? Obviously men as a group have a vested interest in keeping things as they are because it is they who benefit financially from the current arrangements; but this does not explain why individual men do not sometimes find it to their advantage to seek jobs in education other than in administration and why men do not hire women to administrative positions. The field of education might well be a route for upward social mobility for some working-class men. Nevertheless, for many years relatively few males entered education at the elementary school level; and once in teaching they usually did not remain long.

Statistics from a number of years ago indicated that less than 10% of all male teachers had been teaching for 5 or more years (Clark, 1964; Carlson, 1972); in more recent years more men have entered education, and they appear to be staying longer as teachers. However, not being satisfied with the image of education as a woman's profession, they have tried to change this, most notably with attempts to unionize teachers and raise the pay scales (compare Schmuck, 1980b, p. 93). The resistance to hiring women as administrators appears not to be entirely rational, although it may be "rationalized," often in terms of job security, as in the comments of one male principal justifying the exclusion of women from administration: "It's easier to work without women. Principals and superintendents are a management team. It fosters interdependence and mutual support. We need each other for survival. It's no evil liaison—it's just pure politics. I wonder if we could hang together so well if some of us were women. Could she protect my job as well as her own?" (Schmuck, 1976, p. 16). While the principal is saying that by sticking together, men can protect their jobs better, he is really only asserting a belief in sexual segregation—that is, males get along well together, males have solidarity with each other. One wonders why males feel they are better off without women, and why they try to separate themselves from women. Women do not seem to feel the need of a comparable separation from men in order to feel their strength.

We believe there are nonrational reasons operating when men who need work do not enter a field because it is stigmatized as feminine and when men do not seek to have women in their ranks as administrators. Psychoanalysis assumes that it is possible to understand the basis of motivations that appear irrational on the surface; such analysis is especially useful in understanding motivations and subsequent decisions that perpetuate sexual segregation and the devaluation of women. As we outlined it earlier, the male motive to separate men's activities from women's and to devalue women's activities is related to experiences in infancy and early childhood that result in men's defining of themselves as male largely by denying the feminine aspect of themselves. Because men have to maintain their view of themselves as masculine, the mere fact that a profession is defined as female is enough of a stigma to keep them out. Their alternatives are to storm the occupation en masse, to leave quickly, or to move to spots within the profession that are not typed as female and try to change the image and status of the profession.

While males do tend to compete for dominance vis-à-vis other males, their susceptibility to insecurity about their masculinity can also prompt them to seek solidarity with other males and separation from females. Perhaps one element behind this bonding between males is a shared need to feel unthreatened by the feminine power with which they were surrounded as infants. Far fetched as all this may sound, it is commonly observed that one of the most potent motivators for men is the suggestion that they are not quite masculine. Everyday interactions can reinforce this threat of femininity.

IMPLICATIONS FOR CHANGE

We stressed in earlier writings (Stockard & Johnson, 1979, 1980) that changes in family and economic patterns that promote the involvement of fathers as well as of mothers in caring for children are necessary if we are to counteract the motivations that underlie male dominance. If fathers were involved in infant care, young boys might be able to develop a real and more concrete sense of maleness and a conception of themselves as male that would not involve the rejection of femininity as part of being masculine or the need for defensiveness. If fathers themselves were secure, and simply took their biological maleness for granted without stressing the differentiation of sexual roles, there would be no need for defensiveness. Clearly, however, all changes need not wait until men share early child care with women. It is important to continue to press for changes in our everyday interactions and social institutions, especially since the law now requires sexual equality in occupations.

In everyday interactions, feminists can challenge male expectations regarding role differentiation and women's devaluation—and there is evidence that change can be produced when these expectations are challenged. In one western state, the representation of women on the program of the state administrators' meeting grew from 19% in 1976–1977 to 32% in 1979, a difference that was significantly different from the amount of change one might attribute to chance. This group of state administrators had been pressured in 1977 to give greater attention to women, and indeed they passed a resolution promising to do so. On the national level, no such commitment was made, and the national administrators' meetings showed no rise in women's representation over those years. In a number of western states there has also been a dramatic increase in women's representation in graduate programs in educational administration (Stockard, 1980). Although it is probably too early to tell what impact these changes will eventually have on hiring, the mere fact of the greater presence of women in training programs for administrators and in public meetings can challenge the sexual typing in the field.

Although numerous laws now exist that require the end of sexual segregation and discrimination in occupations, the need for consistent enforcement remains. It is necessary to call attention to infractions instead of ignoring them. Beyond this, people must be more prepared to assume nontraditional roles. Data cited earlier showed that women usually aspire to the traditionally female slots in education. A 1978 directory of aspirants to administrative positions revealed that fewer women than men had the required certificates for these posts, specifically for the superintendency (Stockard, 1980, chap. 5). Women must be encouraged to get this training, and undoubtedly more will do so as they perceive that it is possible to get such jobs. We do not anticipate that these changes will be easy or that they will occur rapidly. In Oregon, from 1971 to 1979 the percentage of women in all school administrative positions went from 12.1% to 14.5%; and although this change over the 7-year period is significantly greater than zero, continuing at this rate would mean that an equal number of males and females could not be expected in the area of school adminstration until well into the next century.

Moreover, changes in the total representation of women do not guarantee equal changes in each subarea. This was definitely the case in Oregon in 1978–1979, where in the positions of assistant and deputy superintendents there were no women, and in the positions of superintendents 1.9% were women. Increases in women's representation in educational administration in Oregon occurred mainly in staff administrative positions such as supervisors and coordinators, rather than in the more powerful line positions of superintendents and principals. If the end of sexual segregation and stratification is to become a reality in the profession of education, increased pressure will be needed to bring about significant substantive changes. Because these inequities and the male dominance that accompanies them are reproduced by everyday interactions, in institutionalized patterns, and in sexually differentiated motivations, changes in all these areas are necessary if we are to achieve genuine equality and prevent sexual stratification from arising in a new form.

In spite of the deep rootedness of the problem, several trends provide hope that real equality in the field of education can be attained. First, laws requiring changes in institutional practices and an end to sexual segregation and discrimination in education are on the books (see

Williams, 1980). Second, feminist groups have continued to push for equality in general, and in education in particular (Schmuck, 1980a). Finally there are some indications of a general cultural trend toward nurturance, caring, and sharing, as opposed to aggression and competition as a way of life (Johnson, 1977). Beginning with the antiwar and counterculture movements of the 1960s and continuing with the concern for ecology, arms control, and consumer protection in the 1970s, values ordinarily associated more with the maternal aspects of femininity than with certain aspects of masculinity are coming into prominence in the society as a whole.

In this era of increasing humanistic concerns, education may hold more promise for change than most other professions. Because education is fundamentally and directly concerned with human growth and development, both the men and the women who enter the field thereby commit themselves to tasks and values that are culturally defined as feminine. Many aspects of the jobs that men usually hold, such as the position of building principal, also require the skills of nurturance and human sensitivity. Although these acts are typed as feminine, men often comfort children and ease hurt feelings. As the more feminine values and behaviors embodied in education gain greater ascendancy in the society as a whole, it should help men who are in education feel good about the commitment they have made and reduce any need they may have to disassociate themselves from the women in the field. Thus, an increase in humanistic and maternal concerns in the society as a whole may decrease tendencies toward sexual segregation and stratification in education sooner than in other areas. Perhaps, in tandem, the legal requirements, the actions of feminists, the unique values and commitments within education, and the general cultural trend toward humanistic values will accelerate the move toward greater equality in the education profession.

REFERENCES

Barter, A. S. (1959). "The Status of Women in School Administration—Where Will They Go from There?" *Educational Horizons*, 37:72-75.

Boulding, E. (1979). "Introduction." In *Sex Roles and Social Policy: A Complex Social Science Equation* (J. Lipman-Blumen and J. Bernard, eds.). Sage Publications, Beverly Hills, Calif., pp. 7-16.

Carlson, R. O. (1972). *School Superintendents: Careers and Performance*. Merrill, Columbus, Ohio.

Clark, B. R. (1964). "Sociology of Education." In *Handbook of Modern Sociology* (R.E.L. Faris, ed.). Rand McNally, Chicago.

Cobbley, L. (1970). *A Study of Attitudes and Opportunities for Women in Six Western States to*

Become Elementary School Principals. Unpublished doctoral dissertation, Brigham Young University, Provo, Utah.

Coser, R. L., and Rokoff, G. (1974). "Women in the Occupational World: Social Disruption and Conflict." Pages 490–511. In *The Family: Its Structures and Functions*, 2nd ed. (R. L. Coser, ed.). St. Martin's, New York.

Edson, S. K. (1979). *Differential Experiences of Male and Female Aspirants for Public School Administration: A Closer Look at Perceptions in the Field.* Paper presented to the American Educational Research Association, San Francisco.

Epstein, C. F. (1970). "Encountering the Male Establishment: Sex Status Limits on Women's Careers in the Professions." *American Journal of Sociology,* 75:965–982.

Estler, S. E. (1975). "Women as Leaders in Public Education." *Signs,* 1:363–386.

Finigan, M. W. (1979). *The Influence of Sex Ratio on Group Process in Small Professional Work Settings.* Unpublished doctoral dissertation, University of Oregon.

Fishel, A., and Pottker, J. (1975). "Performances of Women Principals: A Review of Behavioral and Attitudinal Studies." *Journal of the National Association of Women Deans and Counselors,* 38:110–115.

Grimm, J. W. (1978). "Women in Female-Dominated Professions." In *Women Working* (A. Stromberg and S. Harkess, eds.). Mayfield, Palo Alto, Calif., pp. 293–315.

Grimm, J. W., and Stern, R. (1974). "Sex Rules and Internal Labor Market Structures: The 'Female' Semi-Professions." *Social Problems,* 21:690–705.

Gross, E. (1968). "Plus Ça Change . . .? The Sexual Structure of Occupations over Time." *Social Problems,* 16:198–208.

Gross, N., and Trask, A. E. (1976). *The Sex Factor and the Management of Schools.* Wiley, New York.

Hoyle, J. (1969). "Who Should Be Principal—a Man or a Woman?" *National Elementary Principal,* 48 (January):23–24.

Jenkins, W. J. (1966). *A Study of the Attitudes of Elementary School Teachers in Selected Schools in Montgomery County, Pennsylvania, toward the Women Elementary School Principals.* Unpublished doctoral dissertation, Temple University, Philadelphia.

Johnson, M. M. (1977). "Androgeny and the Maternal Principle." *School Review,* 86:50–59.

Johnson, M. M., Stockard, J., Acker, J., and Naffziger, C. (1975). "Expressiveness Reevaluated." *School Review,* 83:617–644.

Kalvelage, J. (1978). *The Decline in Female Elementary Principals Since 1928: Riddles and Clues.* Unpublished paper, Center for Educational Policy and Management, University of Oregon, Eugene.

Kanter, R. M. (1975). "Women and the Structure of Organizations: Explorations in Theory and Behavior." In *Another Voice* (M. Millman and R. M. Kanter, eds.). Doubleday, Garden City, N.Y., pp. 34–74.

LaBarthe, E. R. (1973). *A Study of the Motivation of Women in Administration and Supervisory Positions in Selected Unified School Districts in Southern California.* Unpublished doctoral dissertation, University of Southern California, Los Angeles.

Linton, D. L. (1974). *Teachers' Perceptions of Women as Principals in an Elementary School District.* Unpublished doctoral dissertation, United States International University, San Diego, Calif.

Longstreth, C. H. (1973). *An Analysis of the Perceptions of the Leadership Behavior of Male and Female Secondary School Principals in Florida.* Unpublished doctoral dissertation, University of Miami.

Mansergh, G. (1976). "Attitudes of Teachers toward Women School Administrators and the Aspirations of Teachers for Administrative Positions in the State of Minnesota." *Catalyst for Change,* 5:4–7.

Matheny, P. P. (1973). *A Study of the Attitudes of Selected Male and Female Teachers, Administrators, and Board of Education Presidents toward Women in Educational Administrative Positions.* Unpublished doctoral dissertation, Northwestern University, Evanston, Ill.

McMillan, M. R. (1975). "Leadership Aspirations of Prospective Teachers: A Comparison of Men and Women." *Journal of Teacher Education,* 26:323–325.

Meskin, J. D. (1974). "The Performance of Women School Administrators: A Review of the Literature." *Administrator's Notebook,* 23(1).

Miller, J., Labovitz, S., and Fry, L. (1975). "Inequities in the Organizational Experiences of Women and Men." *Social Forces,* 54:365–381.

Morsink, H. (1968). "Leader Behavior of Men and Women Secondary School Principals," *Educational Horizons,* 47:69–74.

NAESP (1970). *The Assistant Principalship in Public Elementary Schools—1969.* National Association of Elementary School Principals, Washington, D.C.

NEA (1968). *The Elementary School Principal in 1968.* Department of Elementary School Principals, National Education Association, Washington, D.C.

NEA (1973). "Survey Findings." *Research Action Notes—Resource Center on Sex Roles in Education.* 1(4). National Education Association.

Neal, M. A. (1979). "Women in Religious Symbolism and Organization." *Sociological Inquiry,* 49:218–250.

Neidig, M. B. (1973). *Women Applicants for Administrative Positions: Attitudes Held by Administrators and School Boards.* Unpublished doctoral dissertation, University of Iowa.

O'Connor, J. (1977). *Changes in the Sex Composition of High-Status Female Occupations: An Analysis of Teaching:1950–1970.* Unpublished paper, University of Illinois at Urbana-Champaign.

Paddock, S. (1977). *Women's Careers in Administration.* Unpublished doctoral dissertation, University of Oregon.

Pottker, J., and Fishel, A. (1977). *Sex Bias in the Schools.* Associated University Presses, London.

Schmuck, P. A. (1976). "The Spirit of Title IX: Men's Work and Women's Work in Oregon Public Schools." *OSSC Bulletin,* 20(2).

Schmuck, P. A. (1980a) "Context of Change: The Women's Movement as a Political Process." In *Sex Equity in Education* (J. Stockard, P. Schmuck, K. Kempner, P. Williams, S. Edson, M. A. Smith). Academic Press, New York, pp. 165–184.

Schmuck, P. A. (1980b). "Differentiation by Sex in Educational Professions." In *Sex Equity in Education* (J. Stockard, P. S. Schmuck, K. Kempner, P. Williams, S. Edson, M. A. Smith). Academic Press, New York, pp. 79–97.

Schmuck, P. A. (1980c). *Sex Equity in Educational Leadership: The Oregon Story.* Education Development Center, Newton, Mass.

Scriven, A. L. (1973). *A Study of Women Occupying Administrative Positions in the Central Office of Large School Districts.* Unpublished doctoral dissertation, University of Florida.

Stevenson, M. H. (1975). "Relative Wages and Sex Segregation by Occupation." In *Sex, Discrimination, and the Division of Labor* (C. B. Lloyd, ed.). Columbia University Press, New York, pp. 175–200.

Stockard, J. (1980). *Sex Equity in Educational Leadership: An Analysis of a Planned Social Change Project.* Education Development Center, Newton, Mass.

Stockard, J., and Johnson, M. M. (1979). "The Social Origins of Male Dominance." *Sex Roles,* 5:199–218.

Stockard, J., and Johnson, M. M., (1980). *Sex Roles: Sex Inequality and Sex Role Development.* Prentice-Hall, Englewood Cliffs, N.J.

Stockard, J., Johnson, M. M., Acker, J. R., and Goldman, M. S. (1976). *Sex Role Develop-*

ment and Sex Discrimination: A Theoretical Perspective. Paper Presented at the Annual Meeting of the American Sociological Association, San Francisco.

Taylor, S. (1971). *The Attitudes of Superintendents and Board of Education Members in Connecticut toward the Employment and Effectiveness of Women as Public School Administrators.* Unpublished doctoral dissertation, University of Connecticut.

Timmons, J. E. (1973). *A Study of Attitudes toward Women School Administrators and the Aspirations of Women Teachers for Administrative Positions in the State of Indiana.* Unpublished doctoral dissertation, Indiana University.

Tyack, D. B. (1974). *The One Best System: A History of American Urban Education.* Harvard University Press, Cambridge, Mass.

Van Meir, E. J. (1975). "Sexual Discrimination in School Administration Opportunities." *Journal of the National Association of Women Deans and Counselors,* 38:163–167.

Warwick, E. B. (1967). *Attitudes towards Women in Administrative Positions as Related to Curricular Implementation and Change.* Unpublished doctoral dissertation, University of Wisconsin.

Wiles, K., and Grobman, H. G. (1955). "Principals as Leaders." *Nation's Schools,* 56:75–77.

Williams, P. (1980). "Laws Prohibiting Sex Discrimination in the Schools." In *Sex Equity in Education* (J. Stockard, P. Schmuck, K. Kempner, P. Williams, S. Edson, M. A. Smith). Academic Press, New York, pp. 143–164.

Zimmerman, J. N. (1971). *The Status of Women in Educational Administrative Positions within the Central Offices of Public Schools.* Unpublished doctoral dissertation, Temple University, Philadelphia.

Chapter 14

THE IMPACT OF ORGANIZATIONAL
STRUCTURES ON ISSUES
OF SEX EQUITY

Margaret Wheatley

The scarcity of women in the administrative ranks of public school administration is both a curious and a compelling phenomenon. It is curious since women predominate in the initial pool of teachers from which administrators are chosen, and compelling because women rarely make it to administrative posts, and are losing those they even once retained. Public school administration is the only profession in the human services area where women have been losing ground steadily. Female principals and assistant principals are almost always limited to the elementary school level, and the number holding these positions has declined from 37% in 1960 to 21% in 1970 to 13% in 1976. At the high school level, where women have traditionally been less evident, the number of women principals declined from 6% in 1950 to 1.4% in 1976 (Howard, 1975, p. 14; *Sex Bias in Schools*, 1978, p. 7). The number of women teachers in high schools has also been shrinking. As we all remember, the influx of more men into the teaching profession was loudly applauded in the late fifties as one means of upgrading the quality of education. Since that time a slight majority of all high school teachers have been men; in the past decade, there has been a 67% increase in men's representation (Howard, 1975, p. 13).

The higher one looks in the administrative hierarchy, the fewer women one observes. Until quite recently, estimates of the number of

255

women superintendents ranged from 0.1% to 0.5%.[1] Recent statistics from the National Education Association (NEA) show that 5% of all superintendents and assistant superintendents are female, but the aggregation of these two roles makes it impossible to evaluate the gains of women in the more senior role. In a 1972 survey of all state education departments, Clement located 87 women superintendents from among more than 17,000 school districts (1975, pp. 38–43). Forty-six of these women served in districts with fewer than 500 pupils. What is most startling about these figures, however, is that of the 87 women, 43 of them were located in the state of Illinois; the total number of women superintendents distributed throughout the remaining 49 states was 44.

Of the few works that analyze women's small representation in administrative roles, much of the attention has focused on the influence of sex-role stereotyping (see Howard, 1975; Schmuck, 1975). Analysts point to the fact that teaching is an outstanding example of a sex-stereotyped career—a role for which women seem intrinsically well suited. These stereotypes work to prevent men in power from seeing women as suitable candidates for administration. Most people assume that women who go into teaching do so primarily because of limited aspirations, choosing a career that is compatible with home and family demands. Men, on the other hand, are thought to view teaching as a stepping stone to higher positions, either in education or in other fields (Carlson, 1972; Mason, Dressel, & Bain, 1959, pp. 370–383). This stepping-stone pattern for male teachers is cited in explanations of why males become administrators and women do not (Poll, 1978).[2]

There is a great deal of cogency to these analyses, particularly in their explanations of the historical and socialization processes that, in the past, drove women into teaching and then kept them there. These analyses are less satisfying, however, in explaining the present-day losses of women from administrative ranks, because these losses are not the artifacts of a less liberated era, but are increasing at a time when we expect more women to aspire to administrative positions.

This chapter discusses organizational factors that are pertinent to an

[1]Getting accurate statistics on women administrators requires incredible sleuthing and/or perserverance. As recently as 1974, the American Association of School Administrators computerized their membership without listing sex as one of its descriptors.

[2]Poll's research refutes the stepping-stone theory of male careers in education, and the notion that men enter the profession with preformed aspirations for administrative office. In her sample of 32 administrators (15 male and 17 female), 30 had no other aspirations than to be a teacher when they began work. The aspirations of the men changed as they were presented with opportunities.

analysis of women's failure to reach administrative ranks. In the work done by Kanter (1977) in large corporations, specific organizational features were observed to be causes, and therefore explanations of such observed work behaviors as aspirations, career-orientation, motivation, and leadership effectiveness. Although Kanter's theory evolved from studies of industrial corporations, it explains processes that occur in any bureaucratically organized institution. In our analysis of organizational factors in schools, we examine structures of opportunity and power, two major variables in Kanter's framework.

THE OPPORTUNITY STRUCTURE OF SCHOOLS

The Moving and the Stuck

Kanter's definition of opportunity goes beyond the traditional concept of upward mobility. Although promotion prospects are still a primary indicator of opportunity in most organizations, opportunity can also be measured by the extent to which a job allows a person to grow and develop, to use skills and to learn new ones, and to be recognized and rewarded for those skills. A person can remain in the same job over many years and still experience it as a high opportunity position if there has been a sense of growth and development. This concept of opportunity has great significance in low growth or professional organizations such as schools.

High and low opportunity positions tend to breed two very different styles of involvement in work, and thus two different "ideal types" of people. Kanter labels them the "moving" and the "stuck." The moving tend to differ from the stuck in ways that set self-fulfilling prophecies in motion. Those in moving positions are not only in a position of being eligible for advancement, but also tend to behave in ways that confirm the organization's selection of them as people who should be rewarded. Those who are stuck tend, as a result of their situation, to act in ways that confirm the organization's lack of attention to them.

Opportunity affects such key organizational behaviors as aspirations, self-esteem, work engagement, self-preparation, and style of expressing dissatisfaction. The moving tend to have or to develop greater aspirations and to aim for higher positions, largely because they can already see themselves on a path leading to those positions. The stuck, however, tend to limit and lower their aspirations, and appear to be less motivated to achieve, because they lack a sense that better and higher positions are realistically attainable. The moving also have greater self-esteem; they tend to recognize that they have skills and tend to use them more. The stuck tend to think less of themselves as skilled workers; since they devalue their skills and abilities, they are much less likely to make them known or to feel that they can carry out assignments for which they do not already have the experience. Those who are stuck are unlikely to give the organization any indication that they deserve to do more than the job in which they are currently stuck.

The moving are much more likely than the stuck to become highly engaged in their work and even committed to the organization. They are much more likely to talk about work as a major source of life investment and satisfaction, whereas the stuck are likely either to become psychic drop-outs, putting in their time while making major life investments elsewhere; they may actually dream of escaping from the organization into some realm that gives them greater possibilities for growth. The greater engagement of the moving also shows up in the extent to which they begin to prepare themselves in advance for their next job. The stuck are much more likely to invest their energy in perfecting details of their present job. The moving are likely to be much more active about expressing dissatisfaction, much more constructive in their style of protesting and expressing grievance. The stuck often turn into passive gripers, hoping to get something more for themselves, but rarely constructive when it comes to suggestions for improving the organization.

Reinterpretation of Classic Stereotypes

Kanter's images of the moving and the stuck lead to reinterpretation of some classic ideas and research findings about how women's behavior in organizations differs from men's. If women have lower aspirations, lower self-esteem, less investment in work, less interest in self-preparation for advancement, and more passive and conservative styles, these behavioral elements emerge not as characteristics of women, but as characteristics of anyone who is stuck in a job, man or woman. To the extent that women find themselves more frequently in low opportunity situations, then they are more likely to be subject to these tendencies (Kanter, 1977, pp. 129–163). Kanter's elaboration of the behavior of people who are stuck helps explain women teachers' attitudes about careers and their behavior—two factors that have been cited as the source of women's difficulty in reaching administrative posts. If organizational features are responsible for such behavior, it is necessary to understand what particular features of school organizations act to limit opportunity or to distribute it in ways that discriminate against women.

The Interplay of Bureaucratic and Professional Systems

The peculiar structuring of schools, with its mesh of bureaucratic and professional patterns of organization, exacerbates the conditions that limit opportunity. The result is a chronic state of severely limited opportunity that has negative consequences for all teachers, men and women; but particularly, it perpetuates the role stereotypes that continue to haunt women. The entire system, which may itself be seen as "stuck," creates alternative means of conducting business that work to disadvantage women even further. In Bidwell's analysis of the school as a formal organization, he describes two organizational systems, the bureaucratic and the professional, and the tension that exists between them. The professional character of teaching requires autonomy, yet system-wide needs demand routinization and bureaucratization (Bidwell, 1965, pp. 970–977). Bureaucratic and professional systems each have their own opportunity structures. Ironically, it is the existence of the two opposing structures that contributes to the lack of opportunity in school organizations overall.

The bureaucratic system within schools has clear career ladders, although they are few in number at the lower levels. From the viewpoint of teachers, the positions of specialists and department heads represent entry-level administrative positions; these positions exist almost exclusively at the high school level. Once a person is in one of these positions, assistantships and acting positions become available, and these positions lead to principalships. Not all principals are on the ladder to higher office, however, because in most systems, only those from high schools are selected for further moves (Schmuck, 1975, p. 15).[3] Although the relative scarcity of entry-level positions is important to note, what is more crucial is the manner in which these posts are assigned. Certification requirements are common prerequisites, but the selection of department heads and specialists does not rely solely on objective criteria;

---

[3]It is interesting to compare the orientation and styles of elementary and high school principals in terms of Kanter's moving and stuck images. Elementary school principals frequently cite their next career move as a return to the classroom; as leaders, they tend to interact more with their subordinates. In Kanter's terms, they do not anticipate upward movement and thus do not prepare for it by anticipatory behaviors that model administrators; instead, they get more involved in perfecting their craft (the good ones, that is). Middle school principals, who as a group are on an ambiguous career ladder, offer an even more vivid illustration of Kanter's types. Leaving aside those who are merely putting in time, there are two distinct types. Some act quite officially, emulating the administrative behavior more appropriate to a central office; others act with a great deal of informality and even display nurturant behavior. It would be interesting to survey the aspirations of these types to assess the degree to which aspirations correlate with behavior patterns.

instead, criteria are frequently changed to make the job fit the person who has already been selected (*Sex Bias in Schools*, 1978, p. 37).

In spite of the presence of objective criteria and certification demands, decision making about appointments within the bureaucratic hierarchy rests squarely in the hands of particular individuals—it is left to the discretion of principals. With this mode of decision making, informal connections become important; people get selected who are known and who have a prior relationship with those in power. In a male-dominated organization (98.6% of all high school principals are male), this informal system of allocation clearly acts as a strong barrier to women's advancement. Of course, informal systems influence promotion decisions in every organization; but in schools, particular features of the second internal organization, the professional system, act to make the informal system an extremely potent and impenetrable force.

The profession of teaching has been characterized by Miles as a "craftlike occupation," where members rely on intrinsic rewards (1975, p. 237). In such a profession, opportunity obviously means the chance to grow better at one's craft, to become an expert and to gain status and recognition for doing so. Where opportunity is so linked to personal pride in one's work, the organizational structure lacks many external, or hierarchically differentiated, rewards. Within a school, there are only a small number of functions that can be distinguished from one another; instead, we find many people occupying identically defined roles, and performing multiple duties within that role (Schmuck & Runkel, 1972, p. 7). In a school system, extrinsic rewards, such as differences in pay, are minimized. Nothing could be more objectively equal, in fact, than the current method of determining teacher's pay on the basis of training and years of experience. This organization of teaching along professional lines limits the opportunity to receive the extrinsic rewards that are available in other organizations.

All of us know, of course, how tenuous a grasp teachers have on their professionalism. As Lortie has aptly noted (1975, pp. 253, 254, 257, 263), teachers have neither the prestige nor the clout of other professionals. They lack the economic sanctions of a fee-based profession and the effective support of a guild or association. Their professional authority, even within their own classroom, is subject to challenge from school boards and members of the community. The only way they can maintain control over their work is to retreat into isolation. In isolation they can be autonomous, something that other professionals are afforded because of their expertise and their ability to exercise power. "Autonomy-equality supplies teachers with the personal and spontaneous choice which they would have if they possessed the privileges granted those in high prestige, fee-taking professions. . . . It acts to limit the influence of the formal and bureaucratic order."

Patterns of Autonomy and Equality

Lortie distinguishes three norms for how teachers relate to one another and to administrators. Teachers should (1) be free from the interference of other adults while teaching, (2) be considered and treated as equals, (3) act in a nonintervening but friendly manner toward one another. This normative pattern not only serves to discourage contact among teachers but further reinforces the need for all extrinsic rewards to be equal. The rewards of power and prestige must be kept relatively insignificant. With extrinsic rewards equalized, intrinsic rewards are magnified. In the isolation of the classroom, teachers can choose to define their rewards as they will. Lortie's description of prevailing school norms has consequences for a number of educational concerns. In terms of opportunity structures, his analysis offers a succinct portrait of a system plagued by a self-sealing spiral of ever-decreasing opportunity. The logic of this spiral is quite straightforward:

- The teaching profession lacks the opportunities for finding rewards that other professions offer through money, status, and influence.
- The only way for teachers to achieve professional autonomy is by withdrawal, isolation, and avowals of mutual equality.
- These behaviors curtail the possibility of developing opportunities within the system; they force teachers to rely on self-generated rewards.
- But the shaky status of teaching makes intrinsic rewards difficult to find and hard to maintain. Isolation compounds the difficulty.
- Thus, the very factors that force teachers to choose isolation and search for intrinsic rewards are those that predict that few such rewards will be found.

The failure of teachers to feel that they are growing, being challenged and developing their craft is well known and captured in such current terms as "teacher burn out." Clearly, the low opportunity aspect of the teaching profession affects both men and women; but even when large numbers of employees are exhibiting similar behaviors, it is the behaviors of women that become linked to stereotypes describing alleged intrinsic predispositions of their sex. It is especially difficult to refute stereotypes in a profession as historically sex-typed as that of teaching, where stereotypic assumptions about women are validated by continual observation of their behavior. When such powerful stereotypes are operating, when they have been absorbed over time into the culture's image of a teacher, it becomes increasingly difficult for anyone within the school system, male or female, to look for alternative explanations of the observed behavior. Women come to believe what is said about them as much as men believe it, with deleterious effects on their behavior and career prospects.

Status and Rewards of the Informal System

Norms of autonomy and equality do not entirely eradicate a hierarchy among teachers. In fact, there are numerous ways in which teachers compete with one another for status and rewards. Since status differences are discouraged because of the formal organization and its norms, they are then distributed in the informal system by the principal or more senior administrators. The scarcity of such rewards and the manner of their distribution tend to emphasize their importance; seemingly small differences in opportunity can become highly significant. Opportunities vary, depending on the school, but can include such things as:

- Selection for attendance at conferences, important meetings, and meetings where there is favorable interaction with the public
- Assignments to the better classes and the better schedules
- Coaching assignments, especially those that involve a monetary supplement
- Access to "soft money" or any special discretionary funds
- Selection for special training programs, especially leadership training

Such opportunities can contribute to one's sense of professional effectiveness, to one's public visibility, to the development of new skills and the recognition of existing ones, and therefore to the greater motivation, commitment, and aspirations that characterize the positive work behaviors of "the moving." Although it is to the disadvantage of schools that so few opportunities exist for distribution, it is to the particular detriment of women that these few resources lie within the discretionary realm of the principal or other administrators. Wherever rewards are distributed informally, women suffer, because the distributors, predominantly men, favor those most like themselves.

Women are also at a disadvantage when the opportunity shortage in school organizations results in the polarization of stuck workers into single-sex groups. One kind of behavior observed in stuck employees is their tendency to look for other sources of status and reward in the workplace (Kanter, 1977, pp. 164–205). When these are not available in the tasks themselves, stuck workers tend to find them in their relationships with other workers. Peer groups become a source of satisfaction; friendships and good times together become a reason for going to work. Cliques spring up among workers; sports, drinking, and vacations all become salient topics of conversation. Since these tightly knit groups have little to do with work, they do not violate the norms of autonomy. They are safety valves from tedium, sources of status and camaraderie—and they tend to be single-sex groups. A work force that is split into many cliques rather than into task groups only adds to the influence of the informal system in an organization. Important information is communicated via the grapevine, and those with the right connections are those who hear it first. Here, of course, women lose out. Since nearly all senior administrators are male, it is the male groups that are privy to whatever early information is floating about. Women may be excluded, prevented from obtaining essential information, information whose immediacy and details would enable them to respond quickly and/or appropriately. Instead, they may be forced to rely on formal channels of communication, where information arrives late and frequently is of superficial value. Thus, the polarization of a stuck work force into single-sex groups creates additional and severe problems for women.

Summary

The problems of limited opportunities and restricted access to them will occur in any system where there are few differentiated roles or rewards. These problems are magnified in schools because of the unique position of the teaching profession and its struggle to attain greater status. We have seen how efforts to garner professional autonomy lead teachers into an isolated position that further limits their opportunity prospects. Because of the need for equal rewards, any differentiation that could create opportunity is restricted. Opportunities that do exist then surface in the informal system, which operates actively in the selection of entry-level administrators. The informal system is given further potency by the presence of multiple peer groups that arise in response to low levels of worker satisfaction. Critical information circulates within these single-sex groups to those privileged to be members.

Sex-role stereotypes, always endemic to teaching, are nourished by a number of organizational factors. Low opportunity fosters behavior that, when observed in women, reinforces both males' and females' preconceptions of women as workers. Women may not seek after those opportunities that do occur, and men consistently bypass women candidates for roles associated with "male" traits. Where decisions are left to individuals and the informal system is powerful, personally held stereotypes have great influence, and this results in decisions about hiring that continue sex-role stratification. In the stuck systems of the schools, the polarization of teachers into single-sex peer groups prevents the type of shared task-related work that would help individuals see beyond their stereotypic notions.

THE STRUCTURE OF POWER IN ORGANIZATIONS

An understanding of organizational forces helps us explain why public school administration is becoming an increasingly male profession. In any organization, the forces that favor alliances of male colleagues push women further to the sidelines. In the organization of schools, these forces are especially strong. The male alliances that appear in schools gain strength not only from the way the system provides opportunity and equalizes rewards and status through autonomy; such alliances also gain strength from the dynamics of power in the organization. Kanter's explanation of the sources of power in an organization adds to our understanding of the factors that help male administrators get promoted. Although we frequently think of power as an individual attribute, Kanter defines power as a capacity that is structured into a job by virtue of the job's activities and location within the larger system. Power is the capacity not to coerce, but to mobilize the resources—both human and material—necessary to get the job done.

Power results from systemic connections that allow one to perform well. Power is efficacy that accumulates through both formal and informal systems (Kanter, 1977, pp. 164–205). Formal job activities contribute to power when they are *visible* to others, *relevant* to current organizational problems, and *extraordinary*. Job activities are visible when they are linked to people both inside and outside the work unit; when they are in contact with other activities and functions; when they are central in information flow networks; and when their contributions are clearly identifiable and measurable. Job activities are relevant to current organizational problems when they involve handling environmental contingencies and when they are at the center of crises, problematic activities, and current organizational goals. Job activities are extraordinary when they are nonroutine, discretionary, and pioneering.

Power also accumulates through alliances in informal network connections. Informal systems facilitate the practice of looking out for one's friends, and they also play an important role in one's ability to accomplish one's job and thereby enhance one's reputation as a desirable and promotable employee. The three kinds of alliances that contribute to organizational power are those an employee has with subordinates, with peers, and with sponsors. People in a position to supervise accumulate power by promoting the careers of subordinates. Peer alliances are founded on common interests or social similarity; they clearly contribute to power and are the classical source of organizational politics. Alliances with sponsors—those influential people willing to endorse an individual, who bestow reflected power or support careers at critical moments—are also crucial.[4]

Power is important not only because it directly affects one's access to decision making and to resources in the system, but also because of its impact on the behavior and style of leaders. Powerful bosses tend to delegate more and to allow subordinates more discretion and latitude; they engender more cooperation, are better liked, and foster higher group moral. Bosses who have little power tend to perpetuate lower group morale; they are more directive, authoritarian, and controlling; they supervise too closely, restrict opportunities for subordinates' growth and autonomy, use more coercive power, and engage in territorial domination; they are concerned about threats to their authority. If common stereotypes of the "bossy" woman boss are examined, it becomes clear that characteristics often attributed to women are really characteristics of powerlessness. Such stereotypes reflect historical differences pertaining to the location of women in organizations rather than to innate sex-linked factors (Kanter, 1978, pp. 11, 12).

Informal and Formal Sources of Power

To analyze the distribution of organizational power in schools, and how such distribution patterns can adversely affect women, we will look first at the informal systems in operation and then at the formal job activities that help individuals accumulate power and establish reputations. In discussing opportunity structures, we elaborated on some of the major forces that create and sustain a strong informal system within a school; such a system distributes information, favors, and rewards to its privileged members. This system of alliances, however, represents

---

[4]Using Kanter's criteria, the role of principal exemplifies a powerful position. A number of recent studies conclude that it is the principal's leadership that accounts for the substantial differences in quality among schools, rather than the socioeconomic variables stressed in the work of Coleman and Jencks (see *New York Times*, 24 August 1979, p. C-1; *Boston Globe*, 6 April 79, p. 12).

only the internal part of the informal mechanisms that exist to help school administrators accomplish their tasks. Beyond the boundaries of the school, a network of associations is formed with various agencies and citizens, a system of alliances necessitated by the extreme vulnerability of schools to their external environment.

Miles characterized the thin skin of the school organization: "The American public school, even more than other public organizations, is subject to control, criticism, and a wide variety of 'legitimate' demands from the surrounding environment: everyone is a stockholder" (1975, p. 240). School administrators can only hope to cope with this reality through the conscientious building of alliances with a wide variety of officials, public groups, board members, and central office staffs. To cultivate these relationships, it becomes important to be a Kiwanian, a Rotarian, or a Lion; to have friends in the Chamber of Commerce or the town or city council; to meet privately with influential board members. No woman administrator, regardless of her experience or credentials, will have an easy time breaking into these historically male clubs; and even if she gains admittance, her token status in the group can quickly destroy the sense of ease and camaraderie that makes belonging to such groups a pleasant experience for its male members (Kanter, 1977, pp. 221, 222).

The fact that so many of these male groups are central to effective school administration makes the task of a woman administrator inestimably harder. Conservative impulses, which might be successfully countered with separate individuals, accumulate in such groups into a body of resistance that is hard to overcome. Statistics on the number of women administrators in school systems bear eloquent testimony to the strength of the patterns of sponsorship and peer alliances within schools and communities that act to sustain male school leadership. Such forces exist not only in informal systems but in formal job activities as well. When one examines the sources of power in schools, it quickly becomes apparent how many opportunities to work on relevant, visible, and autonomous tasks revolve around activities outside of normal teaching duties, opportunities that are distributed informally by administrators.

Coaching assignments are among the most important extracurricular activities a teacher can perform to acquire more influence in the organization. A coach is exposed to the view of the school, the parents, school boards, and local officials. Coaches receive frequent press notices, they preside at awards nights and sports banquets, and have their names and performance records become local knowledge. This visibility is helpful, and more importantly, their reputation and influence are extended into opportunities for advancement. Those who become coaches are able to demonstrate a different range of skills and to show competence in new areas; these skills are highly relevant to nonacademic issues that are important to the school. Not only do coaches have the opportunity to show their ability to influence and control students and to exact discipline, but they manage funds allocated to sports, they meet with local luminaries, and they sustain close ties with alumni and townspeople. In sum, they demonstrate to a willing audience their potential for management. No wonder the overwhelming majority of superintendents were at one time coaches. A member of one screening committee reported:

> [The screening committee] wants to decide who is the best person for the job. But they don't really know what the job is, so decisions are based on extraneous functions. They want demonstrated competence, and they measure it by the winning football team. They want somebody who can work with the public and who the public knows, and so again it's the winning football coach. Everybody ignores the long lists of criteria and chooses on the basis of a winning football team. The deck is stacked against women [Schmuck, 1975, p. 123].

Although this commentator felt distress that job criteria were ignored, it can also be said that the committee's decision resulted from a list of criteria that were centered on other relevant skills, such as control, discipline, and public relations. We all understand, at various levels of acceptance, how central these skills are to the functioning of schools. As society hands over more and more control issues to schools, there is an increasing demand on school officials to deal with serious behavior problems, with rising vandalism, with more social and public agencies. Political talent becomes necessary; so too does sound fiscal management. Skills associated with these new arenas are, of course, associated with male traits. Even a woman candidate with established competence in one or more of these areas may lose out because of the multiplicity of "male" skills linked to the administrative role.[5]

Four studies reviewed in the work of Schmuck (1975, p. 22) and Howard (1975, p. 31) revealed that under women administrators, teacher performance and student achievement rated higher; the administrators had a more active stance towards problem solving and more

---

[5]In a further twist to women's dilemma, Poll found that certain skills valued in aspiring male administrators were interpreted as liabilities when exhibited by female aspirants. A male teacher's ability to work with parents was applauded; in a female teacher this was seen as dangerous because she might be revealing school secrets to parents. This is an excellent example of why those who are socially dissimilar from the dominant group feel they are not trusted. (see Poll, 1978, p. 17).

bent toward instructional leadership (Gross & Trask, 1962; Hemphill, Griffiths, & Frederickson, 1962; Hoyle & Randall, 1974; Meskin, 1974). In a somewhat oblique manner, these studies underline the fact that the presently relevant skills demanded of school administrators go beyond those which focus on the academic functioning of schools. Unless schools can be relieved of the many social forces that now push them into a posture of exercising control, common stereotypes will continue to exclude women from administration.

Autonomy Norms and Powerlessness

Autonomy (Kanter's third descriptor of power-enhancing jobs) allows people freedom to do nonroutine tasks and thus display their skills and creativity. Such activities include the coaching assignments already described, soft money projects that call for new skills and priorities, the reorganization of systems, new legislation that alters current ways of doing things. However, since teachers seek autonomy to shield themselves from public scrutiny, the autonomy-equality norm that Lortie described acts strongly to limit occasions where they can demonstrate new or unusual skills. Autonomy springs from a need to be left alone, and in isolation, it is difficult to show others how good you are. Autonomy-equality behaviors, closing oneself off, protecting one's territory, and resisting innovation, are symptoms, in Kanter's analysis, of powerlessness.

Powerless workers strive to defend whatever sphere of influence they already have. As they withdraw to their own turf, they lose sight of larger issues and behave only in self-protective ways. Because they lack influence in the larger organization, they rely on rules to coerce their subordinates. Over time, this adherence to rules becomes an end in itself and is typical of the behavior of the petty bureaucrat. The powerlessness of teachers goads them into isolation, denying them those occasions where they could display new and relevant skills. In a cycle similar to that which affected opportunity prospects, the autonomy-equality norm further intensifies the powerlessness it is designed to correct. Those who succeed in gaining power are those who have excelled in other spheres of school activity where such norms do not predominate.

The conclusions that can be drawn from this analysis of organizational power within schools are as depressing as those that became apparent from observing opportunity structures. A strong informal system exists through which favors and opportunities are distributed. Included in those opportunities are the types of extracurricular activities that, because of their visibility, autonomy and relevance, allow individuals to demonstrate their skills and enhance their reputations. A powerful internal system is overlaid with an external system of alliances with community groups that have traditionally been male bastions. Yet these alliances are necessary sources of power for any school administrator.

The pattern of male domination is repeated in the types of job skills valued in today's administrators. Skills related to fiscal control, student control, negotiating, and politicking are assumed to be found only in men. The few women who do advance to administration are frequently placed in low power positions—either as superintendents of small districts under the heavy control of local boards or in staff rather than line functions or as directors of program areas where they administer policies set by male superiors.[6] These women are thwarted from displaying the independent leadership that would enhance their own reputations and those of women in general. Instead, their powerlessness may spawn behavior typical of petty domination and lend credence to common stereotypes of women bosses.

RECOMMENDATIONS

The situation for women in schools is dismal. They work in an organization whose hierarchical structure, normative patterns and community location conspire to create enormously powerful forces of resistance to their advancement. But if an analysis of the school organization yields these depressing conclusions, the same analysis can offer organizational strategies to ameliorate these conditions. Women's progress toward administrative ranks would profit from some steps in the right direction:

- Breaking down autonomy-equality barriers would be helpful. Innovations that stress cooperative behavior are pertinent not only to educational goals, but to women's issues as well. Activities involving team teaching, problem-centered task forces, swap shops, the use of internal teachers as training resources for other teachers, and brief exchange programs with teachers from other schools can promote visibility, enhance reputations, build contacts, and break down single-sex cliques.
- Creating opportunities for task-related groups can be accom-

---

[6]A 1974 study by Fischel and Pottker revealed that women represent 18% of state education department employees; 9% of these are employed as directors, 2% are employed as deputy associates or assistant superintendents; see Schmuck, 1972, p. 16. For the distribution of women superintendents by size of district, see Clement, 1975, pp. 38–43.

plished through task forces, and important committee work, all of which allow people to use new and different skills and to counteract the pressures that create a stuck work force.

- Promoting women's visibility with the public would be made possible by selecting women for tasks that require working with people outside the school and by supporting women in such work.
- Selecting women for committees or task groups would help them become adept at handling important problems, such as budget issues and vandalism. These assignments can draw on existing knowledge and also serve to develop new skills.
- Demystifying administrative tasks would allow women to assess their interests and potential more accurately. The curtain of ignorance that blocks aspirations can be lifted by in-service courses on administration, certain types of committee work, external training programs, occasions to observe various administrators, and meetings with women administrators.
- More equitable distribution (by men of goodwill) of leadership training and conference opportunities would be helpful and noteworthy.
- Giving women resources to distribute would enhance their reputation, since resources attract notice and allies.
- Awarding "acting" administrative posts to women would allow them to demonstrate their competence and to gain experience.
- Developing more publicity for the extracurricular activities of girls would make women teachers more visible; and these activities would thereby gain more public popularity.

This is but a partial list of the types of strategies that could alter the organizational dynamics that affect women. The targets of such efforts to bring about changes are not individuals but the systems and subsystems that distribute opportunities for building successful careers. The strength of such strategies is that they can improve the situations of a number of women simultaneously. Such strategies are necessary if women are to occupy an arena where it is essential for them to be.

REFERENCES

Bidwell, C. E. (1965). "The School as a Formal Organization." In *Handbook of Organizations* (J. G. March, ed.), Rand McNally, Chicago, pp. 970–1018.

Carlson, R. O. (1972). *School Superintendants' Careers and Performance.* Merrill, Columbus, Ohio.

Clement, J. P. (1975). *Sex Bias in School Leadership*. Integrated Education, Evanston, Ill.

Gross, N., and Trask, A. E. (1964). *Men and Women as Elementary School Principals*. Final Report No. 2., Cooperative Research Project No. 853., Graduate School of Education, Harvard University.

Hemphill, J., Griffiths, D., and Frederickson, N. (1962). *Administrative Performance and Personality*. Teachers College, Columbia University.

Howard, S. (1975). *Why Aren't Women Adminstering Our Schools? The Status of Women Public School Teachers and the Factors Hindering Their Promotion into Administration*. National Council of Administrative Women in Education, Washington, D.C.

Kanter, R. M. (1977). *Men and Women of the Corporation*. Basic Books, New York.

Kanter, R. M. (1978). *A Structural Approach to Affirmative Action*. Paper presented at the Conference on Equal Pay and Opportunity for Women, Wellesley College.

Lortie, D. C. (1975). "The Teacher and Team Teaching: Suggestions for Long-range Research." In *Managing Change in Educational Organizations* (J. V. Baldridge and T. Deal, eds.). McCrutchan Publishing, Berkeley, Calif.

Mason, W. S., Dressel, R. J., and Bain, R. K. (1959). "Sex Role and the Career Orientations of Beginning Teachers." *Harvard Education Review*, 29 (Fall): 370–83.

Meskin, J. (1974). "The Performance of Women School Administrators: A Review of the Literature." *Administrators Notebook*, 23: p. 1.

Miles, M. (1975). "Planned Change and Organization Health: Figure and Ground." In *Managing Change in Educational Organizations* (J. V. Baldridge and T. Deal, eds.). McCrutchan Publishing, Berkeley, Calif.

Pellegrin, R. J. (1975). "Some Organizational Characteristics of Multiunit Schools." In *Managing Change in Educational Organizations* (J. V. Baldridge and T. Deal, eds.). McCrutchan Publishing, Berkeley, Calif.

Poll, C. (1978). *No Room at the Top: A Study of the Social Processes That Contribute to the Underrepresentation of Women on the Administrative Levels of the New York City School System*. Unpublished dissertation in sociology, City University of New York.

Schmuck, P. (1975). *Sex Differentiation in Public School Administration*. National Council of Administrative Women in Education, Washington, D.C.

Schmuck, R. and Runkel, P. (1972). *Handbook of Organization Development in Schools*. National Press Books.

Sex Bias in Schools: Evaluating Employment Practices (1978). Institute for Women's Concerns, Arlington, Va.

Chapter 15

HORMONES AND HAREMS: ARE THE ACTIVITIES OF SUPERINTENDING DIFFERENT FOR A WOMAN?

Nancy J. Pitner

The majority of the employees in educational organizations are women, but their numbers decrease with each step up the hierarchical ladder, until at the top there is nearly no representation at all. Tyack (1974) aptly describes school districts as "pedagogical harems." Much of the research that has attempted to uncover the factors responsible for the underrepresentation of women at managerial levels in school districts has focused on two problems: first, on the acculturation that has resulted in role ambiguity and limited aspirations for women (Maccoby, 1966; Coleman, 1961; Horner, 1969; Epstein, 1970; Astin, Suniewick, & Dweck, 1971; Schwartz & Lever, 1973); second, on the barriers society creates that prevent all but exceptional or "lucky" women from reaching positions of leadership (Roby, 1973; Sewell, 1971; Schwartz & Lever, 1973; Epstein, 1970). One percent of all superintendents are these exceptional or lucky women who have managed to pass through the filters of the educational system and the process of obtaining credentials and have arrived at the top.[1] This chapter examines three such women.

METHODOLOGY

Several questions arise when a professional woman enters the male domain of administration: How does she conduct her organizational

---

[1]The American Association of School Administrators (AASA) reported in December, 1979, that approximately 160 out of 15,000 superintendents were women.

273

life? Are the activities different when the superintendent is a woman? Are there differences in the decisions to be made? The dilemmas to be untangled? The preoccupations and concerns that arise? In a study designed to arrive at answers to these questions, three women occupying positions as chief executives in suburban school districts in a western state were observed as they worked during the fall of 1979. A similar study in the spring of 1977 (Pitner, 1978) had observed three male superintendents for the purpose of describing and analyzing the kind of work American school superintendents do in their day-by-day ongoing activities and in the network of relationships of which superintendents are necessarily a part.[2] In both studies, three strategies were employed in order to gather information about the structure and content of the work of superintendents: unstructured observation of incidents; structured observation of the frequency of certain events; and open-ended interviewing about institutional norms, levels of status, and administrative processes. During the observation phase, two types of data were collected: anecdotal data, which included detailed descriptions of critical and interesting activities, exhibits of correspondence, and background notes relevant to activities; and structured data on the pattern of activities throughout every minute of the workday, which were maintained in a detailed chronological record, in a record of all inter- and intra-office correspondence and all incoming and outgoing mail, and in a detailed record of all verbal contacts during meetings, tours, and telephone calls.

Both the 1978 and 1980 studies focused on the observed behavior rather than on the traits and capacities of superintendents, and both focused on descriptions of types of behavior and frequency of occurrence rather than on evaluations of behavior. Before a case can be made for the absence or presence of sexual factors and sex-related differences in the work activities of superintendents, it is necessary to describe how the subjects for both studies were selected, what their demographic characteristics were, and what everyday activities were revealed in the study of male superintendents. When potential subjects were contacted, the studies were briefly described and copies of the research proposal

[2]Not everything a person does on the job is a job-related activity or in a strict sense part of that job. Goffman (1959, p. 100) makes an important and useful distinction illustrating this concern: "I suppose one might want to ask what a salesgirl does in a store by virtue of her being a salesgirl. The test of close analysis, however, is to study what a person who is a salesgirl does in a store that persons who are not salesgirls do not do, for much of what only salesgirls do in stores is not done by them *qua* salesgirls and has nothing to do with sales." Similarly, Drucker (1954) shares Goffman's concern that certain activities of managers are not inherently managerial. Mintzberg (1973), on the other hand, does not make this distinction.

along with an explanatory letter were sent to those superintendents who expressed an interest in both studies. In the first study, participating school districts were limited to those near the large midwestern city in the area. Of the five male superintendents contacted, two agreed to participate initially, and a third volunteered during a second round of contacts.

Reasons for willingness and nonwillingness to participate varied. One copy of the research proposal was returned with a letter: "I am done with PPBS [Planning, Programming, Budgeting, Systems].... This is the time in my yearly workload that I visit schools to observe in the classrooms.... I'm not sure of the effect upon your [sic] staff during visitation." Another superintendent delayed in making a decision, saying, at one point: "Last week would have been perfect for observation; I was busy in negotiations and had meetings every night." It was inferred that he did not want to be observed during an uneventful cycle of activities. Perhaps it was not coincidental that two of the three male subjects arranged to be observed during a week when a regularly scheduled board of education meeting was to be held. The third volunteer tried to recruit additional subjects on his own during a luncheon meeting of district superintendents from his area.

While the 1978 study selected male superintendents from suburbs surrounding one large midwestern city, the 1980 study selected female subjects from suburbs surrounding two large cities on the west coast. One of the four female superintendents initially contacted agreed to participate. Reasons for refusing were not elaborate, and they were delivered by the superintendents' secretaries over the telephone. In one case, a recall vote involving two school board members was underway, and in the other, the threat of a teachers' strike was imminent. The superintendent who accepted supplied the names of colleagues, "feminists" likely to be interested in the research; they accepted. As with the male subjects, two of the three female superintendents arranged to be observed during a week in which a regularly scheduled board of education meeting was to be held. All three had all-day conferences at least once during the period of observation.

In both studies, the superintendents permitted the observer to watch them in almost all types of work situations—during board meetings, staff meetings, individual conferences with subordinates and community members, off-the-record meetings with their peers, and in moments alone. The female superintendents invited the author to extend the observation into their homes, which provided a view in one case of a woman superintendent juggling a complex set of roles— arriving home from the office around 7:00 P.M., catching up on the news with her teenagers, working together with her husband to prepare dinner, reviewing a slide show for a school board meeting, playing a game of backgammon with her husband, and receiving a telephone call from the school board president.

The two samples of superintendents in these studies can be compared with each other and with the superintendent population as a whole. Prior research has suggested that male and female administrators have different careers and different demographic profiles. Male administrators were almost always married and white (Carlson, 1972; Gross, Mason, & McEachern, 1958). Women were generally older and less often married; they had more training and classroom experience and received lower salaries than male superintendents with similar qualifications (Paddock, 1977). In this study male superintendents of the 1978 study shared many characteristics with the female superintendents. Both males

TABLE 15.1

Profiles of Three Male and Three Female Superintendents Studied by Pitner

	Male Subjects (1978)			Female Subjects (1980)		
	A	B	C	D	E	F
Actively affiliated with a religion	0	X	0	0	0	X
Active in professional organizations	0	X	X+	X+	X	X
Attends AASA regularly	0	X	X	X	0	X
40–49 years of age	X	X	0	X	X	X
White	X	X	X	0	X	X
Protestant (as reared)	X	X	X	X	X	X
From rural or small-town background	0	X	0	X	0	0
Married	S	X	X	X	E	W
Has children	X	X	0	X	X	X
Resides in district	X	X	X	0	X	X
Years of tenure in this superintendency	7	4	1	3	1	2
Is adjunct professor in local university	0	0	X	X	X	0

KEY: 0 = no
X = yes
X+ = very active
S = separated (was divorced after observation)
E = engaged (was married after observation)
W = widow
AASA = American Association of School Administrators

and females were in their first superintendency and were career-bound as opposed to place-bound. They had had previous experience in an educational organization and had doctoral degrees in educational administration. While all the males were superintendents of suburban districts where schools were for kindergarten through twelfth grade (K–12), two of the females were superintendents of suburban districts with elementary schools. More detailed profiles of the superintendents and their districts are displayed in Tables 15.1 and 15.2. Females differed from males in one major respect. They traveled the traditional career route from teacher to principal to central office administrator to superintendent; males skipped the principalship.

Integrated accounts of superintendent's daily activities are scarce (Pitner, 1978). Cuban remarked in 1976 that "while we know to the penny what salaries administrators received, what degrees they earned, and where they were born, we know very little about what they, as executives actually do each day" (p.xiv). To answer the question of whether the work of male superintendents differs from that of females we used three studies of male superintendents of suburban districts as a basis for comparison (Campbell & Cunningham, 1959; Mintzberg, 1973; Pitner, 1978). These observation studies provide information about the commonplace activities of a superintendents daily life. In this chapter we present (1) a description of a typical work day for one male and one female superintendent; (2) the characteristics of the work of superinten-

TABLE 15.2

Characteristics of the Districts of Three Male and Three Female Superintendents Studied by Pitner

	Districts of males (1978)			Districts of females (1980)		
	A	B	C	D	E	F
Enrollment	3500	5000	1500	4300	1700	3700
K-12	X	X	X	0	0	X
Suburban	X	X	X	X	X	X
Elected board	X	X	X	X	X	X
Predominantly anglo community	X	X	X	X	X	X
Declining enrollment	X	0	X	X	0	X
Superintendent evaluated by board	0	0	X	X	X	X
Written goals and objectives	0	0	X	X	X	X

KEY: 0 = no
X = yes

dents as revealed in the description of activities; and (3) the crucial alliances maintained to carry out the work. Following the presentation of these materials, a case is made regarding sexual factors and sex-related differences in the work activities of superintendents.

FINDINGS ON THE WORK DAY

A Day in the Life of a Male Superintendent

The observer arrived at the superintendent's office at 8:00 A.M. The superintendent, Dr. Beta, was already meeting with a male high school teacher behind closed doors. Dr. Beta had scheduled this meeting the day before for 7:35 A.M. so it would not conflict with the teacher's responsibilities. Dr. Beta requested that the teacher assume the extra responsibility for the next school year of editing the district newsletter, which is distributed quarterly to all residents of the community. Toward the end of the meeting, voices became audible from behind the closed door. When the door opened at 8:30 A.M., the secretary entered the office. She reviewed for Dr. Beta the day's schedule and the messages that were received during the conference. Dr. Beta began to return calls at 8:25. After an unsuccessful attempt to reach one person, he noted on the message slip the date and time he tried to return the call.

At 8:40 he called his secretary, using the intercom, and asked her to call four people on the phone. He then proceeded to process the items in his IN basket. The telephone rang. The junior high school principal was returning his call. He asked the principal to check on the grade in math for Student X. The superintendent hung up, and returned to his desk work:

- A letter from an alumnus association specifying the agenda for an upcoming meeting was skimmed and filed.
- A courtesy copy of a memo from the chairperson of the physical education department reporting the minutes of the last department meeting was skimmed and put into the OUT basket for filing.
- A brochure from a publishing company, entitled *Essence of Adolescence* was skimmed; a routing slip directed to building principals was attached, and the brochure was put into the out basket.
- A book published by the National Institute of Education (NIE), *Violent Schools, Safe Schools* was skimmed; a routing slip directed to building principals was attached, and the book was put into the OUT basket.

At 8:45 the phone rang. A professor from a nearby university was returning the superintendent's call. The superintendent told the professor that Ms. X was critical of a physical education teacher and he wanted to straighten things out. The professor told the superintendent that the student teacher in question was reprimanded for her unprofessional behavior. At 8:48 the superintendent hung up the phone and returned to processing items in his IN basket.

- From a copy of the student high school newspaper he learned about operations in the high school; the newspaper was put into the OUT basket for filing.
- After reading a luncheon invitation from an elementary school, he wrote a note to his secretary to R.S.V.P.
- A report from a principal informed him about the safety patrol at an elementary school. He was prompted by this to write a note to the administrative assistant telling him to put out another job description.
- A courtesy copy of a memo from the school nurse contained information about the upcoming program on posture; the superintendent glanced at the letter and put it into the OUT basket for filing.

At 8:52 the elementary school principal in charge of special education telephoned and said: "Dave, I sent you a note to have the school psychologist present at the board meeting, but I want to change that." The superintendent was lining up potential board reports. "How about one on what school psychologists do? ... Also, add the speech therapist, nurse, special education ... different programs ... kids going to Delta Schools, and so on. . . . Say, did you get my memo I sent on gifted kids? ... Okay. ...."

At 8:57 the superintendent returned to his desk work:

- He dictated a letter to inform a teacher of the reasons a contract to continue teaching was denied.
- A report from a principal on the status of special education programs in the district was skimmed and put into the OUT basket for filing.
- A letter from a person in the community gave opinions on the recent failure of the bond issue; it was carefully read and put into the OUT basket for filing.
- A form from the state education department announced a course for bus drivers; the superintendent signed it.

At 9:05 the administrative assistant dropped in and inquired about the selection of a teacher for the program for gifted and talented students. He reminded the superintendent that the job announcement had to be posted. While the administrative assistant was talking, the superintendent continued to process his mail. "I have a letter here from a teacher requesting a 2-year leave," he said. "Has that been done in the past?" He asked the administrative assistant to check in the policy book.

- A note from a principal requested information about the procedure for custodians on the last day of classes at a nearby technical school. The superintendent wrote "Check with Marlan" on the note and put the note into the OUT basket.

The superintendent asked the administrative assistant, "Should we pursue the double-session thing?" The administrative assistant said, "We have to be concerned with equitable assignments at the elementary." While he was talking, the superintendent signed approximately 20 forms—absence reports, purchase orders, and supplemental pay forms—and processed several additional items:

- He read a courtesy copy of a letter from the high school principal notifying parents of the suspension of their son.
- He glanced at copies of honor roll lists from the high school and middle school and filed them.
- He skimmed and filed a copy of an "exclusion list," students who did not have required immunizations, that had been sent to him from the middle school principal.
- He signed a letter that he had dictated the day before requesting information from the city solicitor about legal questions.

He continued talking with the administrative assistant while processing the above. "I want to make it difficult for the board to back down," he said. "Get me information on the additional staff we'll need for program expansion, split sessions, and expanded enrollment." The assistant said, "We should change the course on language expression to an elective if you think reading is a higher priority. We must make the change."

The superintendent said, "Let's go to a six-period day."

The assistant answered, "We'd have to cut out home arts."

The superintendent said, "Go to a three-day cycle.... You'd have longer periods."

The assistant asked, "What about problems with standards... have to go to seven-period day to offer reading... require art, music, or language expression.... We could eliminate study halls."

When the administrative assistant left, the superintendent proceeded to file copies of school newsletters from three schools in the district. At 9:30, the middle school principal entered the office and inquired about getting an additional secretary to type purchase orders at the end of the year. The superintendent laughed and agreed to give the principal an extra three days of secretarial time.

A meeting of all administrators scheduled for 9:30 begins.

A Day in the Life of a Female Superintendent

The superintendent stepped into the lobby of the administrative office annex at 8:15 A.M. on a sunny Monday in October. She greeted the receptionist, picked up several telephone messages from her secretary's desk (the secretary was on vacation for the week), and walked into her large but modestly decorated office. After thumbing through assorted messages, she reviewed the activities scheduled in her appointment calendar for the upcoming week. Ordinarily this would have been done with her secretary.

Monday:	Meeting with administrative cabinet
	Appointment with president of retail food company with headquarters in the community
Tuesday:	School tour
	Meeting with administrative team
Wednesday:	School tour
	Luncheon meeting with the press
	Meeting with a parent regarding a complaint
	Dinner with a professional peer
	Meeting of community civic elite at a controversial research center
Thursday:	Meeting with a school board member
	Luncheon with community leaders
	School tour
Friday:	Statewide curriculum conference outside the community

After reviewing the scheduled activities, the superintendent made two phone calls to principals, one regarding a student and the other to schedule a meeting. She spent a few minutes on the final draft of a presentation for the cabinet meeting and left her office to ask the business manager's secretary a question, exchanging greetings with two secretaries and the personnel director on her way. Upon returning to her office, she placed a call to a principal to discuss an upcoming office klatch in his building; she asked whether the press would be there. As she continued to talk on the phone, her back turned to the conference area in her office, which is made up of three tables shoved together, the five male members of the administrative cabinet arrived one at a time for the weekly Monday morning meeting. They engaged in light chatter and sauntered up to the chalkboard to add agenda items to the existing list. Joking ensued about the baseball pool. One man reported that he had won the World Series pool that is run by the custodians. The atmosphere was casual—everyone was on a first-name basis. The superintendent was wearing a pantsuit, and her jacket was on the back of her chair. The male subordinates wore sport jackets and ties.

The superintendent swung her desk chair around to face her subordinates. She smiled and began the meeting, asking first for additional agenda items, then identifying the fifth item on the list, which pertains to a problem that is to be discussed first. It is the name of a teacher who has had a record of excessive absences partly because of personal problems. After discussing several options, for example, whether to reassign her as a substitute and hire a full-time teacher for her position, the superintendent requested that the personnel director "pursue the matter." The superintendent left this agenda item abruptly and inquired about the status of legal action regarding the sale of school-owned lands. Since no one offered any new information, the superintendent went on to another agenda item and announced that a state legislator would be visiting the school district in two weeks. They discussed what he "should see" while he was there. One principal responded, "We'll arrange for you to have a tea . . . ." The business manager arrived and took a place at the far side of the tale. The superintendent requested that he clear his schedule for the state legislator's visit. Throughout the discussion, the superintendent worked with a mimeographed form categorizing the items and outlining the order in which they would be discussed at the upcoming board of education meeting. She made notations on the form as each item was discussed. This was a low-keyed preparation for the board meeting and lasted about 30 minutes.

The meeting was then turned over to the administrators, who brought up items pertinent to their individual situations. The middle school principal delivered a teacher's request for permission to raffle a side of beef, the proceeds of which would be used to purchase instructional materials for the English department. The principal raised the issue of how tight money was in the schools and whether they needed such things as raffles. A discussion ensued about product liability, raffles, and money-raising functions that benefit only one department in a school. The raffle issue was quickly solved by the decision to "call it donations so it's not [seen as] gambling." The question of "who benefits" was more problematic. Normally, money-raising activities that benefit only one department were discouraged. One principal reminded the others that the music department had an annual money-making project to purchase instruments. This case appeared to be within regulations because the music department was a district-wide department and the purchase of instruments was not restricted to one building. Concern was expressed regarding "setting a precedent" and the possible consequences; for example, a raft of fund-raising drives might decrease the importance of the annual drive of the Parent–Teachers Association (PTA). While the discussion trailed off, the administrators decided not to conflict with other established fund raisers and with the district. The "vote" was casual, and it was assumed that there was consensus.

At the close of the meeting, the superintendent quipped, "Who else is suing us?"

"The student with the broken leg," one principal piped up.

"The student with a cut finger," another added.

The business manager summarized. "We have possibly three law suits facing us not. . . ." He included the school-land controversy in his summary.

The regular Monday morning meeting of the administrative cabinet ended after 65 minutes, and the personnel director and business manager remained to discuss in detail items that would be brought up in the executive session of the monthly board of education meeting scheduled for the following week. After 25 minutes of discussion, the superintendent asked the personnel director whether a female teacher in the district was ready for a principalship. The teacher was being considered for a position in another district. The personnel director responded affirmatively.

From 10:58 A.M. to 10:30 P.M., the superintendent's day included 4 more scheduled meetings, 11 unscheduled meetings, 12 phone calls, and the following sequence of events:

10:58: She placed a call to a principal to follow up on a parental request regarding a home-bound student with learning problems and inquired as to the availability of space for the kindergarten-aged child.

11:04: She reviewed mail received the day before and was interrupted by the personnel director, who stopped in to discuss personnel issues. She continued reviewing mail and messages and requested that the secretary arrange a meeting.

11:15: She left the building and drove to an elementary school to drop off materials for the principal. While she was there, she visited the playground to ask a female physical education teacher to attend a meeting she was asked to attend, exchange pleasantries with two secretaries and with the assistant principal, and she stopped to chat with the principal, who brought up the lack of supervision in the boys' locker room since the assignment of a female teacher to the fifth-grade section of physical education.

11:38: She left the building and stopped at a local delicatessen to pick up a sandwich for lunch.

11:55: While eating lunch in her office, she called a woman superintendent in a neighboring district to discuss the personnel problem identified at the morning meeting of the administrative cabinet. She was interrupted by the speech coordinator, who wished to discuss a proposed student-evaluation form.

12:20: She arranged to have a report typed and told the secretary that she was trying to contact a principal. She read her mail.

12:44: She left the building, running into a board member as she was getting into her car; they discussed the progress of teacher negotiation. She congratulated a passing maintenance worker on the recent birth of his child.

12:50: She was called back into the building to take a phone call from a woman superintendent in another district. They discussed a nomination of the screening committee and the settlement that morning of a contract in a district in the area. She stopped in to inform the business manager of these matters.

12:56: Leaving the administrative building, she drove to another district building, dropped off a letter, and then drove to the middle school.

1:00: She spent 1 hour and 25 minutes at the middle school, stopping into every classroom and talking with teachers and also with students, many of whom knew her by name. She spoke for 5 minutes with a male superintendent from the midwest who stopped by to visit as he was passing through the state.

2:25: On the way back to the central administrative offices she stopped at a busy intersection to talk with the patrol aide, who had been having problems with older students from another district.

2:40: She met with the personnel director for 5 minutes and then left the office.

2:45: The superintendent drove 3 miles to the corporate headquarters of the retail food company located in the community for a meeting she had arranged with the president. She put on her jacket as she got out of the car and walked into the large reception area, identifying herself and signing the register. Although the receptionist asked her to be seated, she stood off to the side of the room, admiring the paintings and plants. In 10 minutes two large wooden doors behind the receptionist's area were opened, and the president emerged. He escorted the superintendent to his office, asked his secretary to get some soft drinks, and they sat down in the conversation area. The superintendent commented on the artifacts in the office and the luxury of the space and revealed her knowledge of the company, mentioning the location and the names of stores throughout the west. She quickly moved on to discuss pertinent subjects—the effects of tax reform on schools, the plan of one corporation to set up a trust fund for a particular school district, and the status of the land owned by the school district that was adjacent to the corporation's headquarters. The president remained quite relaxed, one leg over an arm of the chair; he was noncommital. The meeting lasted for about an hour, and as she left, the superintendent toured the computer facilities and the photographic display of the various stores owned by the corporation. After exchanging pleasantries, the president left the superintendent at the double doors to the lobby.

4:15: The superintendent returned to the administration building. Several people had telephoned and she called them back. She scheduled a meeting with a principal; she discussed the upcoming school board meeting with a member and clarified issues regarding jurisdiction and state law; and she called the business manager on the intercom while on the line with the board member in order to get some information. Then she called the business manager back to ask how "candidates night*" went.

4:42: She returned a call to the press, provided information about a letter from the state mediator, and called the business manager on the intercom to ask for the name of the mediator assigned to the district. Leaving the office, made the 45-minute drive home.

9:00–10:30: The superintendent spent the evening reviewing her mail, drafting correspondence, and talking on the telephone with the school board president.

---

*"Candidates night" is a preelection activity in which school board candidates meet with the public to discuss issues and platforms.

CHARACTERISTICS OF SUPERINTENDENT WORK

The activities encountered by male and female superintendents in a typical workday do not reveal an exotic story. Like the activities of other managers (Mintzberg, 1973), the tasks do not approach the lofty ideals of "leadership"; they are characterized by brevity, variety, and fragmentation. Of all the work-related activities engaged in, 60% lasted less than 9 minutes, and only 7% lasted more than an hour. This does not coincide with the image of an executive as a reflective planner. Attending to mail, telephone calls, and meetings accounted for almost every minute from the moment the superintendents entered their offices in the morning until they departed in the evening. The end of one meeting frequently became the beginning of another when subordinates slipped into the superintendents' offices as the door opened. Since superintendents, like other managers, feel compelled to do a great amount of work (Mintzberg, 1973), the amount of time available is a critical factor in determining how much attention can be given to issues and problems. The interruptions of phone calls and drop-in meetings and the frequent need to leave their desk work to attend to the myriad of matters on their mind make the day quite fragmented as a superintendent tries to resolve the current and future concerns of the district. The distribution of time during the day described was typical of that for the rest of the week and was consistent with the experiences of other subjects in both samples. A more complete breakdown of how superintendents distributed their work activities is displayed in Tables 15.3 and 15.4. Although there were similarities in the work of superintendents, differences among individuals, as well as differences between male and female samples, did exist.

For example, while the average work week was 44 hours, the range was from 36 to 55, and two of the three work weeks that exceeded 50 hours were those of women superintendents. All superintendents reported working a 60-hour week, and one male superintendent added that this excluded nightmares. The shortest work weeks were connected to the following factors: the longest tenure in the superintendency (7 years); having a father who had also been a superintendent; being in a suburban district that had the highest socioeconomic status in the study; and previous experience as an executive in a business corporation. Female superintendents spent less time engaged in desk work in the office (11% versus 20%). Desk work is the processing of paper—reviewing the mail, most of which is unsolicited and warrants minimal attention, writing response to requests, initiating written communications. In all cases, the mail was opened and presorted by secretaries so that much of the junk was sifted out. Female superintendents prepared

TABLE 15.3
Distribution of Superintendents' Time

	Percentage of total time		Mean duration of each event (minutes)	
	Males (%)	Females (%)	Males	Females
Activities				
Deskwork	20	11	12	14
Telephoning	8	7	4	4
Unscheduled meetings	10	8	11	5
Scheduled meetings	51	42	70	56
Tours	2	8	12	31
Conferences	0	24		
Personal contact				
Subordinates	47	50		
Board	5	6		
Peers	7	26		
Clients or community representatives	11	30		
Some combination of the above	29	8		

TABLE 15.4
Percentage of Superintendents' Time Spent in Verbal Contacts

Verbal Contacts	Male (%)	Female (%)
Basis of initiation		
Superintendent	56	59
Another party	40	37
Regularly scheduled event	2	1
Mutually arranged	2	3
Location		
Superintendent's office	49	42
Subordinate's office	1	5
Hall or building in school district	16	22
Conference room	23	10
In the community	11	10
Outside of school district	0	31
Number of participants		
2	83	81
3	6	7
4	3	4
More than 5	8	8

their written correspondence and dictation in the evening at home. Males rarely reported doing routing paperwork at home, but they did report doing budget preparations, which requires more attention, either at home or in the office on the weekend; and one ritualistically filled up his attache case each evening with professional literature only to admit the following morning that he never looked at it.

Another difference between males and females was in their use of the observation tour. The amount of time spent and the purpose of the tour are left to the discretion of each superintendent. Female superintendents averaged seven tours per week, each lasting about 30 minutes; males averaged five tours per week, each lasting about 12 minutes each. More importantly, females used their time to visit classrooms and teachers, keeping abreast of the instructional program, while males used the time to walk the halls with the principals and the head custodians, requesting that they follow up on particular concerns. Teachers and students responded favorably to visits by female superintendents, eagerly demonstrating what was going on, including any difficulties they were having. Male superintendents did not visit classrooms during the observation phase of the study except in the case of teachers who had quasi-administrative assignments. During the tours, both male and female superintendents met mostly with professionals of their own sex.

The interest of female superintendents in curriculum and instruction was manifested in their memberships in the Association of Supervision and Curriculum Development (ASCD)—in addition, they belonged to the American Association of School Administrators (AASA). While females were able to articulate the specific ideology and activities that dominated the district's curricular program, men appeared to speak of aspects of organization structure, such as the construction of a new school building, approval of a tax levy, and the graduation of a senior class.[3]

NETWORK OF CONTRACTS

The single dominant pattern that characterized superintendents' activities was their constant communications. They communicated with

---

[3]We must consider that classroom visits might be seen by principals as close supervision, and a violation of the norm Meyer and Rowan (1977) identify as "the logic of confidence"; that is, upper levels of the educational organization assume that what goes on at the technical level makes sense and is appropriate without directly observing it. It is also interesting that male superintendents who had never held the principalship did not trespass into the principals domain, while those who had been principals did so.

municipal authorities, state departments of education, teachers, parents, residents of the community, attorneys, and colleagues, and they spent the major part of their time with subordinates. In their communications with staff members and members of boards of education, there was a tendency to contact individuals who ranked highest in the formal hierarchy. The emphasis was on face-to-face contact and a two-way flow of information. Certain communications involved elements in the environment and here the tendency was to communicate with individuals and groups who were politically and socially influential and "relevant" (males' definitions of this term varied slightly from females').

The contacts of female superintendents differed in four respects. In addition to being more informal, females spent more time with community members who were not parents, such as the president of a local corporation and the advisory board to a scientific research center. They interacted more frequently with their professional peers and almost exclusively with their female counterparts. They were formally involved in the training of administrators holding positions as adjunct professors in local universities and in sponsoring women teachers within the district for leadership positions within and outside of the school district. Women generally spent their unscheduled time handling curriculum and instruction matters, while men were involved with political activities—campaigning for a candidate for office in the state affiliate of AASA, eating lunch in local restaurants, maintaining liaisons with the state department of education, and trying to capture the state teacher-of-the-year award for the district. Women superintendents normally ate alone in their offices or at home rather than in restaurants in the community, while men used luncheon invitations for exposure, visibility, and to make connections. One female did go on one day to a moderately priced restaurant noted for its salad bar. The patrons did not represent the power structure, however; they were predominantly housewives, clerks in retail stores, and secretaries.

On the average, women superintendents were casual in their dress and did not adopt the skirted-suit uniform suggested for women executives (Malloy, 1977). Although their dress was not provocative, frilly, or pink, it was neither expensive nor classic in styling. Men felt that some occasions called for a Bill Blass suit, and some for a corduroy sport jacket. A few of the meetings attended by women called for a more sartorial deportment than they displayed. The more casual dress of the women cannot be accounted for by the casual attitudes of the west coast because their male subordinates consistently wore coats and ties. When one woman accepted the position in the district, the male administrators had asked whether they should wear a coat and tie, and she had replied that it did not matter. The women's informality was also noted in that subordinates (including teachers, secretaries, and custodians) addressed the female school executive by her first name whereas they addressed male central-office administrators and principals by their last names. Females' informality was also evident during meetings with their administrative staffs. Females assumed a more limited control of the agenda than their male counterparts. Males constructed and distributed an agenda several days in advance. Females used an instant agenda, and anyone who wanted to discuss an issue added the item to the handwritten list on the chalkboard just before the meeting began. Males followed the agenda order. Females changed the order to fit their priorities; and the structure of their scheduled meetings, for the most part, neutralized status differences, with all members assuming an equal part in the construction and presentation of the agenda.

The concentration of effort is often not apparent in managerial activities. A great amount of time might be spent on something seemingly superficial, while important decisions might be made swiftly and wigh incomplete knowledge. Much of the day was spent in talking with subordinates about minor things, making rather inconsequential decisions, and holding meeting about ordinary agendas. In essence, superintendents must respond to the little irritants in organization life. It has been argued that while monthly and seasonal patterns exist in certain managerial jobs, there is little evidence of short-term patterns (Mintzberg, 1973, p.31). Those who are around superintendents the most, for example, the secretaries and central-office administrators, noted certain shifts in the content and intensity of activity as monthly board of education meetings approached. Secretaries reported attempting to get ahead of their work before board preparation began. One administrator reported not scheduling activities for the day before the board meetings, which freed him to handle any last minute requests by the superintendent.

SUMMARY AND CONCLUSIONS

We cannot determine whether or not there is a pattern to managerial activities from the evidence and scope of this study. The general finding of the studies described in this chapter is that regardless of the sex of the superintendent, the activities of suburban school superintendents are characterized by (1) brevity, variety, and fragmentation; (2) a preference for oral modes of communication over written and visual modes; (3) contact with four groups—school board members, outside clients and community members, professional peers, and subordinates (teachers, administrators, classified personnel), most of their time being spent with the latter; (4) cycles of either intense or diminished activity; (5) control over a substantial part of their work as they initiate communications, ideas, and programs; and (6) the utilization of time and space as organizing frames, with an emphasis on schedules, segmentation, and promptness (Pitner, 1978). Whether male or female, superintendents' time and energy is for the most part expended on the more routine aspects of their work. Bennis (1976) points out that there is an unconscious conspiracy in organization to bog down a leader in details. Because routine problems are easier, more manageable, require less change and consent on the part of anyone else, and lend themselves to instant solutions that can make an executive temporarily look good, routine work drives out nonroutine work. An insight confirmed in the foregoing observational studies of male and female suburban school superintendents was that the trivial problems may all be dumped on leaders' desks.

While the predominant inference from the numerical data collected in both studies was that work activities are not different when the superintendent is a female, women were less formal in personal style and more directly involved in the instructional program; they established peer relationships predominately with their female counterparts, and usually had lunch alone or in restaurants whose patrons were largely women. The informality of women superintendents was observed in their language and dress and in their encouragement of subordinates to address them by first names.[4] In addition, females exercised less control over the construction of agendas and the outcome of meetings—thinking out loud, questioning, probing, and hooking up ideas as opposed to announcing decisions during meetings. One finds an interplay between the office of the superintendency and the person in it, a combination of official and informal activities, a manipulation of roles to fit circumstances. We questioned whether maleness and femaleness caused any differences for people occupying the executive position

---

[4]When a person takes on an established social role, usually he or she finds that a particular front has already been established for it. Whether acquisition of the role was primarily motivated by a desire to perform the given task or by a desire to maintain the corresponding front, the person will find that he or she must do both (Goffman, 1959). Social front includes such things as the setting, personal appearance, and manner; certain occupations have specific role signs, items that we most intimately identify with the occupation. One can infer from role signs how to behave toward a person with a particular occupational status. Personal front includes insignia of office as rank, clothing, sex, age, racial characteristic, size, looks, posture, speech patterns, facial expressions, bodily gestures, etc.

in an educational organization and whether there were barriers for women. Gross, Mason, and McEachern (1958) rejected the idea of consensus in role definition and noted that there were greater differences within the roles than between the roles of superintendents; in other words, that they have a great deal of choice in their behavior.

One difficulty regarding differences in the range of acceptable role behavior and expression for superintendents is that women are defined, as they have always been, as "the others." Men set, and thus are, the standard. The way men act and talk is normal and reasonable, and anything that deviates is often viewed as strange or illogical. Behavior that is nonmale or different is often though of as "bad." Until recently, it has been an unquestionable compliment to tell a professional woman that she does not act, think, or talk like a woman. After all, it is a compliment to be told you are one of the accepted group, the group that sets the standards. Writers of books suggesting changes in personal style, directing women to be assertive, to be totally feminine, to dress for success, are attempting to show readers how to get the desired reactions from other people.

How do others interpret it when women superintendents behave differently in a role? Key (1975) points out that women are generally in lower status positions and thus likelier to receive first name address from males than to call males by their first names. Many feminists have claimed that, even outside hierarchical organizations, a woman is more likely than a man of roughly equal status to be first named by new acquaintances; the basis for this is not sex or femininity, but rather status distinctions. Such usage is possibly an accurate indicator of the relatively higher status of males, but for several reasons it is not a good way of comparing women's and men's access to power. The first name, which is one of the commonest forms of address used by Americans, carries many varied messages. For example, when first names of employees are used familiarly by employers it can express either power or solidarity. What is expressed when an employee uses the familiar form with an employer and it is not reciprocated might be interpreted as deference in a power-marked dyad; its reciprocal use might denote nonintimacy between power equals. If a female secretary addresses a female executive by her first name and a male by his last name, it may indicate either greater solidarity with the woman boss or less respect for her (McConnell-Ginet, 1978). The situation is confused and confusing if men and women in the same occupational slots are called by different forms of address. A study is need to help sort out the conditions under which first names are used in the social organization known as the school district.

It was previously noted that in their personal style for conducting meetings women used instant agendas and did not dominate the discussion, thus increasing the participation of subordinates. In addition, women seemed to use meetings with subordinates as a forum for considering possibilities. They used verbs like *think, guess,* and *wonder,* which require a specific response and imply uncertainty and hesitancy. During one administrative cabinet meeting a woman superintendent queried, "How many people are suing us?" Observation suggests that a man would have asked this of the appropriate person prior to the meeting and then announced, "We have three lawsuits facing us now," after which require a specific response and imply uncertainty and hesitancy. delegated the responsibility. Hedging and the use of modal forms in language (e.g., "John is sorta tall"; "it's raining outside, isn't it?") give what one is talking about uncertain and shifting properties. Administrators who use such language may be, or appear to be, uncertain about their own judgment or to be indicating that the final decision is to be left up to the other party or parties. The language used by administrators needs to be more closely examined.

The use of the lunch hour by women superintendents warrants some discussion. It is easy to suggest that superintendents, male and female, ought to use the lunch hour to make contacts with the community power structure, which is thought to include government officials, business people, service clubs, and so on, and thought to be limited to males. It is in service clubs that superintendents meet businessmen, who supposedly have power and influence in the community and can be helpful regarding the district's financial issues. It is believed that women's inability to break into a white male club seriously limits their careers. Research suggests, however, that mothers are more instrumental than males are when it comes to voting affirmatively for school levies and bond issues (Piele & Hall, 1973). This finding suggests that males may have other reasons for belonging to services clubs, such as the desire to be thought of as a businessman and to project the efficiency of the school district (Callahan, 1962). Since teaching is a feminized profession, it makes sense that male superintendents may not want to be regarded as a "teacher of teachers."

While this line of argument suggests that superintendents may not need to spend time with businessmen, it still does not address the question of why female superintendents do not visit bars and lunch counters where there are lots of men. Is it because they are excluded? Or because they might be gossiped about and treated as if they were "looking for a good time?" Or what? Attitudes about sexual relations among men and women in this society and about related mundane issues may influence the behavior of both male and female superintendents. They may explain why female superintendents spend more time with female teachers and superintendents and why male superintendents elect to spend their time with principals, head custodians, and male peers. One female superintendent reported that she was visited by a principal's wife the morning after a long board meeting; the wife suspected possible transgressions. It seems that differences in superintendent work do not appear in the surface structure of their activities but in the deeper structures and nuances of their everyday lives.

Kanter (1978) makes a case for the absence of sex differences in work behavior and argues instead that attitudes and behavior at work are a function of one's location in the organizational structure. We have pursued this argument by examining women at the top of the school district hierarchy who have many of the same social characteristics as men occupying the same formal position in other suburban school districts. Our research examined female superintendents as they worked, and we cannot predict how many opportunities for growth and change will come to the subjects. The typical career path suggests that mobile superintendents will move to more attractive school districts (larger or more prestigious, for example) and that a few will move to professorships.

None of the three male and three female superintendents studied expected or desired to spend the rest of their working lives in their present institutional setting. In fact, two years after Pitner's initial study of male suburban superintendents in 1978, all three subjects changed positions. One moved to a larger district with very visible problems in the same county, another to a smaller district in the state, and the third to a professorship in a state university. Are the women subjects just as mobile? Will they advance? Only time will tell.

REFERENCES

Astin, H., Suniewick, N., and Dweck, S. (1971). *Women: A Bibliography on Their Education and Careers.* Human Service Press, Washington, D.C.

Bennis, W. (1976). *The Unconscious Conspiracy: Why Leaders Can't Lead,* Amacom, New York.

Callahan, R. E. (1962). *Education and the Cult of Efficiency.* University of Chicago Press.

Campbell, R., and Cunningham, L. L. (1959). *Observations of Administrative Behavior* (mimeographed). Midwest Administration Center, University of Chicago.

Carlson, R. (1972). *School Superintendents: Careers and Performance.* Charles E. Merrill, Columbus, Ohio.

Coleman, J. S. (1961). *The Adolescent Society.* Free Press, New York.

Cuban, L. (1976). *Urban School Chiefs under Fire.* University of Chicago Press.

Drucker, P. (1954). *The Practice of Management.* Harper & Row, New York.

Epstein, C. F. (1973). "Bringing Women In: Rewards, Punishments and the Structure of Achievement." *Annuals of New York Academy of Sciences*, March.

Epstein, C. F. (1970). *Woman's Place: Options and Limits in Professional Careers.* University of California Press, Berkeley.

Estler, S. E. (1975). "Women as Leaders in Public Education." *Signs*, I:363–386.

Goffman, E. (1959). *The Presentation of Self in Everyday Life.* Doubleday, Garden City, N.Y.

Gross, N., Mason, W. S., and McEachern, A. W. (1958). *Explorations in Role Analysis.* Wiley, New York.

Henley, N., and Freeman, J. (1975). "The Sexual Politics of Interpersonal Behavior." In *Women: A Feminist Perspective* (J. Freeman, ed.). Mayfield, Palo Alto, Calif.

Horner, M. S. (1969). "Fail: Bright Women." *Psychology Today*, 3 (November): 36–62.

Kanter, R. Moss. (1978). *Men and Women of the Corporation.* Basic Books, New York.

Key, M. R. (1975). *Male/Female Language.* Scarecrow Press, Metuchen, N.J.

Maccoby, E. E., ed. (1966). *The Development of Sex Differences.* Stanford University Press.

Malloy, J. T. (1977). *The Woman's Dress for Success Book.* Follett, Chicago.

McConnell–Ginet, S. (1978). "Address Forms in Sexual Politics." In *Women's Language and Style* (D. Butturff and E. Epstein, eds.). University of Akron.

Meyer, J. W., and Rowan, B. (1975). *Notes on the Structure of Educational Organizations: Revised Edition.* Paper presented at the annual American Sociological Association meeting, San Francisco, Calif.

Mintzberg, H. (1973). *The Nature of Managerial Work.* Harper & Row, New York.

Paddock, S. (1977). *Women's Careers in Administration.* Unpublished doctoral dissertation, University of Oregon.

Piele, P., and Hall, J. S. (1973). *Budgets, Bonds and Ballots.* Lexington Books, Lexington, Mass.

Pitner, N. J. (1978). *Descriptive Study of the Everyday Activities of Suburban School Superintendents: The Management of Information.* Unpublished doctoral dissertation, The Ohio State University.

Pitner, N. J. (1980). *Women Superintendents at Work.* (Mimeographed). Center for Educational Policy and Management, University of Oregon, Eugene.

Roby, P. (1973). "Institutional Barriers to Women in Higher Education." In *Academic Women on the Move* (A. Rossi and A. Calderwood, eds.). Russell Sage Foundation, New York.

Schwartz, P., and Lever, J. (1973). "Women in the Male World of Higher Education." In *Academic Women on the Move* (A. Rossi and A. Calderwood, eds.). Russell Sage Foundation, New York.

Sewell, W. H. (1971). "Inequality of Opportunity for Higher Education." *American Sociological Review*, 36 (October):793–809.

Tyack, D. (1974). *The One Best System.* Harvard University Press, Cambridge, Mass.

Chapter 16

THE INFLUENCE OF GENDER ON VERBAL INTERACTIONS AMONG PRINCIPALS AND STAFF MEMBERS: AN EXPLORATORY STUDY

Marilyn Gilbertson

In North America, as in many Western societies, the number of women administrators in education is small. For example, in Canada in 1975–1976, 75% of all elementary school teachers were women, yet less than 20% of the principals on this level were female. Fundamentally different personality characteristics and differences in socialization apparently lead people to adopt at an early age the behavior that is supposedly appropriate for the roles associated with their sex. Such behavior is known to be highly resistant to change. In Western society, masculinity is generally associated with autonomy, aggression, independence, and goal achievement, while femininity implies dependence, passivity, nurturance, and the motive to affiliate with other people. The characteristics of the male role seem to be primarily associated with the occupational world and with gaining the attendant attributions that status implies, attributions that affect both men and their families. The female role is less obviously oriented toward attaining status, and it is typically defined in terms of wife, mother, and homemaker. Additional status more normally accrues vicariously, through association with the status of the husband. In our society, which is ordered according to rank, gender is generally accepted as a prime factor of status. Status can also be achieved through the world of work; but generally men dominate the positions of influence and privilege, and achieved status is also often closely linked with status ascribed to the male gender.

297

Typically, the effects of gender on status can be observed in discussion groups made up of both sexes, where men have been found to be more verbally active, to give more ideas, and to initiate more activities, and women have been found to yield to male opinions, to listen more, and to bring up more subjects that are social and emotional in nature. Lockheed and Hall (1976) found that females tend to defer to males. Women who become leaders in education may be atypical. They have transgressed widely accepted cultural norms and stereotyped beliefs about "appropriate" behavior. Their position of influence contravenes the norms of the ordered ranks of society. Consequently, the normally higher status of males in relationships is often neutralized. Female teachers might be more confident, assertive, and independent with a female principal; they might defer less readily to a female superior than to a male superior. Conversely, male teachers might see a female principal as a threat to their superior masculine status and be less willing to exchange ideas and seek advice from her.

SCOPE OF THE STUDY

Studies have suggested that men in occupational life tend to adopt strategies to use the organization in ways that will enhance their opportunities for career advancement; that organizations have a "male culture" that is reflected, for example, in the interaction of colleagues, in problem-solving techniques, and in methods of competing (Hennig & Jardim, 1976). It follows then that there will be differences between the interactions of female principals with staff members and the interactions of male principals with staff members. The study in this chapter investigates verbal interactions between principals and staff members in one-to-one, face-to-face situations and explores the influence that the gender of the participant might have.

Field Work

Four elementary schools in the metropolitan area of Winnipeg were tested in this study (see Table 16.1). Two schools had female principals and two had male principals. The schools were matched as closely as possible; all had over 500 students, all were in middle-class communities and of open-plan design. Staffs had comparable ratios of men and women. Each of the principals had had a considerable amount of classroom experience before becoming an administrator. They were approximately middle aged (27–50 years of age), had one academic degree, and all but one had been a principal for 12 years or more. Information

299

TABLE 16.1
Gender of Principals and Teachers at Four Elementary Schools

	School A	School B	School C	School D
Gender of principals	Female	Female	Male	Male
Gender of teachers				
Male	5	6	3	5
Female	28	19	24	17

was gathered by observation and interview. The researcher shadowed the principals at four selected periods of the day for 4 days during a period of 4 weeks. Interactions were observed, analyzed, and recorded on a checklist according to place, duration, initiator, and content (see Table 16.2). The lists were collated and converted to either percentages of the total number of interactions or frequencies of interaction (number of contacts per person) so that comparisons could be made. Principals and a representative sample of teachers from each school were interviewed to substantiate trends observed and to pursue particular issues. Simple observations were also made in the staff room during breaks to see whether dyadic verbal interactions in informal group situations were similar to interactions recorded during the formal observation periods.

FINDINGS AND ANALYSIS

A total of 509 interactions were recorded. The data gathered were collated and tabulated to focus specifically on the gender of the principals. The findings are discussed in relation to the number of interactions, the places, the durations, the initiators, and the content.

Number of Interactions

Table 16.3 depicts the influence of gender on the interaction among principals and staff members. While the overall incidence of interaction was 4.8 contacts per teacher, male teachers met more frequently with principals than female teachers did (6.2 versus 4.3 interactions). This is congruent with the findings of Lockheed and Hall (1976) that men talk more and give more opinions than women do in mixed-sex discussion groups. As shown in Table 16.3 the male–female combination was unusually conducive to interactions, and female principals seemed more willing to meet with the opposite sex than male principals did. The findings raise the questions of whether there is a relationship between higher male verbal activity and the kind of jobs men do in schools and

TABLE 16.2
Comparison of the Number of Interactions of Male and Female Principals

	School A	School B	School C	School D	Total
Principals' interactions					
Total	138	113	138	120	509
Males	21	35	24	37	117
Females	117	78	114	83	392
Initiator of interactions					
Principals	85	66	77	80	308
Male teachers	8	10	11	8	37
Female teachers	45	37	50	32	164
Duration of principals' interactions					
0–2 minutes					
Males	15	29	15	33	92
Females	98	64	93	74	329
2–5 minutes					
Males	5	4	8	4	21
Females	17	11	20	7	55
5–10 minutes					
Males	1	1	1	0	3
Females	1	2	0	1	4
More than 10 minutes					
Males	0	1	0	0	1
Females	1	1	1	1	4
Place of principals' interactions					
Principals' office					
Males	5	19	6	11	41
Females	49	43	33	38	163
Staff room					
Males	1	8	9	6	24
Females	9	23	34	11	77
Classroom					
Males	10	0	5	7	22
Females	20	3	19	17	59
Other					
Males	5	8	4	13	30
Females	39	9	28	17	93

how this relates to the work women do. An examination of what topics men and women talk about is presented later in the chapter.

Places of Interaction

Table 16.4 shows that the principal's office was the most common place for principal–teacher interactions (40% of the total), and that the classroom was the least common place (16% of the total). Several teachers stated that they did not like to be disturbed when in class. The

TABLE 16.3
Number of Interactions with Principals per Teacher

	Male principals	Female principals	All schools
Male teachers	7.6	5.1	6.2
Female teachers	4.8	4.1	4.5
All teachers	5.3	4.3	4.8

classroom may not be an appropriate place for interaction. Table 16.4 also shows that 20% of the 509 interactions took place in the staff room. It was generally said that interactions in the staff room were informal and not related to the work but that teachers did take the opportunity to speak to principals in the staff room (especially male principals) if there was a need to communicate about work concerns. The percentages also indicate a modest difference by sex in that female principals were more likely to have verbal interactions in their offices and male principals in the staff room. Other findings suggest too that female teachers tend to prefer the privacy and intimacy of the principal's office when discussing their work; this environment may be more conducive to developing secure, affiliative, and friendly relationships. Perhaps women associate the office with being the appropriate place to discuss work because they are concerned about doing the right thing and being well liked. Men on the other hand, may be more willing to discuss work matters elsewhere because they are less concerned about using the formal *location* of authority. Such a viewpoint would certainly be congruent with what we know of male socialization.

Duration of Interactions

Interestingly enough, no particular variations in the duration of interactions were related to the sex of the principal. Most interactions

TABLE 16.4
Percentage of Interactions by Place

	Male principals (%)	Female principals (%)	All schools (%)
Office	34	46	40
Staff room	23	16	20
Classroom	19	13	16
Other	24	24	24
Total	100	99	100

Note: Total percentage for female principals is rounded off.

TABLE 16.5
Percentage of Interactions by Duration

	Male principals (%)	*Female principals (%)*
0–2 minutes	83	82
2–5 minutes	15	15
5–10 minutes	1	2
More than 10 minutes	1	1
Total	100	100

were very brief. Table 16.5 shows that more than 80% were less than 2 minutes in duration and fewer than 5% were 5 minutes or longer. These facts lend considerable support to the view that teachers are isolated from administrators during their daily work.

Initiations

Principals initiated more interactions than teachers did. Table 16.6 indicates that more than 60% of the 509 interactions were initiated by principals and 38% by teachers. Again, gender of the principal made no difference—male principals initiated 60% as compared with 61% for females. In Table 16.3, we see that male teachers interacted with principals more than female teachers did, disregarding the principal's sex. This raises the question of whether the greater principal–teacher interaction among males was due to initiations by teachers or by principals. In Table 16.6, the data are tabulated in terms of teacher frequencies, paralleling Table 16.3. Male and female teachers did not differ in the frequency with which they initiated interactions with the principal (1.9 interactions apiece); rather it was the principal-initiated interactions that made the difference. Principals initiated more interactions with male teachers than with female teachers (4.2 versus 2.6). This observation holds true for both male and female principals, but the numbers required to demonstrate the fact (by a still further breakdown of the data)

TABLE 16.6
Average Number of Interactions Initiated by Principals and Teachers
per Teacher

	Principal initiated	*Teacher initiated*	*Total*
Male teachers	4.2	1.9	6.2
Female teachers	2.6	1.9	4.5
All teachers	2.9	1.9	4.8

are too small to give dependable results. The evidence suggests that principals do use the privilege of their position or status to initiate more interactions. Moreover, the difference between the frequency of principals' interactions with male teachers and principals' interaction with female teachers again raises the question of how men's jobs differ from women's jobs in schools. If men are perceived to be more assertive and capable at task-oriented matters, perhaps they are requested to do more of these tasks in the school. Possibly, one of the strategies men use to foster closer contact with the principal and to be perceived as potential leaders is to capitalize on this view of males.

Content of Interactions

Interactions were investigated in terms of content; that is, the ideas and information in the verbal message (see Table 16.7). Overall, the most popular topics concerned organizational matters (40%). This was more true for the interactions of male principals than of female principals (48% versus 39%). Male principals not only concentrated more on organizational topics, but they also concerned themselves less with students affairs (12% versus 24%). The sexes were largely alike with respect to personal matters. During interviews, teachers and principals reported that they mostly talked about school-related matters, such as students, parents, progress reports, planning activities, and routine procedural activities. Many more female teachers than male teachers specifically referred to student concerns as those which they most frequently discussed with principals. Teachers said that the principal most frequently talked about organizational matters and initiated such conversations. During breaks in the staff room, discussion tended to center around informal, social matters rather than school matters.

The interactions about organizational concerns are more closely examined in Table 16.8. The data show the per-teacher frequencies cross-

TABLE 16.7
Content of Interactions

	Male principals (%)	Female principals (%)	All principals (%)
Personal subjects	19	20	19
Student affairs	12	24	18
Curriculum topics	19	14	17
Organizational matters	48	39	44
Miscellaneous	2	2	2
Total	100	99	100

TABLE 16.8
Number of Interactions for Organizational Matters per Teacher

	Male principals	*Female principals*	*All principals*
Male teacher	4.8	2.5	3.5
Female teacher	2.1	1.5	1.8
All teachers	2.6	1.7	2.1

tabulated by both principal sex and teacher sex and, although they suffer from only small numbers, the results are nevertheless suggestive. Once again the marginals confirm what earlier tables have shown. Interactions are more common for male than for female principals, and they more commonly occur with male teachers than with female teachers. There is an unusually large incidence of interactions when both principal and teacher are male. This feature can be further highlighted by graphing the data, as in Figure 16.1. This finding and previous findings strongly suggest that the reason for this disparity rests with the principals' inclinations rather than with the difference between the inclinations of male and female teachers.

The findings show a clear tendency for males to be more involved than females are in organizational and management tasks in the school. The evidence substantiates the view that schools typically reflect the cultural norms of sex-role orientation and collectively perceive of men as being more capable in areas of task performance and management. While accepting and carrying out the management role, female principals do not employ a higher proportion of women in the execution of these tasks. Perhaps men seek involvement in the executive aspects of the school in order to be seen as active and potentially successful leaders. This view would be congruent with the concept that organizations reflect a male-dominated culture; that is, they reflect male strategies for fostering their professionalism and developing their careers. Perhaps female principals have adopted this stance as well.

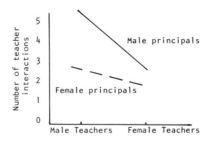

Fig. 16.1.

CONCLUSIONS

Several generalizations emerge from the study of interactions:

1. Male teachers were involved more frequently than female teachers were in principal–teacher interaction. The male–male combination was particularly conducive to interaction.
2. The principal's office was the most common place of interaction. There was a modest difference in that male principals considered the staff room a good place for interaction while female principals did not.
3. Most interactions were very brief.
4. Principals, regardless of sex, initiated interactions more often than teachers did, and they initiated them more with male teachers.
5. The most popular topics of the interactions concerned organizational matters. This was more true for male than for female principals. Male principals concerned themselves less with student affairs.

The findings are consistent with what we know about stereotyped attitudes and beliefs that men are more oriented toward performing tasks and toward achievement and also more influential than women. Principals involved male teachers in interactions more frequently than they involved female teachers, particularly in organizational matters. Men, therefore, were more often involved in the management tasks of the school, a context in which they could be seen as successful and potential leaders. Such actions reinforce the stereotyped belief that men make better leaders than women do. It is important, therefore, that principals ensure female teachers an active role in the school organizational and in managerial tasks so that they are also perceived as being potentially capable leaders. In order for people to aspire to leadership positions, they must obtain information about the organization in which they work and encouragement from their superiors. Conversely, the withholding of information and the failure to give encouragement will sublimate aspirations. Talking with the principal is the most likely way for teachers to receive such support.

Since male teachers were shown to be more verbally active with principals than female teachers were, especially in matters about organization, and since male principals were shown to be more inclined to foster such interactions than female principals were, clearly, women are disadvantaged. They do not receive the same access to or opportunities for obtaining information and encouragement from principals as their male colleagues do. The predominance of male principals in elementary schools perpetuates and reinforces male aspirations for career advancement while sublimating female aspirations. Positive action by administrators is needed to ensure more women of appointments to positions as principals so that this form of covert discrimination is not perpetuated. Principals must make positive efforts to keep women teachers well informed about all aspects of educational and organizational concerns and to provide the necessary encouragement for their career development.

The indication that male principals concerned themselves more with organizational matters and less with student affairs suggests that men and women employ different administrative strategies. Male principals focus more on concerns based on school-wide issues, while female principals focus more on classroom issues. It would appear desirable, therefore, for administrators to staff schools with equal representations of men and women, at both the classroom and senior levels, to ensure a balance of managerial styles. It is important for students and staff members to see male and female behavior in these roles as being equally prestigious and to see that both sexes make equally valuable contributions to the school organization. Continuous and positive efforts to reduce stereotyped attitudes about the concepts of masculinity and femininity are required. Rather than having polarized concepts of "appropriate" male and female behavior, people need to fuse the two and perceive the value of both, whether the characteristics are the empathy, nurturance, and sensitivity associated with females or the independence, activity, and assertiveness associated with males.

Results from the exploratory study of verbal interactions indicate differences between female principals' and male principals' interactions with staff members. However, since the investigation employed only four schools, further research involving a larger and more comprehensive sample of principals and staff members is required to substantiate the findings.

REFERENCES

Hennig, M. and Jardim, A. (1976). *The Managerial Woman* Pocket Books, New York.
Lockheed, M. and Hall, K. (1976). "Conceptualizing Sex as a Status Characteristic: Applications to Leadership Training Strategies." *Journal of Social Issues*, 32(2):111–122.

Chapter 17

THE GENDER OF PRINCIPALS
AND
PRINCIPAL–TEACHER RELATIONS
IN ELEMENTARY SCHOOLS

W. W. Charters, Jr., and Thomas D. Jovick

BACKGROUND OF THE RESEARCH

Do female school administrators manage schools differently from the way male administrators do? Those who have reviewed the research conclude that they do (Fishel & Pottker, 1975; Meskin, 1974). The sparse evidence indicates that female principals concern themselves more deeply with instructional leadership and with affairs pertaining to classroom teaching; that they interact more intensively with the faculty; that they attach greater importance to administrative tasks, use a more participatory (democratic) approach to school decisions, and exercise closer supervisory control of teachers. While such differences might suggest that a female principal would have a favorable impact on staff morale, the few studies that have examined the matter have resulted in inconsistent conclusions about whether this is so.

These conclusions, however, rest on extremely weak empirical grounds. For one thing, the number of studies is small. In their 1975 review, Fishel and Pottker cited only eight studies of the styles in which principals relate to their staff (almost all limited to the elementary school principalship); and the number of studies is barely double that today. For the most part, too, the methods used in the research are of doubtful quality. Questionable measures, inappropriate data-analysis procedures, and the frequent failure to control for alternative interpretations

307

make it difficult to put much faith in the reported findings. Clearly, more research is needed.

The intent of this chapter is to examine, first, conjectures about principal–teacher relations in the elementary school and second, how these relations influence teachers' satisfaction with their work. After a brief description of the sources of the data, we outline our findings concerning the leadership styles of male and female principals and discuss the impact of these styles on staff morale.

Sources of Data

The MITT project (Management Implications of Team Teaching) at Oregon's Center for Educational Policy and Management was funded over a period of several years by the National Institute of Education. The purpose was to study governance and work arrangements in elementary schools undergoing organizational changes. The project staff collected data in the spring of 1974 in nearly 40 schools, some of which subsequently embarked on instituting innovations through major curricular and structural programs.[1] This chapter uses data from the first wave of data collection, before changes had been initiated. Twenty-nine elementary schools formed the core of the MITT study, about one-third with female principals, and we used additional schools for making certain of the analyses that follow. Much of the information came from questionnaire responses of over 300 classroom teachers (90% return rate) who described various characteristics of their work setting, relationships, and sentiments about teaching. Other information was obtained through interviews with staff members and through the use of sociometric types of techniques. We describe the measures in the following sections.

The schools were a purposive rather than a random sample, selected to fit the demands of the design of the larger study. They were heterogeneous in character. All lay in 16 districts east of the Mississippi River, principally in the New England, Mid-Atlantic, and Border states. Some served low-income families in the inner cities, other educated the children from the affluent or not so affluent suburbs, and still others served small agricultural communities. Many schools taught grades from kindergarten through sixth or first through sixth, some included the seventh and eighth grades, and others only the primary grades. They ranged in size from a faculty of eight serving 200 students to thirty

---

[1]Findings of the study, as well as details on the sample and methods, are presented in the final report of the MITT project (Packard, Charters, & Duckworth, 1978).

classroom teachers serving nearly 800 students. Female principals were similar in age to male principals, but they differed in several other important respects. Females had less administrative experience but considerably longer classroom teaching experience. They had been in their present positions a shorter time and were more likely to be assigned to the smaller schools of the sample. These differences are consistent with trends in the career and hiring patterns of elementary principals in the nation at large (NEA, 1973).

LEADERSHIP AND STAFF RELATIONS

The most comprehensive and theoretically sophisticated study of behavioral differences between males and females in the role of principal was conducted by Gross and his colleagues nearly 20 years ago (Gross & Trask, 1964, 1976). They studied 189 elementary principals, nearly half women, selected from a larger sample of public schools in cities of 50,000 or more population during the 1960–1961 school year. The central part of the 1976 publication (chaps. 6–12) reported comparisons of men and women on a number of attitudinal and behavioral variables related to performance as an administrator. Most of their measures were based on the principals' own responses to questionnaires or interviews, although a few came from teachers' reports about the principal, also obtained by questionnaire. The study was especially noteworthy because Gross and Trask made explicit the lines of reasoning that led them to expect particular differences or an absence of differences in performance styles. In a number of instances they were able to test the adequacy of the underlying propositions that led to the prediction of sex differences, and to demonstrate that the differences existed.

Unfortunately, few investigators have pursued the theoretical leads offered by the authors.

In testing their predictions, Gross and Trask made an effort to control for extraneous variables that might explain away observed relationships and correlations, although the statistical procedures they employed in the bulk of their analyses were primitive by today's standards. Typically they relied on simple t tests rather than more suitable multivariate techniques. This is of no concern in most of their analyses, but it casts a doubt on the conclusions they reached on those several occasions when they predicted that sex differences in principals' performances would be conditioned on the level of a third factor, such as the socioeconomic status of the attendance area. More elaborate statistical analyses than *t* tests are necessary to demonstrate contingent relationships. Roughly half of Gross and Trask's predictions were borne out by the data. Of 18 stylistic variables for which they predicted a specific difference between the sexes, 9 were statistically significant in a supportive direction (by the one-tailed test), 7 were nonsignificant, and 2 fell in a direction contrary to their expectations. They predicted no differences between the sexes on three other variables, and all predictions were confirmed. Their relatively low success in predicting may reflect the poverty of theory in the field as much as anything else.

The sexual differences they observed between men and women administrators (whether predicted or not) were generally very small, from any practical standpoint. To estimate the strength of a relationship, we used a procedure recommended by Hays (1960) and McNamara (1978), to calculate the proportion of variance (ω^2) in each Gross and Trasks measure of the performance of principals that was explained by the differences in sex. In only two of their analyses did the sex of the principal explain as much as 5% of the variance in the respective measures: principals showed greater self confidence in their ability to supervise the instructional program ($\omega^2 = 5.5\%$); female principals exercised greater control over teachers' professional activities ($\omega^2 = 9.4\%$), and this was consistently true regardless of the school's size, the principal's age, the teaching experience of the staff, and the judged competence of the staff. This finding about the principal's control is particularly interesting because in contrast to the other sex differences between men and women noted by Gross and Trask and other investigators, the closeness of supervision could be expected to have negative consequences for teachers' affect. We will return to this point later in the chapter. In general, the Gross and Trask study yields an image of the female principal as a firm manager of teachers, oriented to the problems of classroom teaching and the instructional program, interested in the pupils and their individual needs, and personally engaged by the task of administering the school.

The MITT data that bear on managerial features allow us to make similar sex comparisons between men and women principals in four areas: the principal's managerial style, participatory decision making in the school, the interpersonal power exercised by principals, and principal–teacher communication. The Gross and Trask study cautioned us not to expect differences between men and women principals to be detectable by standard significance tests because of the small sample size of the MITT data. Correspondingly, we attended as closely to the strength of relationships as to probability levels.

Managerial Style

To describe their principal's style of school management, teachers in the MITT schools responded to the four subscales of Halpin's Organizational Climate Description Questionnaire (OCDQ) That focus on the principal's behavior (Halpin, 1966). The subscales were *aloofness,* or the extent to which the principal is formal and impersonal and "goes by the book"; *production emphasis,* or the inclination toward close staff supervision and directiveness; *thrust,* or the effect the principal exerts to "move the organization"; and *consideration,* or the extent to which the principal treats teachers "humanly." We aggregated scores of teachers in each school on the subscales; these means could range from 1.0 to 4.0. The Gross and Trask characterization suggests that female principals would show greater production emphasis than their male counterparts, and perhaps greater aloofness and thrust as well. In a study of 30 elementary principals, Kobayashi (1974) found that females received the higher scores on all three of these dimensions, although Roussell's (1974) study of a different administrative position, the department head in senior high schools, was not supportive. Data from the MITT project are shown in Table 17.1.

None of the differences in the means were statistically significant when tested with a two-tailed t-test. Although the difference in means on the thrust subscale was in the expected direction, the relationship was not notably strong. Our further exploration of the influence of factors such as age, length of experience in teaching, and school size, however, turned up no relationships that might have obscured the differences we sought to find. Managerial *style* has the connotation of a

TABLE 17.1

Mean Scores of Male and Female Principals on Four Subscales of the Organizational Climate Description Questionnaire

Subscale	Female $(N = 11)$	Male $(N = 18)$	Difference	t	ω^2
Aloofness	2.19	2.22	.03	<1	
(SD)	(.157)	(.224)			
Production emphasis	2.34	2.35	.01	<1	
(SD)	(.233)	(.257)			
Thrust	3.24	3.04	.20	1.680	.059
(SD)	(.360)	(.293)			
Consideration	2.62	2.40	.22	1.516	.043
(SD)	(.340)	(.409)			

pattern of characteristics. To capture this idea we ran an analysis that considered the four subscales simultaneously rather than separately. To do so we calculated a score to represent the similarity of the subscale profiles for each pair of principals in the sample and conducted a Guttman-Lingoes multidimensional scaling analysis of the resulting matrix.[2] The analysis produces a configuration in which principals with similar profiles will appear close together in the two-dimensional space, while those with dissimilar profiles will be far apart. We looked for indications that men and women principals formed relatively distinct clusters.

The closest approximation to a female cluster is grouping A in the configuration of Figure 17.1, which consists of five female principals and three males (females are represented by circles). The graph below the configuration profiles each cluster on each of the subscales and indicates that the members of Cluster A characteristically scored high on thrust and consideration and around average on aloofness and production emphasis. (The subscores were standardized over the 29 principals of the sample.) Other female principals had quite different managerial styles. For instance, the small four-person cluster labeled B in the configuration, consisting of two females and two males, scored low on all four subscales, but especially low on thrust. The main observation is that the managerial styles of the elementary principals in the MITT sample, at least as measured by the OCDQ subscales, did not simply reflect differences in their sex. This is hardly surprising, since undoubtedly there are a multiplicity of factors, both personalistic and situational, that shape the manager's style, and if sex plays any part at all, its effects are overwhelmed by other determinants.

Participatory Decision Making

While Gross and Trask did not investigate the decision-making system of the school, other research suggests that women principals are more inclined to use a participatory or democratic approach with their faculties than males are (Fishel & Pottker, 1975; Meskin, 1974). The suggestion rests primarily on research of the Florida Leadership Project

[2]Procedurally, we first standardized the subscales (normatively), then calculated a D^2 for each pair of principals by subtracting and squaring their scores on a given subscale and summing these squared differences over the four subscales. The D^2s were computed for all $(29 \times 28)/2 = 406$ pairs. The matrix was analyzed using the Guttman-Lingoes MINISSA-I(M) program (Roskam & Lingoes, 1970). Stress coefficients were .34, .14, and .06, for the one-, two-, and three-dimensional solutions respectively, although we show only the two-dimensional configuration.

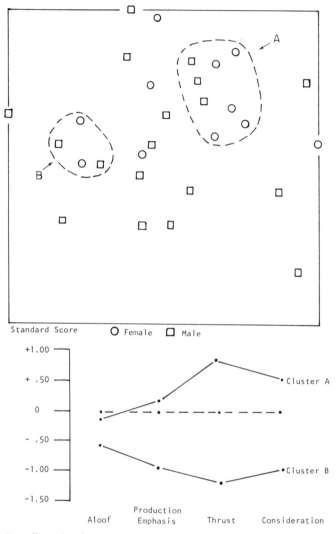

Fig. 17.1. Two-dimensional representation of similarities in managerial style and prototype score profiles for two clusters.

of the early 1950s, in which a questionnaire measure of democratic versus authoritarian behavior in principals was administered to the teaching staffs of some 80 elementary and secondary schools in Florida. Detailed data supporting the claim of a sex difference between men and women were not published by the project, but it appears that important controls were not introduced in the analyses, and in one of the popularized reports of the research, the authors noted that the difference may have been an artifact of school level (Grobman & Hines, 1956). More recent studies, also of dubious quality, yield contradictory findings on the matter (King, 1978; Quinn, 1976). The staff of the MITT project conducted lengthy interviews with knowledgeable informants who were teachers in the schools to determine who made binding decisions in each of approximately 60 arenas of the educational program. The data allowed us to identify four mutually exclusive categories of decision makers within the school: the principal alone (Type P), the principal and teachers together (Type S), the teachers collegially without the principal (Type C), and individual teachers (Type D). Aggregation procedures collapsed the 60 arenas into two domains of issues about which decisions typically are made within the school. The first concerned instructional processes, for example, class scheduling, teaching methods, and the use of curricular materials. The second concerned teacher and pupil deployment, for example, the grade levels of the classes assigned to teachers, the composition of the population of each grade level, and class sizes. Details of the methodology appear in Packard and Carlson (1976) and Jovick (1978).

In these two domains we calculated (on a per-informant basis) the number of decisions for which the four types of decision maker had responsibility and summed the frequencies separately for schools managed by males and females. Because school size based on pupil enrollments is likely to bear on the structure of governance, we categorized schools as small (200 to 450) and large (500 to 800) in order to examine relationships while size was held reasonably constant. Females managed 7 of the 17 small schools and 4 of the 12 large schools. Table 17.2 shows the tabulations in percentage form. Generally they suggest differences exist between decision making in schools under male and under female principals. With school size constant to assess the statistical dependability of the trends, we conducted log-linear analyses of the frequency tables for each decision domain, following methods developed by Goodman (1970) and Kullback (1974) for analyzing multidimensional contigency tables.

The procedures require that one formulate specific models, or hypotheses, regarding the independence or association of the variables—in the present cases, principal sex (A), school size (B), and decision type (C). A computer program generates the cell frequencies expected under a given model and calculates an information statistic representing the amount of discrepancy between the observed frequencies and the expected values. A chi-square test of the information statistic provides a probability level for assessing the goodness of fit to the

TABLE 17.2
Percentage Distribution of Types of Educational Decisions Made by Male and Female Principals

	Principals of small schools		Principals of large schools	
	Female (%)	Male (%)	Female (%)	Male (%)
Instructional processes				
Decision type				
Principal alone	9	6	20	9
Shared by principal and teachers	11	11	5	6
Collegial among teachers	13	8	9	11
Discretion of teacher	67	74	66	74
Number of decisions	(645)	(893)	(363)	(738)
Teacher and pupil deployment				
Decision type				
Principal alone	38	45	38	51
Shared by principal and teachers	15	19	9	9
Collegial among teachers	33	21	39	21
Discretion of teacher	14	15	14	19
Number of decisions	(590)	(782)	(370)	(736)

dates. In the interest of concentrating upon the substantive aspects of the log-linear analyses, we present the conclusions drawn from it but forego the statistical details. These details are available upon request from the authors.

The analysis for decisions about instructional processes indicated that the association between the decision-making procedures and the sex of the principal was of a different character in small and large schools of the sample. Other computations produced by the analysis indicate that in the small schools, more decisions than expected were made by the principal alone, if the principal were male, and more were of the collegial variety, if the principal were female. The reverse held true in large schools: collegial decisions were more common under male principals, and decisions by the principal alone were more common under female principals. (The mean of the scores of the entire faculty represented the rating of a principal's influence on school affairs.) The second set of items asked teachers to rate the principal's influence over their own classroom practices in five areas:

1. Enforcing school rules and regulations
2. Grading students

3. Planning curriculum
4. Teaching specific lessons and classes
5. Controlling and disciplining students

Scores representing the principal's influence in the classroom were formed as described above, and these were an assessment of how closely he or she supervised the work of teachers. Teacher responses to an additional instrument provided an indicator of the location of the principal's influence in the informal power structure of the school. Teachers were asked to name particular people in the school whose support it would be most worth enlisting to gain acceptance of an idea or proposal. They could name as many people as they wished, but typically they named no more than two or three. We tallied the number of nominations received by principals and by the next five more frequently mentioned staff members and summed the numbers separately for schools managed by male and schools managed by female administrators. Data from 34 schools were available for this analysis.

The results of the teachers' ratings can be seen in Table 17.3. Female principals were regarded as having a greater influence over school affairs than male principals had. Males and females were not significantly different in their influence over the teacher's own classroom; the difference explained less than 4% of the variance in the ratings, considerably less than the 9% found by Gross and Trask on a similar measure. The analysis for decisions about teacher and student deployment indicated that the association between decision-making—procedures and sex of the principal was the same in the large and in the small schools. Further computations revealed that in large and small schools alike, more decisions than expected were of the collegial variety under female principals, while more decisions were made by the principal alone under male principals. Thus, differences between male and female principals in the way they made decisions about deployment issues were like those

TABLE 17.3

Mean Ratings of Male and Female Principals' Influence over School and Classroom Affairs

	Female (N = 11)	Male (N = 19)	Difference	t	ω^2
School affairs	4.09	3.86	.23	2.168	.113
(SD)	(.251)	(.301)			
Classroom affairs	3.38	3.21	.17	1.423	.034
(SD)	(.325)	(.307)			

of instructional decisions, in the small schools, namely, more solo decisions when the principal was a male.

In sum, if participatory decision making means a process in which teachers together with the principal decide on educational issues, data from the MITT study reveal no differences between schools run by men and women. For issues about either instructional processes or deployment of teachers and students, male and female principals did not differ in the extent to which they involved teachers in decisions making. However, if we are talking about a decision process in which groups of teachers assume responsibility without the principal's participation, differences between male and female principals showed up for both issues, and, for matters involving instructional processes, depended upon the size of the school.

The Principal's Power within the School

As indicators of the principal's influence among faculty members two sets of items rated by teachers and responses to one other instrument were used. For the first set of items, teachers rated the extent of the principal's influence in five areas of school affairs:

1. Determining educational goals and objectives
2. Establishing rules and regulations
3. Planning general curriculum
4. Setting up practices for grading students
5. Establishing procedures for the control and discipline of students

Ratings for each item ranged from 1 for no influence to 5 for a great deal of influence. The average rating over the five items formed an individual's score. The distributions of power according to teachers' nominations are depicted in Figure 17.2. Not surprisingly, principals received more nominations on the average than any other staff member, although this was not true in every school. In a few schools, another person, such as the vice-principal or a long-tenured teacher, received substantially more nominations than the principal. The distributions suggest that female principals were more likely to monopolize the power nominations than were male administrators. On the average, 43% of the teachers nominated the female, and 31% nominated the male principal.

These results require qualification, however. Because females tended to manage the smaller schools, the difference in influence ratings and in power nominations may actually reflect differences that are sim-

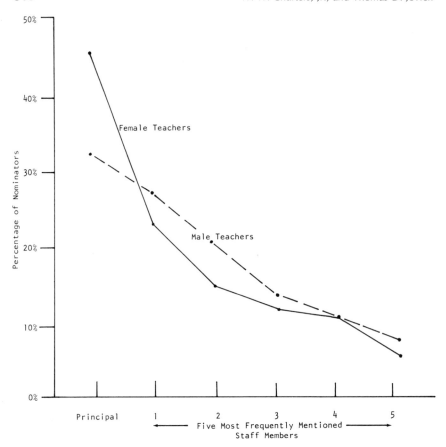

Fig. 17.2. Distribution of power nominations.

ply the result of school size. To test that possibility, we employed a multiple regression procedure to determine the independent effects of the size of the school and the sex of the principal on each set of influence ratings and on the number of principal nominations (in separate analyses). Table 17.4 presents the results. After controlling for staff size, the sex of the principal explained a large proportion of the variance in the measure of influence over school affairs (16.3%), but not in the measure of the principal's influence over teachers' classroom activities nor in the principal's receiving power nominations.

Principal–Teacher Communication

Apart from Gilbertson's investigation in this book, researchers have not studied the differences between male and female principals concern-

TABLE 17.4
Regressions of Three Indicators of Principal's Influence on Sex of Principal and Staff Size

	Beta	R^2	R^2 increment	F
Principal's influence on school ($N = 29$)				
Independent variable				
Number of teachers in school	.129	.001		
Sex of principal[a]	−.414	.164	.163	5.059[b]
Principal's influence on classroom				
Independent variable				
Number of teachers in school	−.315	.129		
Sex of principal[a]	−.193	.164	.035	1.100
Number of power nominations				
Independent variable				
Number of nominators	.745	.444		
Sex of principal[a]	−.257	.504	.060	3.726

[a]Male coded 1, female 0.
[b]Statistically significant beyond .05 level.

ing differences in the frequency of their interaction with faculty members. Characterizations of the differences between men and women principals' interests and orientations would lead one to expect females to have higher frequency rates for such verbal exchanges. Gross and Trask's approach to this was indirect (1976, chap. 10). Their teacher questionnaire measured the "social distance" maintained by principals in their interactions with teachers inside of school and outside. The items reflected the extent to which principals behaved as though they preferred teachers to show them deference and to acknowledge their rank. Gross and Trask found no sex differences in social distance within schools, but male principals tended to manifest a greater social distance in out-of-school relations. The MITT measure simply focused on the frequency and extent of principals' communications with teachers about matters of mutual interest. Teachers and principals wrote down the names of staff members with whom they talked regularly about classroom activities, school-wide matters, and matters unrelated to school or teaching and indicated the frequency with which discussions occurred.

To analyze these sociometric type of questionnaire responses, we ignored instances where one party claimed regular communication on a topic and the other party did not confirm it. Special rules were invoked to assign a frequency value to the verified communication when the parties disagreed on frequency. To compute a principal's communication score, we summed the number of teachers for whom the principal verified contacts of "several times weekly" or "daily," giving double weight to daily contacts, and divided by the number of responding teachers in the school. Thus, higher scores reflect both the larger proportions of the staff with whom the principals communicate and the greater frequencies of communication with them. Table 17.5 presents the regression analyses for the relationships of sex of principal to the three topics of communication after removing the influence of staff size (measured as the number of teachers of grade-level classes). We added the controlled staff size variable to control for the possibility that principals might talk with higher proportions of teachers and with greater frequency in schools that had fewer faculty members, a premise that proved to be true, as shown by the negative beta weights for staff size in the table.

The results show the strongest "sex effects" we encountered in our investigation of the principal–teacher relationship. Female principals communicated much more with their faculties than did male principals, with school size constant, and the sex differences accounted for 15%, 37%, and 43% of the variance in communication scores on classroom, school, and nonwork topics of communication, respectively. These strong differences led us to make a more detailed examination of principal–teacher communication, taking account of the teacher's sex as well as of the principal's. We had two questions in mind. Is the greater interaction observed among female principals also a characteristic of female teachers in their communications with principals, irrespective of

TABLE 17.5
Regressions of Principal Communications with Teachers on Staff Size and Sex of Principal[a]

Communication topic	Beta	R^2	R^2 increment	F[b]
Classroom activities				
Independent variable				
Number of teachers	−.252	.093		
Sex of principal	−.391	.243	.150	4.551
School affairs				
Independent variable				
Number of teachers	−.293	.141		
Sex of principal	−.617	.514	.373	17.684
Nonwork matters				
Independent variable				
Number of teachers	−.097	.034		
Sex of principal	−.663	.466	.432	18.595

[a] $N = 26$; male coded 1, female 0.
[b] Significant beyond .05 level, 1/23 df.

the principal's sex? Is there evidence that communication between male teachers and male principals and between female teachers and female principals is more common than communication between the sexes? As Gross and Trask suggested, one might expect that the one-sex pattern would be the more prominent, especially in out-of-school, nonwork interactions, since such face-to-face interaction is likely to be governed by similarities in general interests and societal constraints are most likely to be operative (1976, pp. 155–156).

We constructed a three-dimensional contingency table for each communication topic, classifying teachers by sex and by the sex of their principal and counting the numbers who were and were not in communication with their principal at least several times weekly. The raw numbers are given in Table 17.6. In order to eliminate sampling bias in these analyses, we included only schools with at least one male teacher on the faculty. This left 9 schools with female principals and 13 with male principals. Even with this restriction, only 43 of the 350 teachers were male, a fact that limits the generalizability of results. Log-linear analyses provided the method for answering our questions, and the details of the procedure are available upon request. The analyses show no evidence for either one-sex or two-sex trends in communication patterns. In addition, disregarding the principal's sex there was no evidence of communication differences between male and female teachers with regard to discussions concerning classroom and nonwork matters.

In the case of communication about school-wide affairs, the analysis revealed a statistically significant association between sex of teacher and communication. The difference in information statistics is significant at the .003 level. Inspection of the relevant numbers in the contingency

TABLE 17.6

Contingency Table for the Presence or Absence of Teacher Communication with the Principal at Least Several Times a Week, by Sex of Teacher and Sex of Principal

Communication topic	Sex of teacher	Number of teachers under female principal		Number of teachers under male principal	
		Contact	No contact	Contact	No contact
Classroom activities	Female	44	72	44	147
	Male	6	9	8	20
School affairs	Female	44	72	23	168
	Male	9	6	9	19
Nonwork matters	Female	33	83	6	185
	Male	6	9	3	25

table (Table 17.7) reveals the nature of the association. Where 42% of the male teachers interacted with their principal (18 out of 43), only 22% of the female teachers did so (67 out of 307). So where our previous analyses had shown that female principals were substantially more communicative with their faculties than male principals were, the same sociability did not extend to female teachers. With respect to discussions about matters of school-wide concern, at least, it was the male teachers who manifested the greater interaction with their principals.

Leadership and Staff Relations in Sum

The fact that stands out most clearly from the foregoing investigations is that the average woman principal of the MITT sample was more prominently and personally involved in affairs related to the program of the school than was her male counterpart. The main empirical findings are summarized by the following points.

MANAGERIAL STYLE. While there was some indication that female principals outranked males on the trust and consideration subscales of the OCDQ, management styles did not appear to differ importantly between them.

PARTICIPATORY DECISION MAKING. More participatory decision making appeared in female-managed schools, if the idea of "participation" includes decision making without the principal's involvement. An exception occurred in decisions regarding instructional issues in the large schools, where female principals used less participatory structures than male principals did.

POWER AND INFLUENCE. Female principals were regarded as more influential with respect to the affairs of their school than male principals were, and they seemed more likely than males to be dominant in the school's internal power system, although this tendency nearly disappeared with school size controlled. Contrary to the Gross and Trask findings, the sexes barely differed on measures of the closeness with which they supervised classroom instruction.

PRINCIPAL–TEACHER COMMUNICATION. Female principals engaged in substantially more face-to-face communication with their teachers than did male principals. At the same time, male teachers interacted more with their principals on matters of school-wide concern, although the sexes were alike in communication about classroom and nonwork matters. Taking account of the sexual difference in the communication of principals, the incidence of a male teacher's interaction was not substantially greater or less if the principal were also male.

CONSEQUENCES FOR STAFF MORALE

Apart from the Gross and Trask work, few studies have deliberately examined the effect of the school administrator's sex on teacher morale, and none has done so with appropriately sensitive data analysis procedures. In this section, after describing the Gross and Trask approach, we report on the two issues we pursued in reanalyzing the MITT data. One issue concerns the direct relationship between the sex of the principal and a teacher's job satisfaction. In the process of testing for a relationship, we considered the possibility that the principal's sex affects male teachers differently from the way it affects female teachers. The second issue connects teachers' job satisfaction to the differences in managerial behavior and relationships that we discussed in the preceding section, specifically questioning whether these differences act as intervening variables between sex of principal and staff morale.

Gross and Trask proposed that the morale of workers in an organization depends to some degree on the ability of the supervisor to facilitate the work of subordinates. They hypothesized, too, that women principals, by virtue of their greater interest in, and technical knowledge of, elementary school teaching, were better able than men to serve in such a facilitative role. This line of reasoning led them to expect higher levels of morale under female principals. Counterbalancing this, however, was the idea that, because of the cultural prejudice of subordinates against female supervisors, especially among male subordinates, morale would tend to be lower in schools with female principals.[3] In view of these contradictory influences, Gross and Trask declined to predict how these would balance out in their study. They merely presented the comparative data.

They used a rather indirect procedure for measuring morale; it re-

[3]While Gross and Trask could cite little research regarding prejudice against female supervisors at the time they were writing, empirical evidence on the point has accumulated since then for the work force at large (references in Wolf & Fligstein, 1979, p. 237) and for school teachers in particular (references in Stockard & Schmuck, forthcoming, chap. 5). When asked simply to express a preference for a male or female supervisor, the standard research technique, on the average, teachers respond more favorably to the male. Whether and how much such hypothetical preferences for the sex of a supervisor relate to satisfaction of the teachers with their concrete work settings remains an open question.

lied on teachers' estimates of the satisfaction levels of others. Specifically, six questionnaire items asked teachers to give the percentage of the teaching staff who enjoyed working in the school, respected the judgment of the administrators in the school, and so on. The means in the responses of schools were obtained by averageing the percentage estimates of responding teachers to the six items. The Gross and Trask comparisons revealed no differences between schools administered by women and schools administered by men principals, in the means in responses concerning satisfaction; nor did differences appear within subclassifications of schools by region, by school size, by age of principal, by mean age of teachers, and various other factors. We should point out, however, that the controls Gross and Trask exercises over the relevant attributes of teachers were necessarily crude, inasmuch as their investigation was conducted using the school rather than the individual teacher as the unit of analysis. Thus, crucial attributes such as a teacher's age and years of teaching experience were controlled as the mean age of the staff and the mean length of teaching experience. In the MITT data on which we now report, satisfaction was measured for individual teachers, and it was possible to exercise much closer control over other individual attributes that could potentially affect the levels of satisfaction in teachers.

Sex of Principal and Teachers' Job Satisfaction in the MITT Sample

The MITT project provided two measures of the satisfaction of teachers. One set of questionnaire items emphasized satisfaction with the teaching career. Included were questions about the teacher's interest in changing to a job outside of education, his or her satisfaction with teaching as an occupation, and the likelihood of choosing teaching again if given the chance to start over. The five-item summative scale, whose scale values could run from 5 for highly dissatisfied to 22 for highly satisfied, had a reasonably high reliability estimate of .80 (coefficient alpha). Teachers in the MITT sample exhibited scores for career satisfaction toward the upper end of the scale; it was the rare teacher who scored as low as 14.

The other scale emphasized satisfaction with the immediate work situation, and in this regard was more similar to the scale used by Gross and Trask. The 10 items of the scale asked about the pleasantness of the teacher's relationships with administrators, fellow teachers, the willingness of administrators to offer the teacher help when needed, the extent to which the teacher's efforts were recognized by others, the progress the teacher was making toward his or her professional goals, and so on. Response alternatives were in a Likert format and scale values, averaged over the ten items, ranged from a low of 1 to a high of 6. The scale for work satisfaction yielded a reliability of .75 (coefficient alpha). Teacher responses to this scale, too, were negatively skewed. Details of both scales are given in the final report of the MITT project (Packard, Charters, & Duckworth, 1978).

We used hierarchical multiple linear regression to test the effect of the differences in the sex of the principals on the career satisfaction and the work satisfaction of the teachers. As part of the analyses, we controlled for the effects of school size (indicated by the number of teachers) and two teacher attributes known from other studies to be associated with job satisfaction—age and sex. (We did not attempt also to control for length of teaching experience, because its correlation with age was so high in our sample as to make it unnecessary.)

The regression procedure also allowed us to test the statistical interaction between the sex of the principals and the sex of the teachers—specifically, the hypothesis that the satisfaction of teachers would be more adversely affected when males served under a female principal

TABLE 17.7

Regression Analyses of Career and Work Satisfaction on Principal's Sex

	Beta[a]	R^2	R^2 increment	F	df
Career satisfaction (N = 226)					
Independent variable					
Staff size	−.046	.002			
Age of teacher	.229	.062			
Sex of teacher[b]	−.123	.077			
Sex of principal[b]	−.177	.107	.030	7.479[c]	1/221
Interaction[d]		.109	.002	.488	1/220
Work satisfaction (N = 221)					
Independent variable					
Staff size	−.070	.006			
Age of teacher	.237	.071			
Sex of teacher[b]	−.131	.090			
Sex of principal[b]	−.223	.138	.048	12.020[c]	1/216
Interaction[d]		.138	.000	.010	1/215

[a]Coefficients for regressions without the interaction term.
[b]Coded 1 for male, 0 for female.
[c]Significant beyond .05 level.
[d]Interaction of principal's sex times teacher's sex.

than when females did. Because of our interest in this issue, we limited our analyses to schools with at least one male teacher on the staff, reducing our sample to 6 schools with female principals and 11 with male principals. At that, there were only 27 male teachers in all, so that conclusions remain highly tentative.

Results of the regression analyses appear in Table 17.7. The interaction term made essentially no contribution to the explanation of variance in scores in either regression, thereby discounting the hypothesis that the sex of the principal made a difference. The main effect of the principal's sex on staff morale, however, was statistically significant, and the signs attached to the beta coefficients indicate that teachers' satisfaction levels were higher under female principals than under male principals. While the effects of the principal's sex reached statistical significance (by virtue of the sizable degrees of freedom available in the analyses, they were not very strong. The principal's sex independently explained 3% of the variance in scores for career satisfaction and nearly 5% for work satisfaction.

Leadership Attributes as Intervening Variables

The other issue we examined in reference to job satisfaction brings the findings of the first part of the chapter into consideration. There we reported that the principals in our sample differed strongly in certain aspects of their faculty relationships and leadership attributes; in particular, female principals were in closer personal communication with their teachers on affairs of the classroom and school than were men principals, and they were also seen by teachers to be more influential in affairs of the school. These attributes of supervisors, on theoretical grounds, could be expected to enhance the job satisfaction of the workers under them. One of the strands of reasoning advanced by Gross and Trask was that they are indicative of the supervisor's capacity to facilitate the work of subordinates. Unlike the principals of the Gross and Trask study, MITT principals did not differ by sex in the closeness with which they supervised teacher performance, a kind of behavior bound to depress levels of job satisfaction. The question we now raise is whether these particular qualities of female principals indeed accounted for the higher levels of satisfaction among their teachers or whether other more subtle (or perhaps just unmeasured) characteristics of the females produced the differences in satisfaction.

To answer the question we employed the same technical procedure as in the previous analyses, hierarchical multiple regression; but here the underlying logic is reversed. After entering into the regressions the controls over size of staff, age of teacher, and sex of teacher, we next entered the measures of the influence of the principal and principal–teacher communication, followed by the coded value for sex of principal. In this case, if sex of principal no longer adds significantly to the explanation of variance, it would signify that the intervening variables had explained *how* the sex of the principal worked its influence on job satisfaction. For present purposes we used data for teachers in 29 schools of the study, not restricting ourselves to those with male teachers. Table 17.8 displays the results. Among them, the three measures of leadership characteristics accounted for about 3% of the variance in scores for career satisfaction and work satisfaction (beyond the 6–7% explained by the control variables). While the proportions are not great, they are significant beyond the level of the .05 criterion. More crucially, the results also indicate that sex of principal contributed less than 1% of additional explanation, which is statistically insignificant even with the large number of degrees of freedom in the analyses.

TABLE 17.8

Regression Analyses of Career and Work Satisfaction on Principal-Staff Relationships and Sex of Principal

	R^2	R^2 increment	F	df	p
Career satisfaction ($N = 319$)					
Independent Variable					
Size of staff	.002				
Age of teacher	.046				
Sex of teacher[a]	.056	.056			
Principal's influence[b]	.058 ⎫				
Principal's communication, class affairs[c]	.064 ⎬ .027		2.947	3/310	.033
Principal's communication, school affairs[c]	.083 ⎭				
Sex of principal[a]	.090	.007	2.615	1/311	>.10
Work satisfaction ($N = 314$)					
Independent Variable					
Size of staff	.001				
Age of teacher	.055				
Sex of teacher[a]	.069	.069			
Principal's influence[b]	.083 ⎫				
Principal's communication, class affairs[c]	.083 ⎬ .029		3.297	3/307	.021
Principal's communication, school affairs[c]	.098 ⎭				
Sex of principal[a]	.105	.007	2.585	1/306	>.10

[a] Coded 1 for male, 0 for female.
[b] Mean influence on school affairs.
[c] Mean principal communication score.

SUMMARY

We conclude that it was because of the female principals' specific leadership qualities that their faculties exhibited higher levels of job satisfaction. Presumably, if the male administrators had been able to establish such close personal relations with teachers and had exerted as much influence over the educational affairs of the school as the women did, their faculties would have shown equally high levels of satisfaction. The question of why there is a difference between the administrative behavior of men and women principals in the first place remains unexplored here. It is pertinent to remark how little the variables of the analyses improved our understanding of teachers' satisfaction. All seven variables taken together, including the personal attributes of teachers, the size of the school, and the characteristics associated with the principal, explained only 9% of the total amount of variance in the scores for career satisfaction, and only 10.5% in those for work satisfaction. Obviously, our simple measures did not capture many features of the work setting, of the personal circumstances of teachers, of the times, and so on, that produced the wide spectrum of differences in satisfaction levels.

Behavioral scientists believe that many conditions are influential in shaping the performance of leaders and in determining job satisfaction; these conditions can be classified, and they require volumes for their elucidation. It is little wonder that investigations that focus narrowly on one specific attribute of these matters, such as the leader's sex, can only capture a small portion of the wonderous variation that people exhibit in their working-day lives. Perhaps the greater wonder is that a single attribute reveals any association at all with leadership qualities and job satisfaction, especially when the samples are small or when other major determinants remain uncontrolled, as is so often the case in the kind of studies we have been investigating. Our findings concerned the association of the principal's sex with characteristics of the principal–teacher relationship and with teacher morale; they were based on our reanalysis of data from 30 or so elementary schools collected in the course of a study of team teaching and educational governance.

Female principals were said by their teachers to be more influential in the educational affairs of the school; they were shown to have had more extensive person-to-person interaction with the teaching faculty than male principals had. However, the differences were smaller or nonexistent, once pertinent outside factors were controlled. We found few important differences on the four subscales of the OCDQ, a questionnaire difference concerning the principal's position of power as measured by teacher nominations, and conditional evidence regarding the greater incidence of participatory decision making in schools managed by female principals. Male and female principals did not differ in the closeness with which they supervised teaching performance, a surprising finding in the light of the Gross and Trask results.

Another small but notable sex effect we reported concerned the job satisfaction of the faculties. Teachers in schools managed by women manifested significantly higher levels of satisfaction on the two scales we had at our disposal—a measure of teachers' satisfaction with their careers and a measure of satisfaction with the more immediate work circumstances. In a special analysis we were able to demonstrate that male teachers as well as female teachers exhibited greater satisfaction levels under women administrators, despite the suggestion sometimes encountered in the literature that male subordinates experience discomfort in relating to female superordinates. If they did, it was not of sufficient importance to affect their satisfaction levels, although, as we pointed out, the number of men teachers in the sample was too small to support dependable conclusions.

We were able to show that a prime reason for the different levels of satisfaction was the very difference in the principals' manner of relating to teachers that we had encountered earlier. That is, the more prominent and personal involvement of the female principals in the day-to-day affairs of the school was largely responsible for the higher morale of their staffs. One might speculate that had the female principals of our small sample reflected the differences in closeness of teacher supervision that Gross and Trask found, we might not have noted any differences in levels of staff morale either, because closeness of supervision was a strong depressant of job satisfaction; previous analyses we made of the data (not reported here) abundantly testify to this, and this factor could have offset the favorable influences of the female style of relating. Whatever the case, the sex variable affected teacher morale in ways that are consistent with our general understanding of relationships between superiors and subordinates, and this removes some of the mystique that surrounds the male–female distinction.

One important question that has not been considered in this chapter is why men and women behaved differently vis-à-vis their staffs. Gross and Trask, in their thoughtful work, suggested a number of sources for the differences they observed between male and female principals, and they put some of them to empirical tests. Their ideas centered primarily on careers as sources, that is, particular experiences males and females encounter and the capabilities they acquire in the course of their markedly divergent passages into teaching and beyond. Parts of the Gross and Trask work documented the wide disparities in occupational histories and career aspirations in detail (see this volume for more recent research). An important task for research would be to systematize and test the adequacies and shortcomings of other explanations of differences between males' and females' styles of relating. As investigations unravel the sources of differences between the sexes in leadership performance, the mystery of the sex variable will be further reduced.

REFERENCES

Fishel, A., and Pottker, J. (1975). "Performance of Women Principals: A Review of Behavioral and Attitudinal Studies." *Journal of the National Association for Women Deans, Administrators and Counselors,* Spring, 110–117.

Goodman, L. A. (1970). "The Multivariate Analysis of Qualitative Data: Interactions among Multiple Classification." *Journal of the American Statistical Association,* 65:226–256.

Grobman, H., and Hines, V. A. (1956). "What Makes a Good Principal?" *Bulletin of the National Association of Secondary School Principals,* 40 (November):5–16.

Gross, N., and Trask, A. E. (1964). *Men and Women as Elementary School Principals.* Final Report No. 2, Cooperative Research Project No. 853, Graduate School of Education, Harvard University, Cambridge, Mass.

Gross, N., and Trask, A. E. (1976). *The Sex Factor and the Management of Schools.* Wiley, New York.

Halpin, A. W. (1966). *Theory and Research in Administration.* Macmillan, New York.

Hays, W. L. (1968). *Statistics for the Social Sciences.* Holt, Rinehart and Winston, New York.

Kobayashi, K. A. (1974). *Comparison of Organizational Climate of Schools Administered by Female and Male Elementary School Principals.* Doctoral dissertation, University of the Pacific, Stockton, Calif. Dissertation Abstracts, 35:129–30A.

King, P. J. (1978). *An Analysis of Teachers' Perceptions of the Leadership Styles and Effectiveness of Male and Female Elementary School Principals.* Doctoral dissertation, University of Southern California, 1978. Dissertation Abstracts, 39:2658–A.

Kullback, S. (1974). *The Information in Contingency Tables.* Technical Report, National Technical Information Service (AD-785 599/2GA).

Jovick, T. D. (1978). *Creating Indices from the Control Structure Interview through Data Collapsing and Multidimensional Scaling: Approaches to Data Analysis in Project MITT.* Technical Report, MITT Project, Center for Educational Policy and Management, University of Oregon, Eugene.

McNamara, J. F. (1978). "Practical Significance and Statistical Models." *Educational Administration Quarterly,* 14(1):48–63.

Meskin, J. D. (1974). "The Performance of Women School Administrators–a Review of the Literature." *Administrator's Notebook,* 23(1):1–4.

Meyer, J., and Cohen, E. (1971). *The Impact of the Open-Space School upon Teacher Influence and Autonomy: The Effects of an Organizational Innovation.* Technical Report No. 21, Stanford Center for Research and Development in Teaching, Stanford University, Calif.

NEA, 1973 *26th Biennial Salary and Staff Survey of Public School Professional Personnel, 1972–1973.* National Education Association Research Division, Washington, D.C.

Packard, J. S., and Carlson, R. O. (1976). *Control Structure in Elementary Schools: Measurement and Findings.* Technical Report, MITT Project, Center for Educational Policy and Management, University of Oregon, Eugene.

Packard, J. S., Charters, W. W., Jr., and Duckworth, K. E. with Jovick, T. D. (1978). *Management Implications of Team Teaching: Final Report.* Center for Educational Policy and Management, University of Oregon, Eugene.

Roskam, E., and Lingoes, J. C. (1970). "MINISSA-I: A Fortran IV(G) Program for the Smallest Space Analysis of Square Symmetric Matrices." *Behavioral Science,* 15:204–205.

Rousell, C. (1974). "The Relationships of Sex of Department Heads to Department Climate." *Administrative Science Quarterly,* 19:211–220.

Stockard, J., Schmuck, P. A., Williams, P., and Kempner, K. (1980). *Sex Equity in Education.* New York: Academic Press.

Wolf, W. C., and Fligstein, N. D. (1979). "Sex and Authority in the Workplace: The Causes of Sexual Inequality." *American Sociological Review,* 44(April):235–252.

Quinn, K. I. (1976). *Self-Perceptions of Leadership Behaviors and Decision-Making Orientations of Men and Women Elementary School Principals in Chicago Public Schools.* Doctoral dissertation, University of Illinois. Dissertation Abstracts, 1977, 37:6199-A.

INDEX

EDUCATIONAL PSYCHOLOGY

continued from page ii

Norman Steinaker and M. Robert Bell. The Experiential Taxonomy: A New Approach to Teaching and Learning

J. P. Das, John R. Kirby, and Ronald F. Jarman. Simultaneous and Successive Cognitive Processes

Herbert J. Klausmeier and Patricia S. Allen. Cognitive Development of Children and Youth: A Longitudinal Study

Victor M. Agruso, Jr. Learning in the Later Years: Principles of Educational Gerontology

Thomas R. Kratochwill (ed.). Single Subject Research: Strategies for Evaluating Change

Kay Pomerance Torshen. The Mastery Approach to Competency-Based Education

Harvey Lesser. Television and the Preschool Child: A Psychological Theory of Instruction and Curriculum Development

Donald J. Treffinger, J. Kent Davis, and Richard E. Ripple (eds.). Handbook on Teaching Educational Psychology

Harry L. Hom, Jr. and Paul A. Robinson (eds.). Psychological Processes in Early Education

J. Nina Lieberman. Playfulness: Its Relationship to Imagination and Creativity

Samuel Ball (ed.). Motivation in Education

Erness Bright Brody and Nathan Brody. Intelligence: Nature, Determinants, and Consequences

António Simões (ed.). The Bilingual Child: Research and Analysis of Existing Educational Themes

Gilbert R. Austin. Early Childhood Education: An International Perspective

Vernon L. Allen (ed.). Children as Teachers: Theory and Research on Tutoring

Joel R. Levin and Vernon L. Allen (eds.). Cognitive Learning in Children: Theories and Strategies

Donald E. P. Smith and others. A Technology of Reading and Writing (in four volumes).

> Vol. 1. *Learning to Read and Write: A Task Analysis (by Donald E. P. Smith)*
> Vol. 2. *Criterion-Referenced Tests for Reading and Writing (by Judith M. Smith, Donald E. P. Smith, and James R. Brink)*
> Vol. 3. *The Adaptive Classroom (by Donald E. P. Smith)*
> Vol. 4. *Designing Instructional Tasks (by Judith M. Smith)*

Phillip S. Strain, Thomas P. Cooke, and Tony Apolloni. Teaching Exceptional Children: Assessing and Modifying Social Behavior